# SEX

TAKE a WALK on the Wild Side

Masterpieces of erotic fantasy photography

SEX: *Take a Walk on the Wild Side*

Design copyright © 2002 by Carlton Publishing Group
Text copyright © 2002 by Tony Mitchell

Published in the United States by
Thunder's Mouth Press
An Imprint of Avalon Publishing Group Incorporated
161 William St., 16th Floor
New York, NY 10038

Published in Great Britain by Carlton Books Limited



Library of Congress Cataloging-in-Publication Data is
available for this title.

ISBN 1-56025-363-0

9 8 7 6 5 4 3 2 1

**Design:** Adam Wright/Mike Spender
**Picture Research:** Faye Parish
**Production:** Gary Lewis

Printed and bound in Italy
Distributed by Publishers Group West

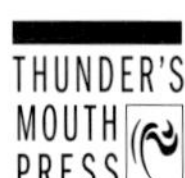

# SEX

## TAKE a WALK on the Wild Side

Masterpieces of erotic fantasy photography

Tony Mitchell

# CONTEN[TS]


INTRODUCTION ... 6
THE PHOTOGRAPHERS ... 10

## DRESSING FOR PLEASURE
Cat Woman: Claws 1992 ... 20
Cat Woman Jumping 1993 ... 22
Untitled ... 23
Untitled ... 24
Rachel Weisz ... 25
Miss T 1980s ... 26
Rubberball 2000 ... 27
David, Transman, Berlin 1998 ... 28
On Fire ... 29
Untitled ... 30
Angel ... 31
Untitled 1998 ... 32
Katrina 1999 ... 33
Devil 2001 ... 34
Emily 1999 ... 35
Roller Girl 2001 ... 36
Untitled 1998 ... 37
Untitled 1997 ... 38
Upskirt # 2 2000 ... 39
Upskirt # 1 2000 ... 40
Trainspotting # 2 1999 ... 41
Untitled ... 42
Untitled ... 43
Untitled ... 44
Serena - Full Mask, November 1999 ... 45
Evil Family, February 2001 ... 46
Full Blosson, February 2001 ... 47
Sweet Aloma, April 2000 ... 48
Untitled July 2001 ... 49
Untitled July 2001 ... 50
Untitled July 2001 ... 51
Untitled 1999 ... 52
Untitled 1999 ... 53

Perfect Doll, July 2001 ... 55
Bath, March 2001 ... 56
Vamp, November 1997 ... 58
Sunbathing, January 2000 ... 59
Nun in the Cellar, Bremen 1999 ... 60
The Nun 1998 ... 61
Danny's 2001 ... 62
Witch Lillith - The Bride of Death, Oslo 2000 ... 63
Red Moon 1998 ... 64
Bizarre Beauty 1998 ... 65
Masuimi, Hollywood 2001 ... 66
Emily Marilyn, Hollywood 2001 ... 67
Natasha Sweet, Hollywood 2000 ... 68
Before the Shower ... 69
In the Park, July 2001 ... 70
Teddy Bear in Paris 1999 ... 71

## DOMINATION AND DISCIPLINE
Charlie 2000 ... 72
Nell 2000 ... 74
Emeryville 1993 ... 75
Whip Me Sweetly 1999 ... 76
Steps by Steps Paris 1998 ... 77
Ingrid in Morocco 1999 ... 78
Catherine & Emily 2000 ... 79
Taylor & Marnie 2001 ... 80
Simone Kross Steps on a Slave 2001 ... 81
Torturella, Damien & Slave 2000 ... 82
Police Woman No. 3 ... 83
Nurse No. 2 ... 84
Notting Hill Gate 1998 ... 85
Berliner Dom 1998 ... 86
Untitled 1998 ... 87
She Whips ... 88
Untitled ... 89

Untitled ... 91
Dita on Polished Wood, February 2000 ... 92
Dita - Red Wall, April 2001 ... 93
Isabella Waiting, April 2000 ... 94
Sitting Pretty, April 2000 ... 95
Isabella Mirror, December 1998 ... 96
Mistress Aves, May 1995 ... 97
Red Room, September 1999 ... 98
Sinful Daughter, July 2000 ... 99
Vanessa, House of Harlot 1999 ... 100
Charlie, House of Harlot 1999 ... 101
Payback is a... 2001 ... 102
Intimate Inquisition 2001 ... 103
Mirror Mirror 2001 ... 104
Friends, October 1997 ... 105
Beguiled ... 106
Dita Blue ... 107
The Bargain ... 108
Lost Weekend ... 109
Dawn Witch ... 110
Sascha ... 111
Distant Cairo ... 112
Zastrozzi ... 113
Untitled 1999 ... 114
Untitled 1999 ... 115
Milk, July 2001 ... 116
Untitled, July 2000 ... 117
Untitled, July 2000 ... 118
Untitled, July 2000 ... 119
Untitled 2000 ... 120
Art & Shay 2000 ... 121
The Amazon and Espen Thoresen Watching TV, Oslo 2001 ... 122
The Amazon and Bored Espen Thoresen, Oslo 2001 ... 123
Untitled 2001 ... 124
Untitled 2001 ... 125

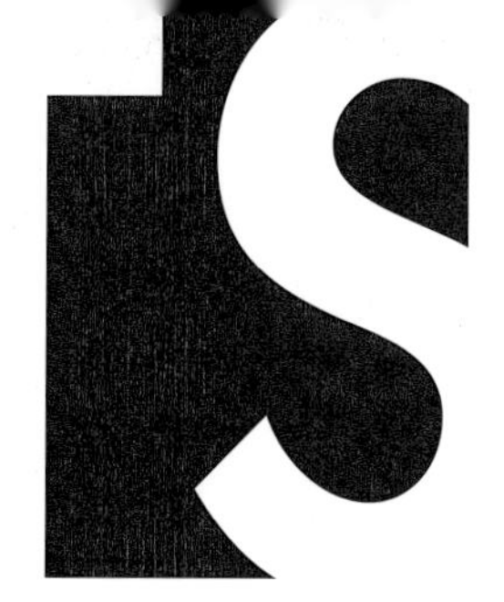


## BONDAGE GAMES

| | |
|---|---|
| Untitled | 126 |
| Untitled | 128 |
| Untitled | 129 |
| Untitled | 130 |
| Pretend Bondage | 131 |
| Time Out | 132 |
| Basement Games | 133 |
| Reptile Eden | 134 |
| Presentation Sexually 1999 | 135 |
| Antonia 2001 | 136 |
| San Francisco 2001 | 137 |
| San Francisco 1996 | 138 |
| San Francisco | 139 |
| San Francisco | 140 |
| Ariane on the Wheel, London 2001 | 141 |
| Persephone, London 1992 | 142 |
| Libidex Hood 98 | 143 |
| Untitled, September 1997 | 144 |
| Cat Burglar 2000 | 145 |
| Dungeon 2000 | 146 |
| Valeria 2001 | 147 |
| Gangster's Moll 2000 | 148 |
| Double Cross 2000 | 150 |
| Homage to Sweet Gwendoline 2001 | 151 |
| Perfect Teese 2001 | 152 |
| Sweet Tangerine 2000 | 153 |
| Anticipation 2001 | 154 |
| Pink Kittens 2001 | 156 |
| Blonde on the Bed, Bremen 1999 | 157 |
| Behind the Boots, 22 February 2000 | 158 |
| Off Duty II, 29 April 2001 | 160 |
| Finger Play, 22 May 2000 | 161 |
| Taped, 18 July 2001 | 162 |
| Cautious Approach, 17 January 2001 | 163 |
| The Martyr, 17 January 2001 | 165 |

| | |
|---|---|
| Off Duty I, 29 April 2001 | 166 |
| Untitled, August 1999 | 167 |
| Untitled 1996 | 168 |
| Untitled 1997 | 169 |
| Untitled 1997 | 170 |
| Untitled 1996 | 171 |
| Sawa Futaoka Tied Up by Nawashi Murakawa 2000 | 172 |
| Aokigahara Forest Near Mount Fuji 1996 | 173 |

## EXTREME MEASURES

| | |
|---|---|
| Simone Kross & Slave 2001 | 174 |
| Untitled September 2000 | 176 |
| Historical Moment 1996 | 177 |
| Metal Hell 2001 | 178 |
| Within My Chains 1998 | 179 |
| Soft Entity 1998 | 180 |
| New York 2001 | 181 |
| Zooey, December 2000 | 182 |
| Ariane the Magical, London 2001 | 183 |
| Zipped Open - Taking a Peek, Bremen 2001 | 184 |
| Untitled | 185 |
| Untitled | 186 |
| Faces, June 1999 | 187 |
| Torture Table, April 2000 | 188 |
| Untitled August 2001 | 189 |
| Restraint, December 2000 | 190 |
| Untitled | 191 |
| Untitled October 2000 | 192 |
| Untitled | 193 |
| Untitled | 194 |
| Untitled | 195 |
| Zentai Girl, Holly wood 1999 | 196 |
| Blow-Up Girl at the Fountain, Bremen 2000 | 197 |

| | |
|---|---|
| Hugging Christmas, Bremen 2000 | 199 |
| Masked Greta, Bremen 1999 | 200 |
| Mirrored Rubberdoll, Hollywood 1997 | 201 |
| Tiffany and Myrna, March 2001 | 202 |
| Tiffany, October 2000 | 203 |
| Lily & Zoe at Jade's Dungeon, December 1999 | 204 |
| Tomoko Haunted by Serial Killer, London 1999 | 205 |
| Rapesfield 1997 | 206 |
| Black Room 446 - 01 2000 | 207 |
| Kiss Me!, July 2001 | 208 |
| I C through U, June 2001 | 209 |
| Benson Boobs, November 2000 | 210 |
| Standing Tall, November 2000 | 211 |
| Yuka, Yuki and Friend, after Performance at the Röntgen Art Space 1994 | 212 |
| Akiko, Sendai Harbour 1995 | 213 |
| Nun with Cross 2000 | 214 |
| Rubber Cyborg 1999 | 215 |
| Melt Down 1999 | 216 |
| Oxygen 1997 | 217 |
| Art & Shay 2000 | 218 |
| Todd & Paulette 1999 | 219 |
| Red Mistress with Black Slave 1999 | 220 |
| Natira, May 1999 | 221 |
| Untitled 1996 | 222 |
| Untitled 2001 | 223 |
| **CONTENTS BY PHOTOGRAPHER** | 224 |

## A Brief History of Tying

It wasn't so very long ago that sex was regarded as a shameful secret. Moral censure was usually based around the notion that sex should be functional rather than enjoyable. Many viewed it as "dirty" (which it is, at least if done properly, according to Woody Allen). But with the emphasis in the Western world now shifted firmly towards fun rather than procreation, the sexual palette of the new millennium is a somewhat richer affair.

The evidence of this is clearly reflected in the changing way photography has been able to deal with erotic subject matter in recent times. Human sexuality presents an intriguing menu of visual possibilities to the curious camera and the fact that at any given time, a particular taste or activity may be regarded as too perverse and bizarre for depiction by legitimate photography has rarely prevented photographers from exploring it. It has merely meant that, until mainstream culture catches up, those who document what's happening at the periphery risk provoking censorious reaction from assorted guardians of public morality.

There is no doubt that, in our voyages of discovery to the wilder erotic terrains, fetishism and BDSM (the collective term for bondage & discipline, domination & submission, and sadism & masochism) are increasingly popular destinations. In the last couple of decades, the public profile of kink culture has grown steadily and as a consequence, its depiction has moved further into the realms of legitimate photography. Thus, today, we are regaled with many technically accomplished and highly creative images of a subject area that not so long ago was the preserve of a mixed bag of amateur enthusiasts and professional pornographers, neither of whom have traditionally been motivated too much by artistic concerns.

Although modern photography has brought greater creative and technical skills, not to mention technological resources, to the production of fetish imagery, some of the best modern pictures perpetuate visual traditions of the genre that were first established 50 or even 100 years ago. Photographers have been fascinated by so-called deviant sexual imagery almost since the invention of photography. Victorian pornographers were not slow to see the potential of the camera, and many early producers of erotic photographs included such images in their repertoire. Though generally categorised under the heading "fladge" (for flagellation, the Victorian perversion of choice) many of these early images contained, in addition to caning, whipping or spanking, clearly recognisable elements of fetishism, bondage, dominant/submissive rôle play or other sadomasochistic behaviour.

This trend continued into Edwardian times and beyond, the 1920s seeing a significant increase in the market for deviant literature and imagery as a result of the establishment in Paris of The Olympia Press and other specialist publishers of erotica, all of whom considered such material fair game. In the 1930s, Britain joined the fray significantly, if somewhat belatedly, with the launch of a magazine whose articles, drawings and photographs focused specifically on fetishism, especially women in high heels, gloves and boots. Called *London Life*, it had a relatively small and anonymous circulation but was to have a major influence on the next wave of pervy publishing activity which would begin many thousands of miles away.

Europe's apparent monopoly on the practice and portrayal of twentieth-century perversions finally crumbled when America got in on the act shortly after the Second World War. At the turn of 1946/47, ex-pat British artist and photographer John Alexander Scott Coutts, who had been working in Australia under the soubriquet John Willie, chose New York as the launchpad for *Bizarre* magazine. *Bizarre* was Willie's answer to *London Life* for those who (unlike *London Life*) liked their women not only fetishistically attired but also tightly bound. He published

# UCTION

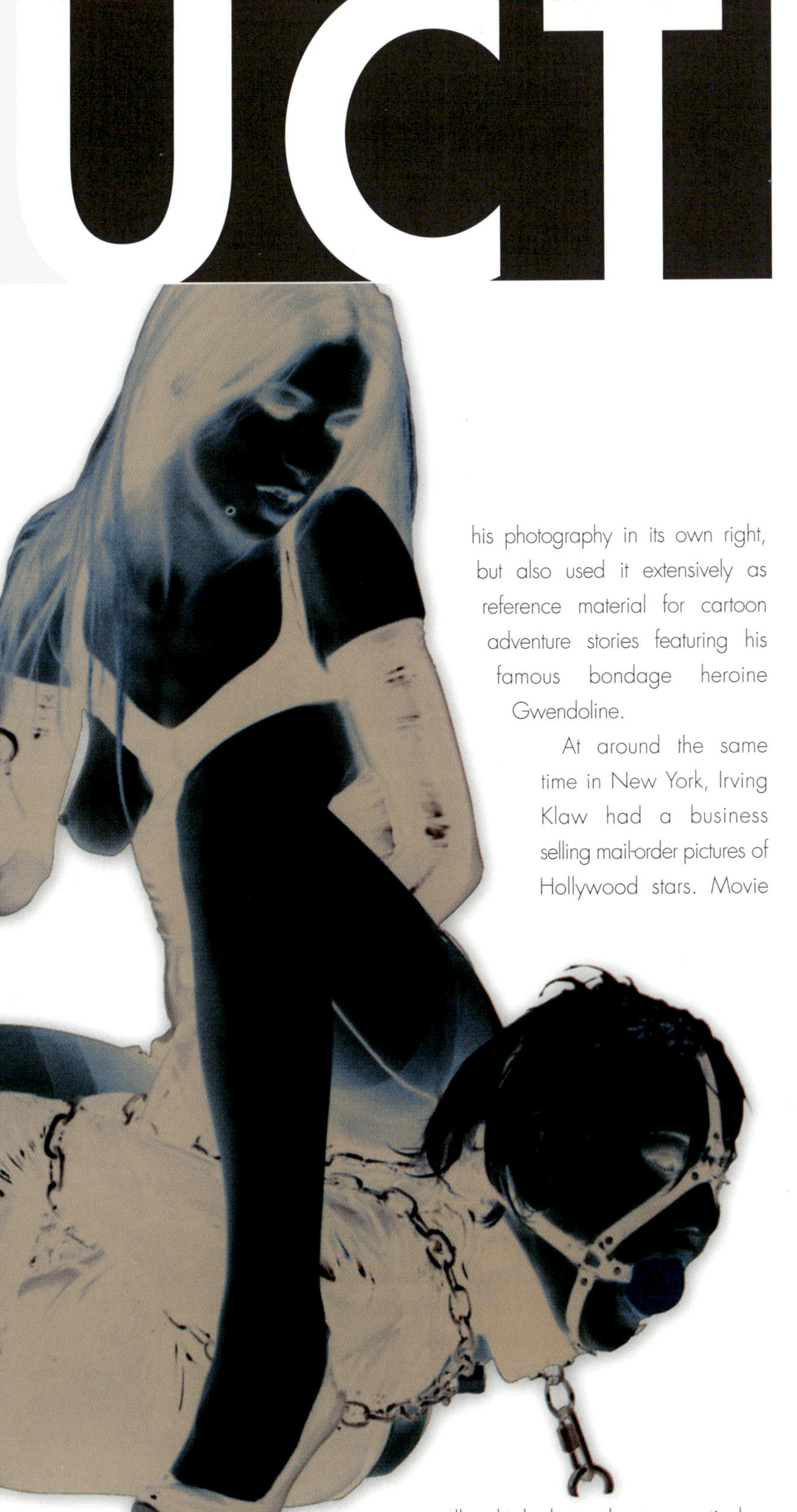

his photography in its own right, but also used it extensively as reference material for cartoon adventure stories featuring his famous bondage heroine Gwendoline.

At around the same time in New York, Irving Klaw had a business selling mail-order pictures of Hollywood stars. Movie stills which showed actresses tied up were particularly popular with certain clients and when one of these offered to finance a private photo session if Klaw would organise a photographer and book models, Klaw readily agreed. When he put some shots from the session into his next mail-order catalogue, he was overwhelmed by demand for the pictures. Klaw began to arrange regular bondage shoots and business boomed – especially when he began to feature his latest discovery, a feisty young model from Tennessee by the name of Bettie Page.

Between them, Klaw and Willie were largely responsible for establishing what is today considered the classic look of bondage-fetish photography. Models were (un)dressed in contemporary cheesecake style – fancy lingerie, garter belts, seamed nylons – and tied up with white clothes line in solo or girl-on-girl situations. The models were always well covered and apart from their ultra-high heels and the odd leather corset, very few specialist fetish garments or props were employed. There was never any suggestion of sex *per se*, the most invigorating consequence of bondage generally being an over-the-knee spanking with a hairbrush.

Although fetishes for industrial materials such as rubber were explored in some of this earlier imagery, the lack of specialist suppliers meant it was generally on a "make do" basis, with models sometimes shown wearing a rubber bathing cap, girdle or gumboots in an attempt to cater for such tastes. It was not until the 1960s and the widespread introduction of synthetic clothing materials such as PVC that the market for "shiny, black and sexy" opened enough to support specialist costumiers. Several companies sprang up in Britain and Germany to cater for the growing European fetish for tight-fitting rubber clothes, selling early versions of the fetish fashions that are commonplace today, but foremost among fetish/BDSM specialists was John Sutcliffe's London-based company Atomage. It quickly established an international reputation for being able to make any piece of clothing or equipment the customer could imagine, however outlandish. A forerunner of today's multi-skilled fetish organisations, Sutcliffe also published catalogues and magazines, collaborating in the production of some of the decade's most bizarre deviant imagery.

Sixties Britain experienced quite widespread cultural flirtation with fetishism, from fashion's kinky boots to *The Avengers* to the pop art of Allen Jones, but the decade also saw the genre's proprietory imagery becoming more hard-edged, moving away from the cute, playful naughtiness of Irving Klaw's bondage babes towards more aggressive and explicit subject matter. This was especially true of America, where the decline in traditional producers of fetish and BDSM imagery meant that, when the genre resurfaced there in the early 1970s, a significant slice was in the hands of hardcore pornographers. Their output – ugly, brutal and sexually explicit – would have horrified Klaw and Willie, whose bondage heroines were essentially damsels in distress, chaste and romantic.

However, the 1970s was by no means an entirely bad-hair decade for pervery. The excesses of the new BDSM porn created much nostalgia for the values of the 1950s pioneers, and in the second half of the 1970s it finally found expression when New York's Bélier Press and a few other like-minded publishers such as Harmony in California began to reprint the original Klaw and Willie material. In Britain, continental Europe and the States, this material started to appear not just in adult bookshops, but also on the shelves of trendy alternative bookstores. Still deemed illegal in Britain, it was seized upon by a new, sexually curious generation and appropriated as visual propaganda by London's punk movement, who gleefully flaunted it as part of their confrontational anti-fashion, anti-establishment stance.

But in terms of fetish chic, the 1970s really belong to *Vogue* photographer Helmut Newton. Newton had been experimenting with a provocative, overtly erotic approach to fashion photography since the beginning of the decade, and publication of the best of this work in his books *White Women* (1976) and *Sleepless Nights* (1978) had an enormous impact on the aesthetics of kink. Combining sexual allure, fashion, and touches of SM decadence in a highly stylised, technically peerless package, Newton's work was a quantum leap for fetish imagery, and though he has always denied any personal fetishistic leanings, there are few photographers in the fetish genre today who do not quote him as an influence.

Seventies feminists despised Newton for (as they saw it) objectifying women, but once he had stuck his head above the parapet, other mainstream fashion photographers began to follow, and by the beginning of the 1980s, influential men's magazines like *Playboy*, *Oui* and *Lui* were also broadening their vanilla sensibilities to accommodate a little SM. In London, punk had by now given way to synthesiser pop and the dandified New Romantics, who had their own special clubs for dressing up in. In such a climate, the idea of starting a fashionable fetish club no longer seemed unthinkable, and when Skin Two opened its doors in January 1983, it attracted a hard core of young clothing designers, musicians, media types, photographers and artists whose presence quickly dispelled the myth that fetishism was the sole prerogative of middle-aged suburban swingers. Top music and style photographer Peter Ashworth shot the club's promotional photography using rubber clothes by innovative designer Daniel James. Together they created for rubber fetishism what it had always lacked until then: *fashion potential*.

Top London photographer Bob Carlos Clarke, whose book *Obsession* (1981) featured the kinky photo-montage work he had been creating since the mid-1970s, was not slow to see the potential in Daniel James's designs. The two began a creative collaboration which bore fruit in Clarke's next book *The Dark Summer* (1985) and the pocket-sized *Maid in London* (essentially a Daniel James catalogue). Clarke's fine art approach established him as the absolute master of the shiny rubber moment and ensured that his work, like Helmut Newton's before him, would inspire a whole new generation of fetish photographers.

Meanwhile, in the wake of the fetish club's success, *Skin Two* magazine was launched in 1984 – its mission to provide an intelligent alternative to BDSM exploitation-porn and general fetish amateurism. It quickly became the established vehicle for the genre of photography pioneered by Ashworth and Clarke and enthusiastically embraced by newcomers such as Trevor Watson. Within a few years other European titles such as <<O>>, *Secret* and *Marquis* followed *Skin Two* into the market, all of them providing exposure to the growing fetish photography phenomenon. These magazines supported and were supported by an explosion in fetish subculture which spread outwards from London through Europe to America and beyond. By the early 1990s, with its own well established fashion designers, clubs and magazines, the fetish scene in Britain had become a fully fledged alternative culture, and one whose influence on mainstream culture was becoming increasingly visible.

At this point, however, the scene's own magazines still provided the main exposure for fetish photography. The big book publishers were not convinced that fetish imagery was a good business

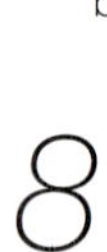

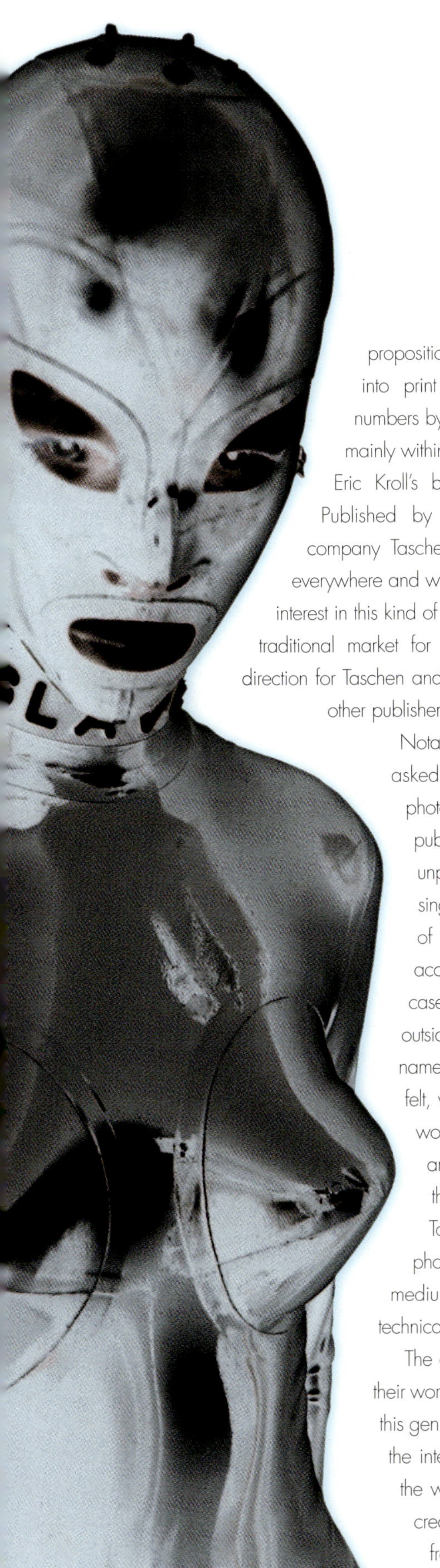

proposition, so the few books that did make it into print were generally produced in low numbers by small fetish/erotica specialists selling mainly within their specialist markets. But in 1994, Eric Kroll's book *Fetish Girls* changed all that. Published by the international art and erotica company Taschen, it appeared in major bookstores everywhere and was an immediate success. Proving that interest in this kind of imagery had grown way beyond the traditional market for fetishism, it provided a fertile new direction for Taschen and helped to opened up the market for other publishers.

Notable among them was Carlton, who asked me to edit an anthology of photography for them called *Fetish* that was published in 1999. *Fetish* gave me an unprecedented opportunity to present, in a single volume, the work of a large number of photographers whose work was acclaimed within the genre but in many cases, had received scant recognition outside it. Alongside the book's well-known names were many others whose talents, I felt, would be equally admired if only their work could reach a mainstream audience, and I think the subsequent popularity of the book has proved my instincts correct.

To say that the right exposure is vital in photography is to express a truth about the medium that extends beyond the mere technical process of letting light fall onto film.

The difficulty of securing suitable outlets for their work is undoubtedly why photographers in this genre have so comprehensively embraced the internet as a promotional medium. True, the web may not offer the permanence or credibility of the printed page, but it has freed fetish photographers from their reliance on the patronage of a relatively small number of magazine and book publishers. Today, fetishism and BDSM of all kinds thrive on the internet, and while a lot of it is, admittedly, no more than exploitative commercial porn, the genre also boasts a relatively large proportion of websites showcasing serious photography.

In fact, when I began systematically surfing the net for possible material for this book (I know – it's a dirty job, etc.), I was surprised by just how much great new work I discovered, hiding in plain view as it were. If not for their websites, I would not have known about – and thus not been able to include in this book – the photography of Fetish Eyes, Alexander Horn (L-A-Tex), Martin Perreault (Latex Lair), No Mercy or Rubber Brain. Had their websites not first brought them to the attention of *Skin Two*, I might not have known about Carlos Batts, Lee Higgs, Kevin Hundsnurcher, Dave Naz or Jim Weathers.

I am pleased to say that, alongside all this new talent, we are once again able to present more great work by familiar names from *Fetish* and *Skin Two* – people like Bob Carlos Clarke, Emma Delves-Broughton, Steve Diet Goedde, James & James, Christophe Mourthé, Doralba Picerno, Gary & Pierre Silva, Del LaGrace Volcano, Trevor Watson and Ben Westwood. I'm pleased also to welcome such prolific exponents of the genre as Peter W. Czernich and Roman Kasperski, both stalwarts of the European fetish press, and Justice Howard and Tony Ward, whose work has long been wowing 'em in the USA.

In the biographies which follow I have mentioned relevant books by each photographer and, as every single one of our contributors now has a website, I have listed their URLs too. So if you like what you see here, you have the means to discover more – and I hope you will take the chance to do so.

I hope it is clear by now what is meant by a walk on the wild side: it is, at the very least a flirtation with fetishism, a touch of tying-up, a dalliance with domination… but maybe a lot more. Each of these themes has been assigned its own chapter. "Dressing for Pleasure" explores the fantastic world of fetish fashion, "Domination and Discipline" focuses on the dynamics between people acting out a scene, "Bondage Games" shows us some of the exciting possibilities of erotic restraint, while, last but not least, "Extreme Measures" takes a tour of the outer fringes, showing us that beyond slinky catsuits, romantic ropework and sensual submission waits an even more bizarre world of inflatable rubber outfits, industrial strength bondage and scary SM dungeons for those who dare to venture there. Enjoy the trip!

**Tony Mitchell, October 2001, London**

# PHOTOG

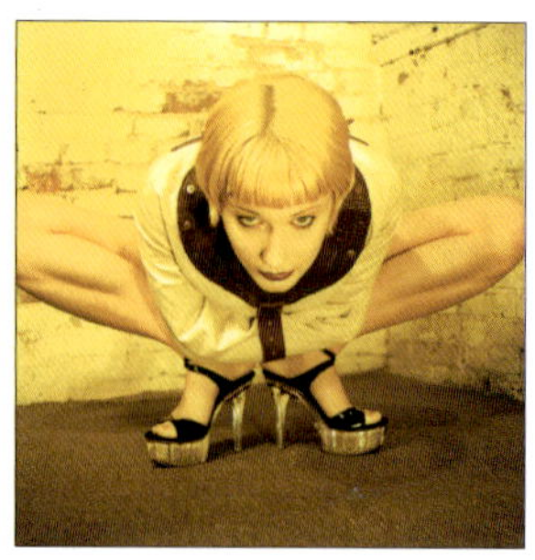

### CARLOS BATTS *www.cbattsfly.com*

For ten years, American Carlos Batts has been creating vibrant erotic and fetish imagery influenced by a strong fashion sensibility. This Baltimore native has produced a wide range of editorial and commercial work for clients as diverse as DC Comics, Agfa and *Leg World*, has directed adult films, and has created album art for an eclectic mix of music acts. Now based in Los Angeles, Batts uses cubist geometry, 1970s exploitation themes, bizarre lighting techniques, textured backgrounds, slice and dice editing, and "a keen eye for beauty in its many forms" to create his bold, engaging fetish images. His book *Wild Skin*, collecting together the cream of his erotic and fetish work, was published by Edition Reuss in 2001.

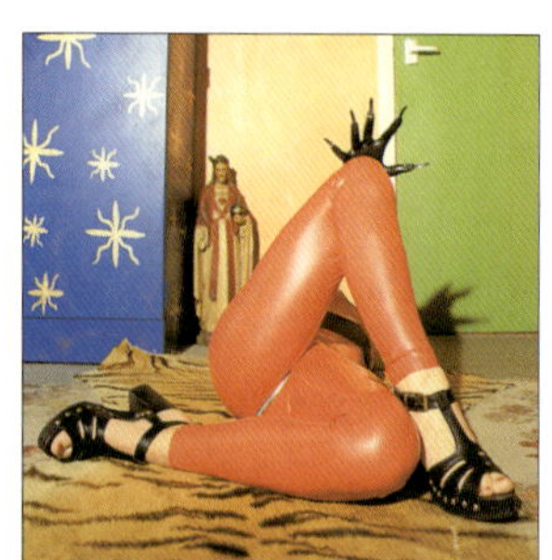

### ALVA BERNADINE *www.bernadinism.com*

Born in Grenada, West Indies, in 1961, Alva Bernadine moved to London at the age of six. When he became seriously interested in photography at the age of 21, his first pictures were of London tourist spots, but within a year he had begun practising his present surrealist style. He is self-taught and has never been an assistant. Working mainly in the editorial field for the last 18 years, he has been published in France, Spain, Italy, USA, Australia, Germany and, of course, Britain, where he was an early contributor to *Skin Two*. Alva was joint winner of the Vogue/Sotheby's Cecil Beaton Award in 1987 and has been twice nominated as Erotic Photographer of the Year. His book *Bernadinism* (Edition Stemmle) was published in 2001.

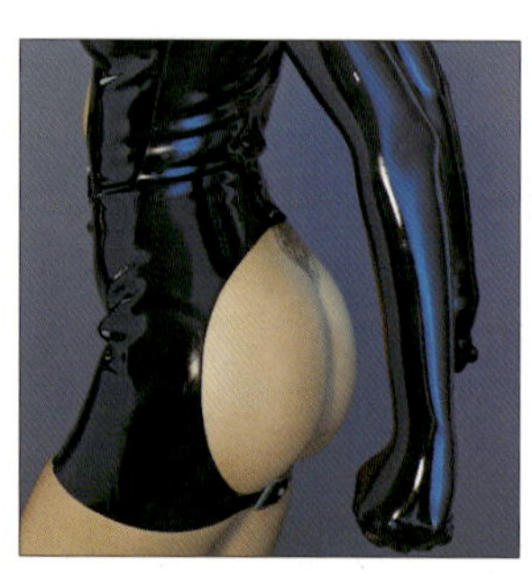

### BOB CARLOS CLARKE *www.bobcarlosclarke.com*

Born in Southern Ireland in 1950, Bob Carlos Clarke came to England in 1964 to study art and design, and became interested in photography, which he subsequently pursued at The London College of Printing and the Royal College of Art. Living and working in London, he has won numerous awards and international acclaim for high-profile advertising campaigns, photo-journalism, celebrity portraiture, and highly collectable fine prints. His B&W images of 1980s fetish fashion are considered among the best ever produced in the genre. He has produced four books: the *Illustrated Delta of Venus* (1979), *Obsession* (1981), *The Dark Summer* (1985) and *White Heat* (1990, with chef Marco Pierre White). A further two – *Insatiable* and *Shooting Sex* – are imminent.

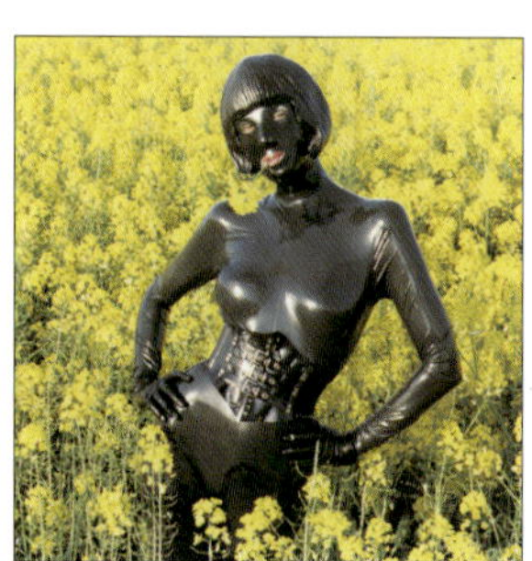

### PETER W. CZERNICH *www.marquis.de*

The man behind the original Anglo-German fetish magazine <O> and its multi-lingual successor *Marquis*, Peter W. Czernich was born in 1953 in Germany. He studied graphic design and worked in advertising agencies in New York and Germany before starting his first fetish publishing venture in 1987. As well as publishing and editing *Marquis* and sister titles *Heavy Rubber* and *Terminatrix*, he directs all his company's prolific fetish output including books and videos, and his crisp, vividly lit rubber photography has graced hundreds of editorial pages since the mid-1990s. Other notable creative ventures Peter has undertaken include designing rubber fashion collections and hosting Germany's *Ball Bizarre* parties and *Art Bizarre* festival.

# RAPHERS

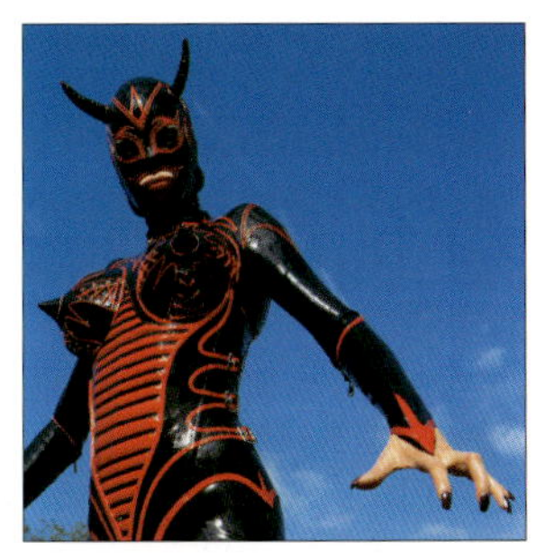



## EMMA DELVES-BROUGHTON *www.emmadelvesbroughton.com*

Emma combines her interests in portraiture, fetishism, fashion and beauty to produce distinctive fine art fetish images. Her B&W work draws on a wide range of specialist skills including toning and hand tinting on fibre-based papers. Colour features prominently in her commercial work, and attention to detail is enhanced by her skills as a make-up artist and stylist. Her first solo exhibition, *Lipstick & Lashes*, was held in 1998 at the f-stop gallery in Bath and later in London at the Skin Two Rubber Ball. Her client base extends to Japan, she is a regular *Skin Two* contributor, and photo anthologies she has contributed to include Carlton's *Fetish* (1999), *The Bottom* (2000) and *Love Lust Desire* (2001).

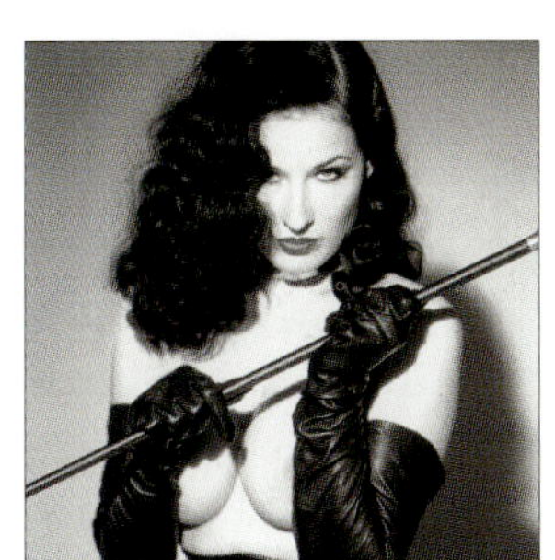

## JOHN DIETRICH *www.lolaart.com*

Born in 1957, John Dietrich first took an interest in photography in his early twenties, but after flirting with formal training, decided to take his lead directly from heroes such as Hollywood's George Hurrell and Britain's Terence Donovan. In 1983 he began photographing professionally as a fashion and beauty specialist, quickly coming to the attention of *English Vogue*, and in 1989 won the Ilford Award, both as photographer and printer. A B&W specialist who prints, tones and manipulates all his own work, he has been commissioned by the likes of Bryan Ferry, U2 and Ozzy Osbourne and is widely recognised as a leading exponent of erotic art photography. A classic selection from this side of his work can be found in his book *The Unrepentant* (Lola Art, 1999).

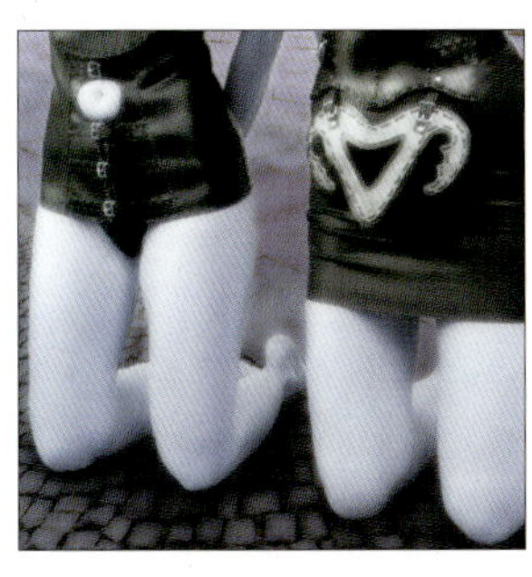

## FETISH ART *www.fetish-art.nl*

Collective name for the Amsterdam creative partnership of photographer/computer artist Robin Cay and fashion designer Doesjka Bee, Fetish Art was born in 1997 with a mission to combine art and eroticism in a fresh, exciting way. Their first commission was for a men's fetishwear catalogue but the emphasis quickly moved to creating computer-manipulated images of their own designs. Notable for placing fetishised images of semi-nude models against backgrounds of outdoor architecture, their work was quickly picked up by the art, style and fetish press around the world and led in 2000 to publication of their first book *Fetish Art* (Edition Stemmle). However, the couple still prefer their work to be seen as a combination of images and designs in galleries.

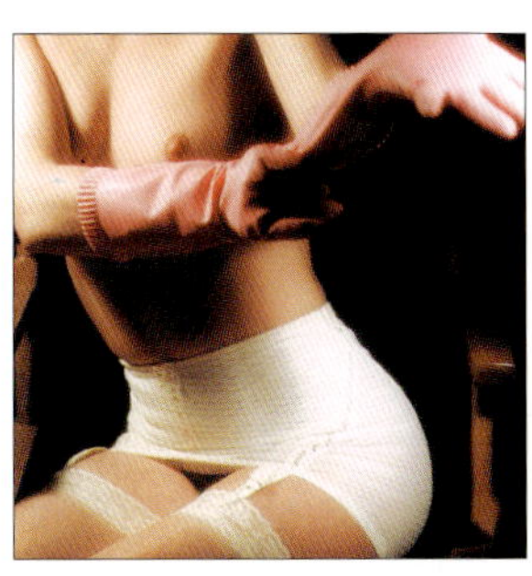

## FETISH EYES *www.fetisheyes.com*

Featuring the work of Alikat and Keital – two leading modern exponents of classic "pre-fashion" fetish photography – and designed by fellow lensman and creative director Hamish Hutchison, the Fetish Eyes website has attracted a huge following after, as Hutchison puts it, "rustling and squeaking onto the cyber stage" in 2000. The team and their contributors offer a smorgasbord of fetish galleries on the site, but are most notable for photography that affectionately evokes the style of 1960s British and European fetish imagery. From vintage wetsuits to rubber mackintoshes, swimcaps to riding boots and gasmasks to girdles, Fetish Eyes presents the classic subject matter of fetishism in a slick, professional and totally modern package.

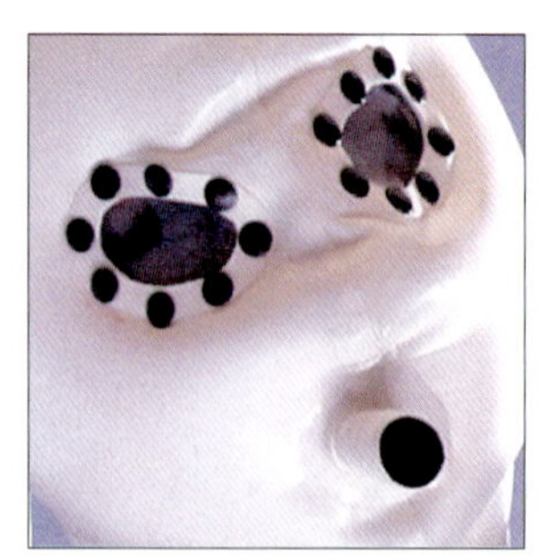

## JOHN FITZGERALD *www.gwenmedia.com*

Growing up in the Pacific Northwest of the United States, photographer John Fitzgerald moved to Los Angeles in the early 1980s and began a career as a professional cinematographer in mainstream Hollywood. Though enjoying work on various feature films, commercials and music videos, John had always sought to bring his talents to fetish photography. After he met Robert Zak, owner of latex clothing store Whiplash! in 1998, the two set out to create GwenMedia, a company that would focus specifically on "the beauty of latex and fetish". Under its auspices, the two partners apply their skills to fetish film production and web design as well as still photography, producing some of the most stylish images of "extreme rubber" to be found.

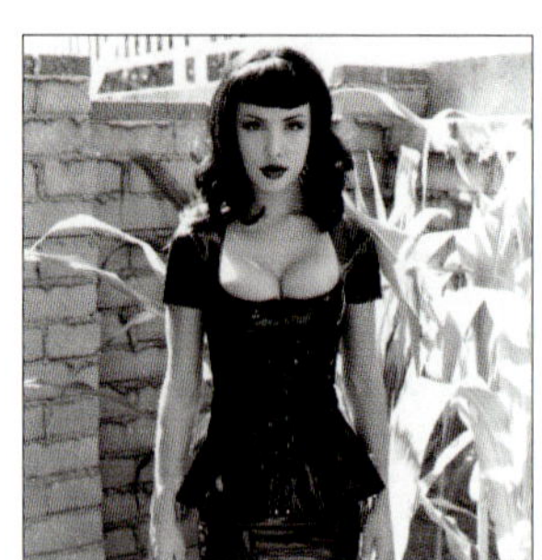

## STEVE DIET GOEDDE *www.stevedietgoedde.com*

Steve Diet Goedde (pronounced "Geddy") has been doing fine art fetish and erotic photography for close to ten years. He started in the early 1990s in Chicago, but in 1998, he relocated to Los Angeles where he currently lives and works. Though renowned for his "fetish eye", Steve says his interest lies primarily in the art of photography, his priorities being tone, composition and mood. He sets out to capture the personality of his subjects and as a result, believes his models – the cream of California's perverati – exhibit a more human demeanour than is seen in most fetish work. His first book *The Beauty of Fetish* (Edition Stemmle, 1999) is already regarded as a fetish classic, and its sequel, *TBoF Vol 2*, (2001), looks set to achieve similar status.

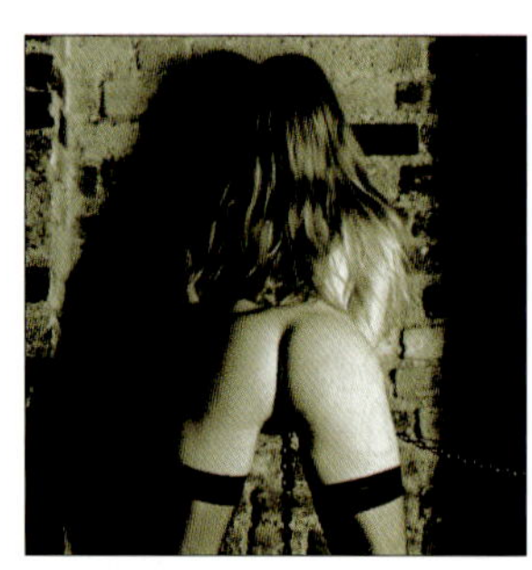

## CHINA HAMILTON *www.chinahamilton.com*

Fascinated by photography from the age of eleven, London-born China Hamilton completed a diploma in art and design and soon began to focus on life drawing, painting and photography of the female nude. An accomplished and respected erotic art photographer whose work is exhibited, published and collected internationally, he is recognised for his creative darkroom techniques and skilful hand-printing. Applied to the creation of SM and fetish images (as it often is), his style evokes the other-worldliness of darker sexual fantasies in a tantalising and uniquely atmospheric way. China's publishing credits include numerous anthologies as well as two monographs from the Erotic Print Society, *A View from Behind* (1997) and *Woman* (1999).

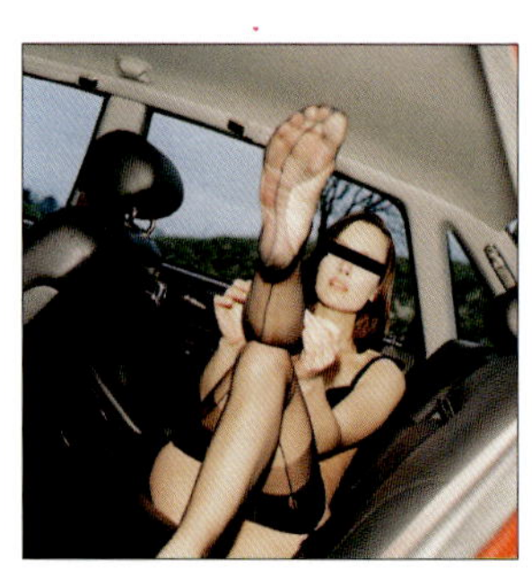

## ERIK HANSEN-HANSEN *www.ocular1.dk*

Photographer, producer and multimedia artist Erik Hansen-Hansen is co-owner of visual productions company The Ocular One in Copenhagen, the city where he was born in 1966. Though known for its glamorous and erotically aggressive fashion photography, the company today is equally involved with internet streaming video and multimedia productions. Adoring "the potential fetish kink in fashion" but despising "the inherent stupidity" of the pro fashion world, Erik is now shifting away from commercial work and trying to push his boundaries in the art genre instead. Fascinated by the new 21st-century fetish for mass-produced designer objects, his goal is "to make a perverse visual exploitation of these postmodern fashion signs".

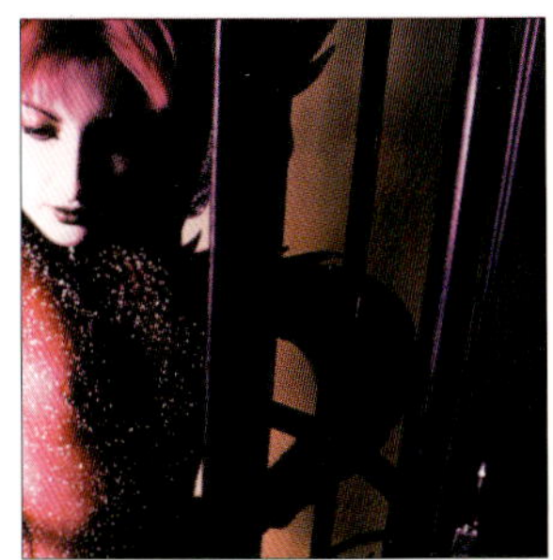

## LEE HIGGS *www.kinkymachine.com*

Born in 1956 in Virginia, Lee Higgs had a very conservative upbringing but was always in a lot of trouble at school. His high school days were in the early 1970s, "at the end of Vietnam and the beginning of Disco". Now based in Chicago, he started taking pictures as a student at New York's Columbia University but did not start to photograph women until much more recently. Influenced by Ginsberg, Burroughs, Nietzsche and Jimi Hendrix, he claims to know very little about photography, having "always been more influenced by books and music". A *Skin Two* discovery, Lee says photography for him is "an act of love and an act of subversion". That double act is showcased in his book *Generation Fetish* (Goliath, 2000).

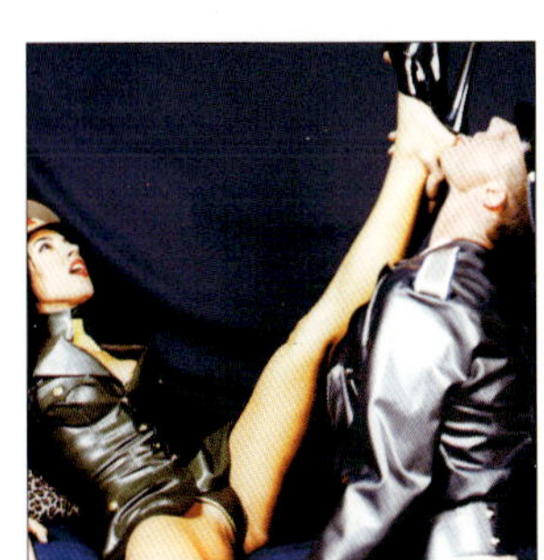

## DAVID HINDLEY *www.rubberduckinc.com*

Manchester-born David Hindley honed his skills in London, gaining experience with such top names as Eve Arnold and Annie Liebowitz. He developed his craft in the music industry, primarily covering live work. This set the stage for his current style of studio-lit club pictures depicting the whole gamut of alternative subcultures, and his work with *Skin Two* and Torture Garden clearly illustrates his ability to connect with the pervy party animal in its natural habitat. David's high level of technical ability, particularly in cross processing, is now married with the advanced photo-manipulation skills of Glaswegian designer Roderick Ramage. The first product of this important collaboration – a major visual exploration of the alternative scene – should be published soon.

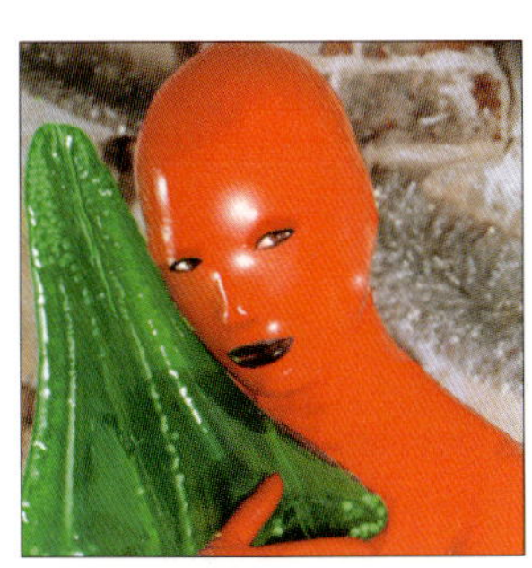

## ALEXANDER HORN *www.l-a-tex.com*

A world-wide web pioneer from as early as 1992, Alexander Horn turned his hobby into a profession when he could not find the fetish pictures online that he was looking for: "stylish and lively fetish pictures without any sleaze or pornography, capturing the essence of latex fetishism as I see it". Professionally a producer of music videos and commercials in Germany, Alexander started his L.A.TEX website in 1995 using his own photography. He continued improving the site both in quality and quantity, and today it is one of the very few free websites with original fetish pictures that is updated frequently – making it one of the most popular on the web. Horn also uses his production skills and technology to produce short fetish clips for his website.

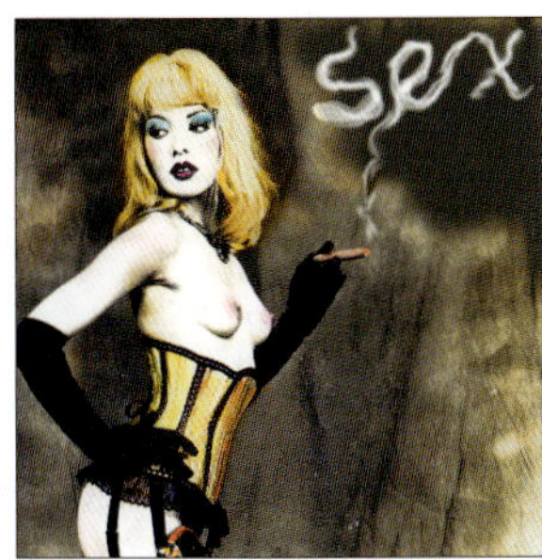


## JUSTICE HOWARD *www.justicehoward.com*

Though she's rightly renowned in fetish circles for her classic portraits of women from LA's BDSM community, Justice Howard's artistic reach stretches far beyond this one genre. Published in 25 countries, she boasts a client list that includes Marilyn Manson, Siegfried & Roy, Dave Navarro, Waylon Jennings, Rich Little, Blue Man Group, Julie Strain and the dozens of other *Playboy* Playmates and *Penthouse* Pets who have been captured by her lens. Creator of hundreds of magazine features and exhibitions and contributor to many anthologies, Justice now follows the success of her *Sirens* calendars with her own book dedicated to female pulchritude: *Sirens: The Photos of Justice Howard* (Foto Factory).

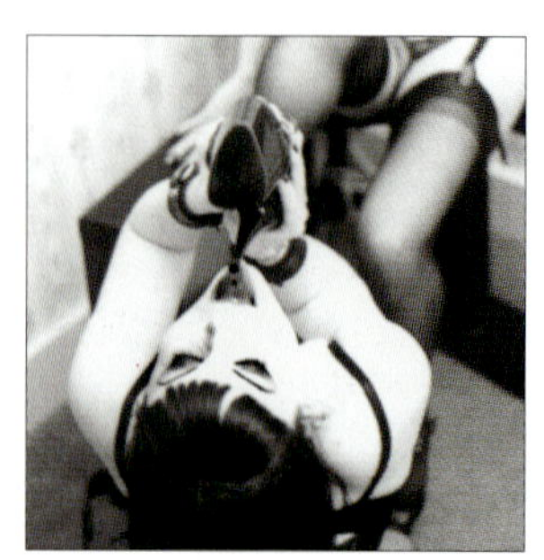

### KEVIN HUNDSNURCHER *www.elaisted.com*

For the last four years, Kevin Hundsnurcher has photographed the denizens of his local Seattle fetish scene. "A critic once told me that I'm an opportunist photographer," he says. "I guess that's why I carry my camera with me in my backpack. Late nights on the weekends, I'll meet girls at the clubs and convince them to let me take their picture." He likes to shoot them in public, always interested in how things will turn out when they pose in full view of an unprepared audience. Until recently Kevin promoted his efforts entirely through his website, a showcase for his mastery of Flash animation. But his approach to the photography itself is surprisingly untechnical. "I usually just try to get a shot of the models when they're at their most natural and sexiest," he confesses.

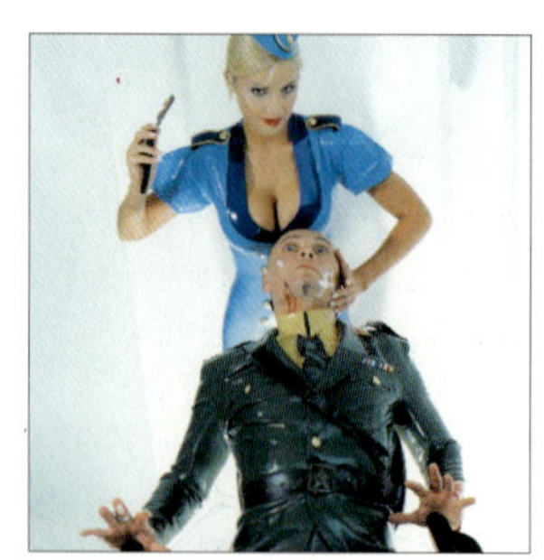

### JAMES & JAMES *www.jamesandjames.co.uk*

Based in London but originally from the north of England, James and James have been working together for six years, "We met in Blackpool, moved to France, and bred chickens before coming to London in '94," explains James Stafford, who wields the camera while partner James Green does the computer retouching. They work regularly for *Cosmopolitan* and British music magazines such as *Smash Hits* and *Kerrang*, but pursue a diverse range of personal projects too, such as shooting nudes of 1950s sex kitten Mamie Van Doren and famous Italian hermaphrodite Eva Robins. *Skin Two* published their first collaboration and they continue to work with the magazine, currently producing more of its cover images than any other photographer.

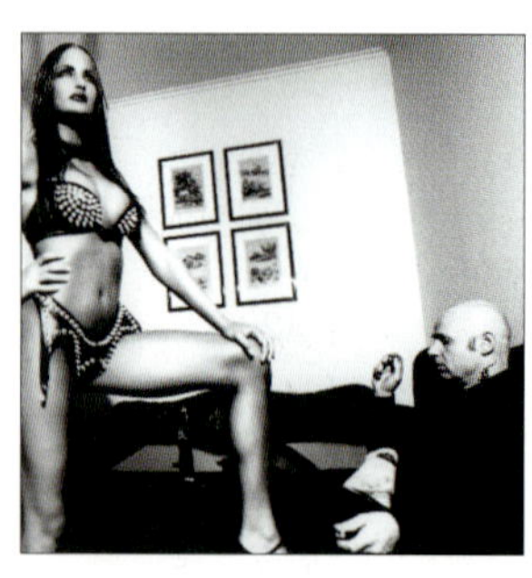

### SANDRA JENSEN *www.sandra-jensen.com*

Hailing from Oslo, Sandra Jensen is a 26-year-old Norwegian/Polish multimedia artist with a taste for bizarre and beautiful images. Under the name Black Factory, she covers a wide range of photographic subjects from fetish to portraiture to fashion. She also works with film, performance and music, writes poems, texts and lyrics, draws, does make-up and styling, creates *objets d'art*, designs clothes and accessories, and, most recently, has been working as a TV reporter making short films about fetish and other underground topics. Initial exposure in *Skin Two* led to publication in numerous other magazines and inclusion, so far, in eight photo anthologies. Her first book – a collection of B&W photographs, poems and drawings – is to be published soon by Secret.

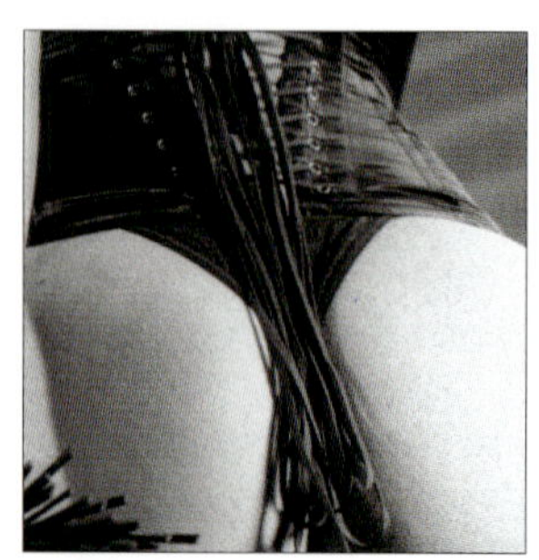

### ROMAN KASPERSKI *www.romankasperski.de*

The close relationship between eroticism and pain is a connecting thread through the personal work of German photographer Roman Kasperski. Born in 1972, he works as a photo-designer in the mainstream, so the fetish images he creates provide not only necessary balance to his commercial work but also expression for his own ideas. He explains: "For me, sado-masochism is visualising the simple beauty of sorrow, power and helplessness – and the fusion between Death and Eros plays an important part." Roman's fetish pictures are the result of "seven years of intensive research" in the fetish world. He showcases them via his website, and his work has been widely published and exhibited in Europe.

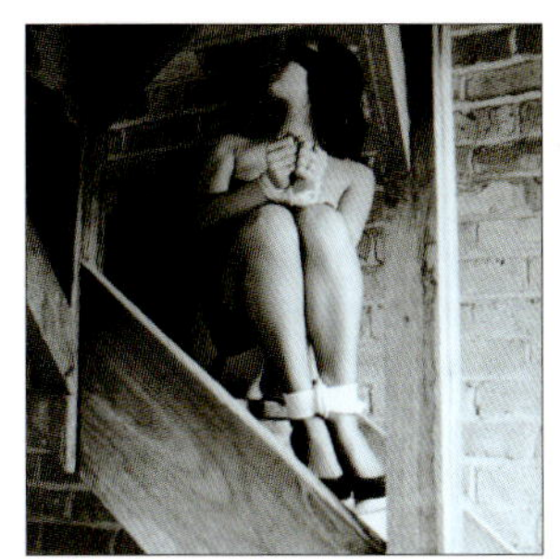

## RAIMUND LAVENDER *www.lightray.co.nz*

London-born Raimund Lavender has lived in New Zealand since he was 14, and began his professional life there as an industrial designer. During this time he bought his first SLR camera, set up his own darkroom and began to teach himself photography so as to create something out of an admitted "infatuation with the female form". His preferred medium is black and white, because "it's about defining the shape and form by light or shade – it is structural". Colour, he feels, makes an image too familiar, too real. Working with non-professional models only, Raimund will happily fabricate garments and "build any set to achieve the shot". Images once created purely for private pleasure are now on his website showcasing 10 years of fetish work.

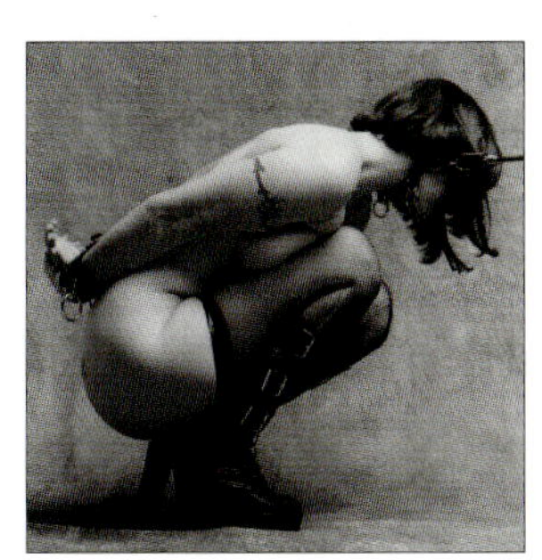

## CRAIG MOREY *www.moreystudio.com*

Born in 1952 in Fort Wayne, Craig Morey studied at Indiana University from 1970–74 under the noted Bauhaus artist Henry Holmes Smith. After moving to California, Craig helped found pioneering nonprofit photography centre San Francisco Camerawork, winning many prizes for his work during his time there. He left Camerawork in 1981 to go freelance, since producing work for hundreds of magazines and a wide range of corporate clients. Craig's book *Studio Nudes* was published in 1992, followed by two Japanese titles, *Body/Expression/Silence* (1994), and *Linea* (1996). His most comprehensive collection, *20th Century Studio Nudes*, has just been published with trilingual text by Glaspalast in Germany. An extensive selection of all his work can be viewed free on his website.

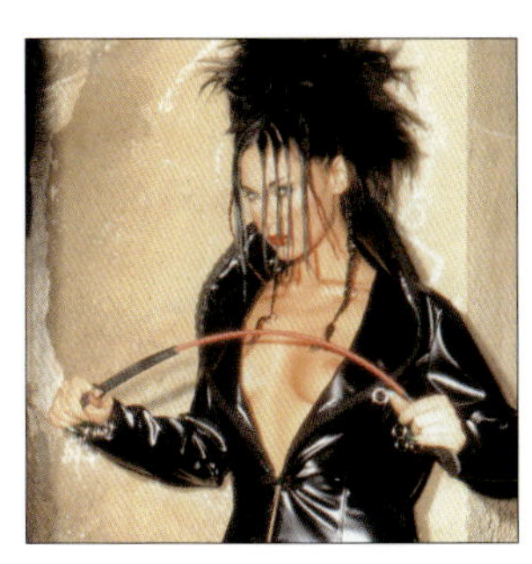

## CHRISTOPHE MOURTHÉ *www.christophemourthe.com*

Christophe Mourthé began his professional life in the theatre and a strong sense of the theatrical still pervades all areas of his work. In 1983, at the age of 24, he met hair and make-up artist Denis Menendez and thus began a lasting creative partnership whose distinctive style was soon in demand for celebrity, glamour and fashion photography across Europe. In 1991 Christophe focused on fetishism and the result was the groundbreaking book *Phyléa* (1993) produced with a Paris fetish store. This led to further collaborations with Patrice Catanzaro in Paris, Boutique Minuit in Brussels and Vero Over in Amsterdam, as well as to independent projects such as *Marlene* and *Fetish Dream*, and to acclaimed work with the high profile fetish model Dita von Teese.

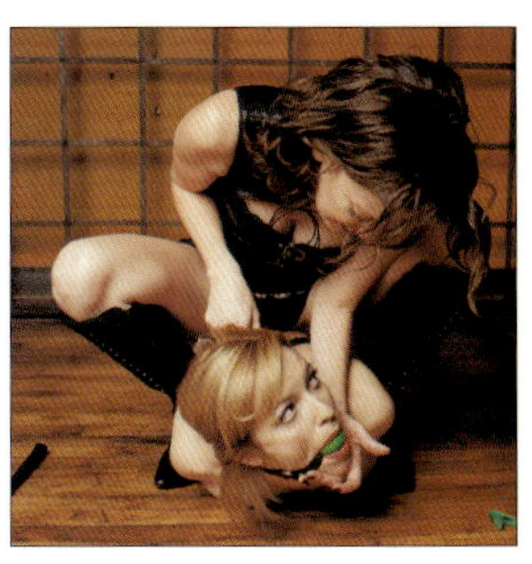

## DAVE NAZ *www.davenaz.com*

An ex-touring musician living in Los Angeles, Dave Naz started photography to keep his sanity after his best friend committed suicide. At first exploring a wide range of subjects, he came to fetishism in 1997, developing a friendship with a famous dominatrix through which he was able to build a substantial portfolio of scene pros and players. "Most people with fetishes are creative," he says. "Imagination becomes reality and I love capturing that reality on film." Much of his fetish photography exhibits a playfulness not found often enough in the genre: a result, perhaps, of the fact that it is not his main business. But it is the camera – especially the dungeon camera – that brings him artistic fulfilment. His first monograph is due for publication by Goliath in 2002.

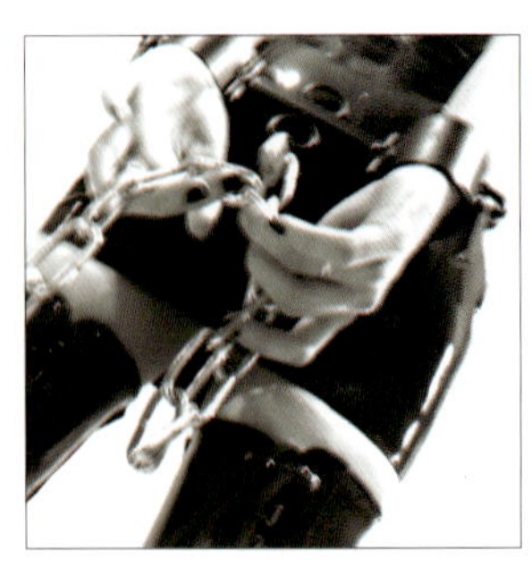

## NO MERCY *www.nomercy.at*

Vienna's No Mercy Project consists of a photographer and model who are also husband and wife, and a perfect example of true fetish talent that might have stayed hidden had it not been for the world wide web. "Johann" and "Sister" (as they must be known for the present) began creating fetish images as a private experiment for fun, but were amazed by the positive response after they decided to put some of their striking, high contrast pictures on to a website at the end of 2000. "I like to wear high-heels, latex and suchlike," says Sister, "so our pictures are honest as they show our own fantasies and obsessions." "Our passion lies in taking those kind of pictures we'd like to see and enjoy ourselves," adds Johann. "This way we want to inspire the viewer's fantasy and imagination."

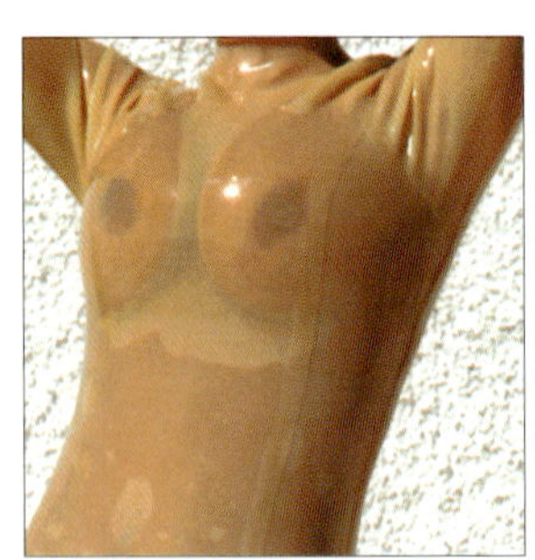

## MARTIN PERREAULT *www.latexlair.com www.latexlover.net*

Martin Perreault is a young French-Canadian photographer who started exploring fetish photography in the mid-1990s. A major turning point for him was in 1998 when his long-time partner Bianca Beauchamp started to pose for him in rubber. She rapidly became his muse and together they used their highly rated websites LatexLover.net and LatexLair.com to share their vision with millions. Since their collaboration began, Martin's work has been published in *Marquis* and *Heavy Rubber* magazines, and on various book covers by Virgin Publishing. He says of his work: "My goal is to capture the essence of latex eroticism through fetish photography. I never get tired of it because it's simply irresistible."

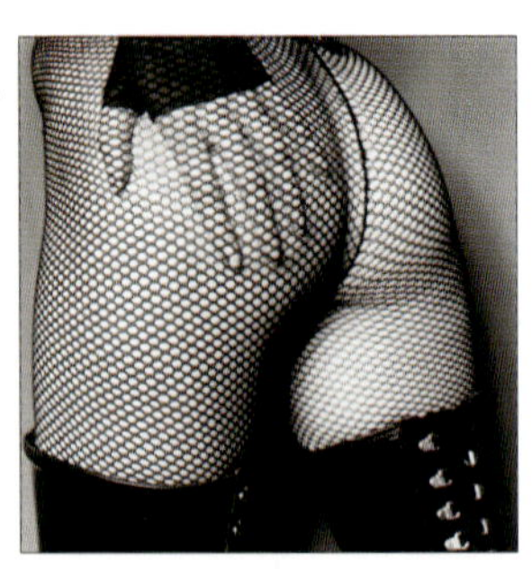

## DORALBA PICERNO *www.doralba.com*

Italian photographer Doralba Picerno has found in London her spiritual home – a place where she is able to document subcultures such as the fetish and the tattoo and piercing scenes that have long fascinated her. Alongside regular fashion shoots and club reportage for *Skin Two*, she has published a portrait book on body piercing and works for rock magazines *Kerrang!* and *Terrorizer*. She puts her success in fetish photography down to the fact that she is not afraid to glamorise women, and doesn't "shy away from strong and assertive females". An established talent-spotter, Doralba has been instrumental in discovering several models who have gone on to become major names both within in and outside the London fetish scene.

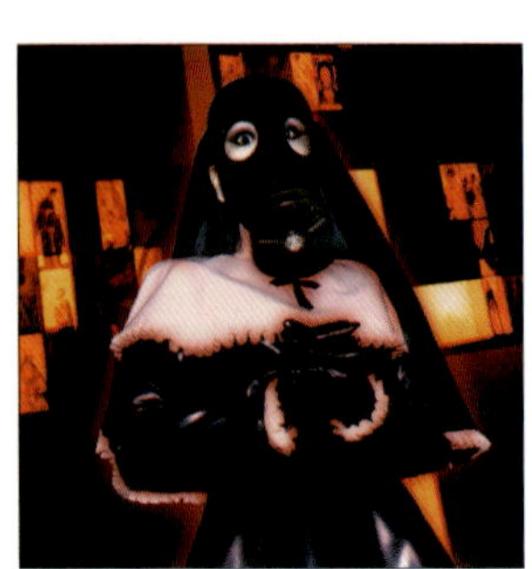

## RUBBER BRAIN *www.rubberbrain.net*

Tokyo-based website designer and occasional model Yu started the website Rubber Brain in 1996 to deal with the growing phenomenon of serious rubber fetishism in Japan. The intention was to depict rubber as a fetish art and to exploit the full visual possibilities of a site, including presenting participants in the Japanese scene in its galleries. At Rubber Brain, explains Yu, "the beauty of the second skin is pursued not only through photography but also through digital effects". The majority of the site's photography is by Yu's friend, Gum Itoh, who we are assured is not only a talented exponent of the camera but also a "real rubberist". Yu chooses the best work from Mr Itoh and digitally manipulates it to create strikingly beautiful results.

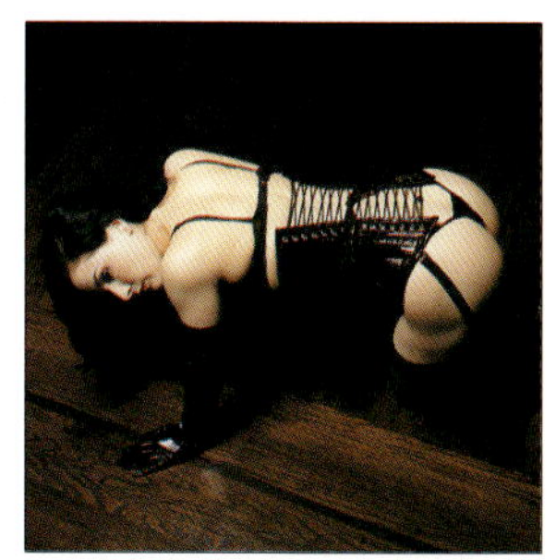

## GARY & PIERRE SILVA  www.silvaphoto.com

A husband and wife team based in Los Angeles, Gary and Pierre Silva find the raw material for their images at LA dungeons, private play parties, fetish clubs, cemeteries and "the personal/secret lives of those who truly live the pervy life". Both actively participate in the LA fetish community. They work as they play, and their lust for life combined with a fine art approach to their work produces images of dark beauty and biting reality. The Silvas' fetish work can be found in such anthologies as *Fetish* (Carlton); *The Fetish Photography Anthology* (Secret), *Breasts* (Carlton) and *Extreme Fetish* (Secret), and their first monograph is due soon from Secret. The pair stage annual exhibitions in LA and also do commercial photography.

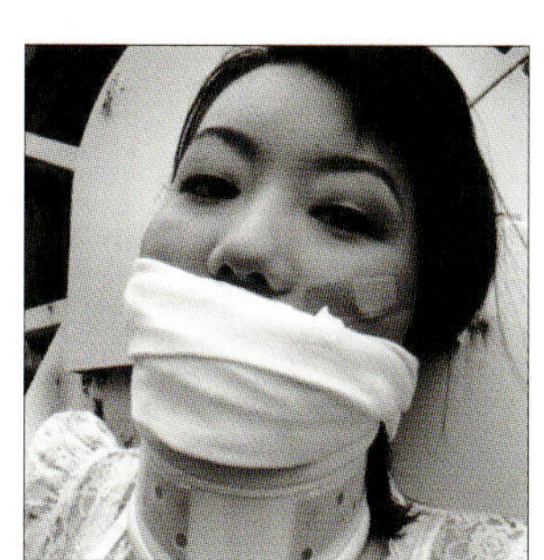

## ROMAIN SLOCOMBE  www.primalinea.com

An award-winning French artist, writer, photographer and film-maker who lives in Paris with his Japanese wife, Romain Slocombe has a long and distinguished history of celebrating Japanese culture. His photography has been exhibited in major cities around the world, and he recently won "Best Foreign Film" at the BBC British Short Film Festival 2000 in London for *Weekend in Tokyo*. The same film also received awards at several European festivals. Renowned in fetish circles for his pictures of Japanese girls in "bandage bondage", Romain recently returned to Japan to shoot images of modern sexuality in all its forms for his latest book, *Tokyo Sex Underground* (Creation, 2001). A feature film is one of several projects he has scheduled for 2002.

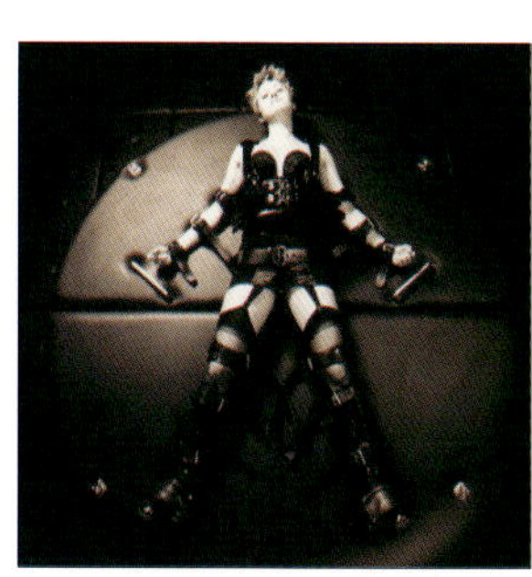

## DEL LAGRACE VOLCANO  www.dellagracevolcano.com

Formerly known as lesbian photographer Della Grace, Del LaGrace Volcano is an American gender variant visual artist who has lived in London since 1982. Del studied filmmaking in California before majoring in photography at the San Francisco Art Institute in 1979. He gained a Masters in Photographic Studies in 1992 from Derby University and has exhibited throughout the world. Del has three monographs – *LoveBites* (Gay Men's Press 1991), *The Drag King Book* (Serpent's Tail 1999), and *Sublime Mutations* (Konkursbuchverlag 2000) – and countless anthologies to his name. Films include *Pansexual Public Porn* (1997), *A Prodigal Son?* (1998) and *Journey Intersex* (1999). A feature-length documentary, *The Intersex Files*, is currently planned.

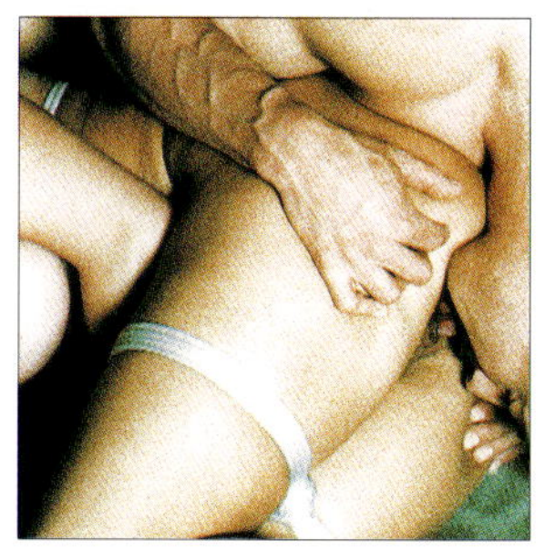

## TONY WARD  www.tonyward.com

With a Masters degree in Fine Arts from The Rochester Institute of Technology, New York, Tony Ward began his professional career in 1979 as staff photographer for a major pharmaceutical company. He continued corporate/industrial photography until 1993 when, aged 38, he returned to fine art work, quickly establishing himself as one of the decade's most accomplished and bold erotic photographers. With countless exhibitions and editorial features to his name, Tony was finally able to present his provocative vision of sexuality and in all its beautifully textured B&W glory with the 1999 publication of *Obsessions* (Edition Stemmle). A year later, he pushed the erotic envelope further with his second book, *Orgasm* (Alixe, 2000). He is now turning his attention to fashion.

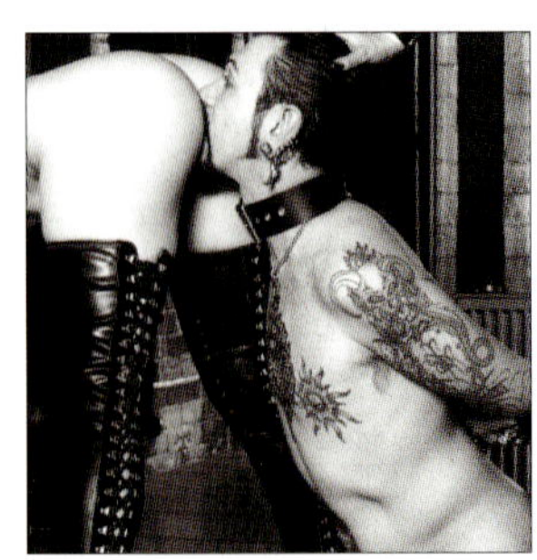

### TREVOR WATSON *www.twphoto.u-net.com*

A fetish photographer since the beginnings of the London scene in the early 1980s, Trevor Watson has been one of the genre's most prolific exponents for two decades. Although self-taught (he didn't pick up a camera until he was 30), he quickly established himself as a master of B&W darkroom technique and by the mid-1980s, his erotic work was to found everywhere, from Athena posters to the pages of *Skin Two* and much more hardcore titles. As fetish magazines moved from B&W to colour so did Trevor, and more recently, he has successfully added video to his repertoire. A regular contributor to anthologies, he produced his first monograph, *Girls Behaving Badly*, for EPS in 1998, followed by *Cheek!* (EPS 2000). The definitive Watson tome is due from Edition Olms in 2002.

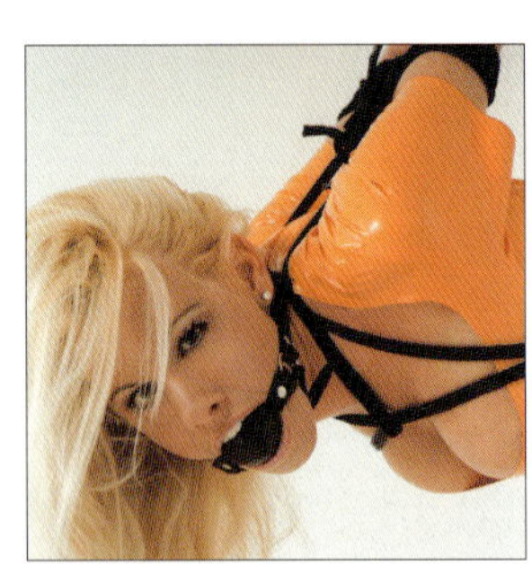

### JIM WEATHERS *www.bondagecafe.com*

The man behind two of the most stylish bondage sites on the world wide web, American Jim Weathers grew up in London and took a decidedly British sense of kink back home to California. His first efforts in the fetish field were stories written just for fun and posted on the internet. But, feeling that the medium lacked quality bondage imagery, he teamed up with fellow enthusiast Cory Thompson to put matters right. Their joint venture Shortfuse was a notable success, presenting bondage glamour in the style of John Willie – exquisite ropework combined with stylish contemporary fetish clothing. In 2001 Jim left to launch current venture Bondage Café, where even more glamorous models are to be found deliciously bound in catsuits, corsets, seamed nylons and heels.

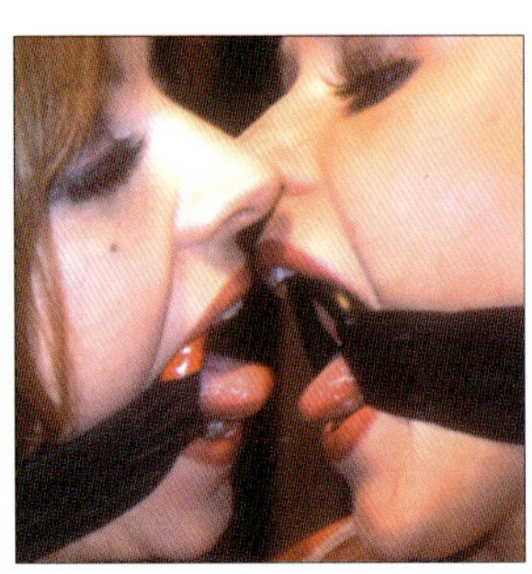

### BEN WESTWOOD *www.pin-up.dircon.co.uk*

Too sexy for fashion and too stylised for porn, Ben Westwood's early photography found a home in *Skin Two*, where his 1950s fetish influences were well understood. He began to pursue photography as a career after realising that shots he had done of his then girlfriend Sarah Stockbridge, who was house model for his mother, Vivienne Westwood, were "pretty good". He used them to start a portfolio which attracted other models of similar calibre to pose for him, thus initiating a unique branch of fetish photography in which the shoes are Vivienne Westwood and a lot of the lingerie is designed by Ben himself. He exhibits regularly and aims eventually to publish his own magazine. His first book, *Ben Westwood*, was published by Treville in 1999.

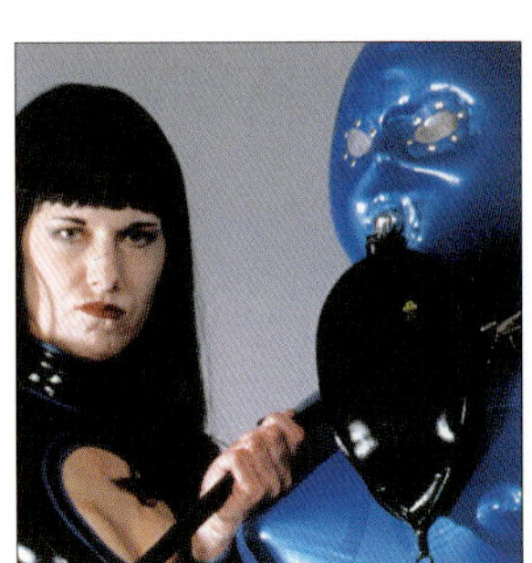

### WHIPLASH! *www.whiplashusa.com*

A fetish clothing and equipment firm would not normally feature in a photography anthology but an honourable exception is Bob Zak's Whiplash! The company has not only brought the cream of rubber designer labels to the USA from Britain and Europe, but also has become an important producer of imagery in its own right – especially at the "heavy rubber" end of the spectrum. When he's not occupying the producer's chair at GwenMedia (the video label he owns with John Fitzgerald), Bob Zak works with various "house" photographers on building up Whiplash!'s archive of bizarre fetish images. The photographs in this book were created for Whiplash! by "Gen", a regular contributor to its website and catalogues.

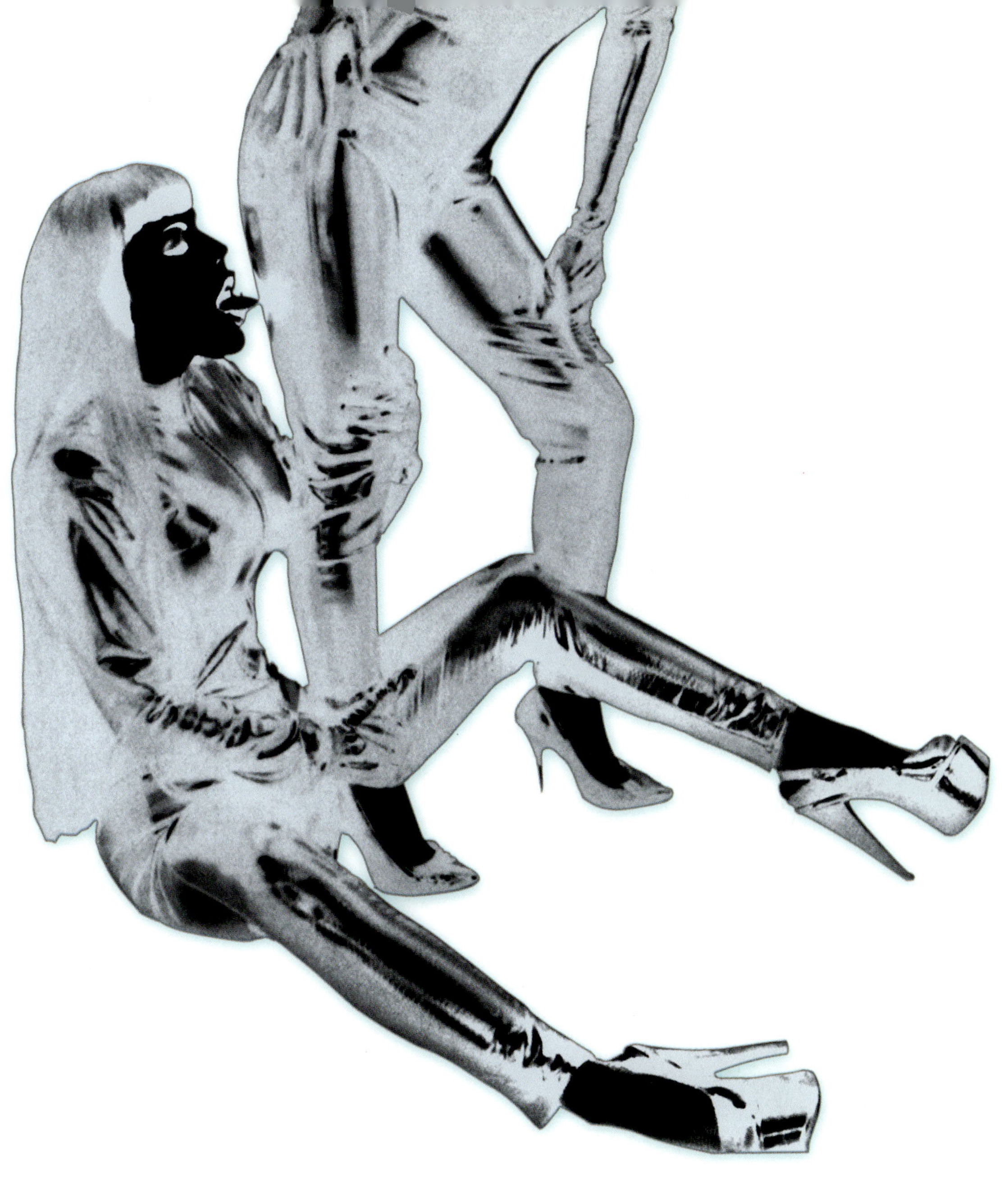

# DRESSIN
# P

Any exploration of the more exotic terrains of sexuality really must begin with a long cool look at fetishism. This once secret activity got a thorough makeover in the 1980s, and in the modern sexual climate, a taste for rubber, leather, corsets, stockings, suspenders or high heels is much more widely accepted as a valid expression of the erotic imagination. Fetishism and fetish fashion have developed into an international subculture over the past two decades, and photography has found this scene to be an endless source of intoxicating subject matter.

Fetishism today embraces many styles of garment and many materials, but the single fabric that has come to epitomise modern fetish fashion is rubber (or latex if you're an American). Rubber's unique ability to cling to and mould the body like a second skin, and the mirror-like sheen it displays when polished, make it a seductive but challenging proposition to the photographer. Great rubber photography requires great lighting skills and the work of Bob Carlos Clarke (such as in *Rachel Weisz*, p.26) has long provided the benchmark.

If rubber is the ultimate fetish fabric, then the quintessential rubber fetish garment must be the catsuit, whose head-to-toe coverage provides a second skin in the most literal sense. Catsuits are usually the most popular item in a rubber designer's range, and while basic black is a perennial favourite, perhaps teamed with matching gloves and boots (Martin Perreault's *Bath* pp.56–57), they come in many shades, from the intriguingly clinical semi-transparent (John Fitzgerald, pp.50–51) to the brightest colours (Peter W. Czernich's *Bizarre Beauty*, p.65) and some, such as the hooded, horned suit of Emma Delves-Broughton's *Devil* (p.35), are incredibly complex and decorative affairs.

Before it became fashionable, a popular public perception of rubber fetishism was that it meant dressing up in a diving suit or perhaps donning a pair of household rubber gloves. Such notions may seem odd now, but in some quarters a fascination for functional rubber clothing still exists – and no one caters for it more affectionately than the photographers of Fetish Eyes (pp.43–45). If you've always wanted to understand the sex appeal of luminescent green bobbly bathing caps, then have I got a website for you.

Though rubber's stretchiness makes it perfect for skintight clothing, it can also be used much like a regular clothing fabric, and plenty of the styles available from today's designers can just as easily be worn for dinner in a restaurant as for dancing in a fetish club. This certainly applies to the outfits photographed by Steve Diet Goedde on pp.66–67, though perhaps not to Gary & Pierre Silva's see-through dress on p.49 (though this might save time on a visit to the doctor).

And rubber lends itself extremely well to uniforms, which of course have a major part to play in our fetish fun. Any uniform that you find sexy in its original form will be far more powerful and seductive if rendered in rubber. This particular rôle is explored more fully in our "Domination and

# G FOR EASURE

Discipline" chapter, but for an early taste, check out Emma Delves-Broughton's cute roller-skating rubber waitress (*Roller Girl*, p.37) and Alexander Horn's rubber nun (*Nun in the Cellar*, p.60).

Clothing fetishism in general can be traced back to the sexually repressive Victorian era, but today, the most widely fetishised Victorian garment is the corset. Not the *faux* styles of recent fashion, but the real, steel-boned, tight-lacing, waist-cinching, back-straightening article. Unlike their austere forebears, the decorative modern corsets photographed by Doralba Picerno (p.30), Emma Delves-Broughton (p.36) and Steve Diet Goedde (p.68) are obviously designed to be seen. But in every other respect they are as the originals: to get into them is a labour of love, and to stay in them is to endure unremitting bondage!

If the Victorian era stirred up a sexual interest in underwear, then it was surely the 1950s that produced its quintessential expression. Women's underwear fashions of that period seems to have achieved a particularly tantalising balance between modesty and revelation, restriction and liberation, functionality and decorativeness. The sort of stuff Bettie Page wore to get tied up for Irving Klaw is guaranteed to quicken the pulse of many a young modern, but retro lingerie is now such a common element of mainstream glamour photography that sometimes only the most stylised kind of fetish photography can still evoke the original sinfulness of those 1950s underpinnings. In Britain, Ben Westwood is an acknowledged master of that art. His images of girls in basques, big knickers, stockings and suspenders such as those on pp.24–25 transport the viewer back instantly to an earlier, golden age of frivolity, frills and thrills.

For many of us though, the outstanding contribution the 1950s have made to modern fetishism is not the whole lingerie experience so much as one specific element of it: stockings. The wearing of stockings is one of the most widely understood symbols of flirtatiousness and erotic promise, and this language of legs is fluently spoken both within and outside fetish circles. But as even ordinary men ago weak at the knees at the very mention of stockings, fetishists have had to refine their tastes. Real stocking enthusiasts only accept proper stockings, and that means vintage-style, non-stretch, seamed nylons with all the trimmings: the reinforced heels, the doubled-over tops and those little holes at the back. Erik Hansen-Hansen is a man who understands this well, as you can see on pp.38–39. Erik also appreciates (*Upskirt 2*, p.40) that a well-turned leg can have just as much fetish appeal in a slinky pair of tights. Are they not, after all, another kind of second skin?

We cannot finish without a word about shoes, boots and heels, which are to be found throughout this chapter and the rest of the book. Heels are indispensable to the fetish experience. For most pervs, no outfit is complete without them. For some, no outfit is necessary with them. Take your pick.

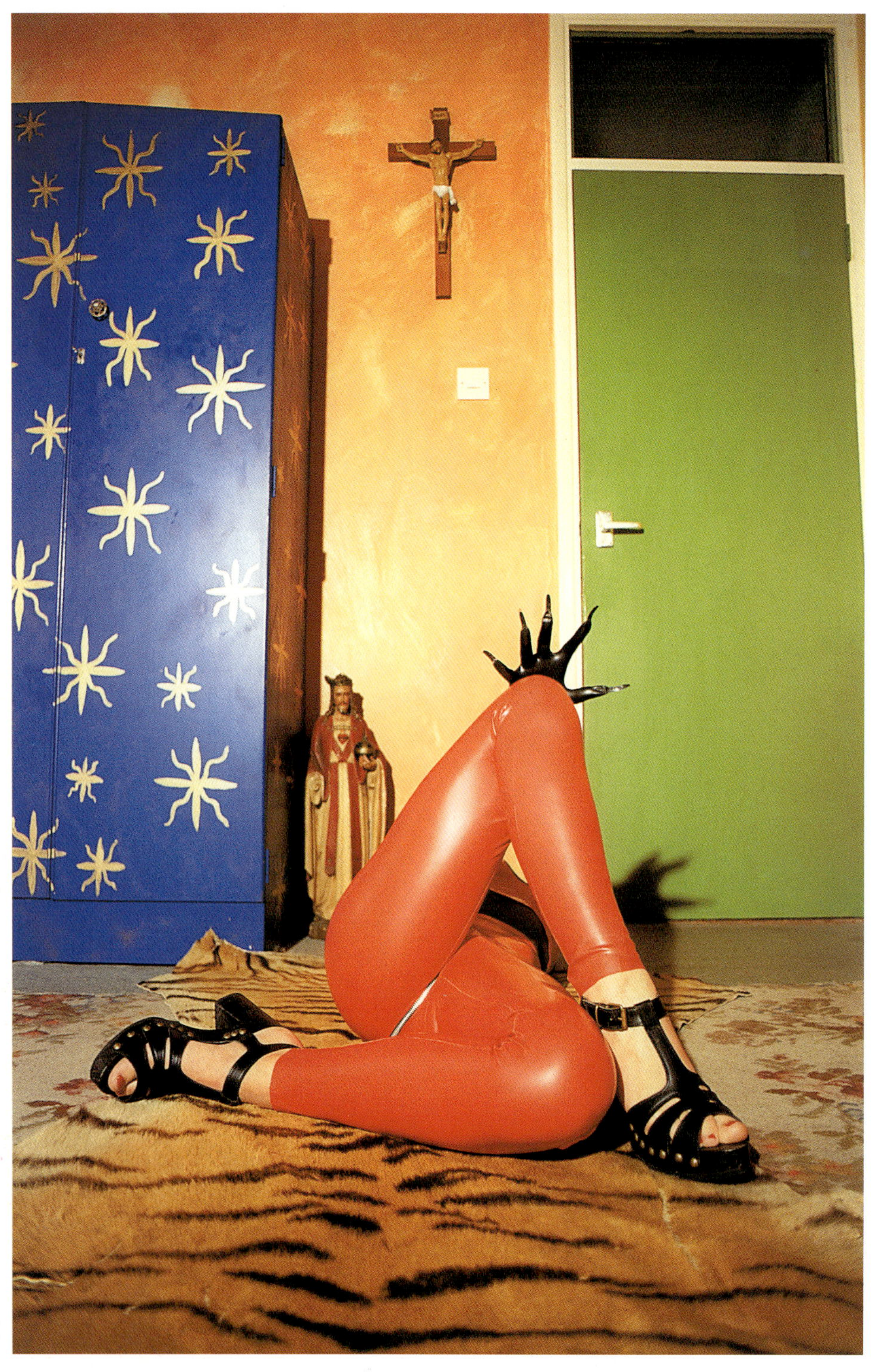

 Alva Bernadine

Opposite Alva Bernadine

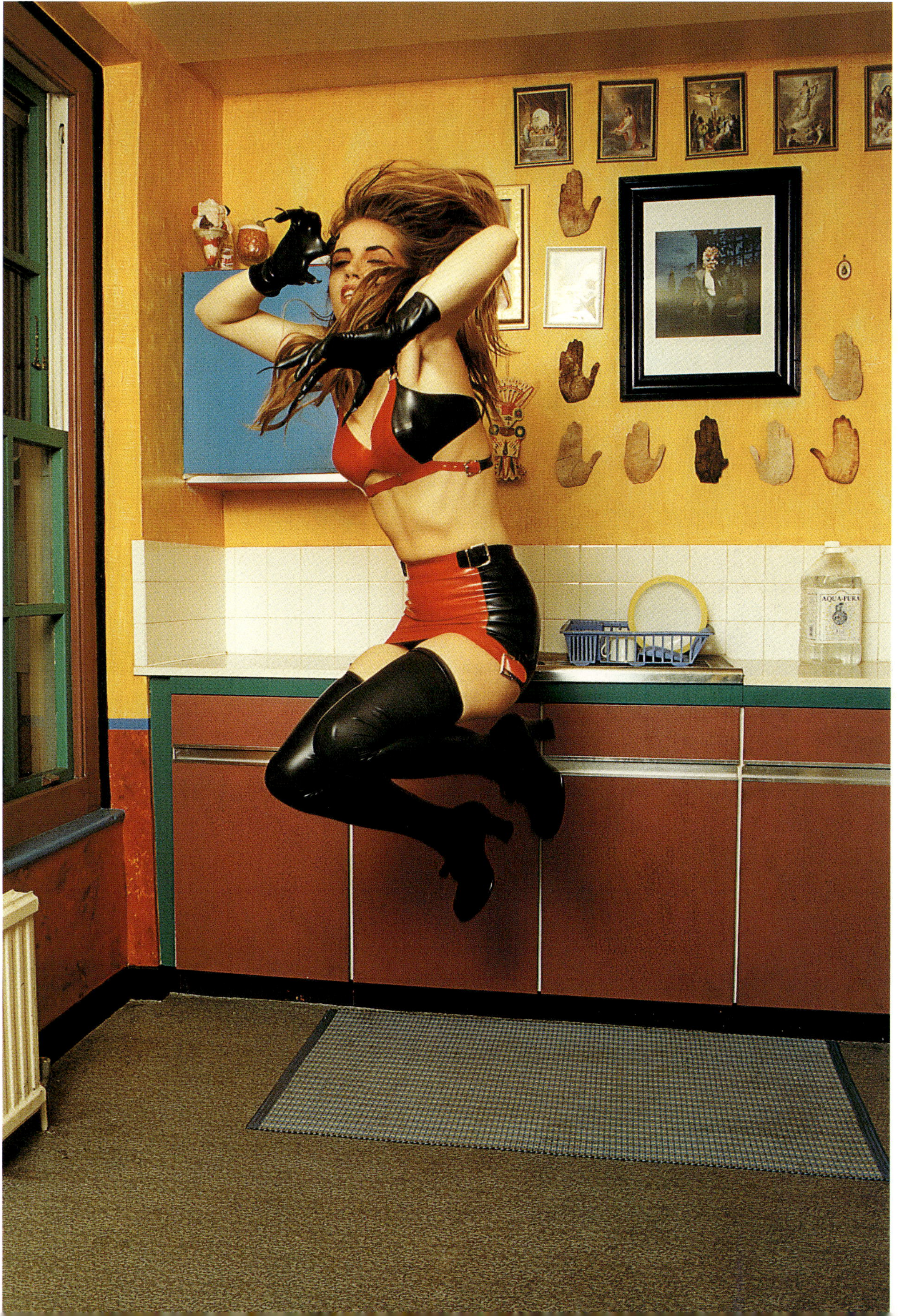

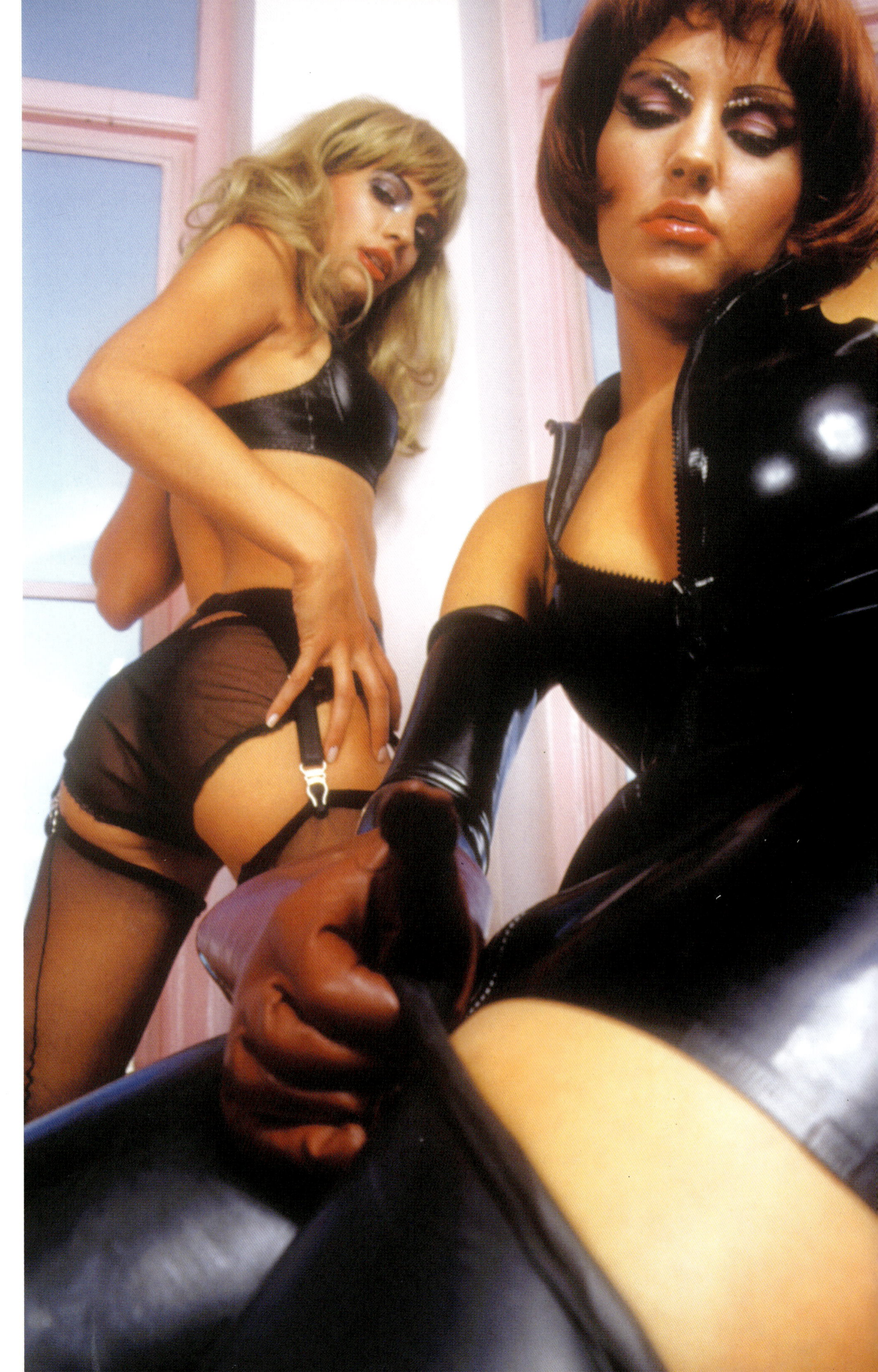

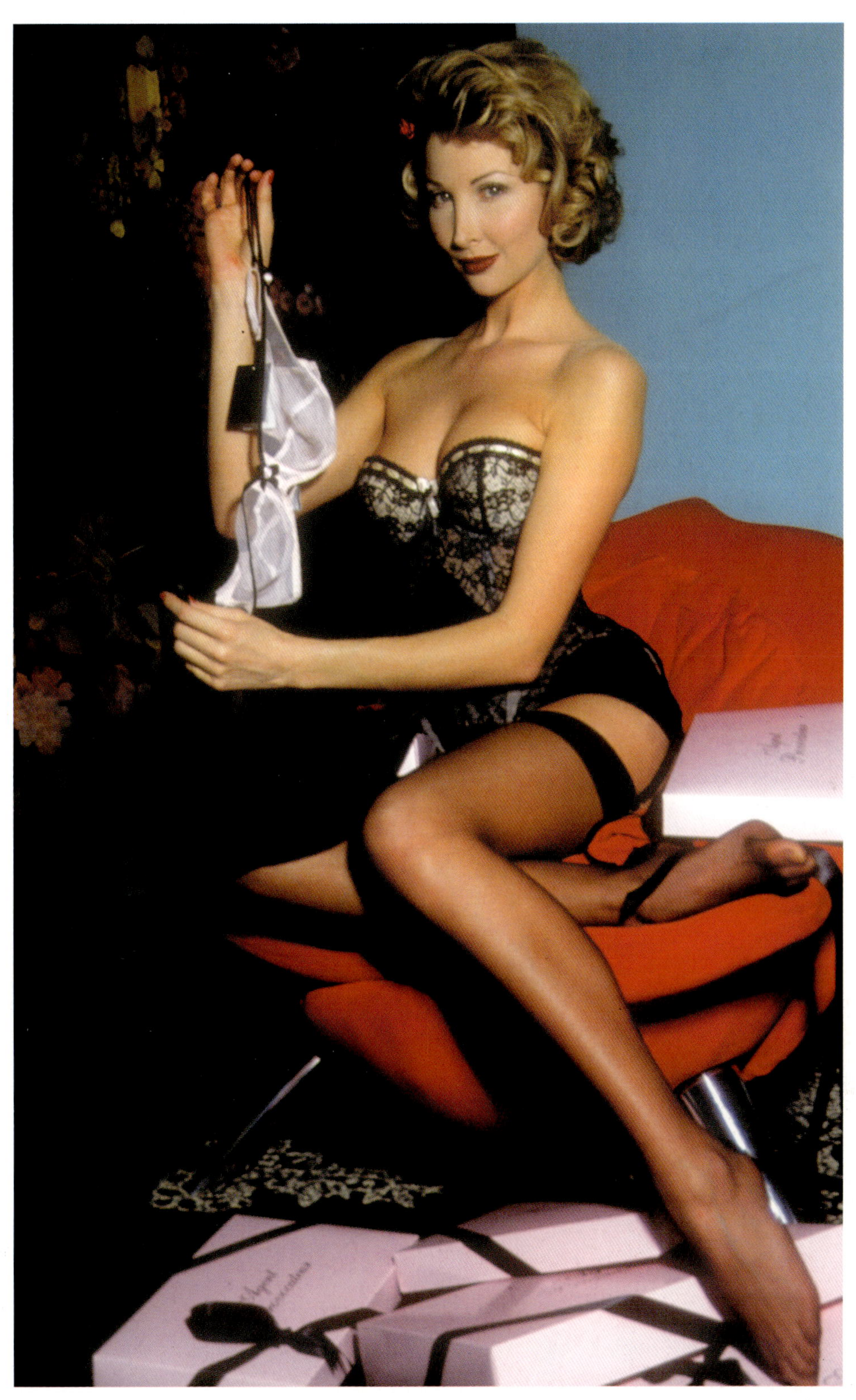

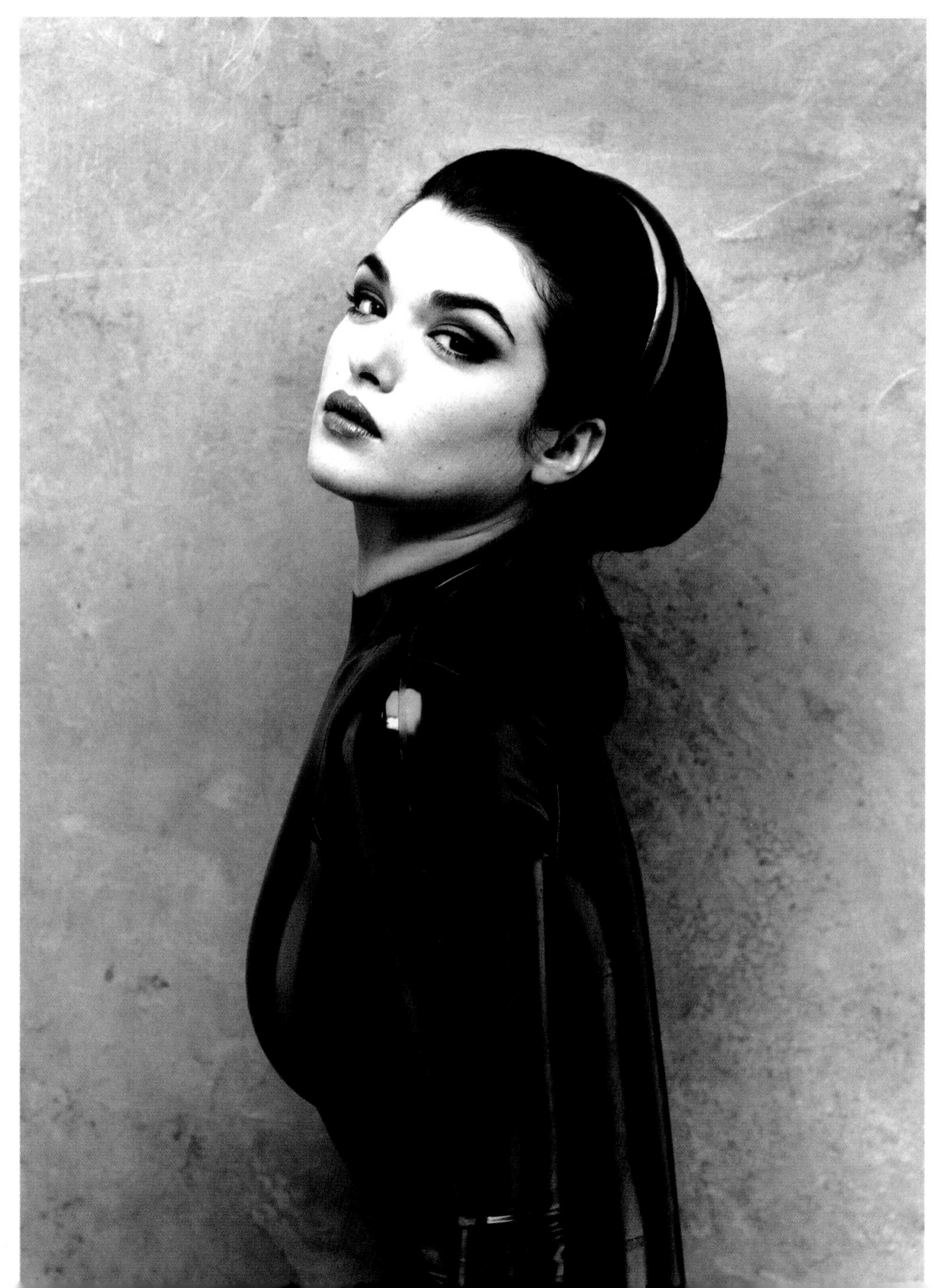

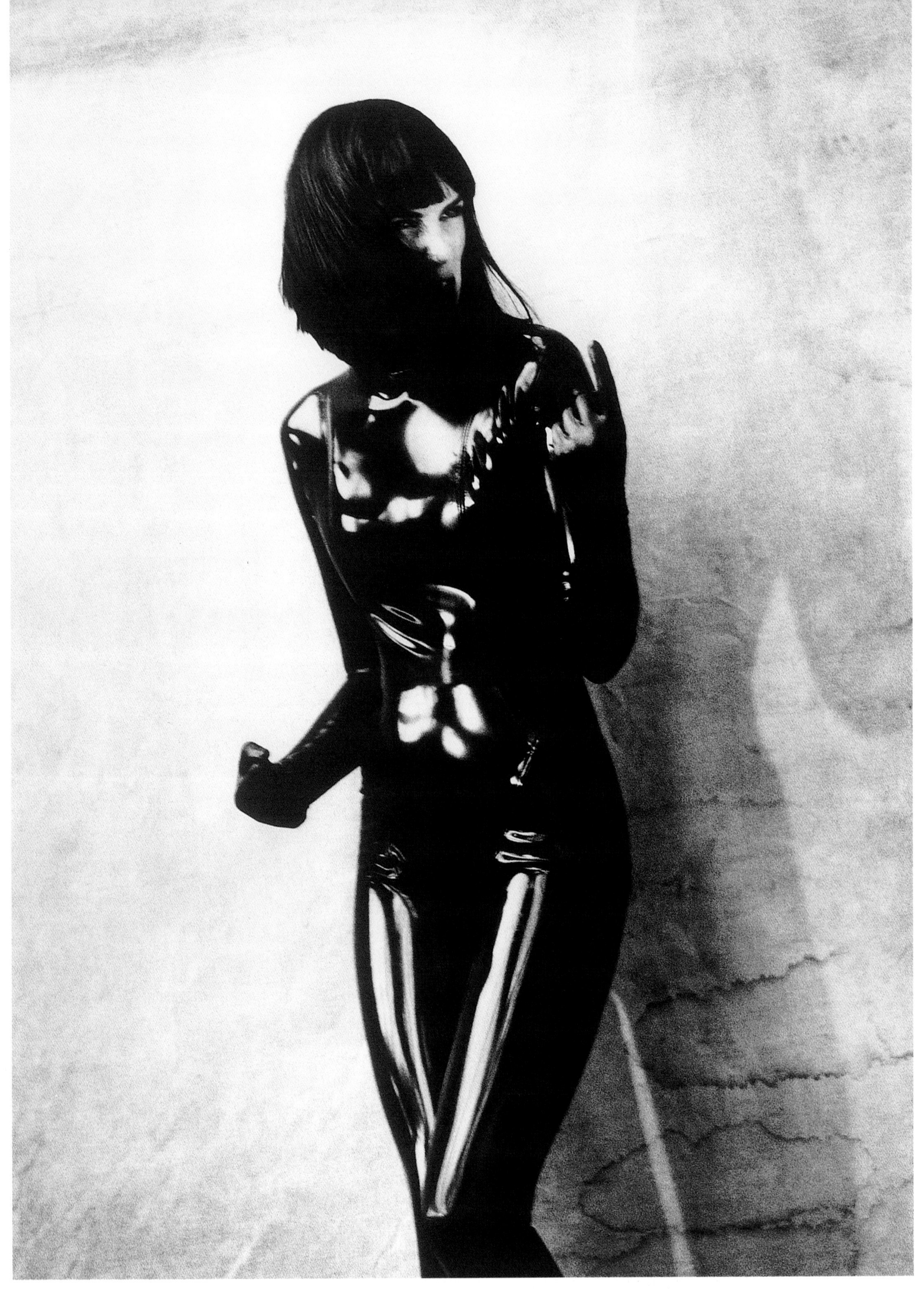

Opposite Bob Carlos Clarke

Bob Carlos Clarke 27

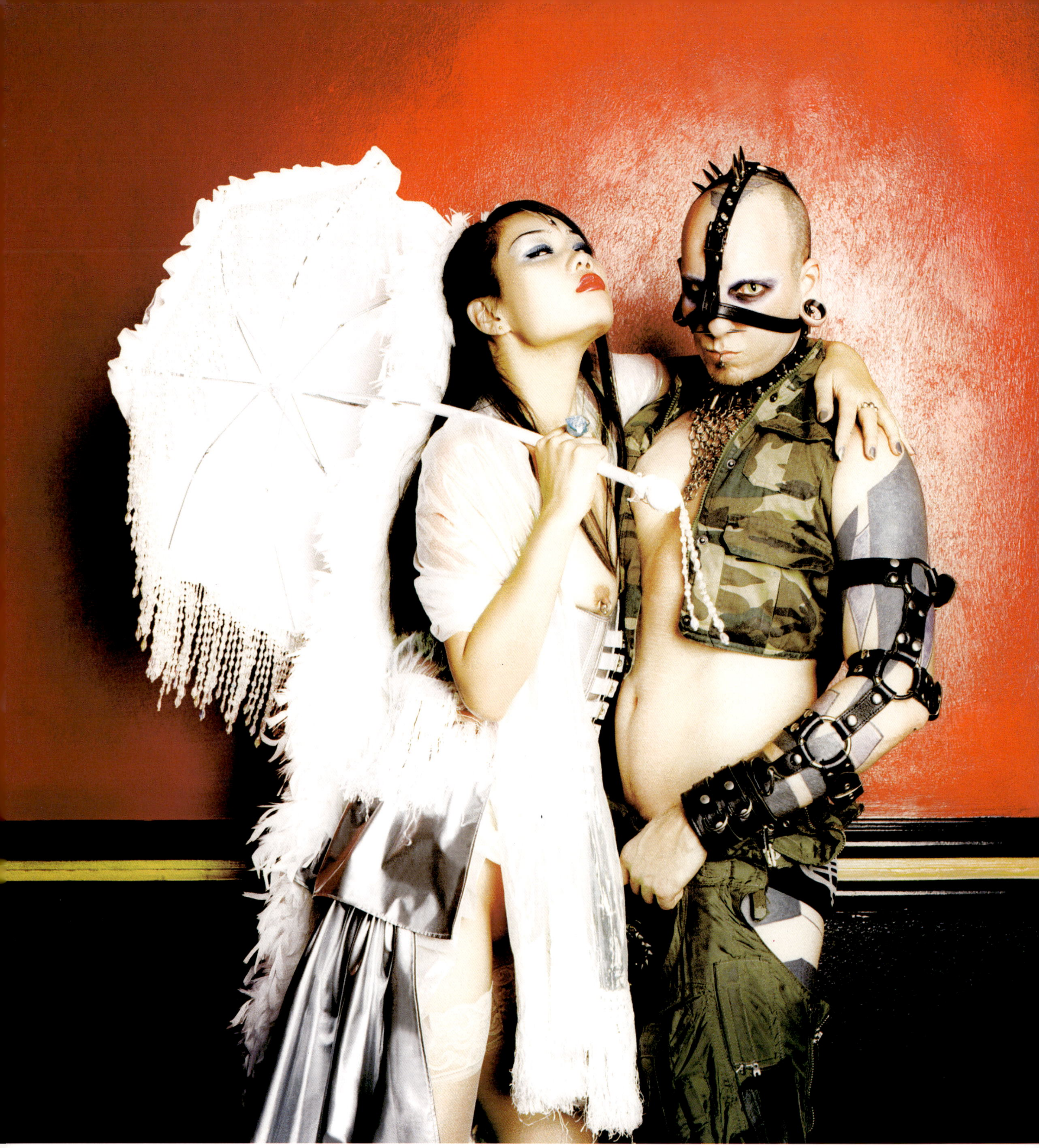

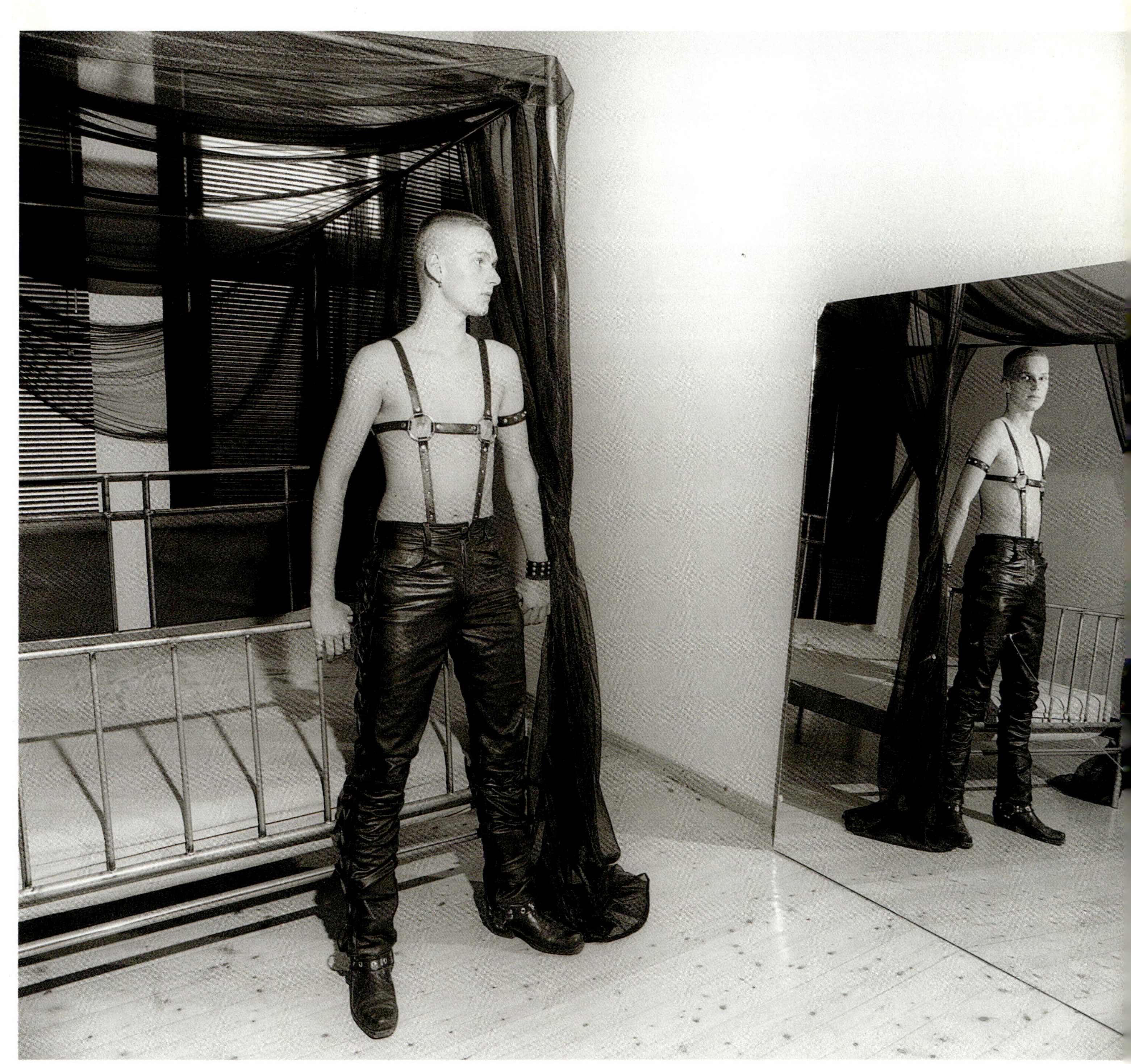

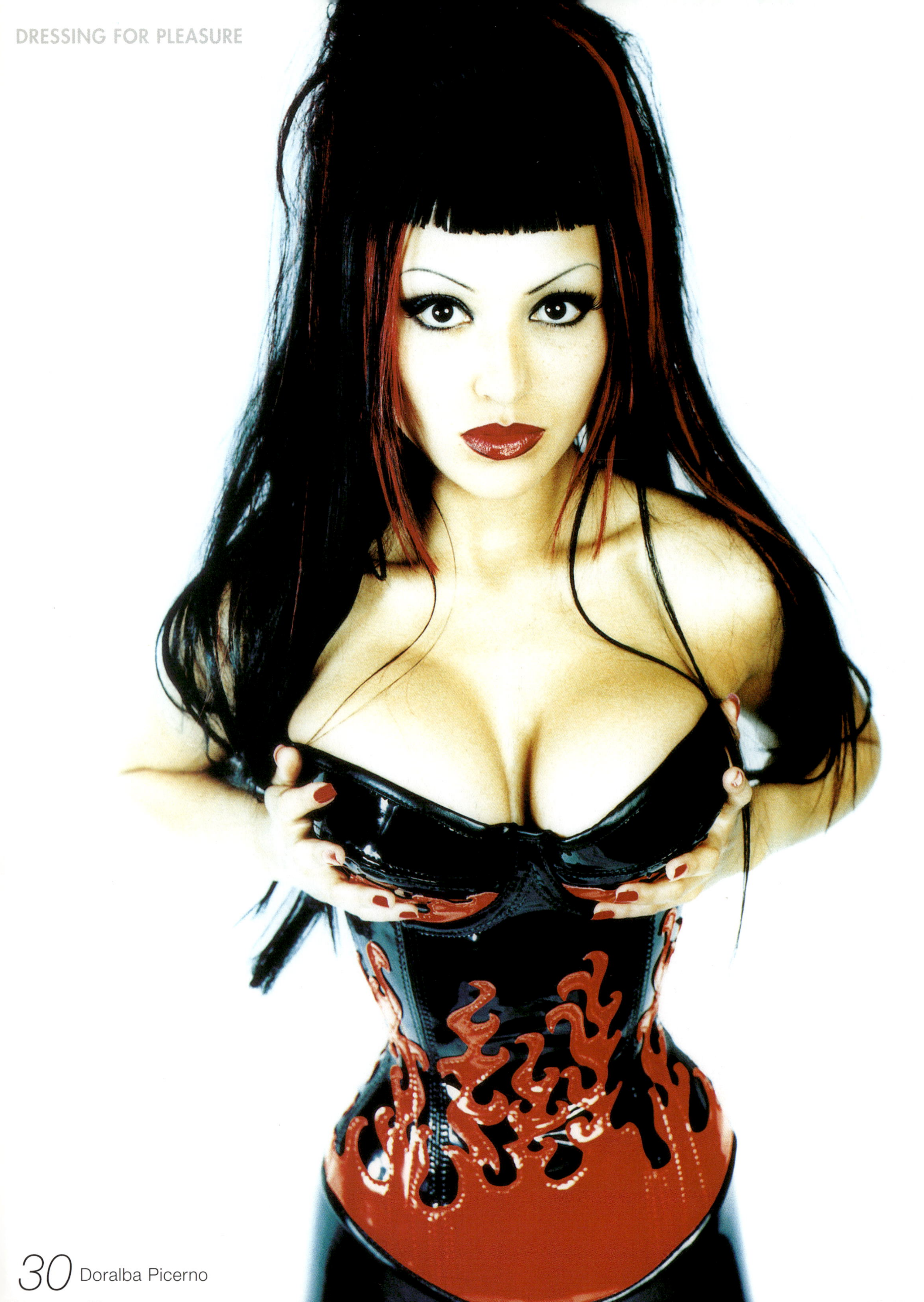

30  Doralba Picerno

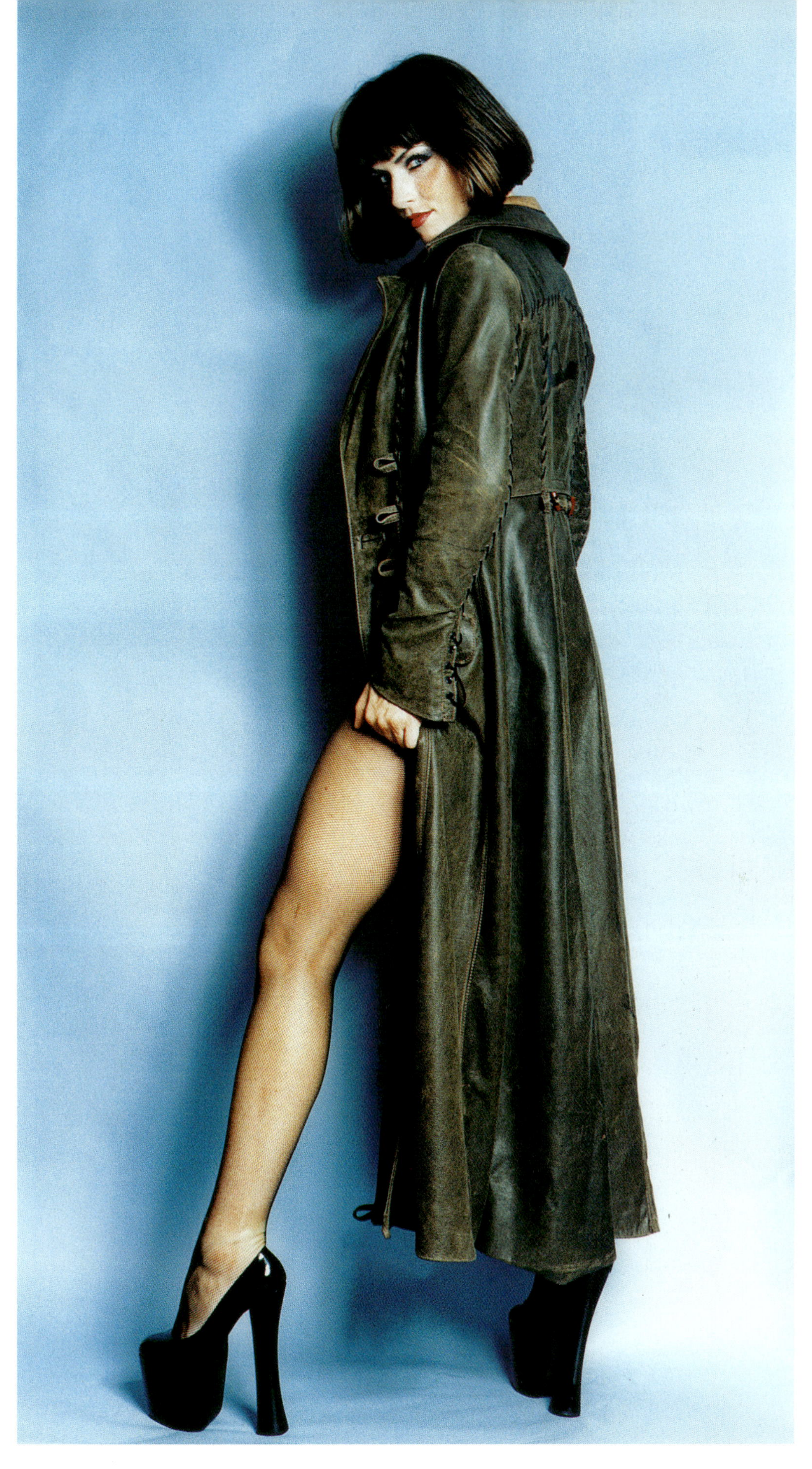

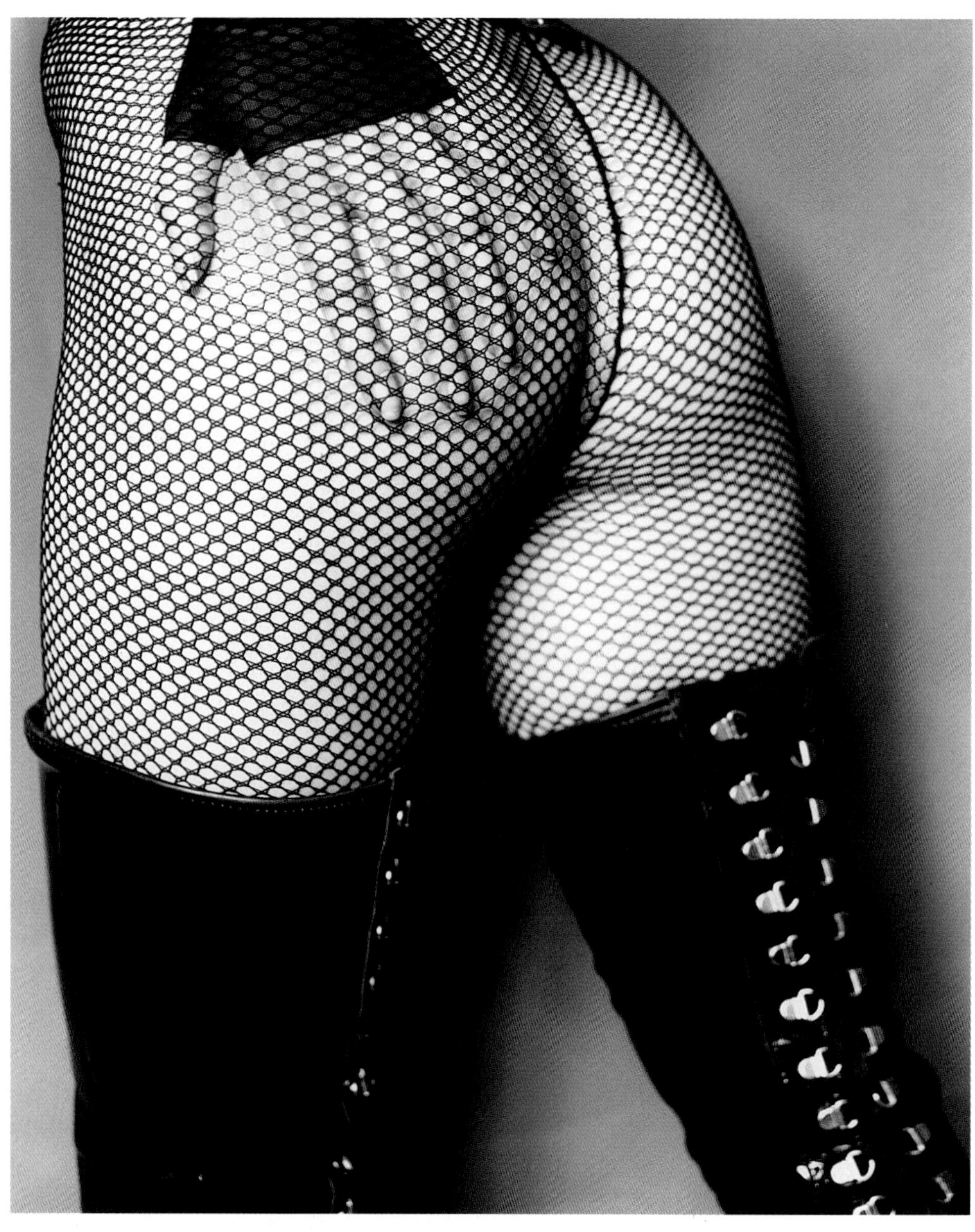

 Doralba Picerno

Opposite Trevor Watson

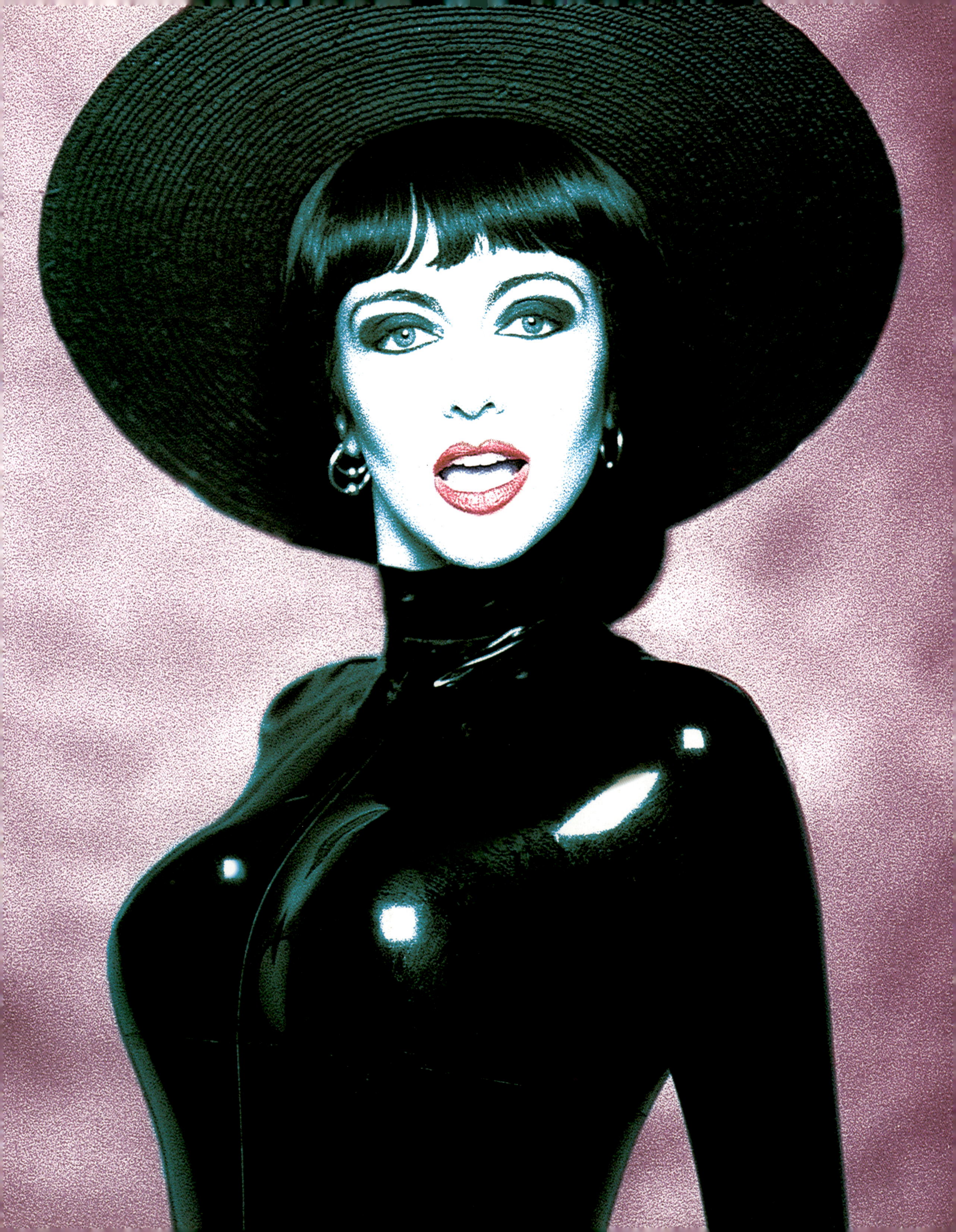

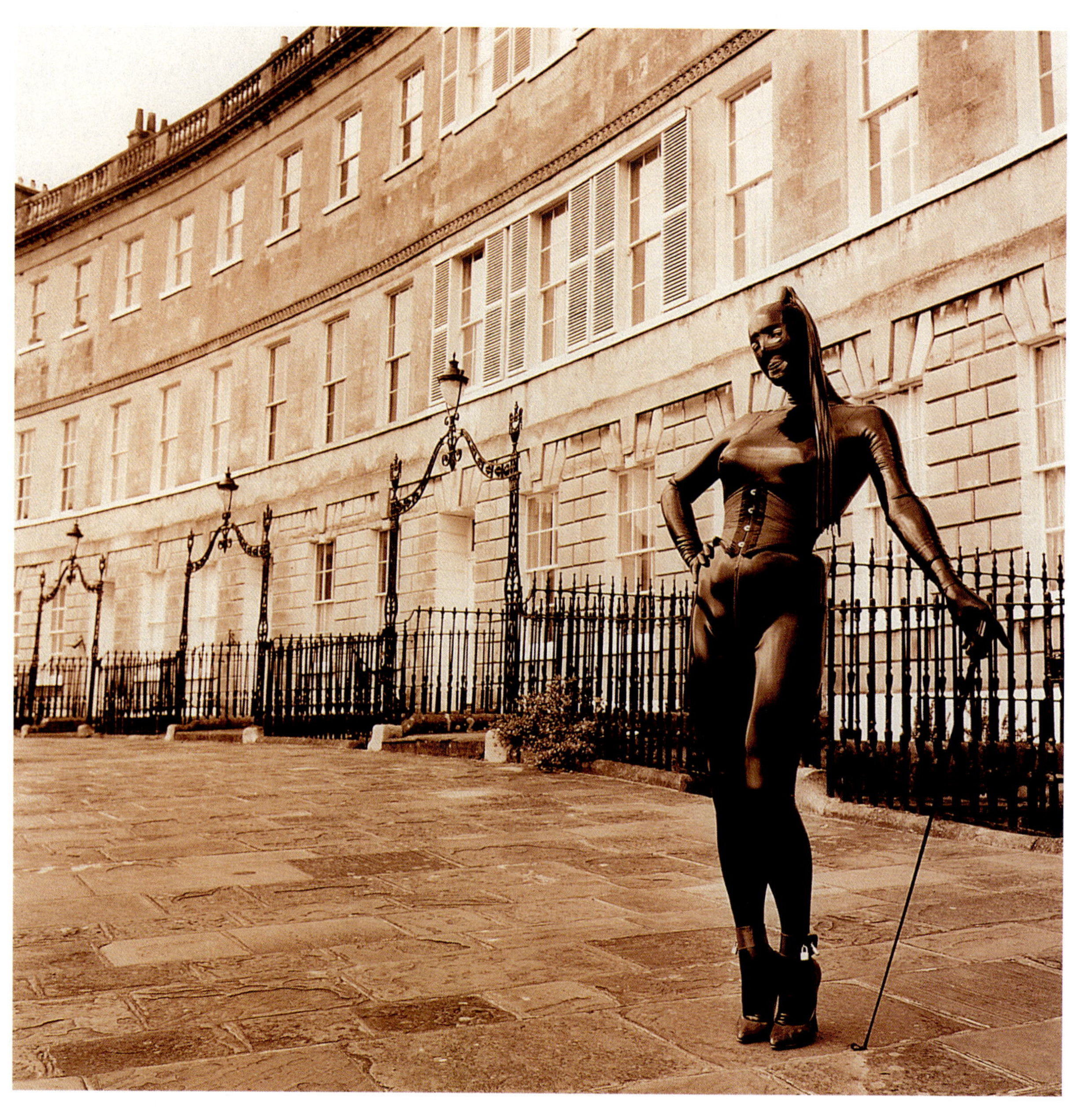

 Emma Delves-Broughton

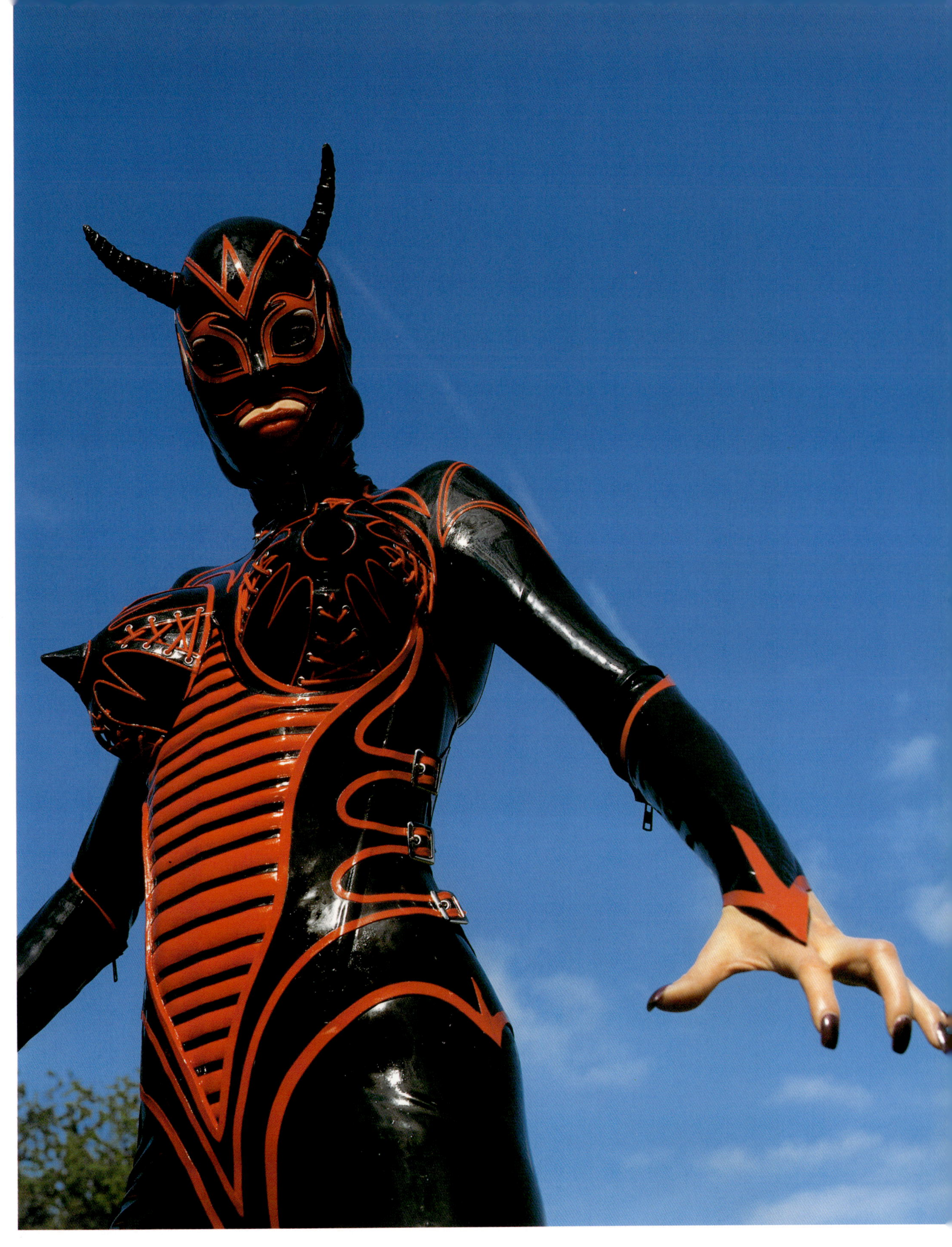

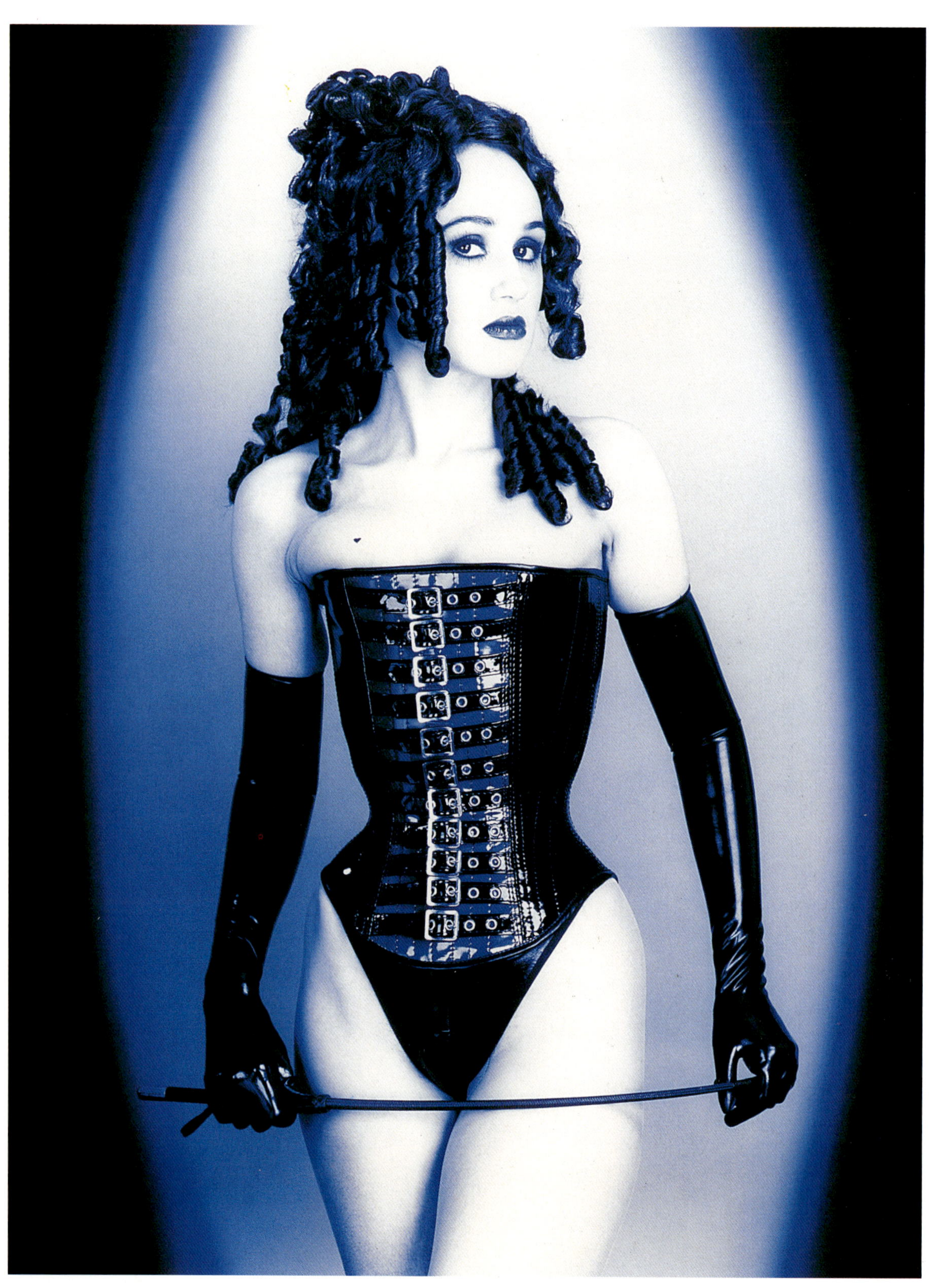

 Emma Delves-Broughton

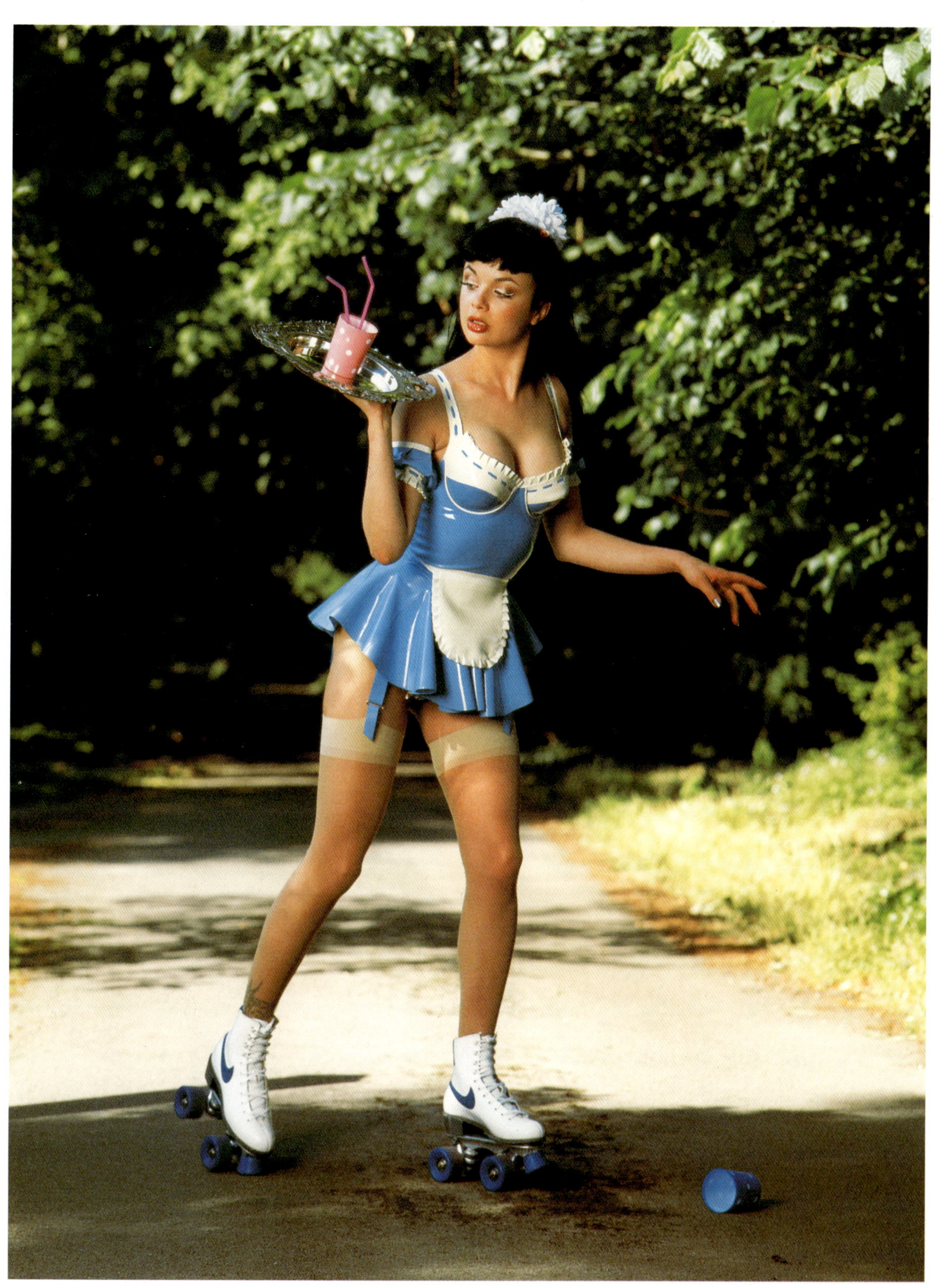

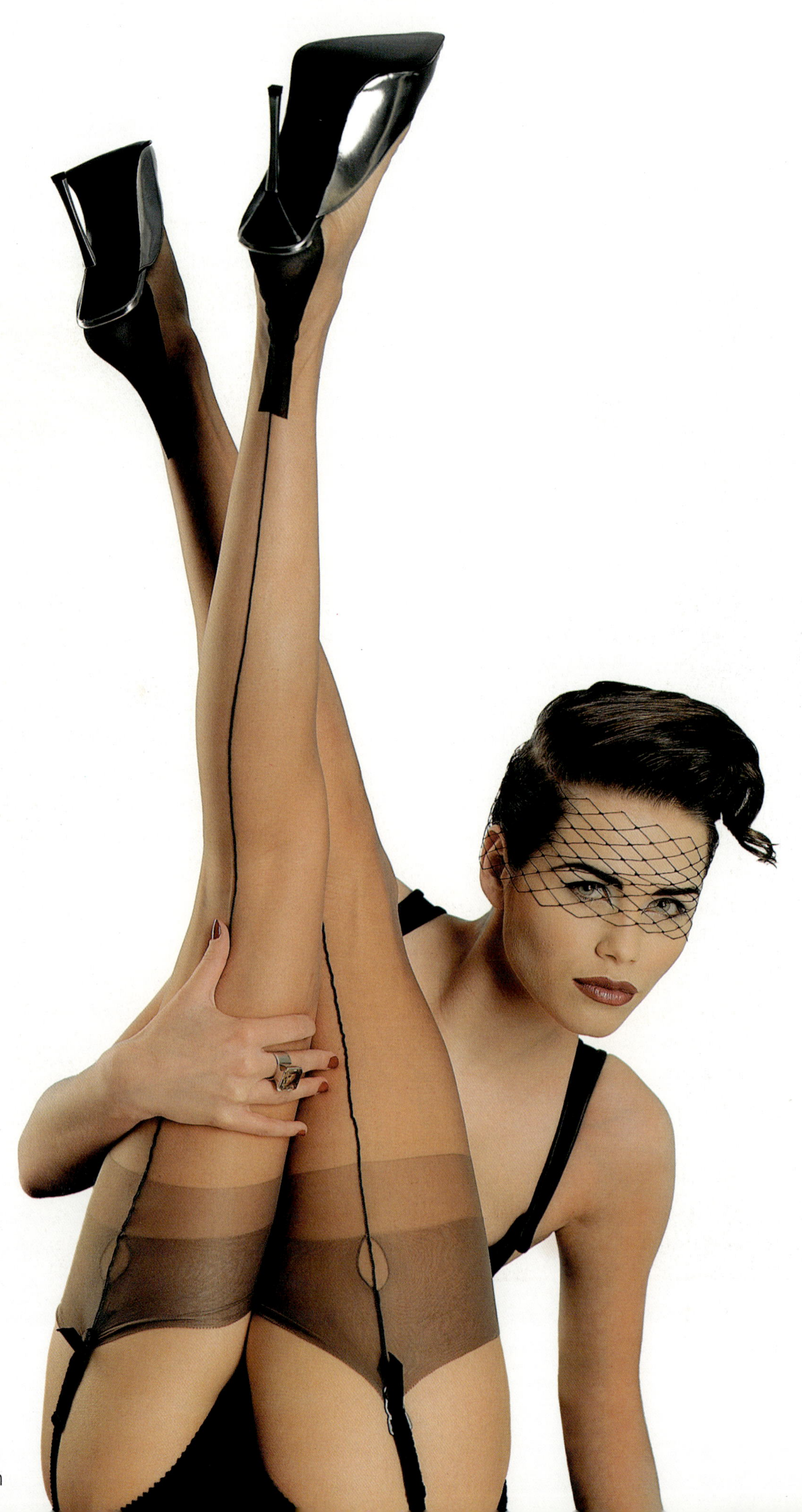

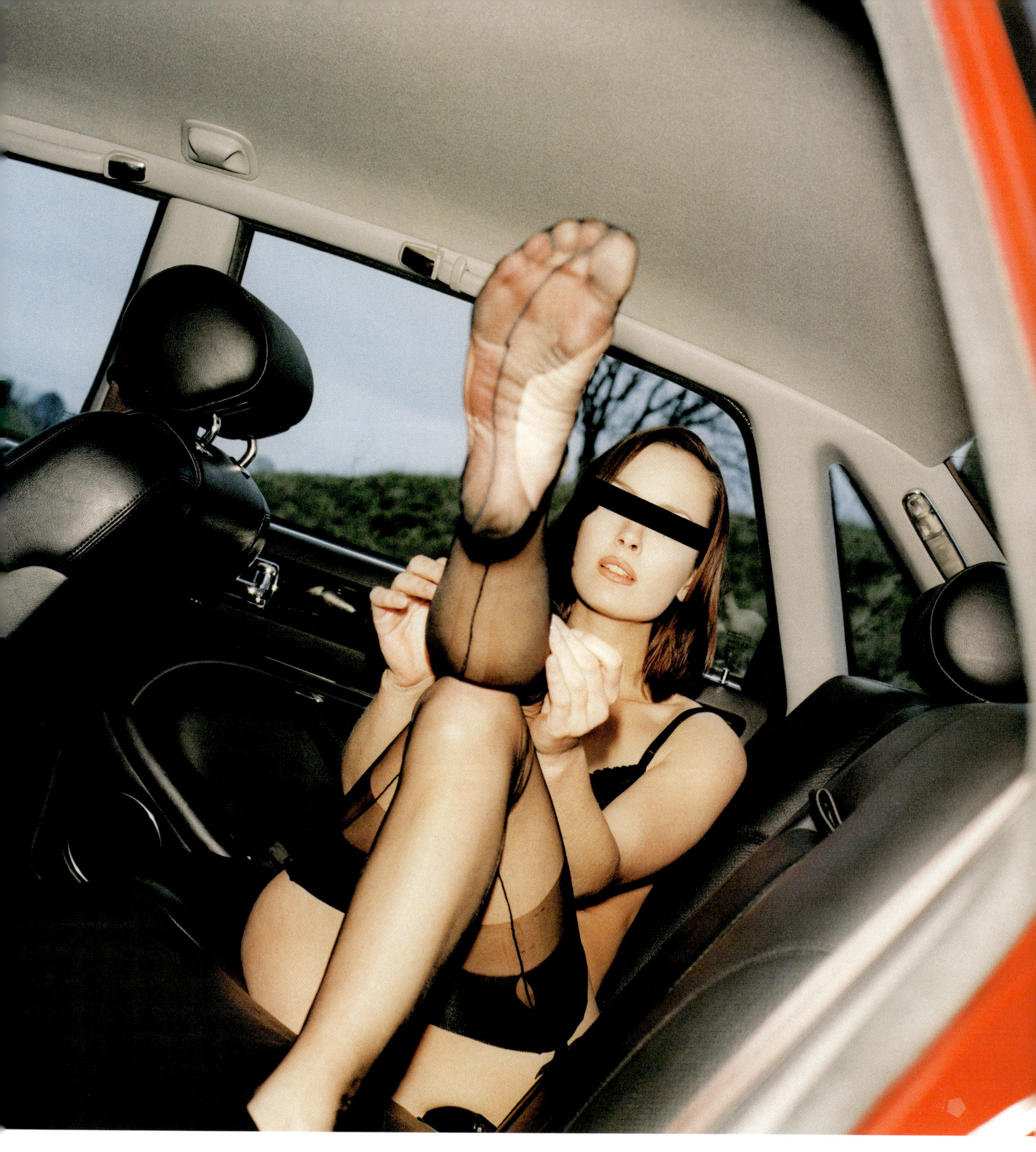

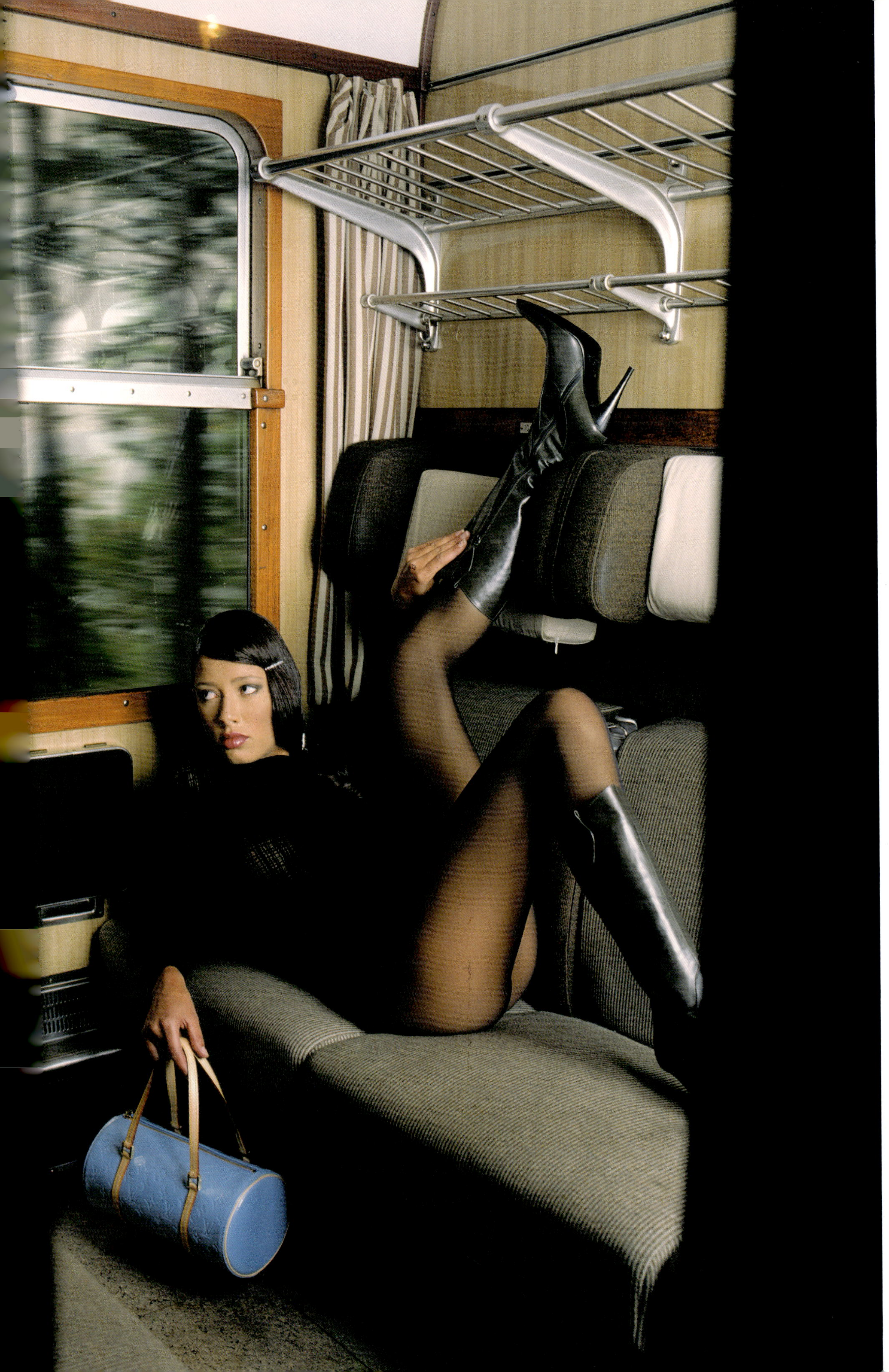

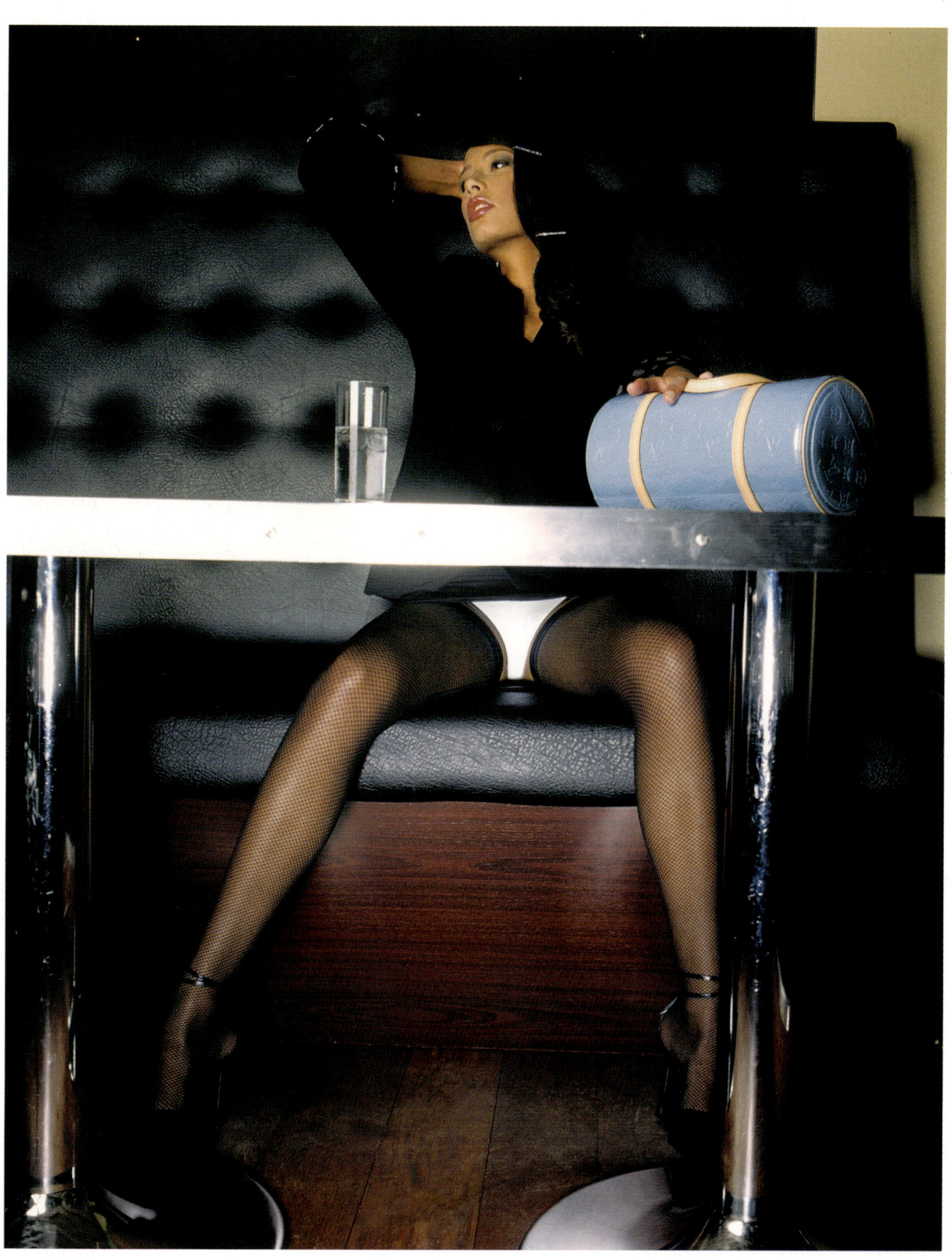



Erik Hansen-Hansen *41*

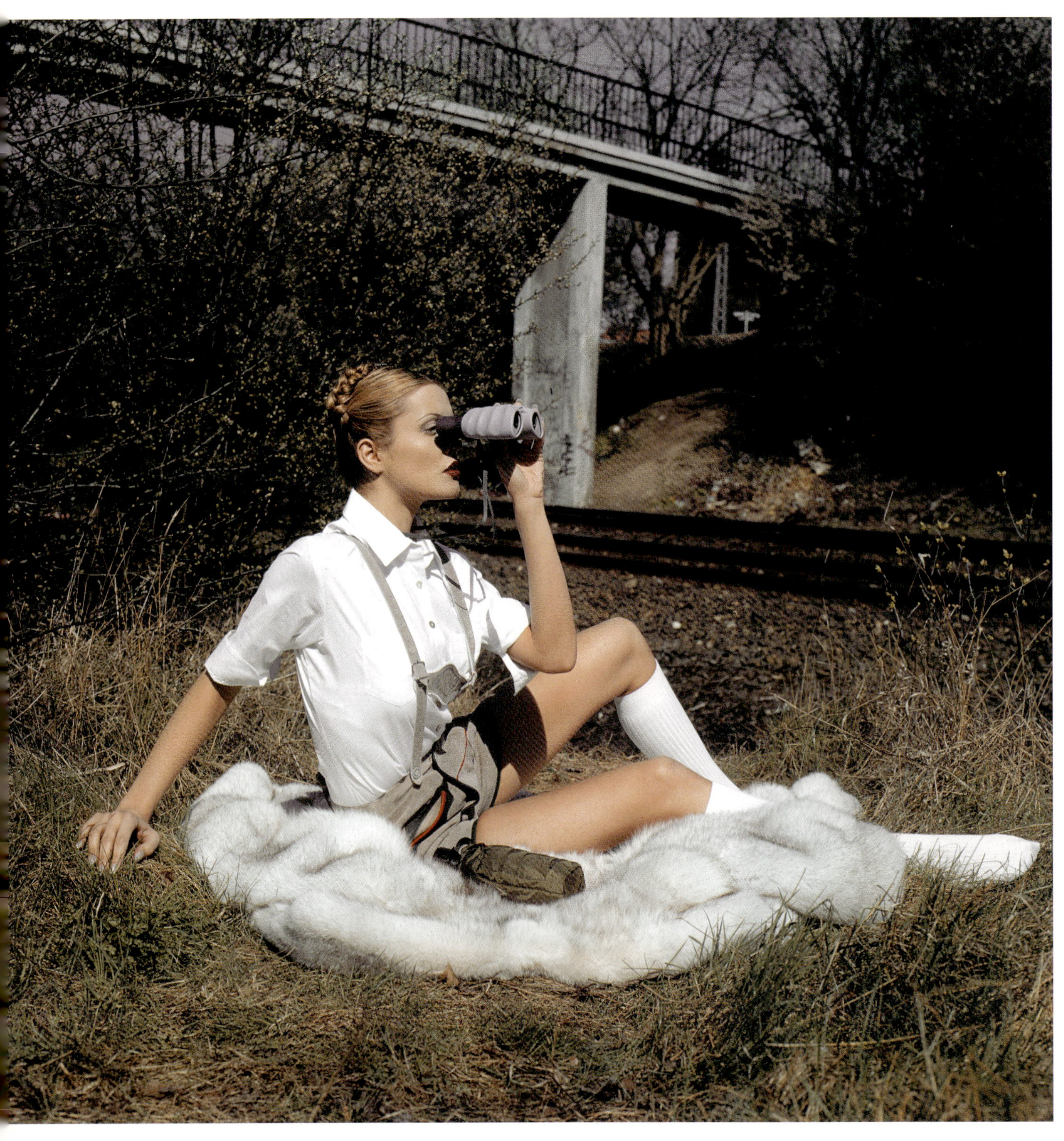

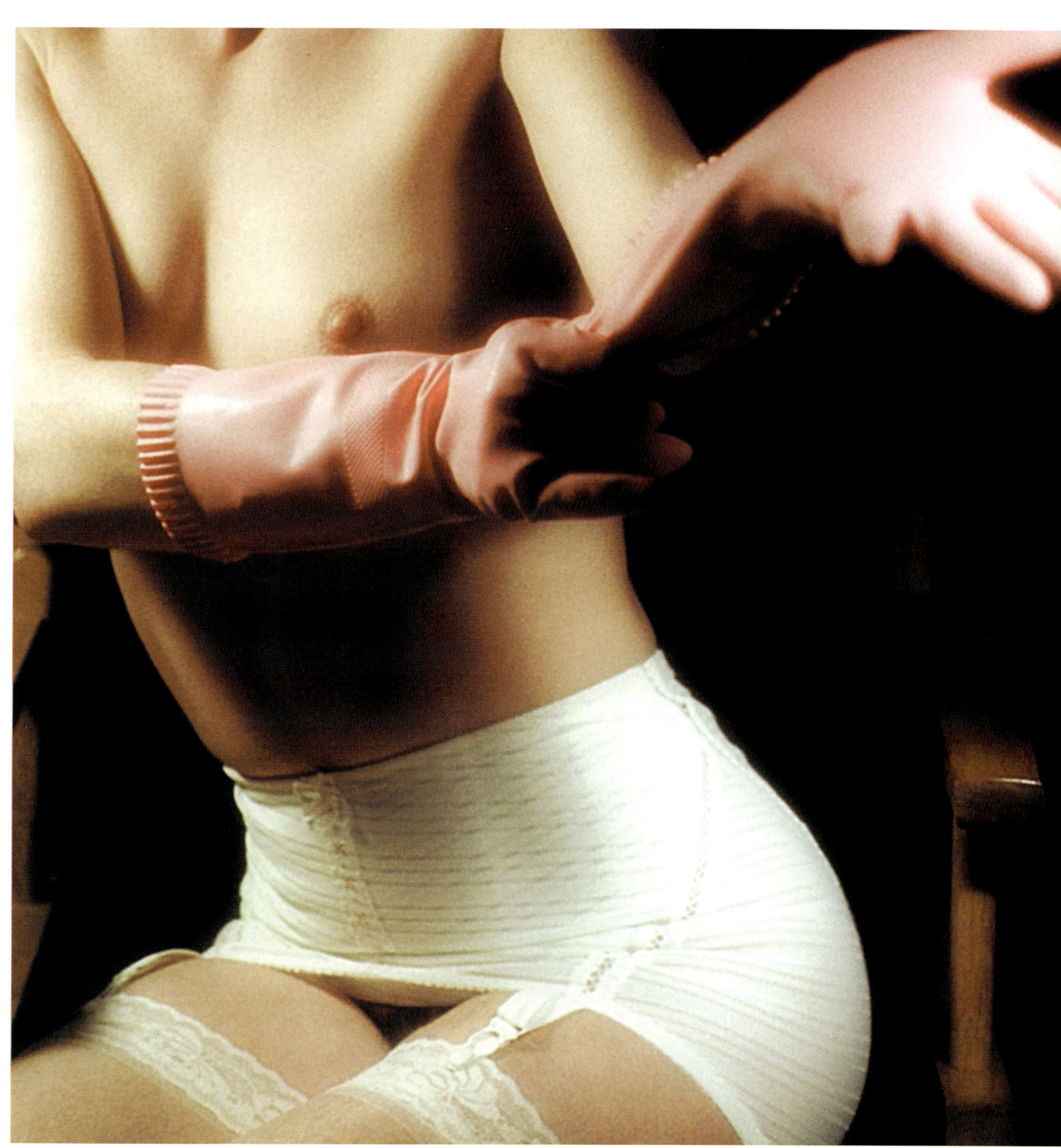

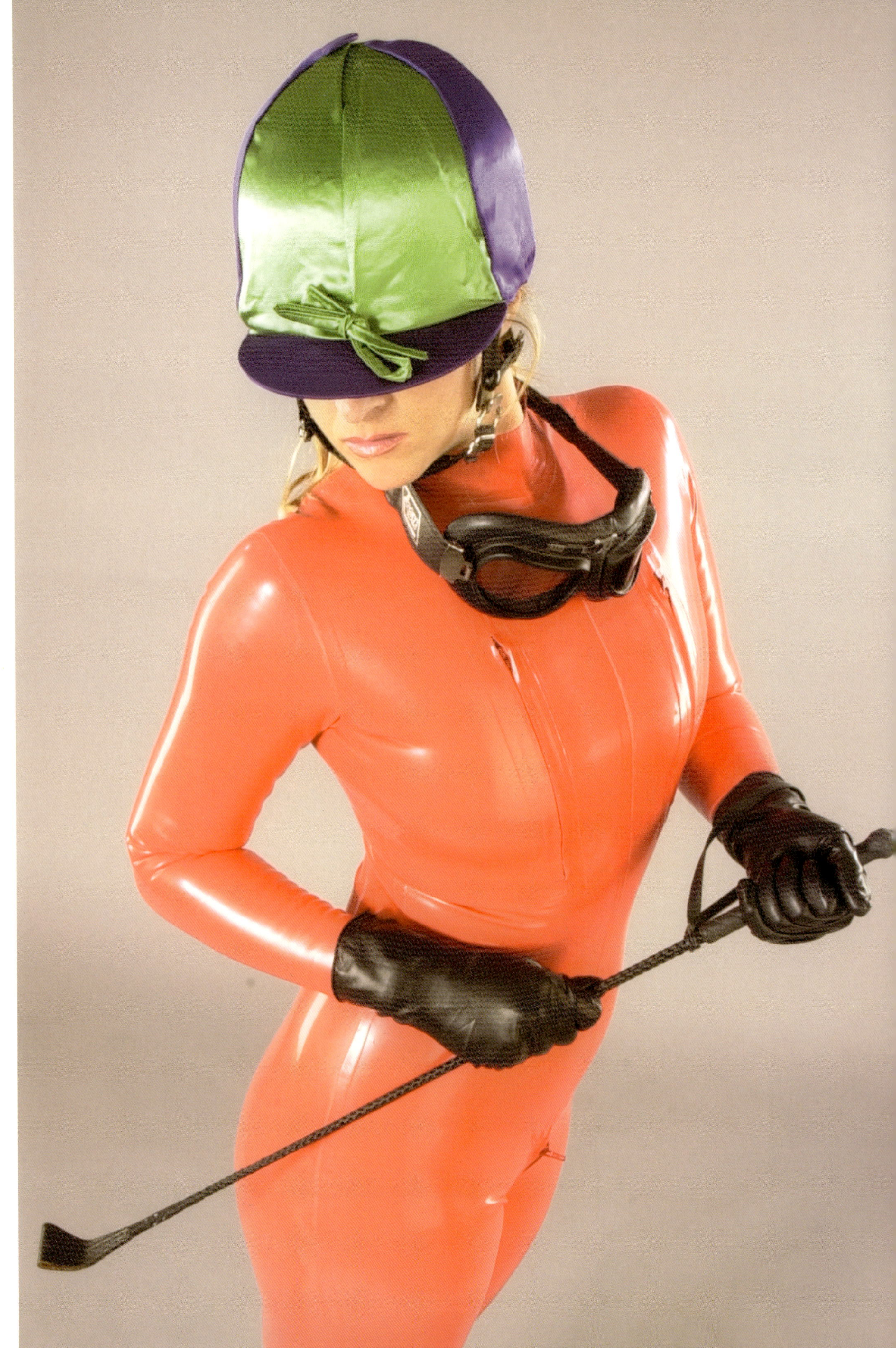

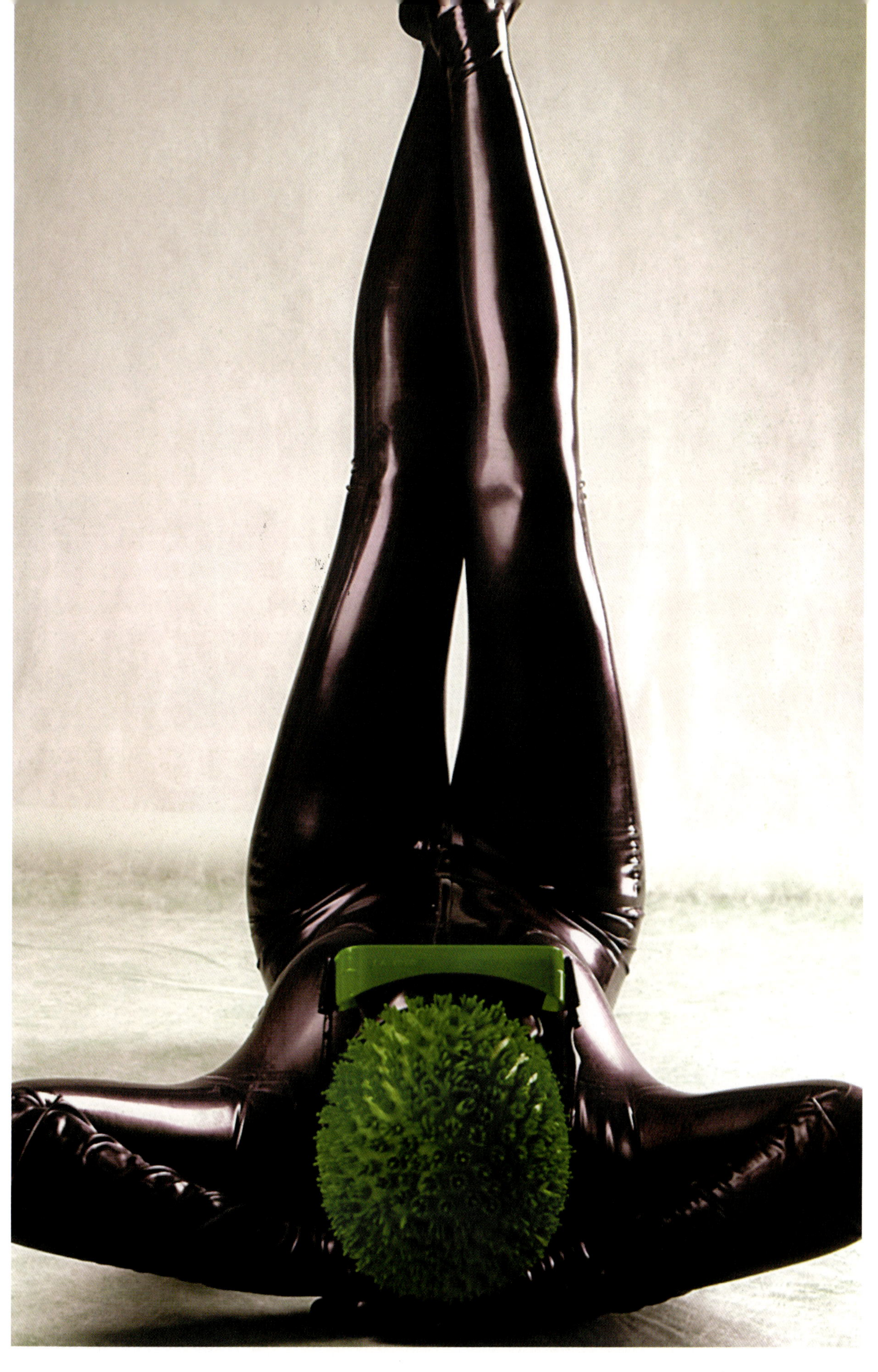

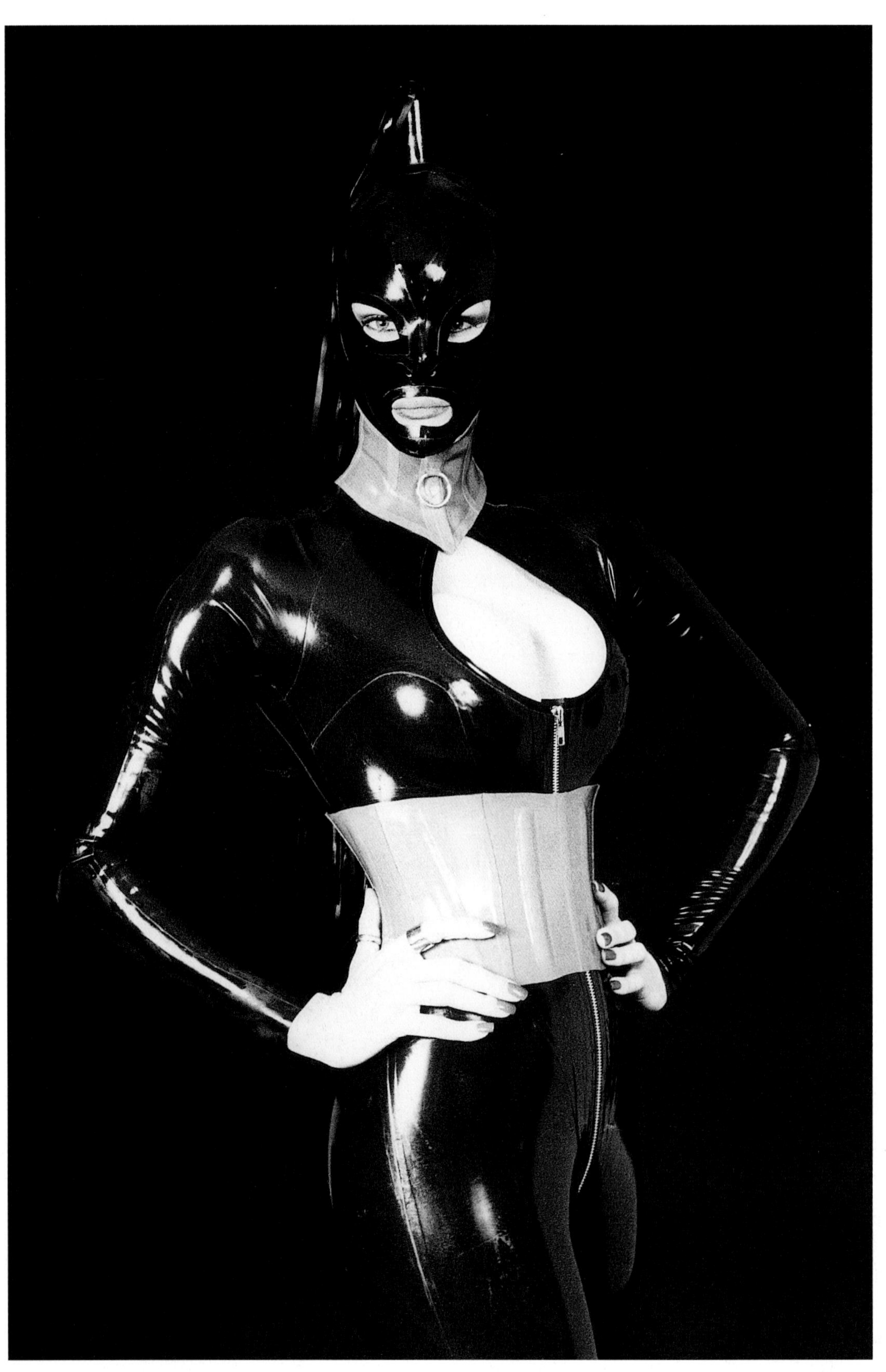

 Gary & Pierre Silva

Opposite Gary & Pierre Silva

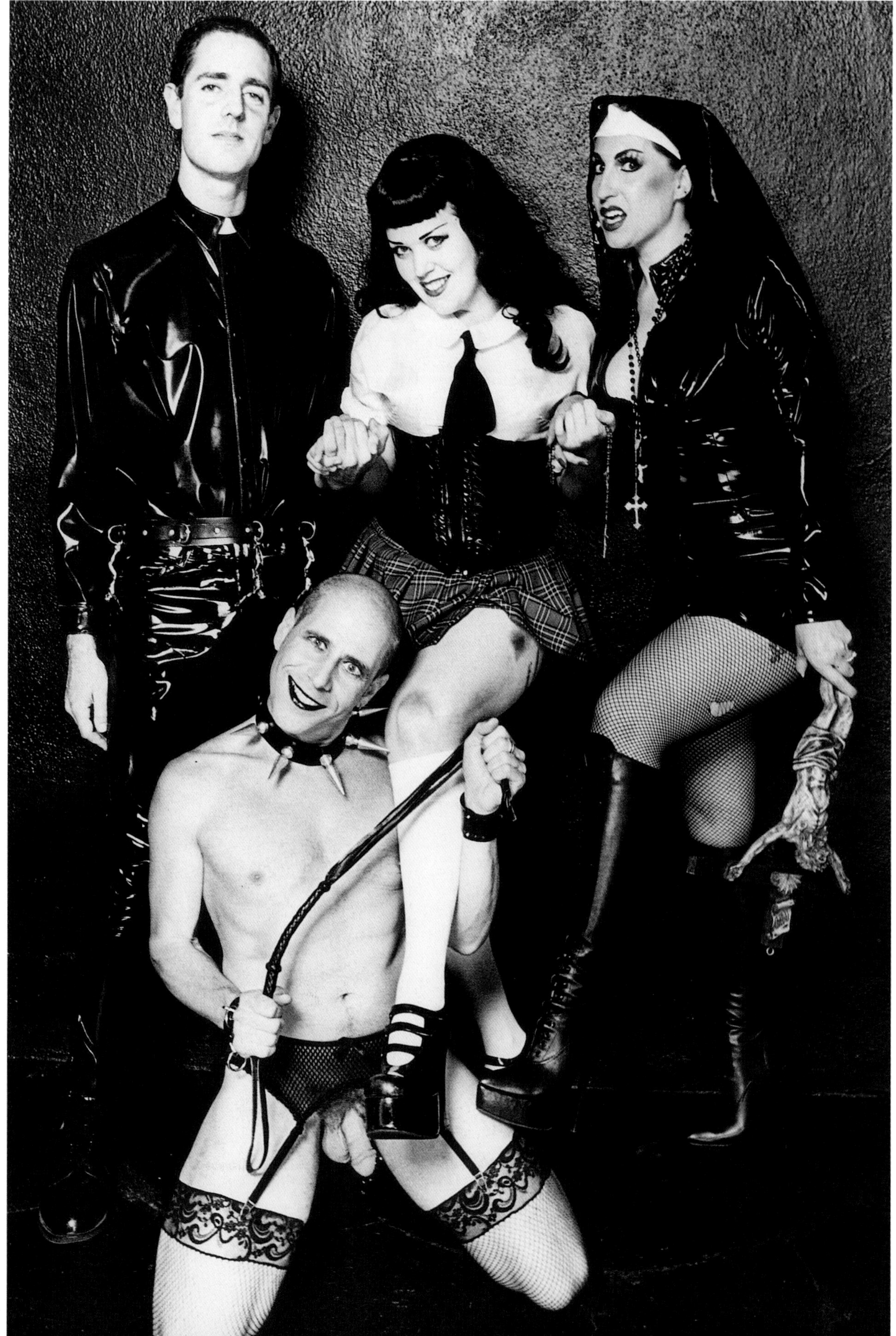

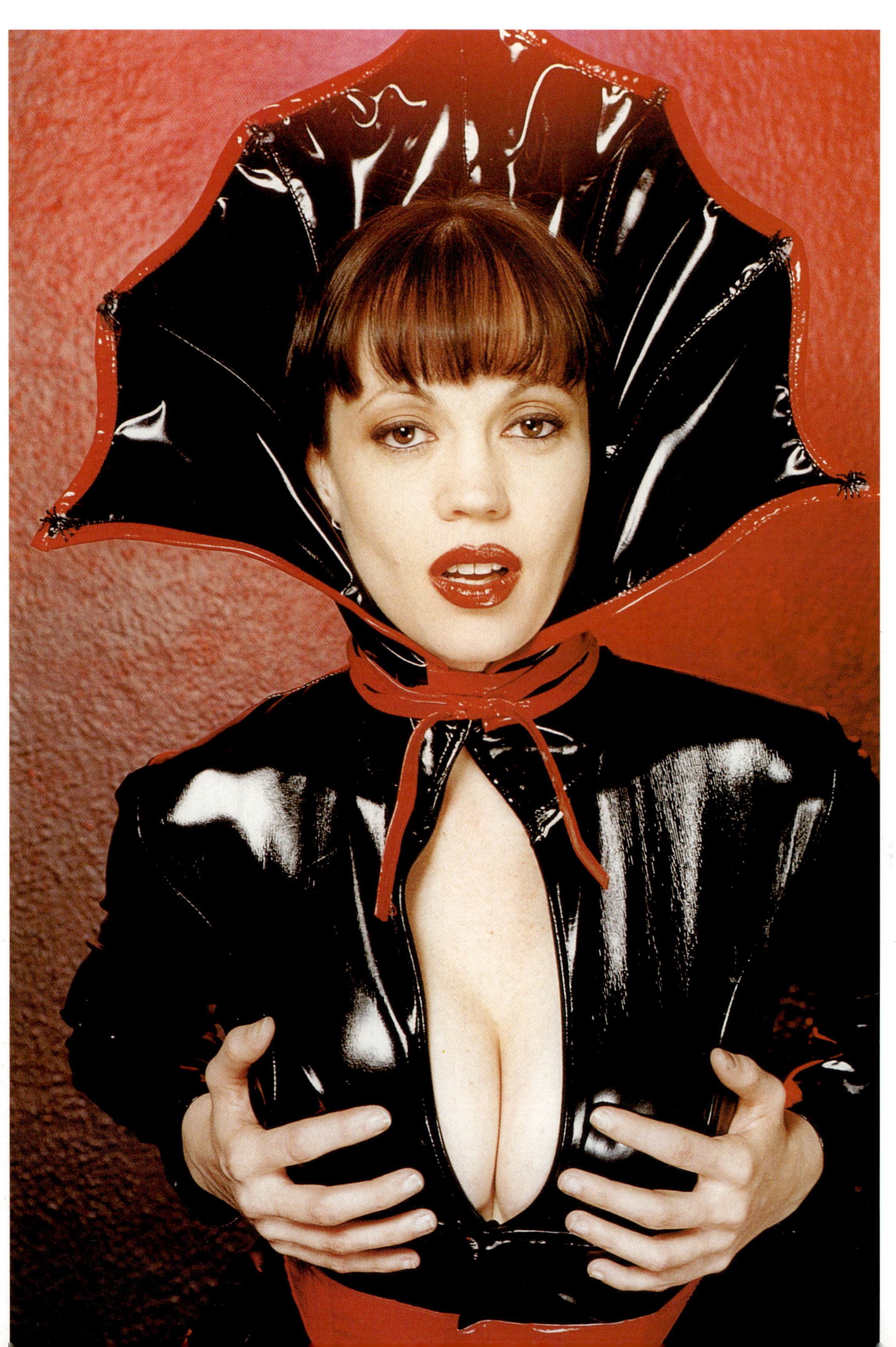

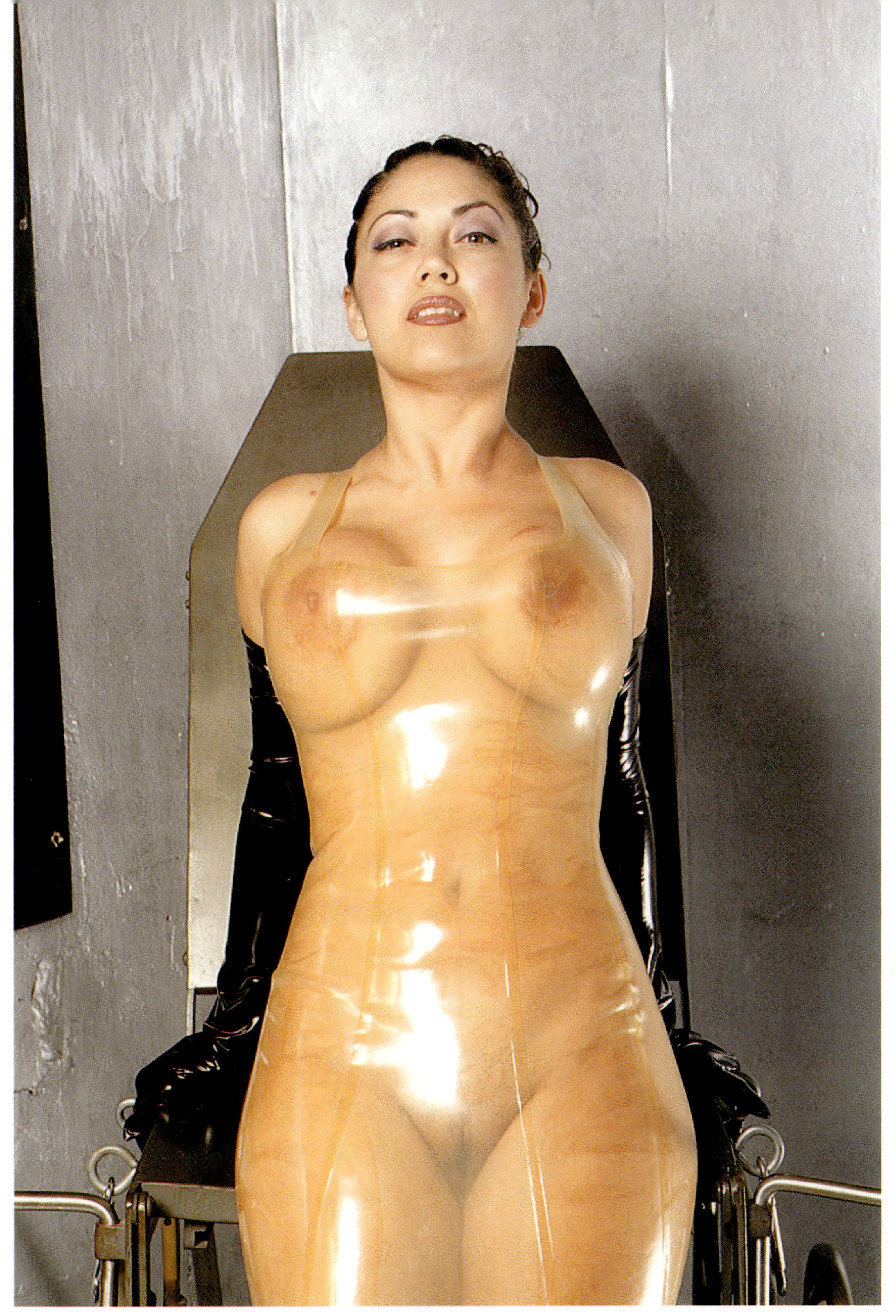

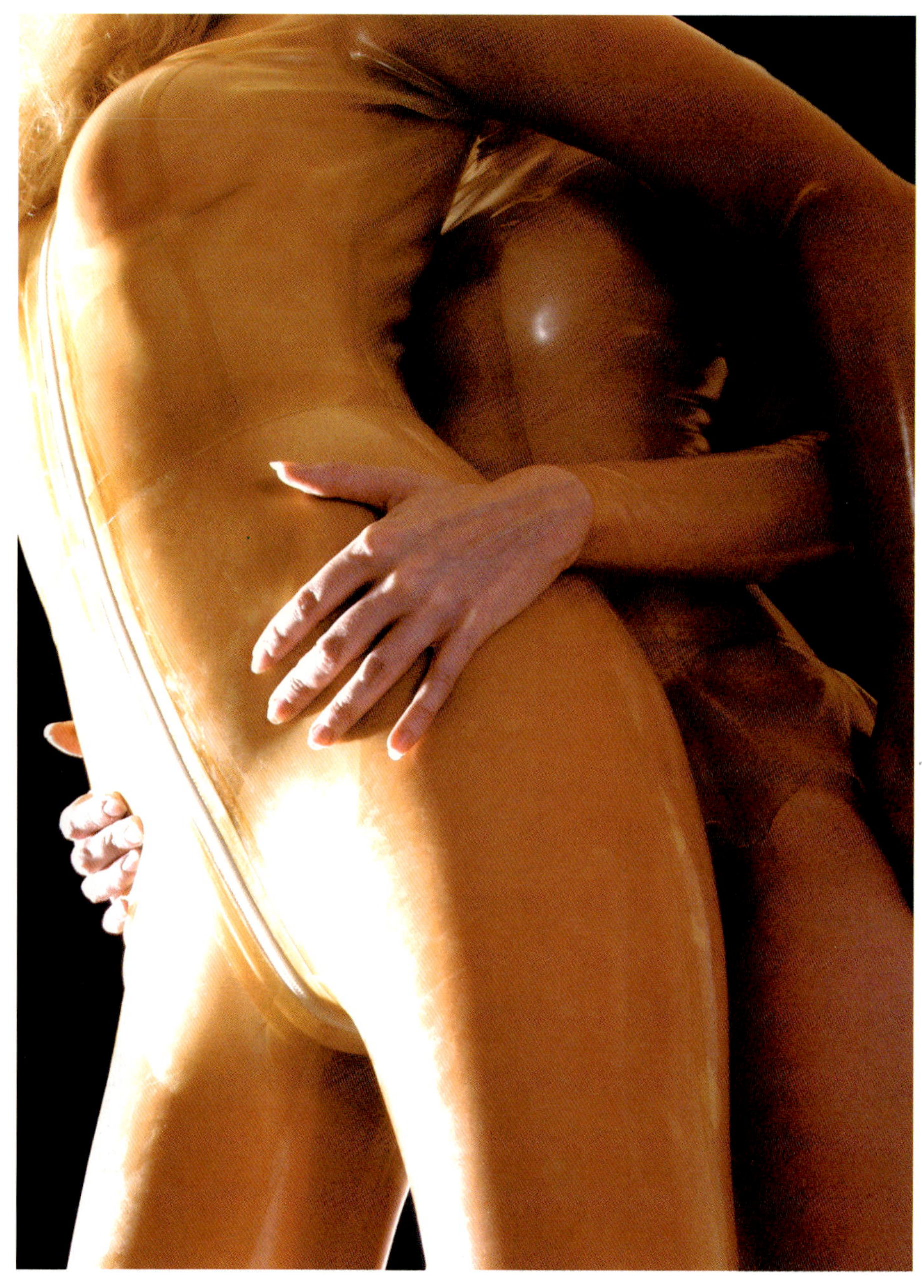

 John Fitzgerald

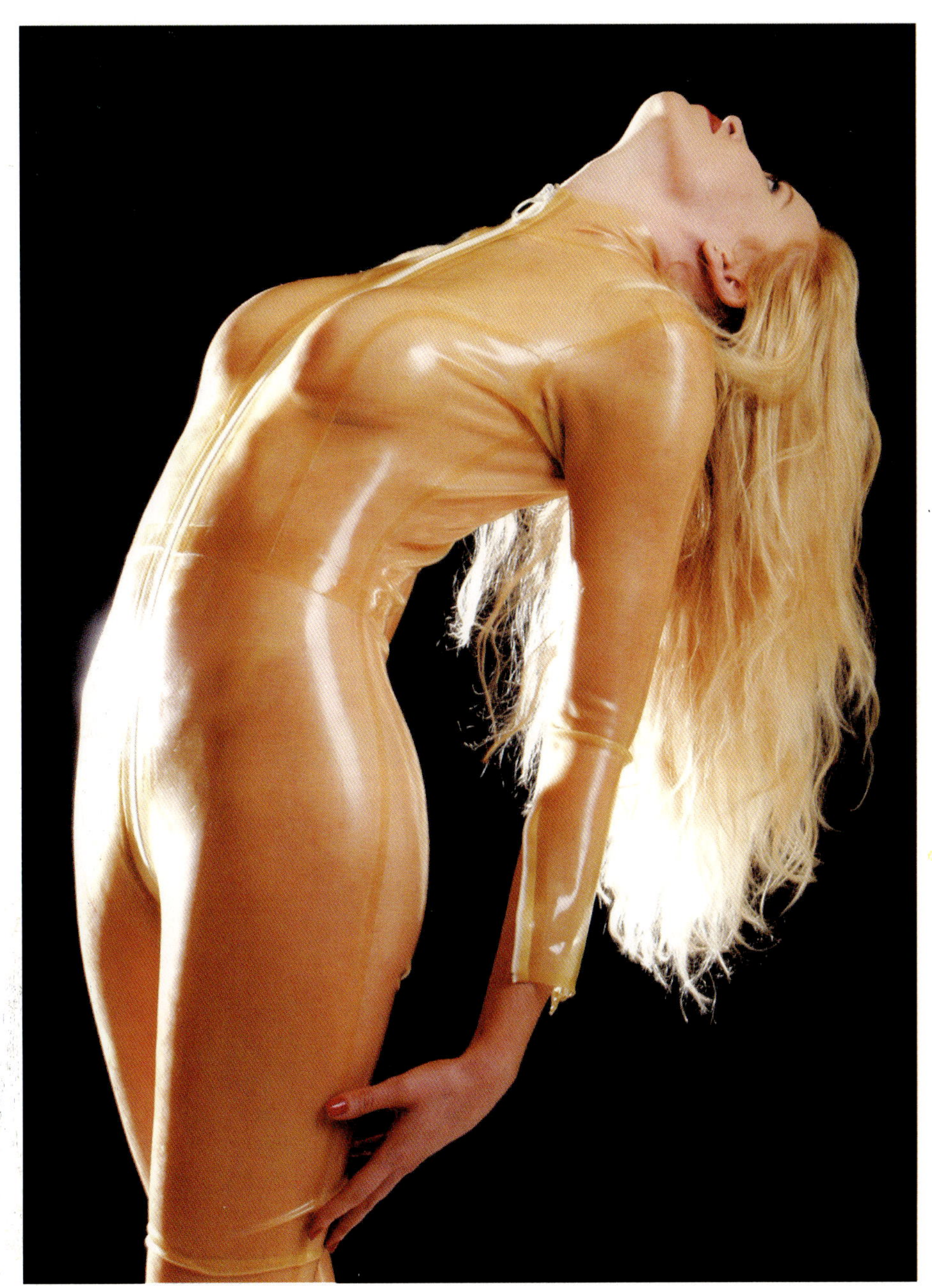

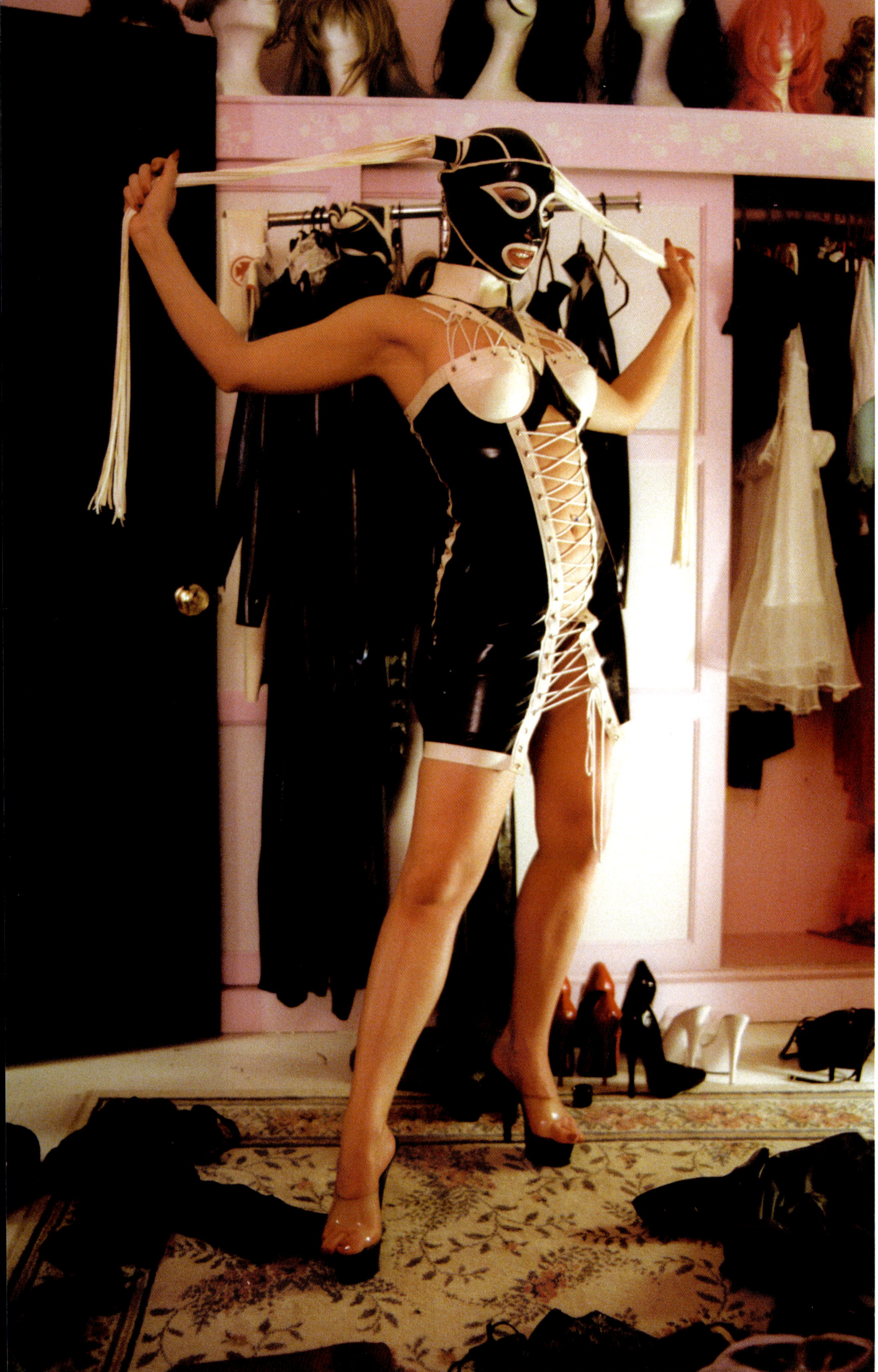

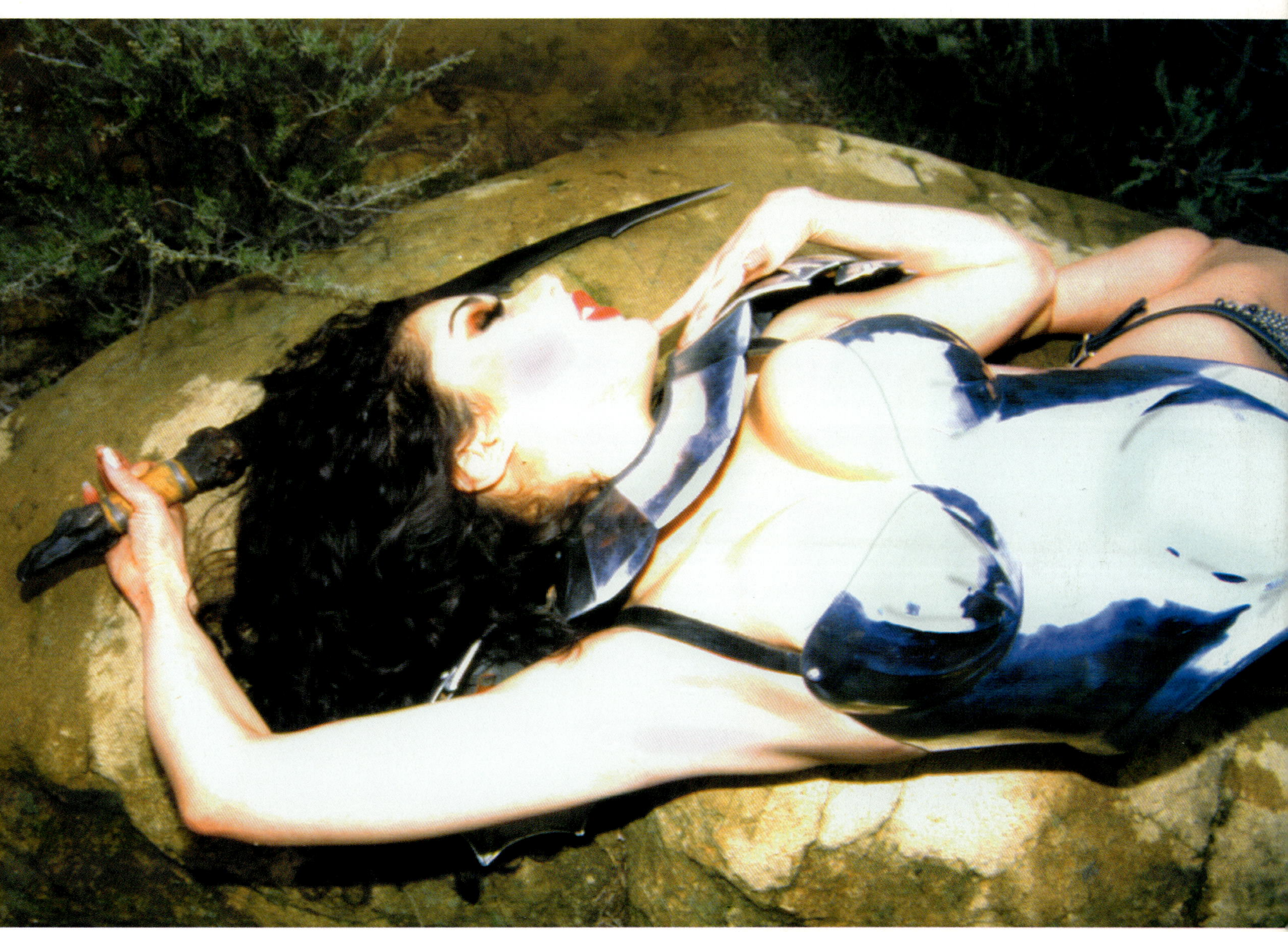



Justice Howard  53

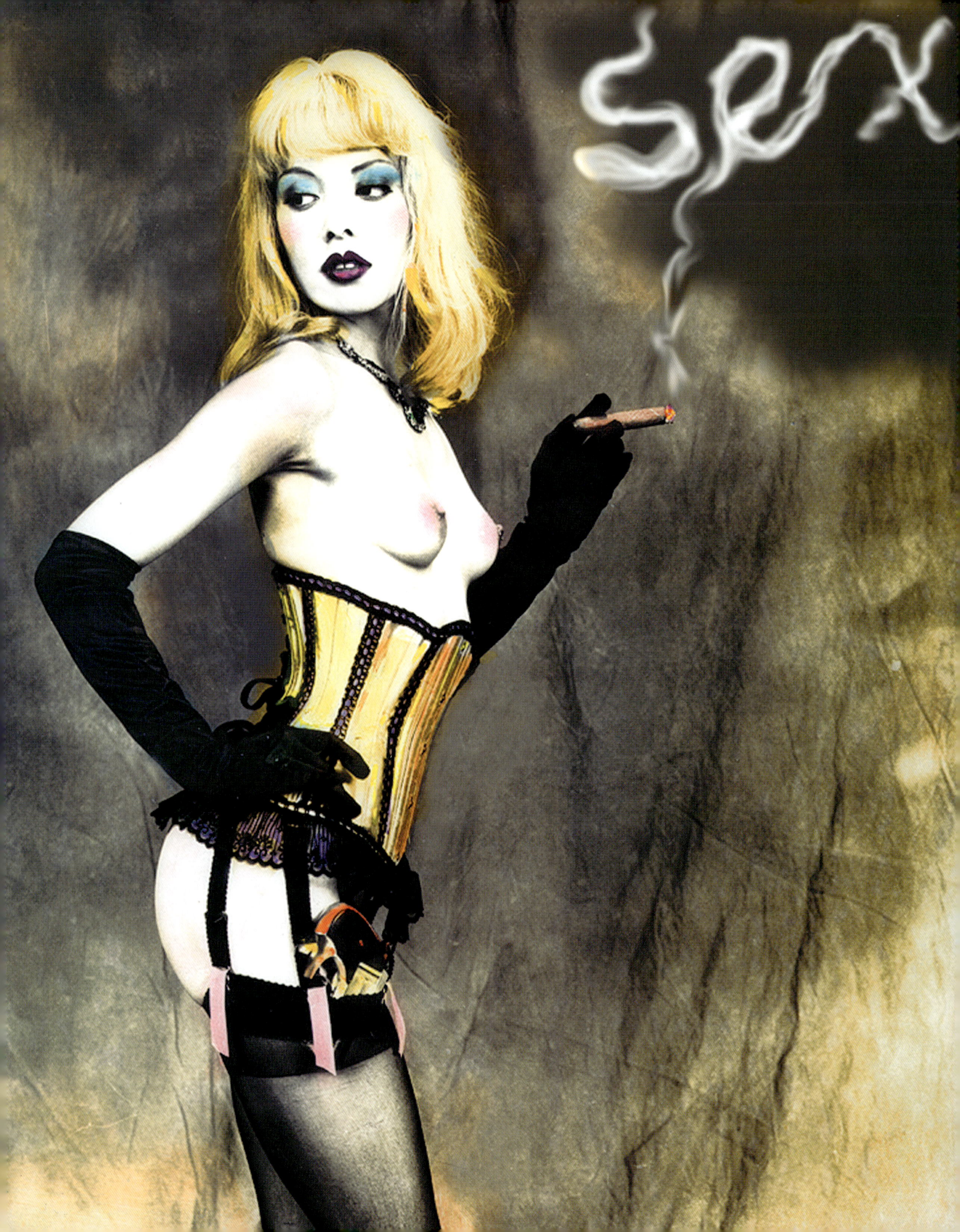
sex

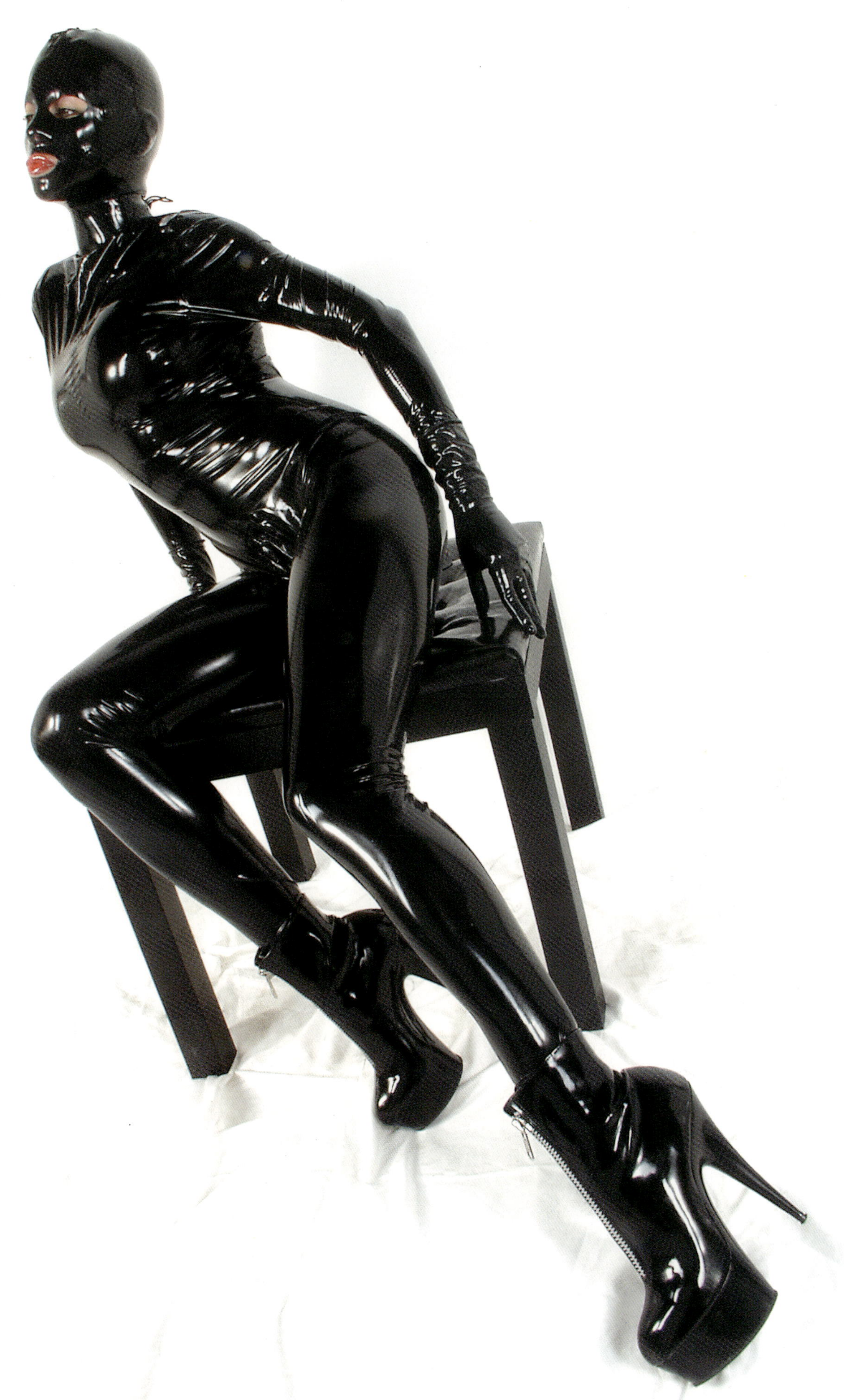

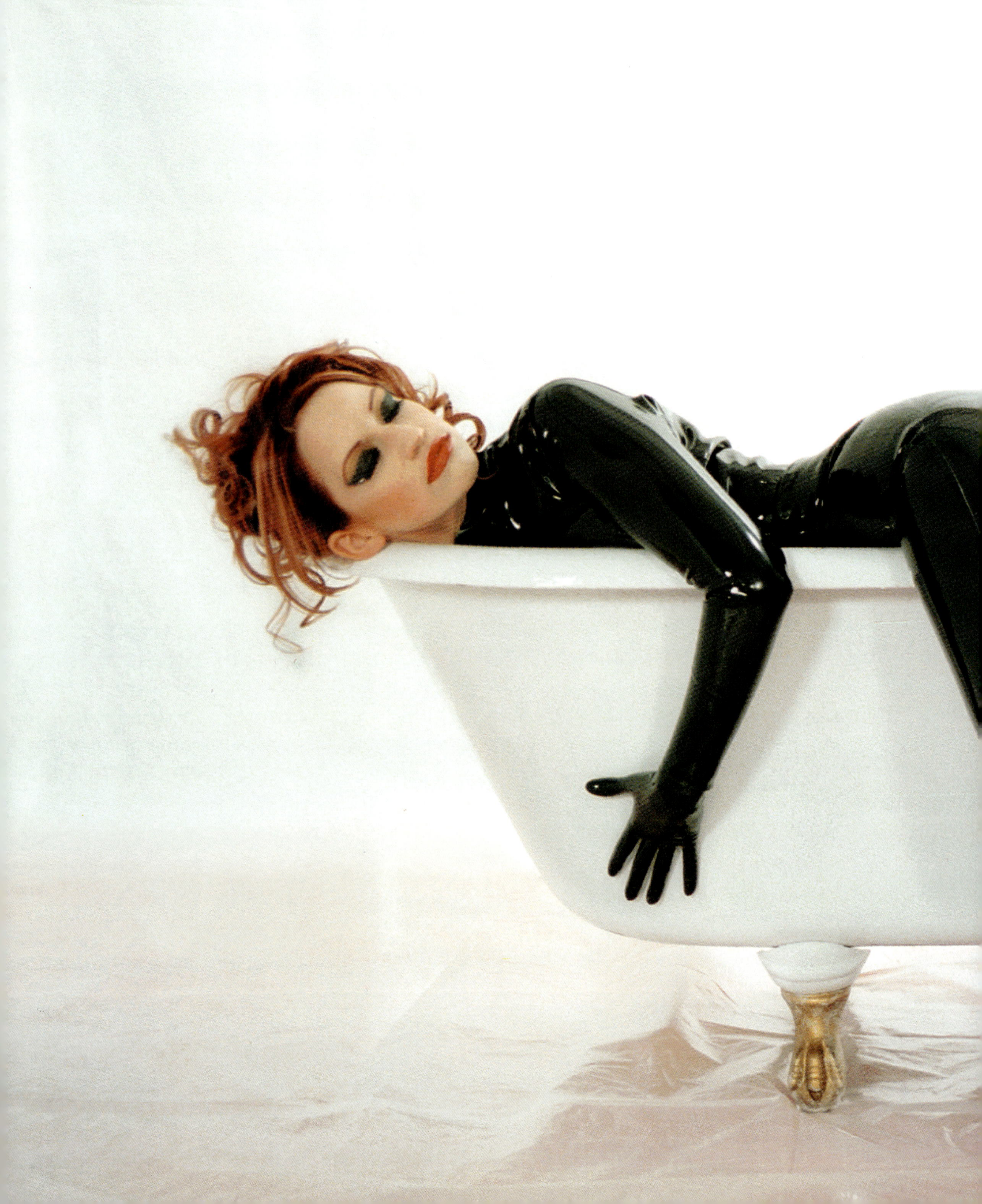

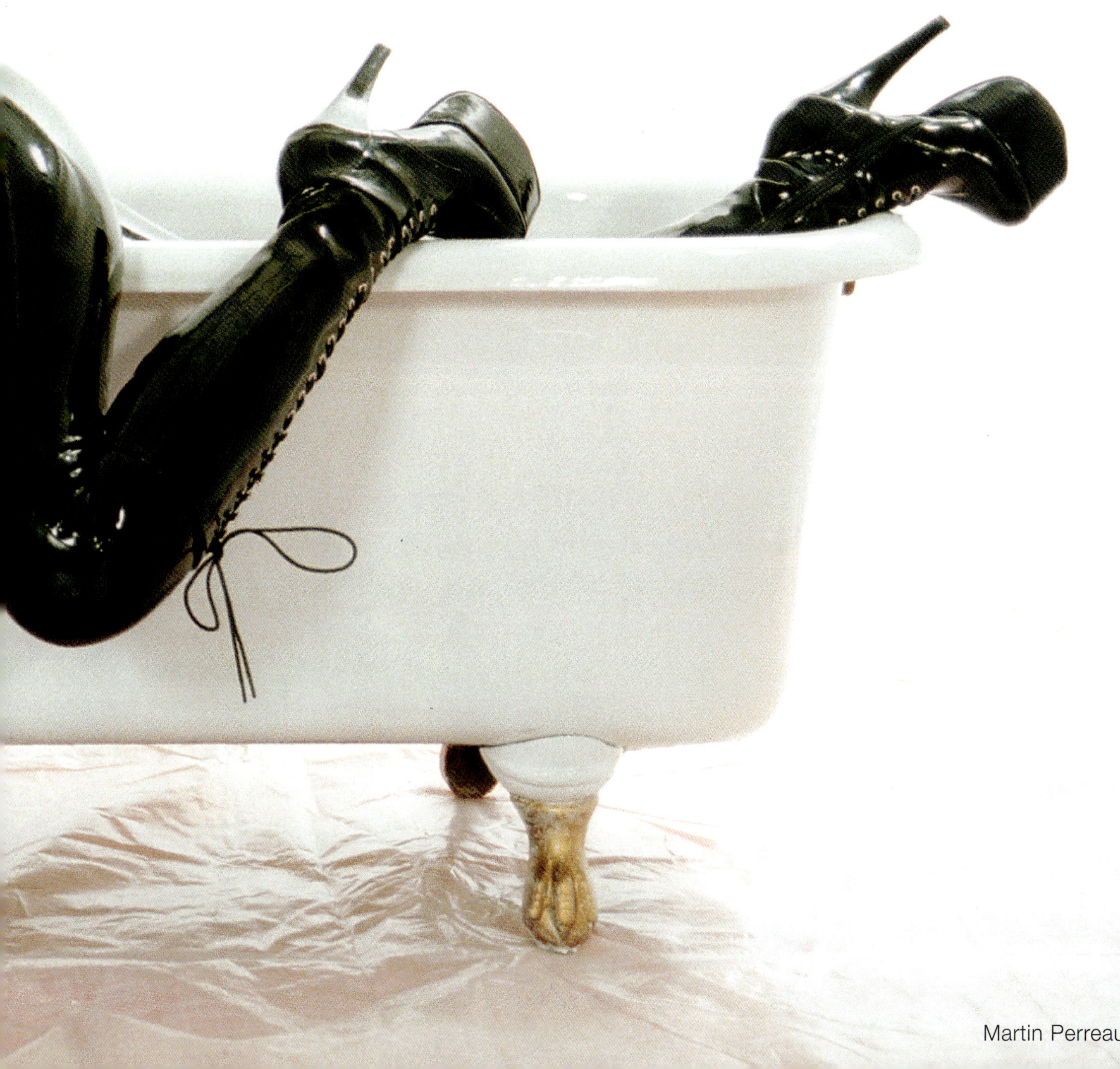

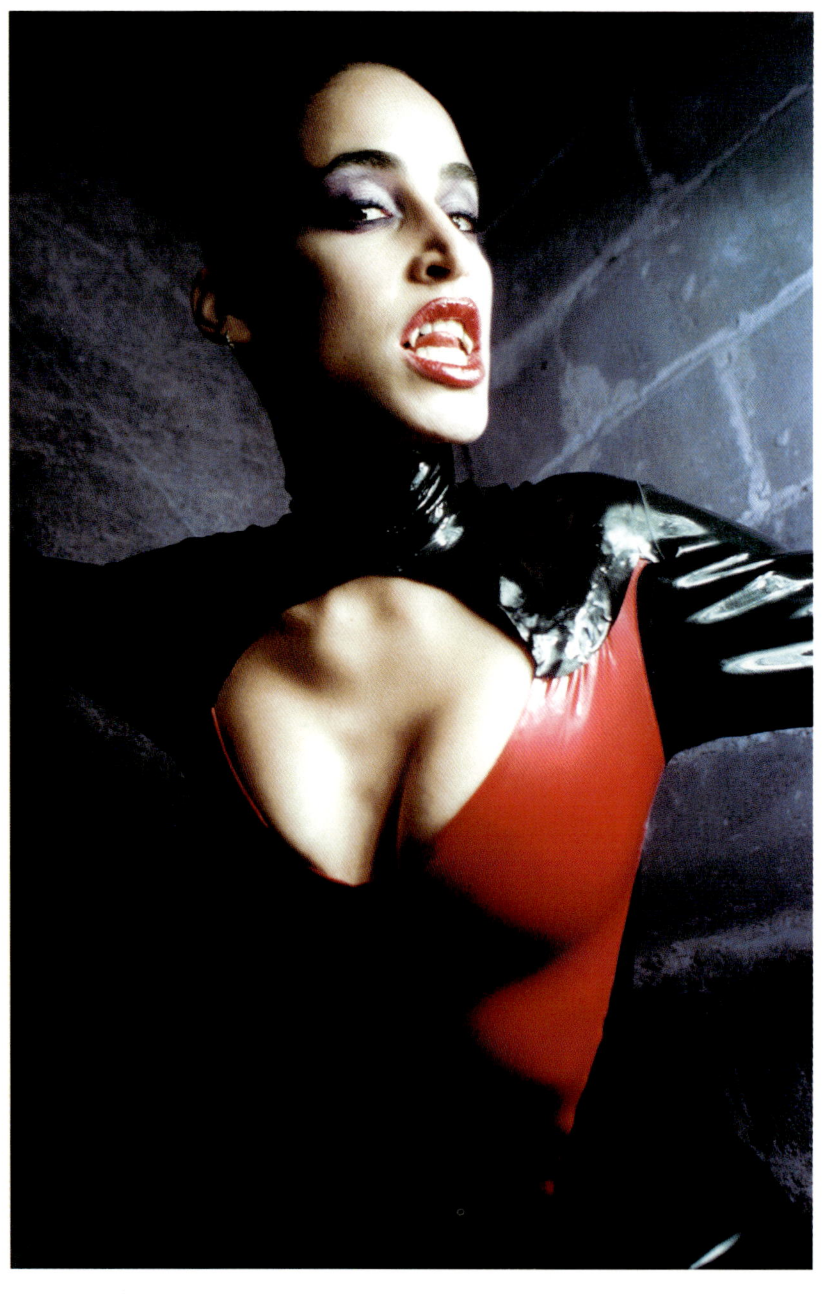



Opposite Martin Perreault

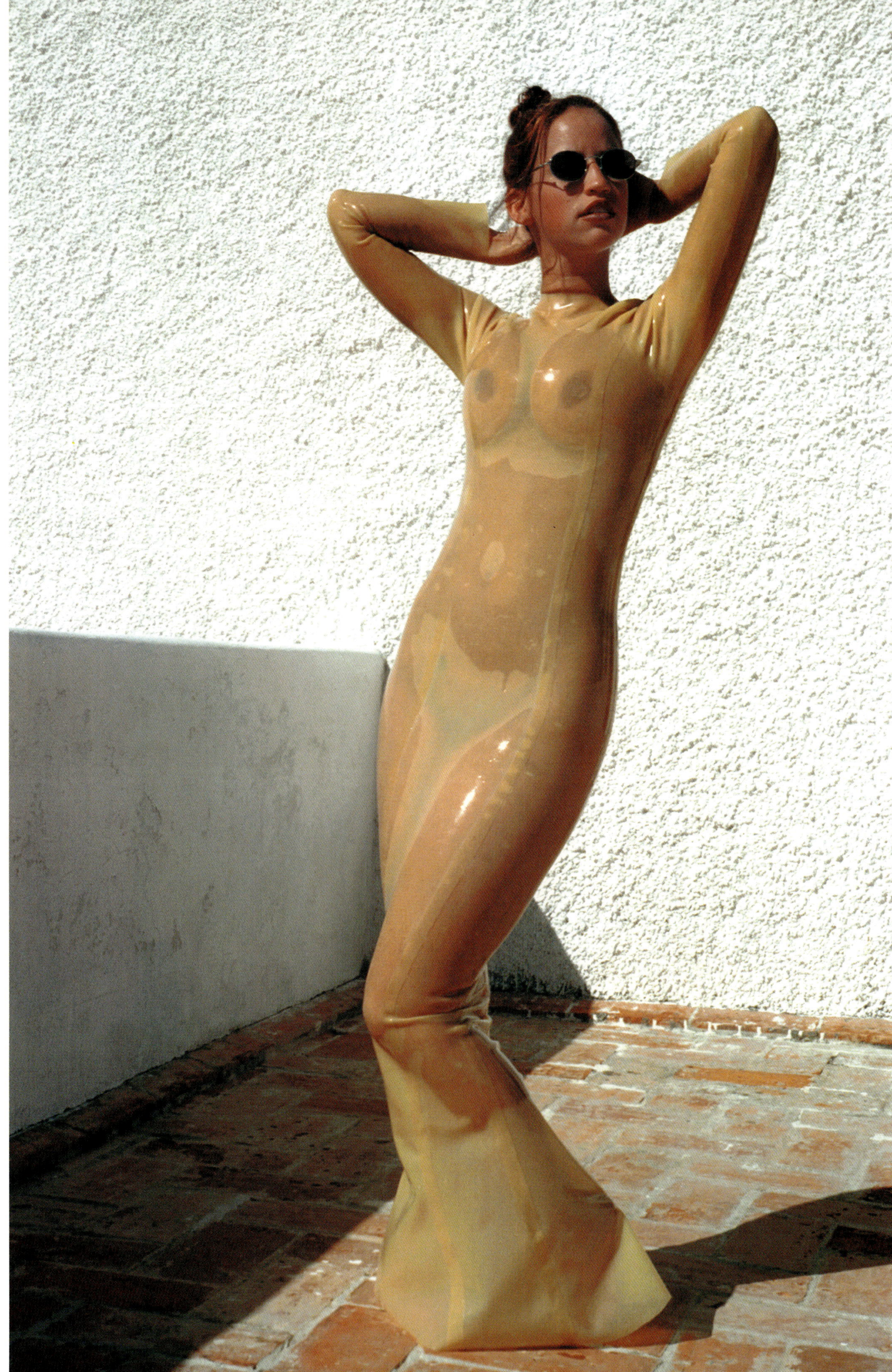

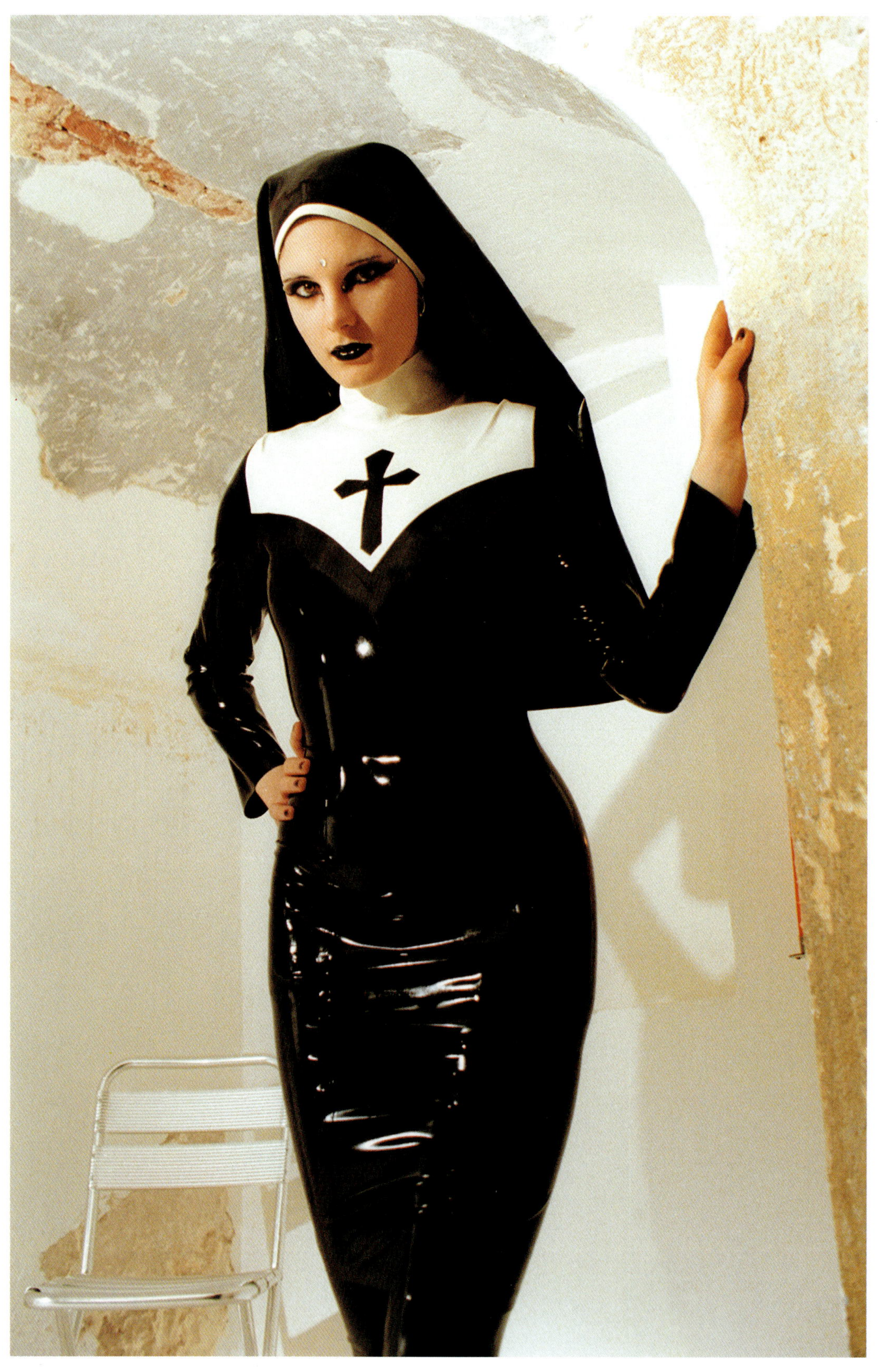

 Alexander Horn

Opposite Tony Ward

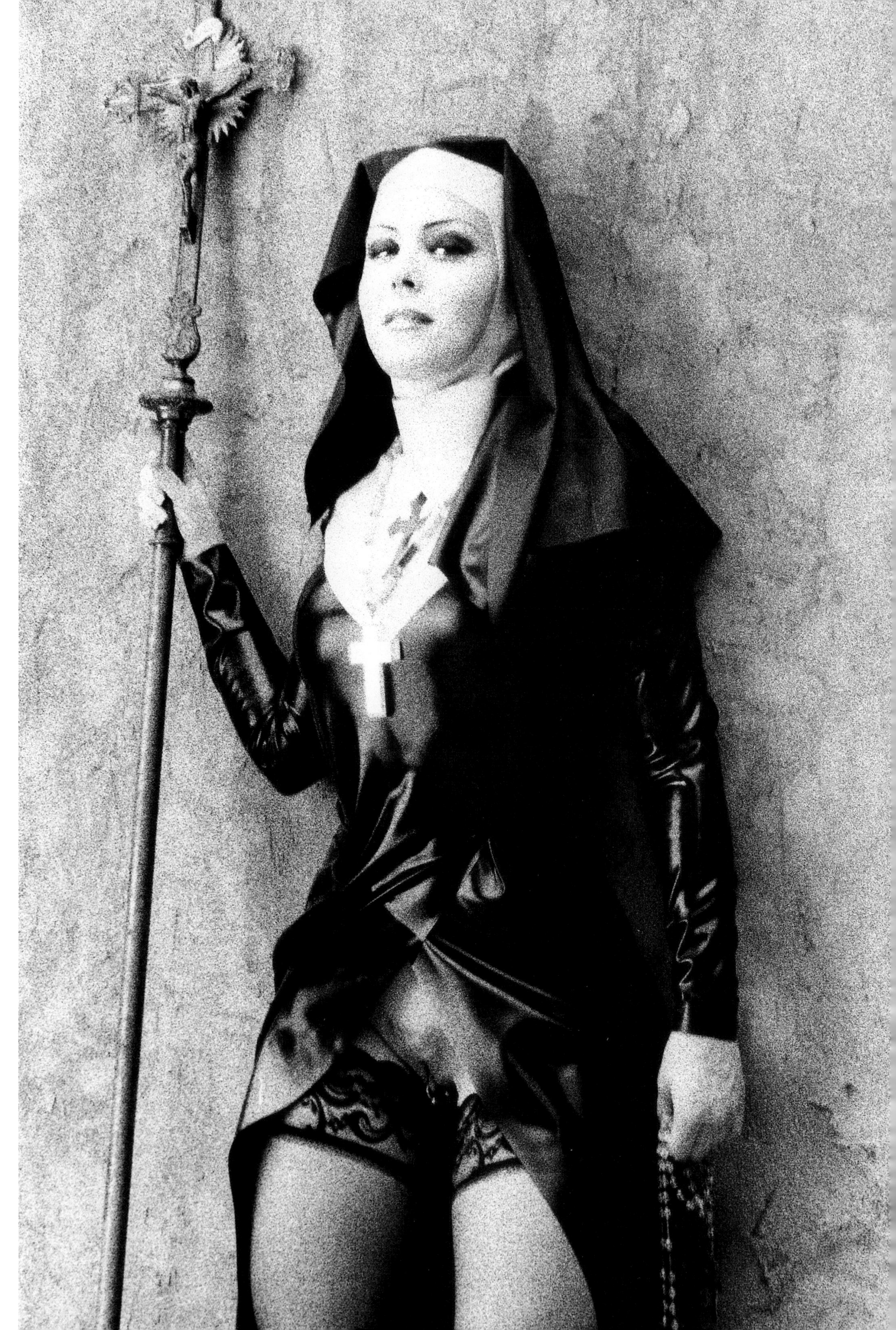

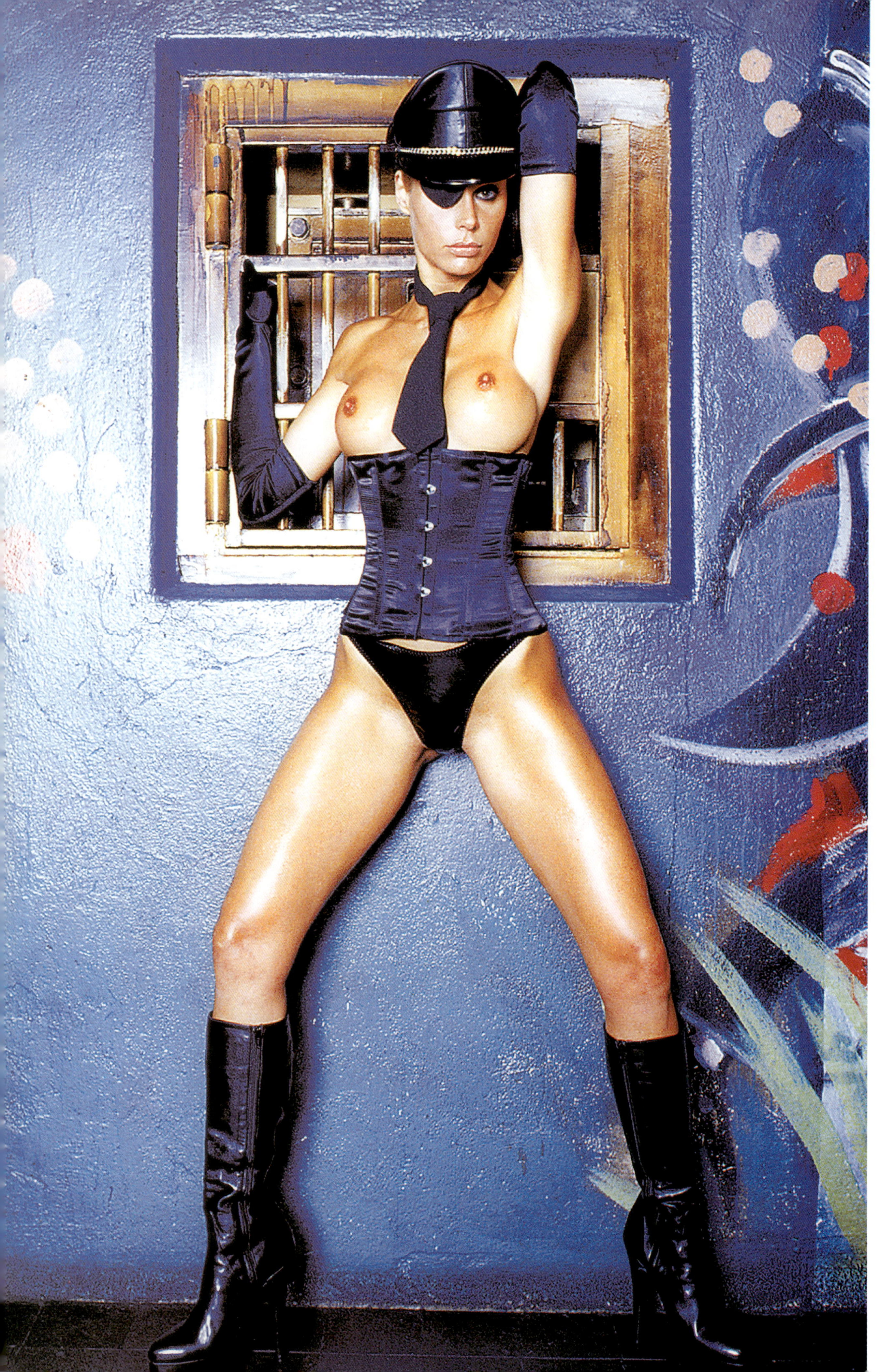

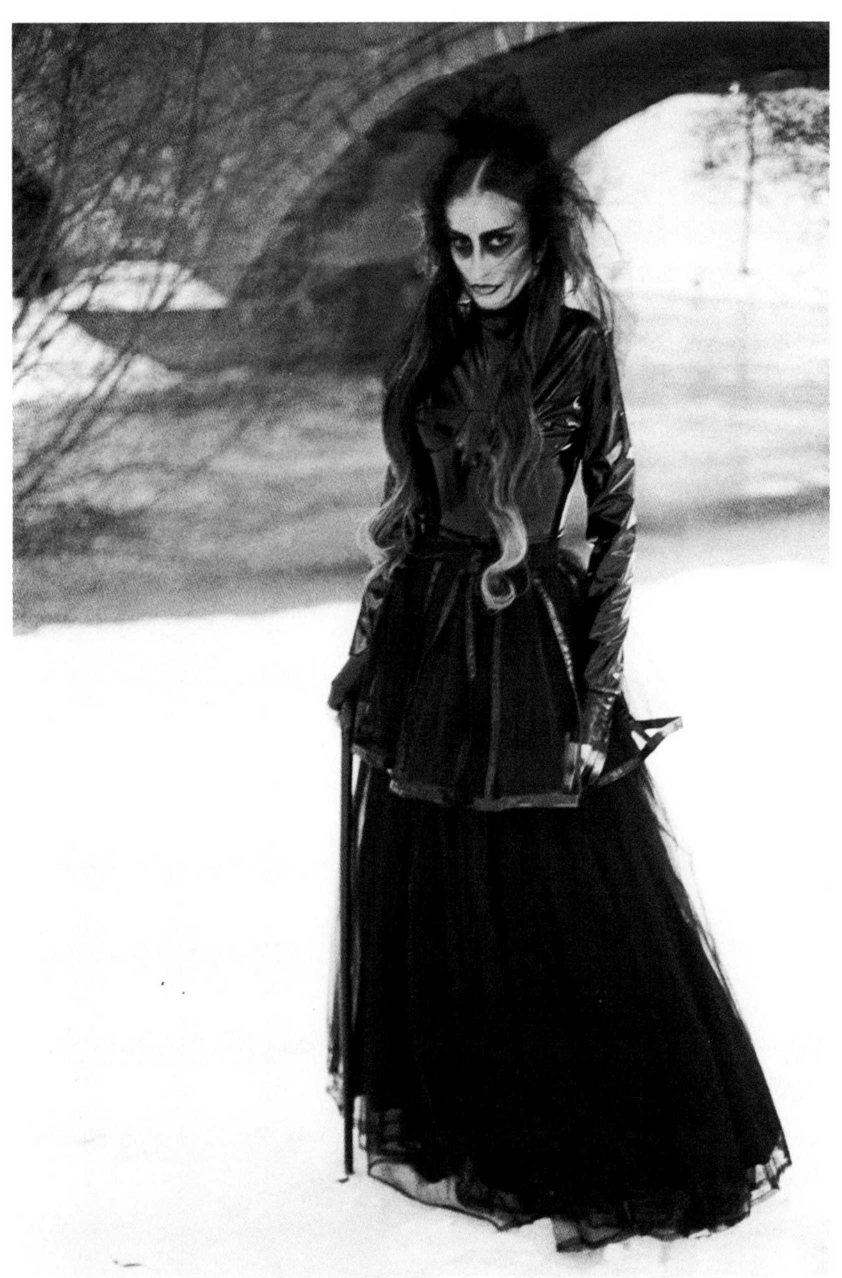

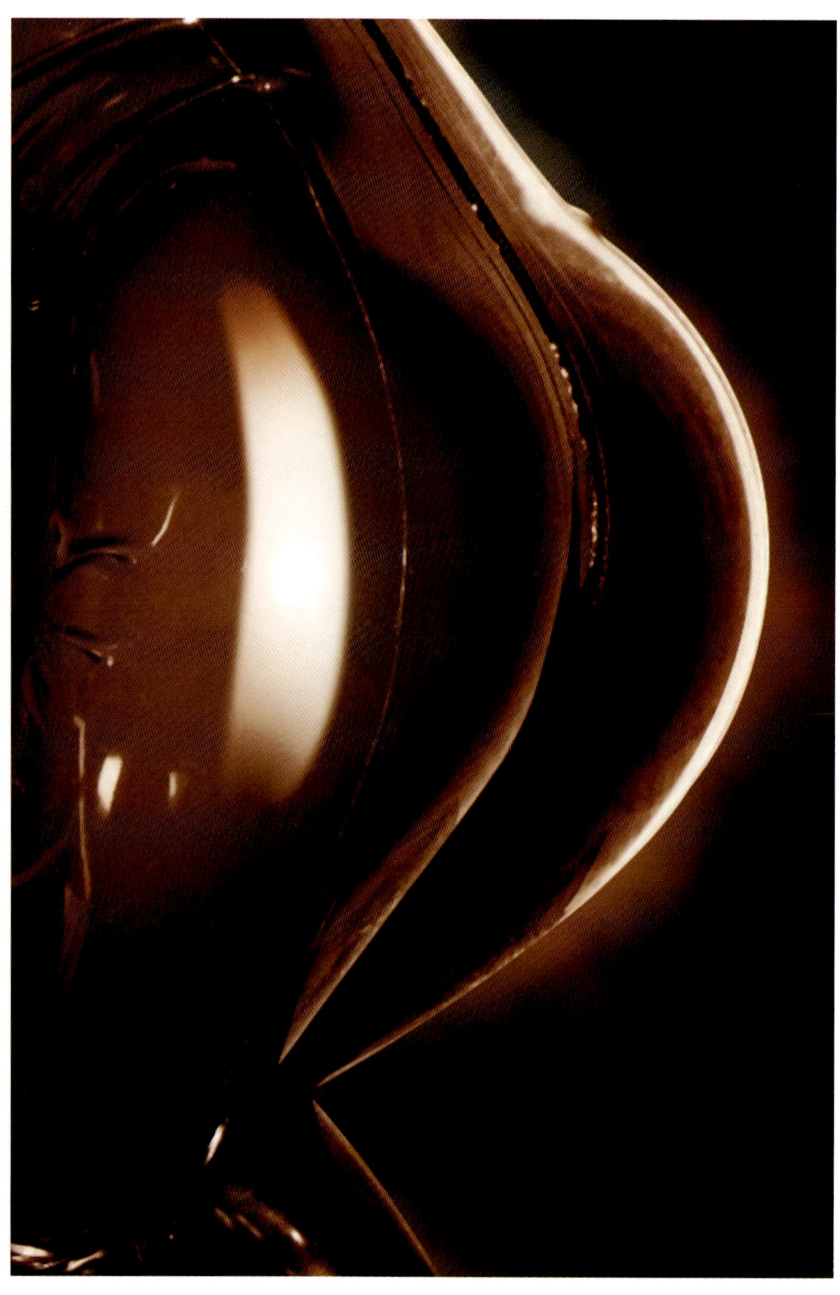

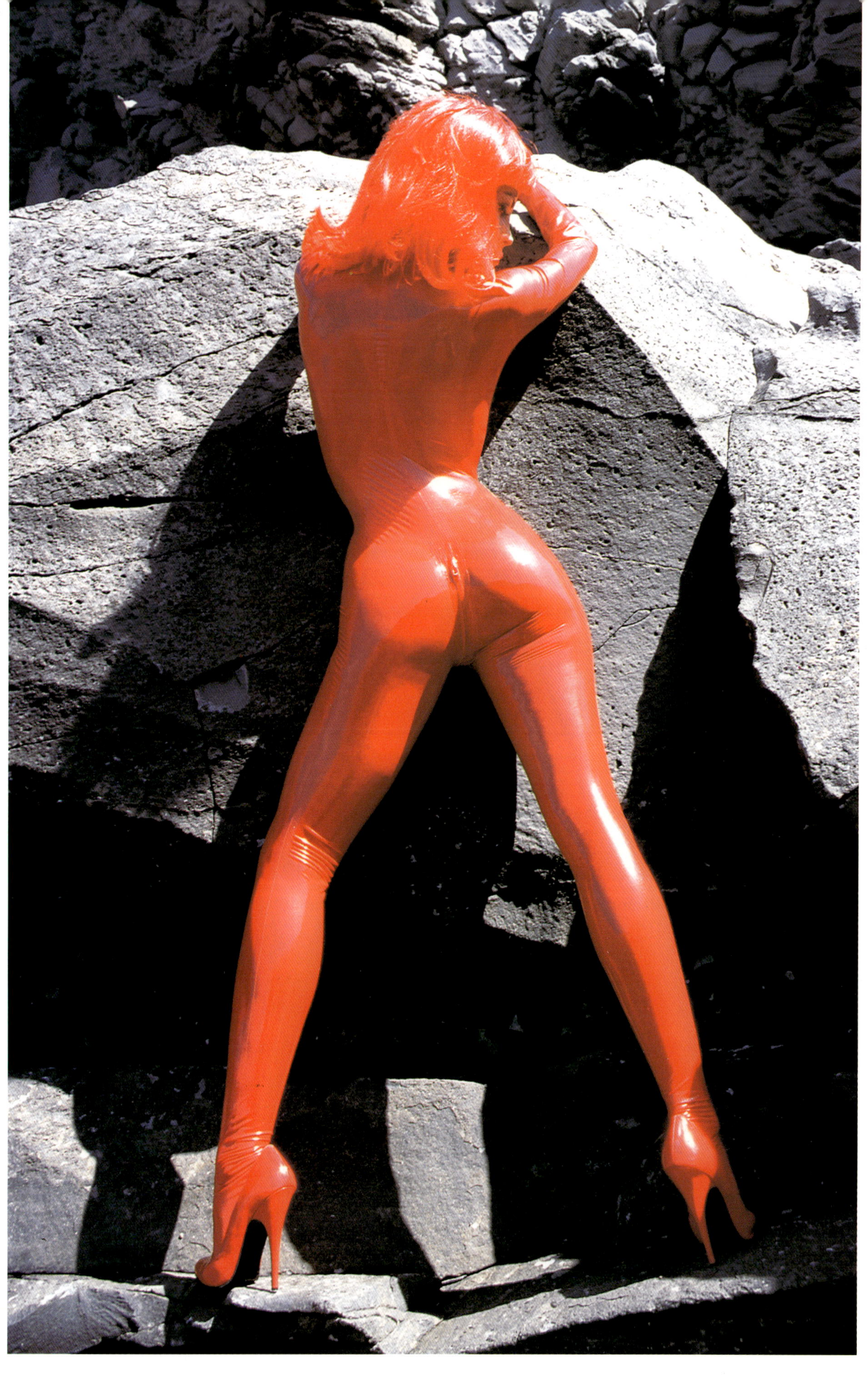

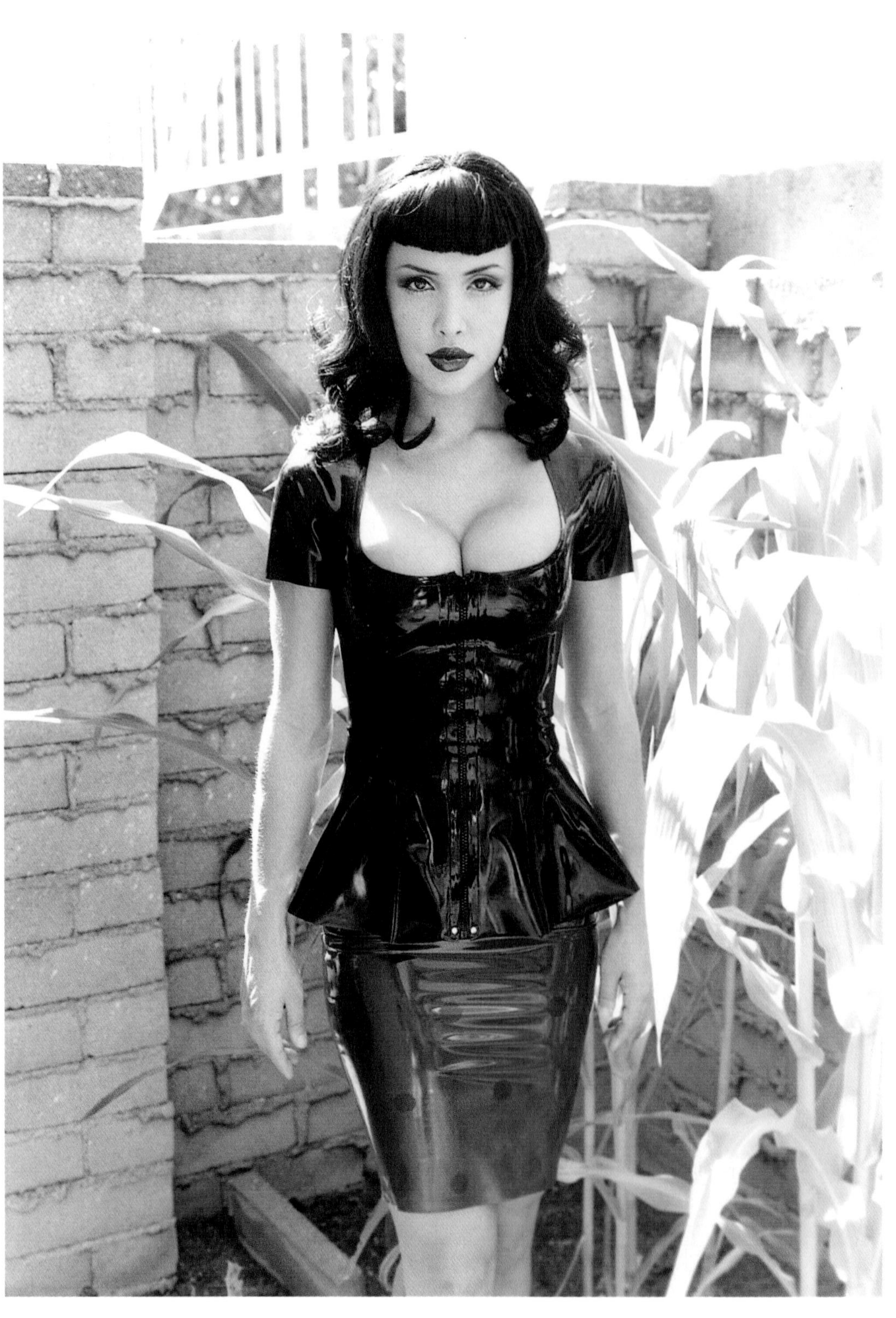

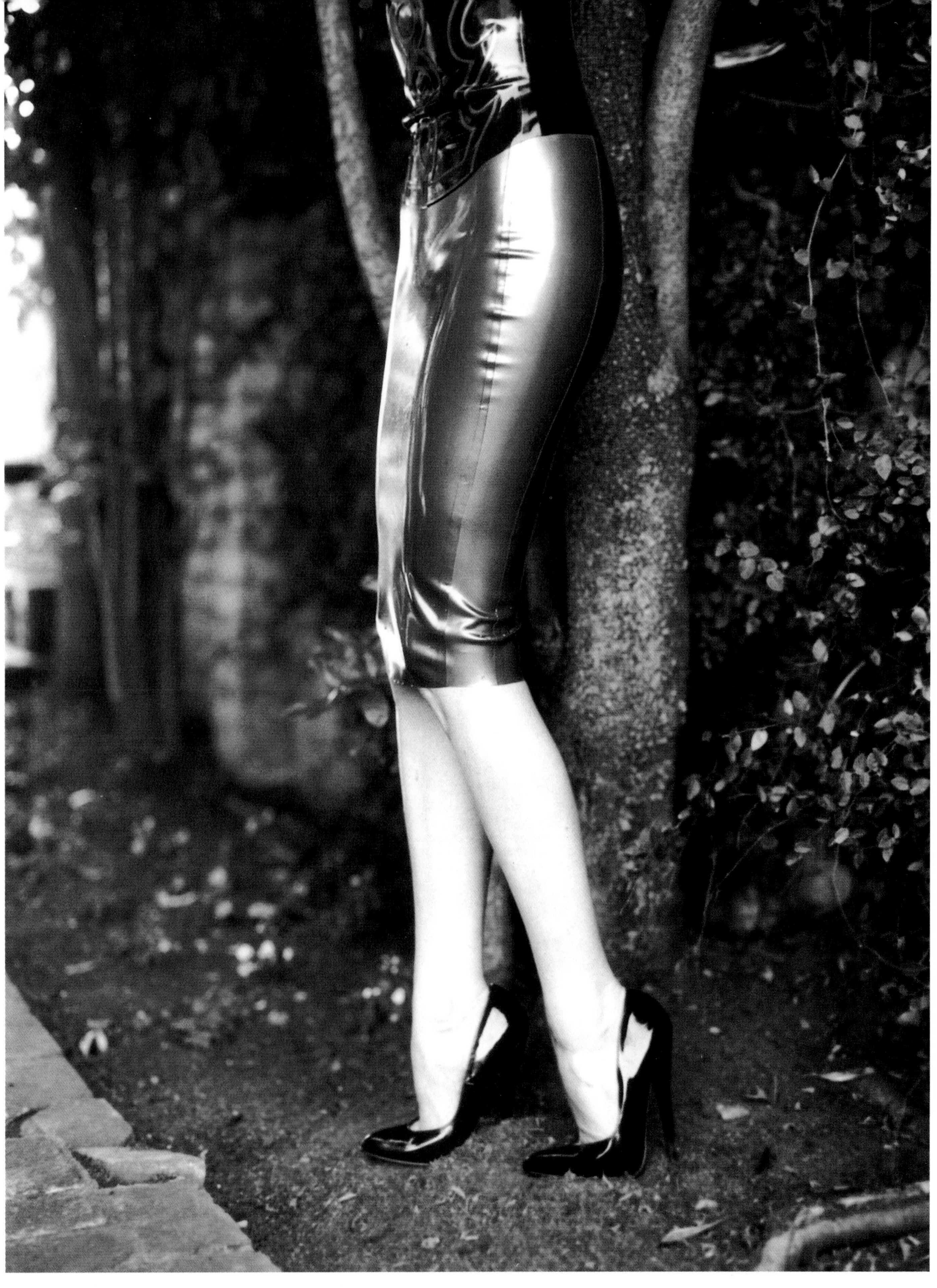

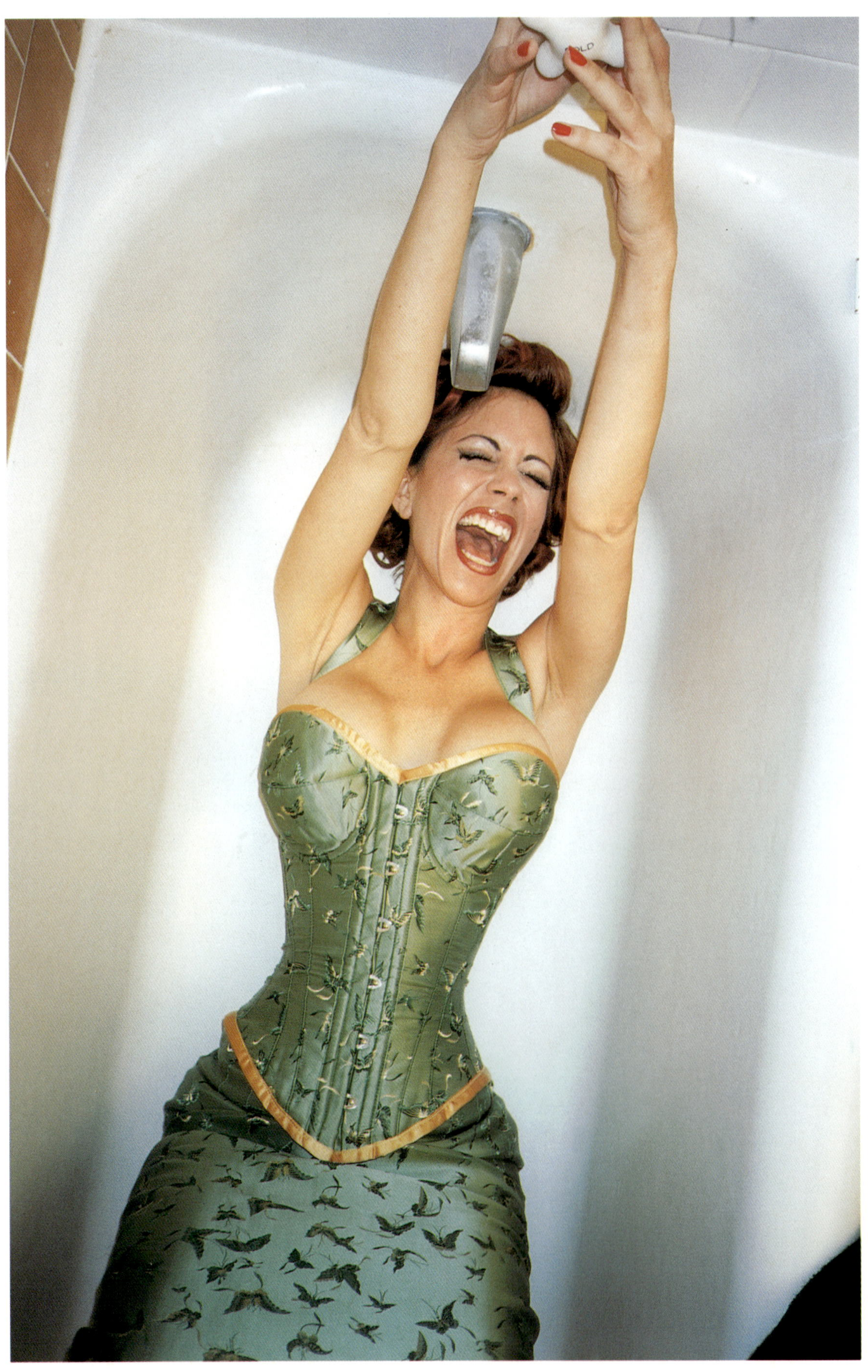



Opposite Carlos Batts

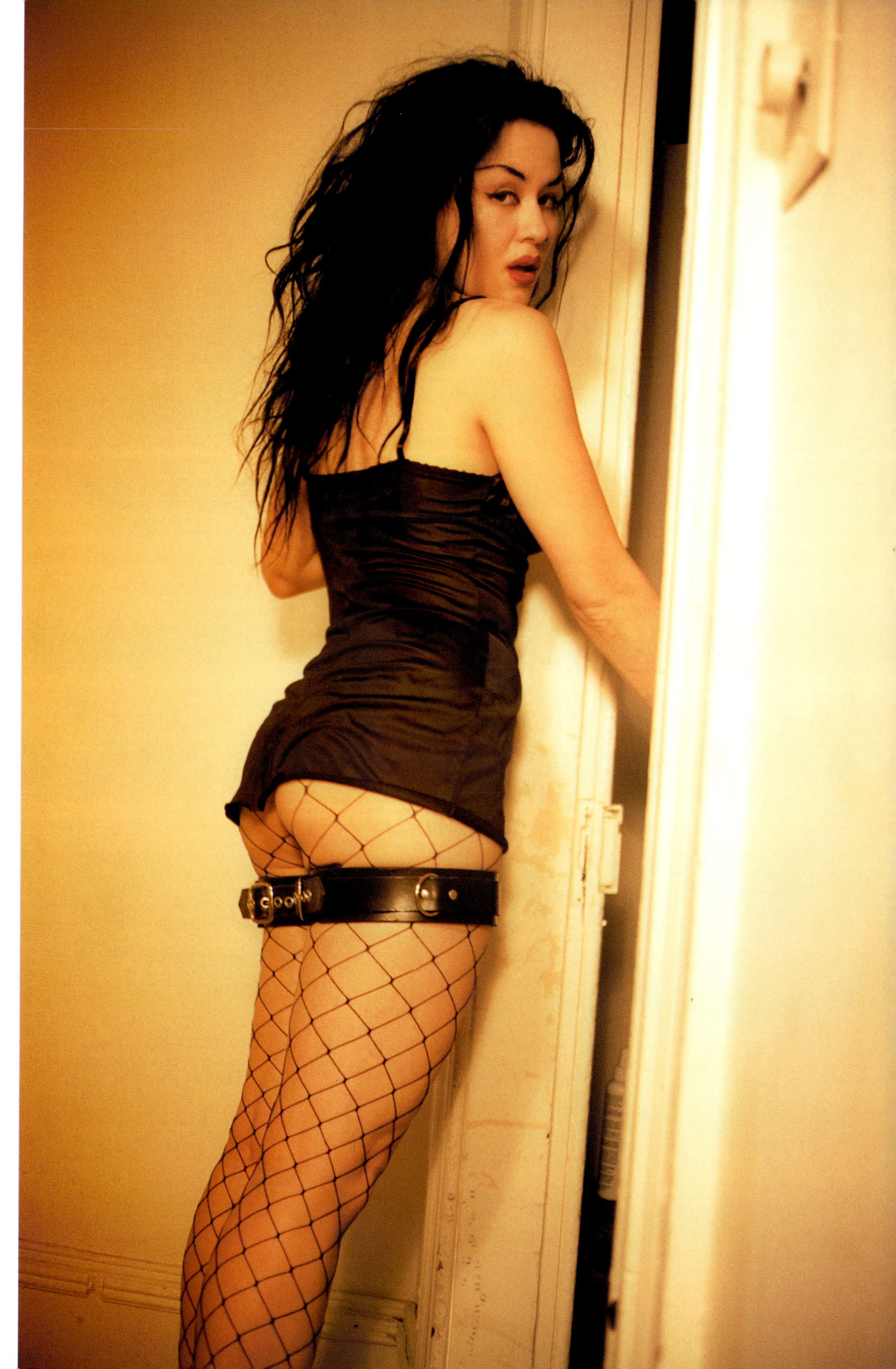

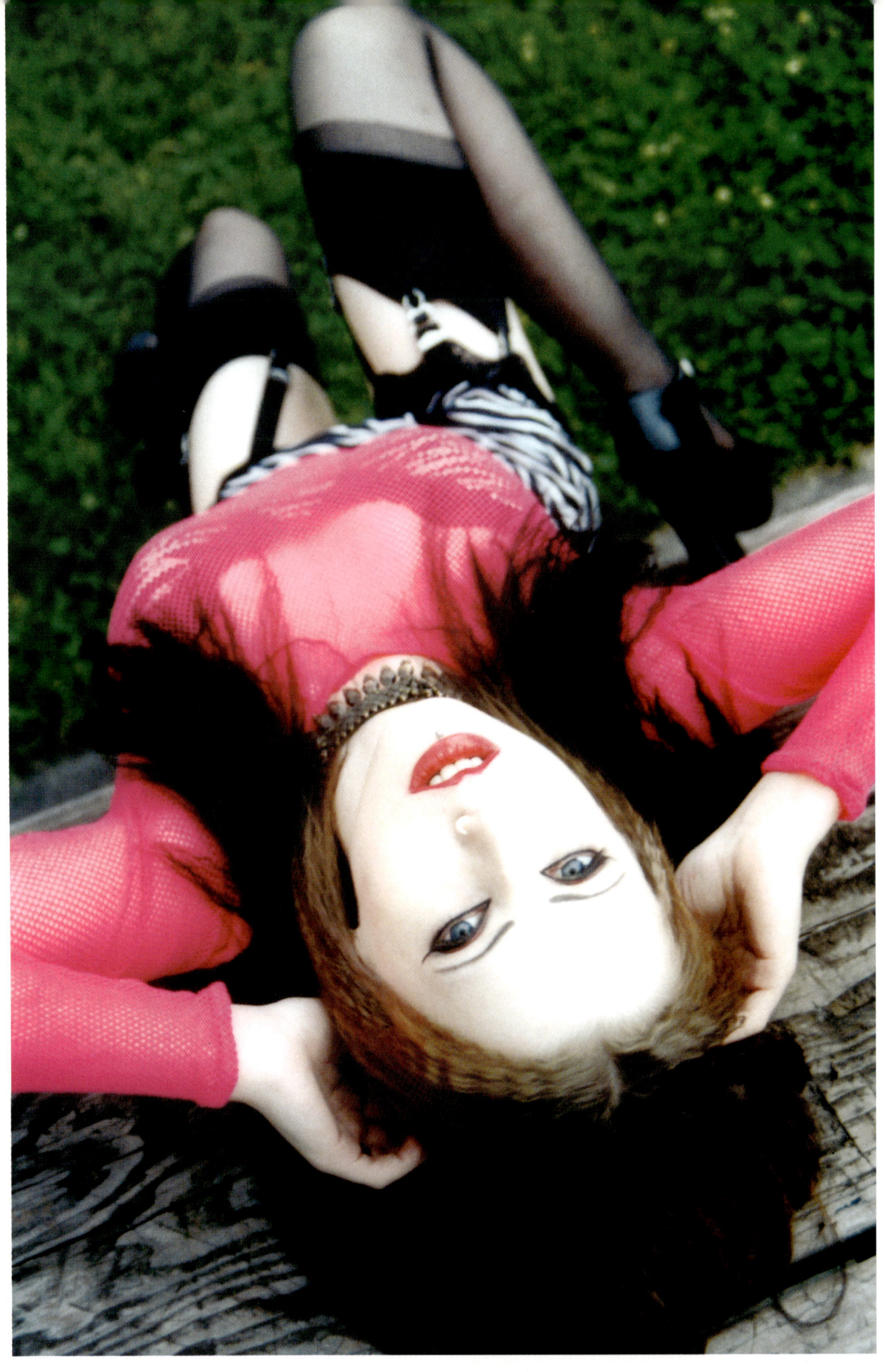

70 Kevin Hundsnurcher

Opposite Christophe Mourthé

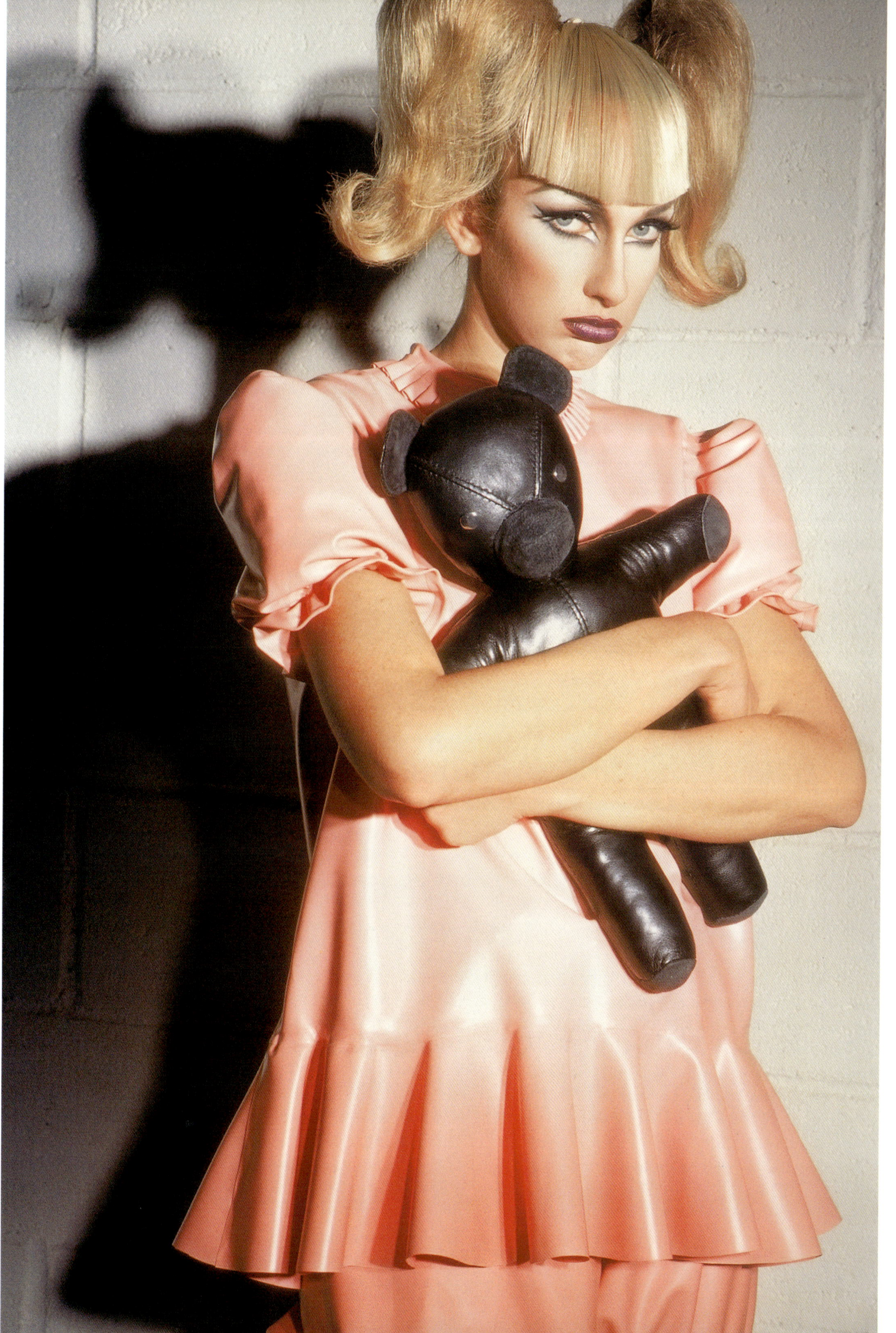

# DOMINA AND D

While dressing for pleasure can be a private solo activity, domination and discipline are games that only two (or more) can play. For some of us, the idea of submitting to another person's erotic power, of being controlled by them and perhaps being punished for our "transgressions" is a fantasy that goes way beyond mere sex. For others, the idea that, temporarily at least, another human being might willingly volunteer to become our quivering slave and perform any task, sexual or otherwise, that we demand, is incredibly exciting. Domination and submission, and the intimate rituals of discipline and punishment often associated with them, can allow us to act out, in a safe space, mutual desires and feelings that "normal" social and sexual etiquette do not permit. The dynamics between participants in such situations can provide wonderful subject matter for the voyeuristic camera.

It would be difficult to find a more powerful single icon to represent the whole world of sub-dom fantasy than the dominatrix. Hence this classic whip-wielding, thighbooted, leather- or rubber-clad goddess figure maintains a powerful presence in modern imagery. When you look like the women in Dave Naz's *Torturella, Damien & Slave* (p.83), Gary & Pierre Silva's *Isabella Mirror* (p.96) or John Dietrich's *Dita Blue* (p.107), there can be little doubt of your intentions. However, the classic dom look is only one way of getting the message across. Practically any uniform that invests its wearer with authority can be adapted to similar erotic purpose, hence the pervy camera calls upon a whole cast of other characters — fetishised versions of cops, nurses, schoolmistresses and so on — usually showing them brandishing the instruments of office that confirm their peculiar power to control, restrain, punish or, at the very least, frighten us.

Even when the rôles of both members of a sub-dom couple are well signposted in the photograph, different pictures can suggest very different narratives. The pose of the dominatrix in Dave Naz's *Simone Kross Steps on Slave* (p.82) suggests that it is all over for her bound client, while for the bound women contemplating female captors portrayed by Erik Hansen-Hansen on p.88 and Jim Weathers' *Intimate Inquisition* on p.103, it looks like things are just about to begin. The stern dominatrixes portrayed by Gary & Pierre Silva (*Mistress Aves*, p.97) and John Dietrich (*The Bargain*, p.108) clearly tolerate no nonsense from their charges, while for Trevor Watson's sporting couples on pp.124 and 125, fun is clearly a major part of the package.

While, in real life, rituals of domination and discipline require at least two participants, photography often focuses on just one side of the equation, allowing us to use our imaginations to providing the missing element of the story. Sometimes the other participant is a person just outside the frame of the image, as implied by Fetish Eyes' schoolmistress (p.90) or John Dietrich's supine blonde (*Lost Weekend*, p.109). But sometimes, as with Bob Carlos Clarke's rubber maid *Charlie* (p.74) the pose and gaze address us directly, so that the viewer becomes the other participant in the scene.

# TION
# ISCIPLINE

While photographers frequently use uniform as a literal pointer to their characters' SM orientation, it is not always a reliable guide. Ambiguity has its place in sub-dom photography just as it has in real sub-dom scenes and relationships, where the question of who is really in charge – the one issuing the orders, or the one allowing himself to be ordered around – is eternally debated. Ambiguity ups the ante: it makes things far more interesting. Wearing a maid's costume, for example, is normally unequivocal evidence of submissiveness, but with her imperious expression, aggressive body language and flexed riding crop at the ready, Clarke's maid appears anything but submissive. So is she simply "out of type" – a dominant maid? Perhaps, though, there is in fact a third possibility recognised within the sub-dom mindset – that her tough pose is actually a challenge to "use this crop on me if you think you're man (or woman) enough".

Context can also change the meaning of the uniform. In conventional male fantasy, nurses are depicted as naughty, promiscuous, sexually available. In sub-dom fantasy, however, nurses are invariably dauntingly powerful figures, equipped both by medical training and natural inclination to do humiliatingly invasive things to those who deserve it. With that glint in her eye, that knowing smile and those hands freshly gloved, no one could doubt which team Doralba Picerno's *Nurse No. 2* (p.85) plays for. And yet by putting the same character under glass like an Allen Jones mannequin (*Vanessa*, p.100, James

& James have turned the tables on the stuff of fetish fantasy. Meanwhile, other photographers have explored this idea of interchangeable rôles within a single image. The carefully matched looks of Christophe Mourthé's women in *Steps by Steps* (p.78) and Kevin Hundsnurcher's dungeon duo (pp.118 and 119) suggest that, whatever the participants' rôles at the precise moment captured on film, there is obvious potential for trading places.

Some readers looking through this chapter may wonder why the genre does not include more images of men, and particularly of men dominating women. Historically, there has always been more interest in images of women in sub-dom situations, whether on their own or in girl-on-girl pairings. Modern photographers have continued in this vein partly because most are personally more interested in photographing females, and partly because it is what the market likes. Also, it should be noted that in the 1980s when the modern fetish photography genre was establishing itself, it was far less acceptable politically to show women being sexually submissive, except to other women.

However, the phenomenon of "out and proud" submissive women that has been gaining momentum since the late 1990s has encouraged photographers to re-evalute their views. Consequently, the sub female now increasingly takes centre stage, as in Kevin Hundsnurcher's *Milk* (p.116), or shares the spotlight with obviously dominant men, as in John Dietrich's *Distant Cairo* (p.112) and *Zastrozzi* (p.113). This is a trend that looks set to continue for some time to come.

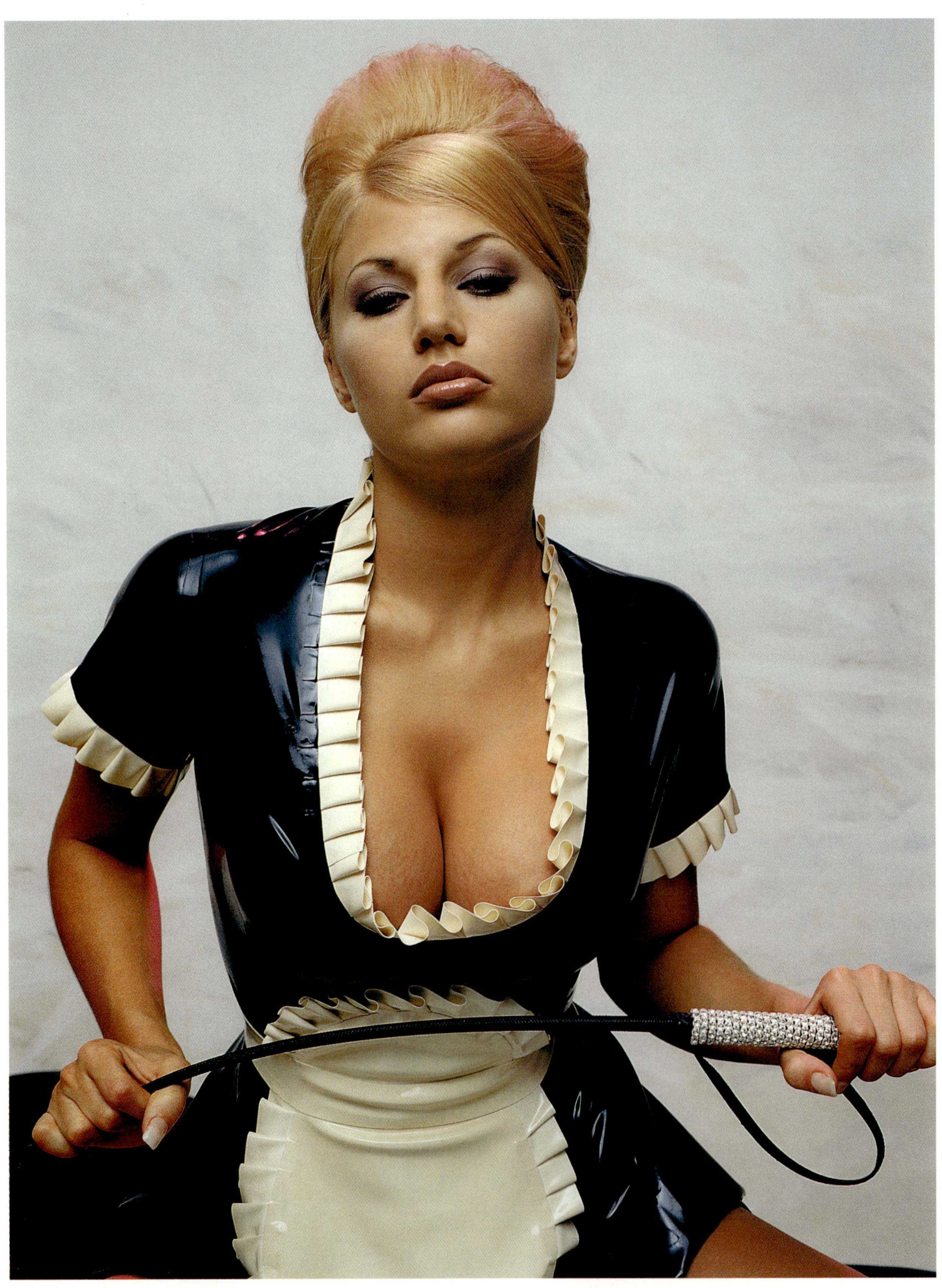

 Bob Carlos Clarke

Opposite Bob Carlos Clarke

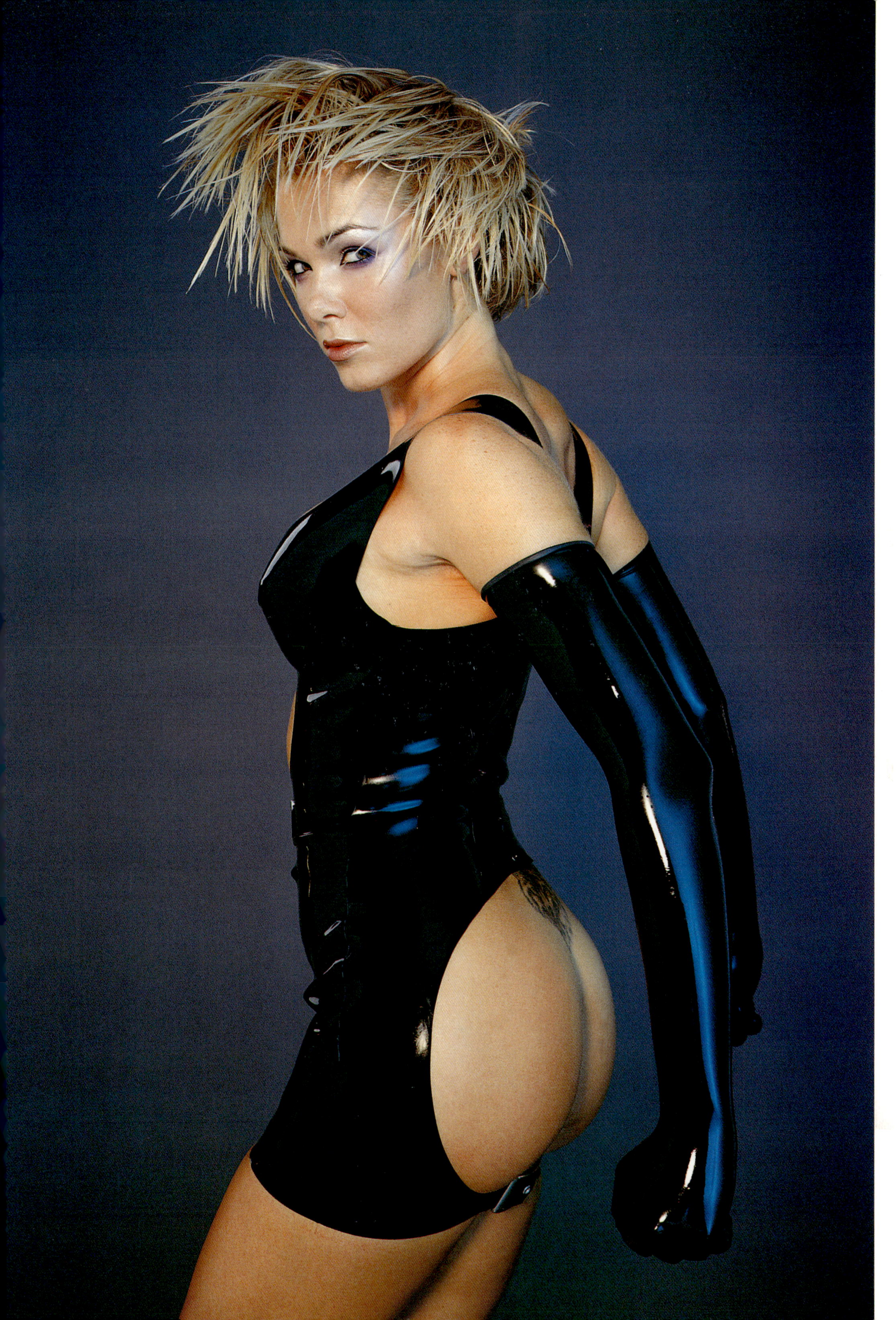

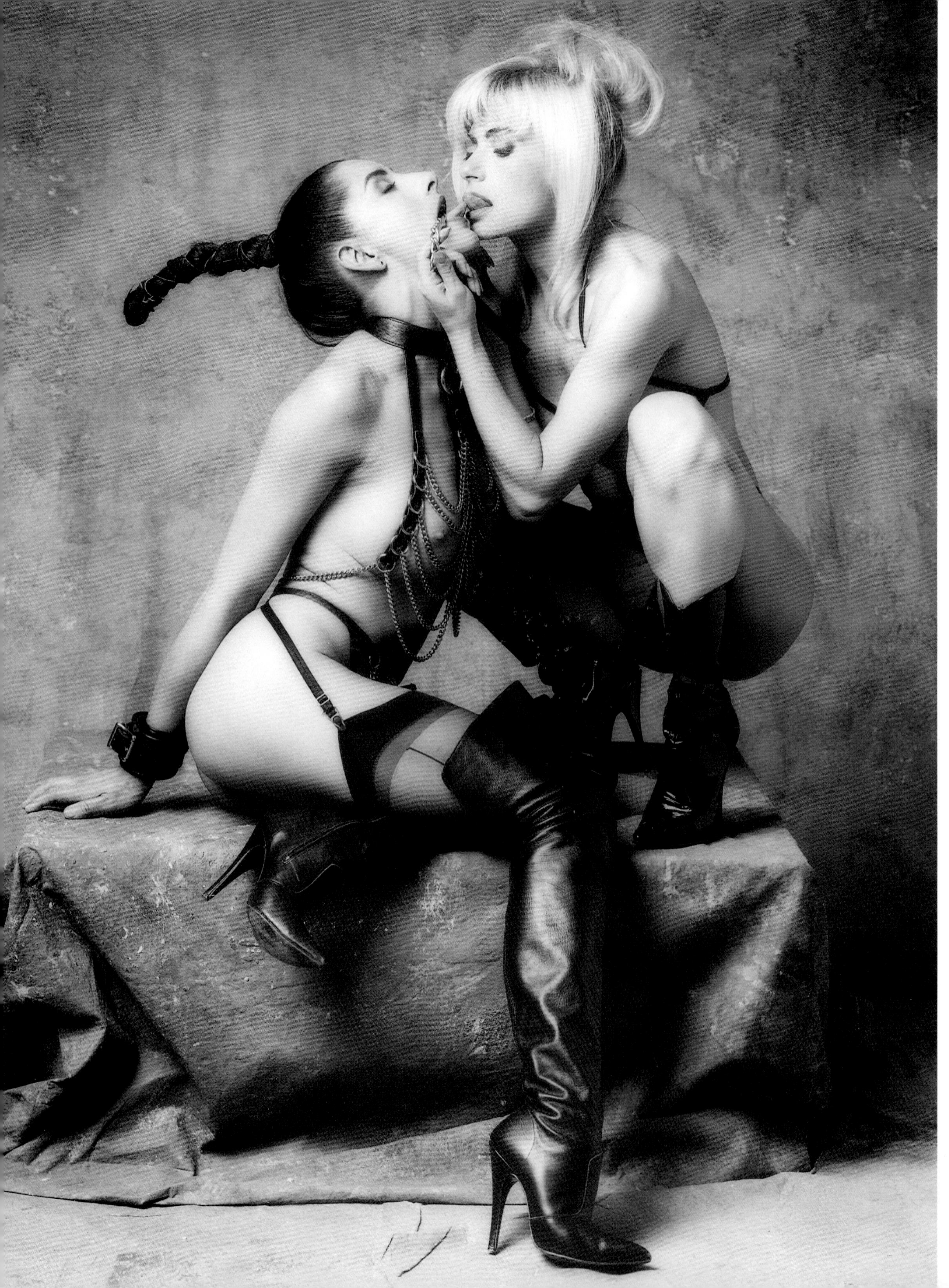

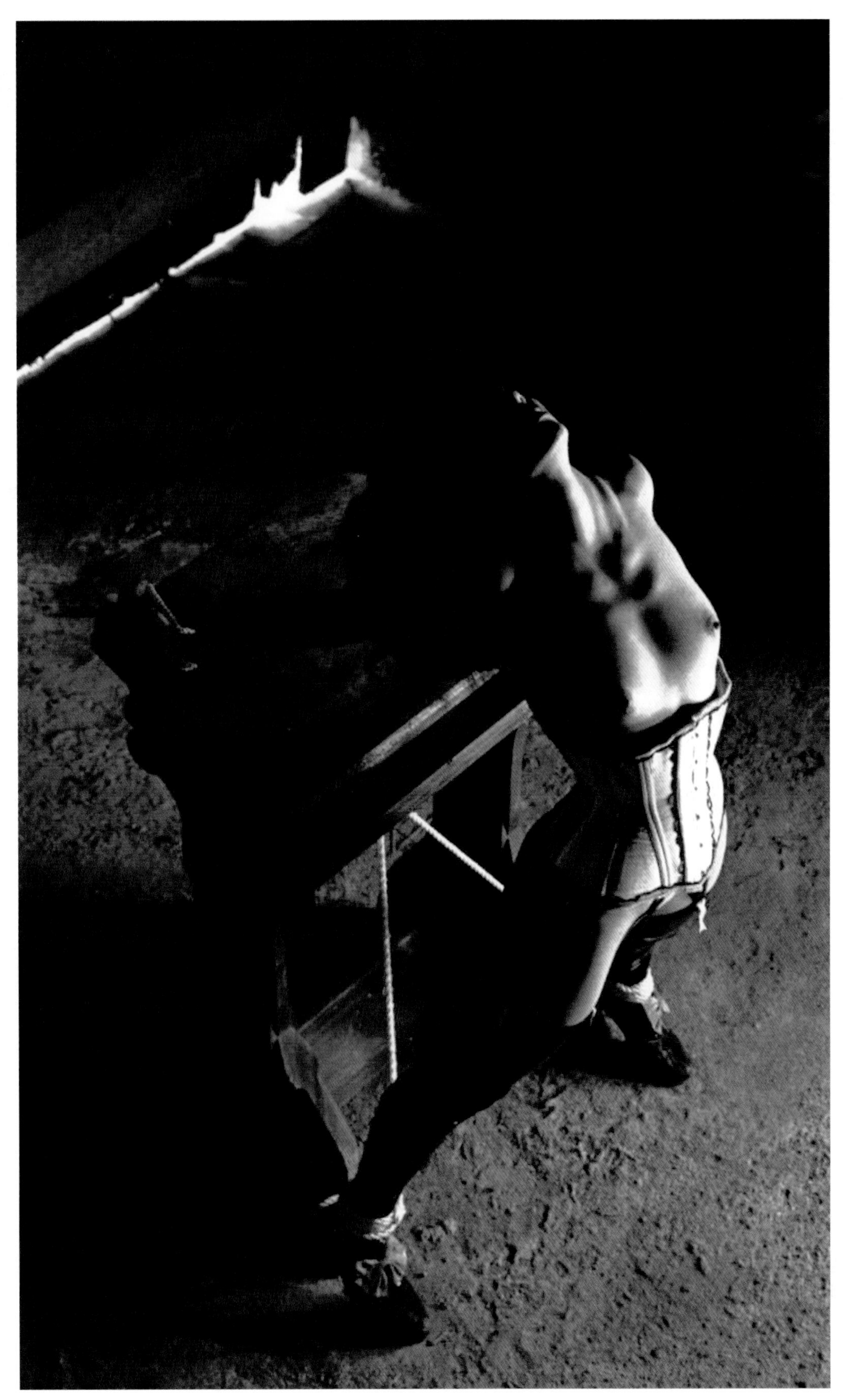



China Hamilton 

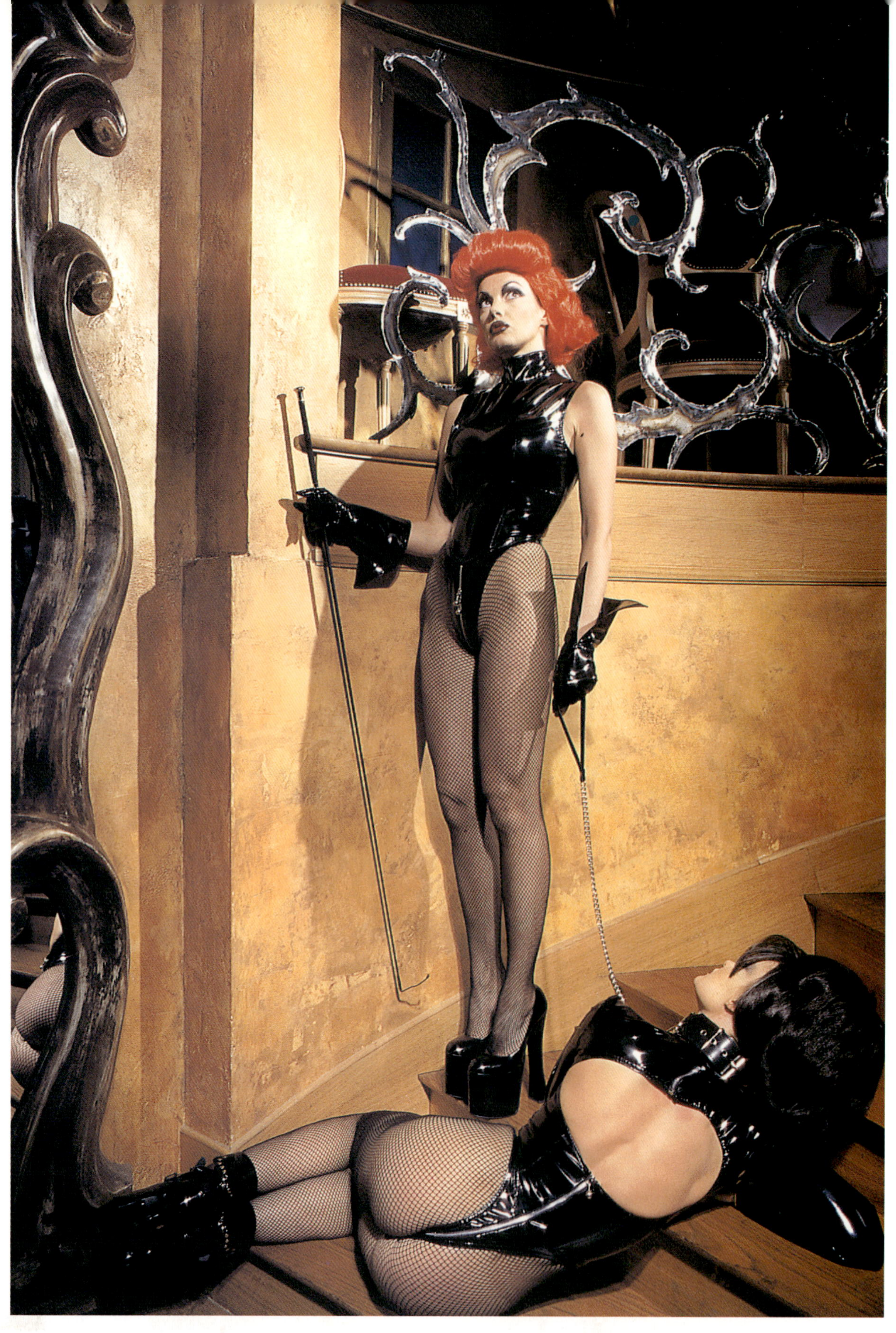



Opposite Christophe Mourthé

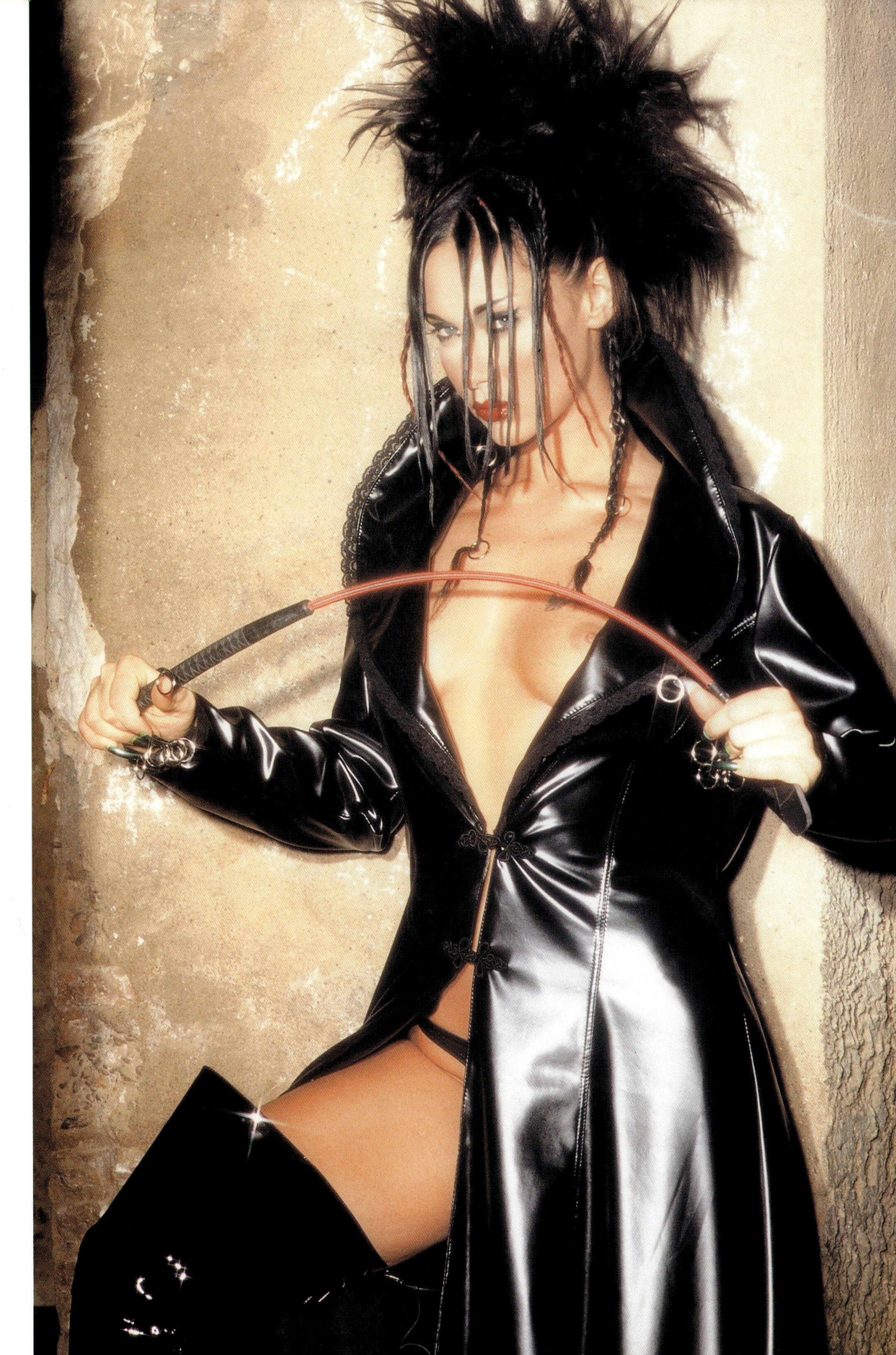

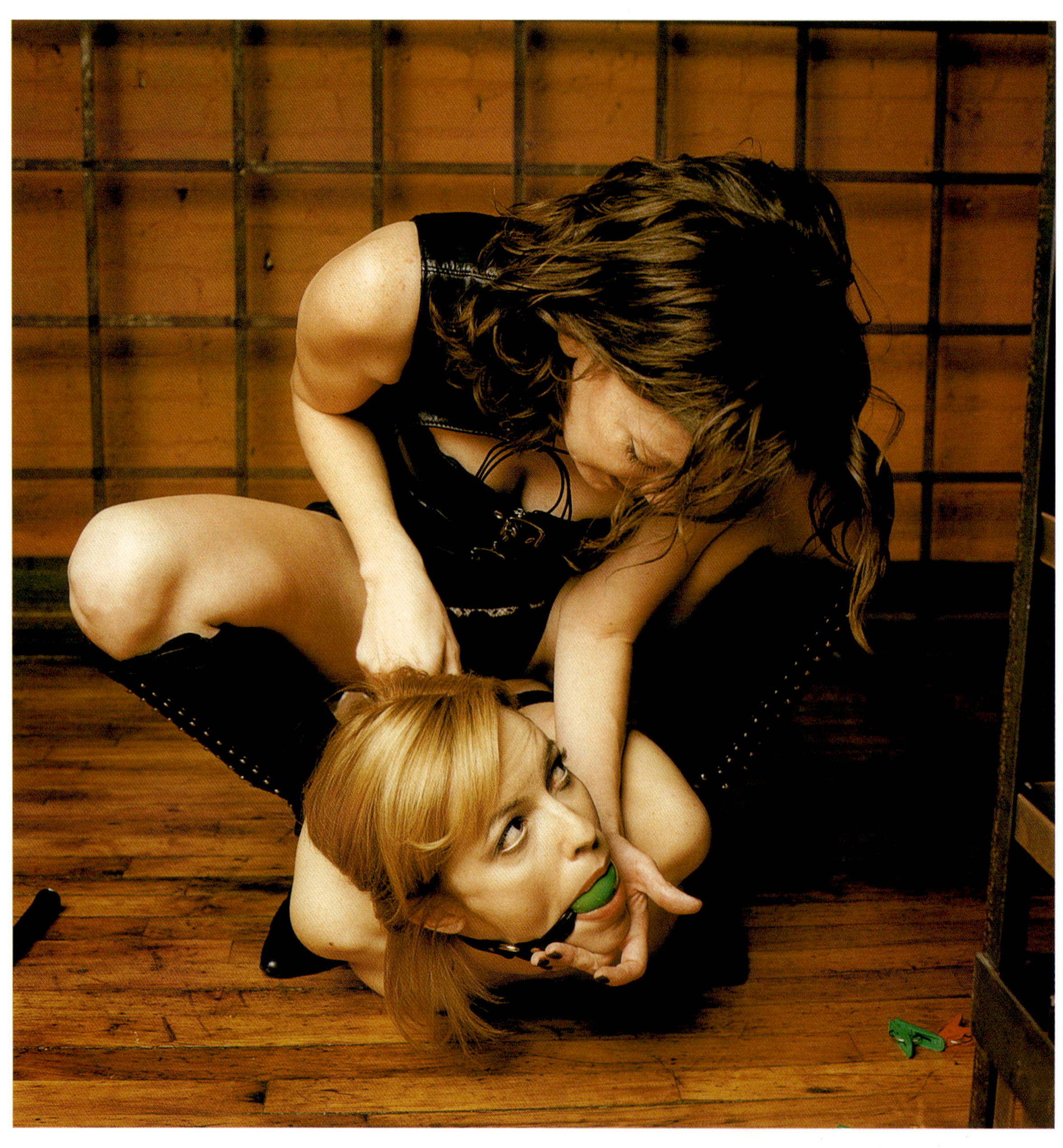

 Dave Naz

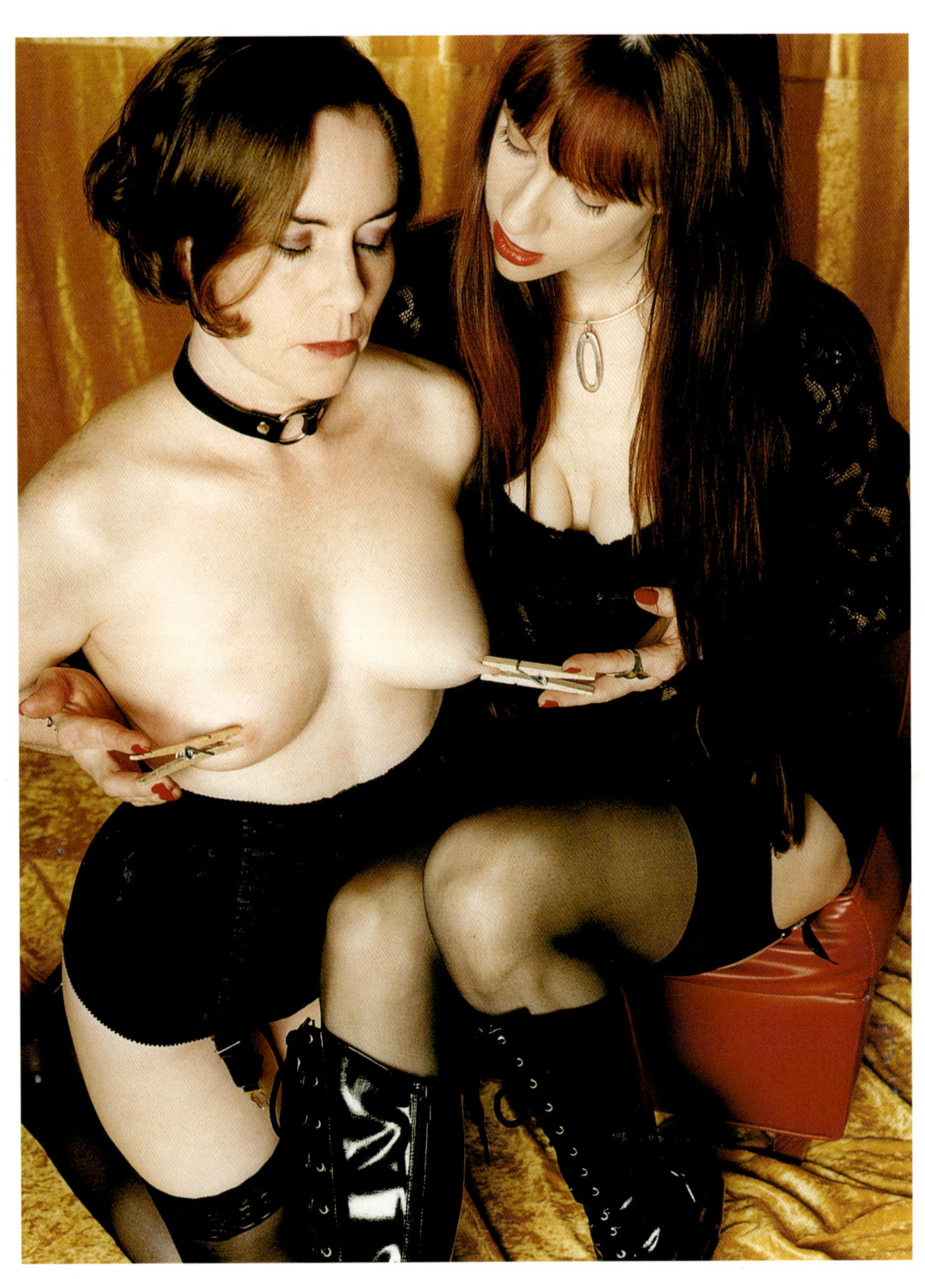

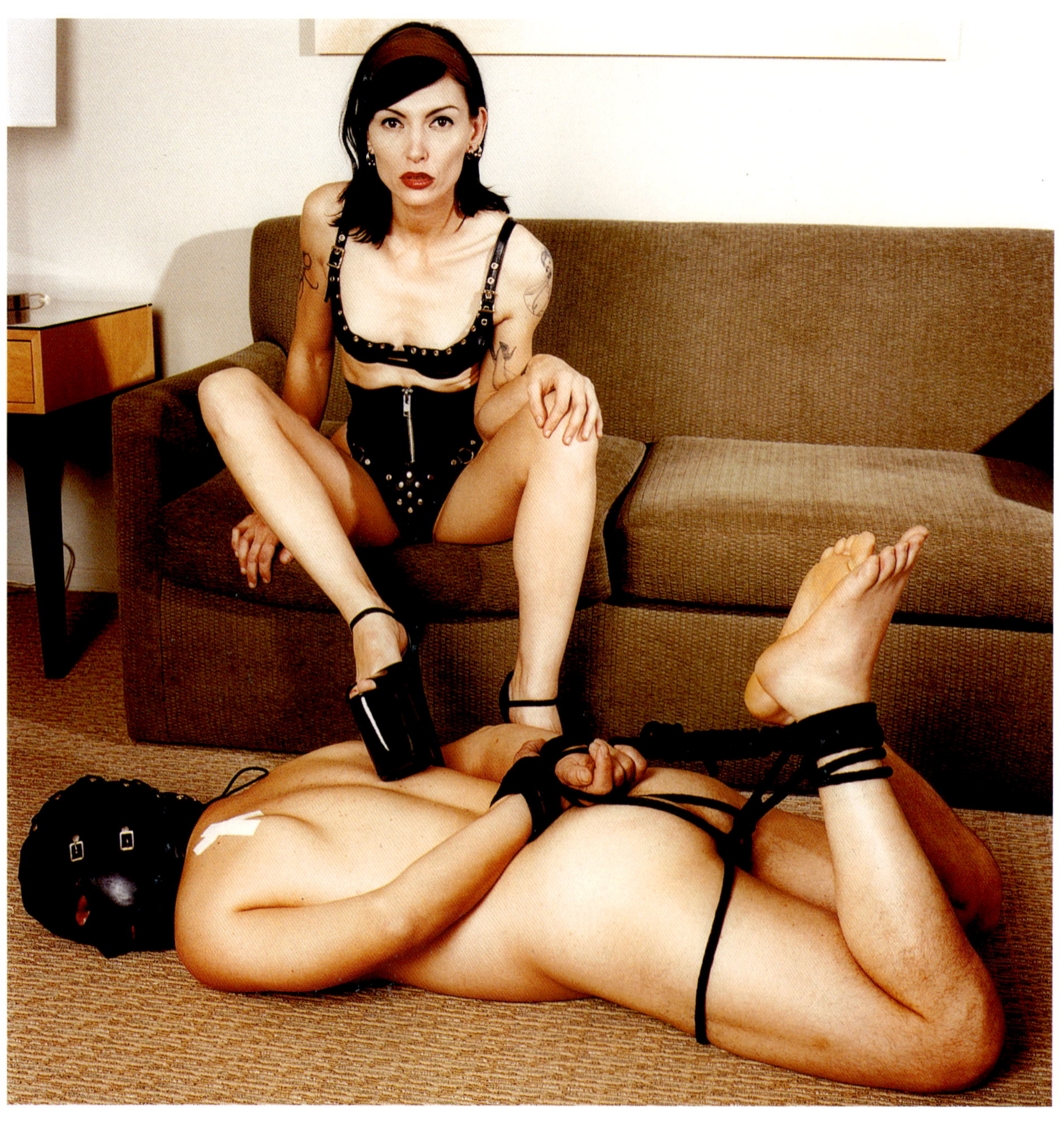

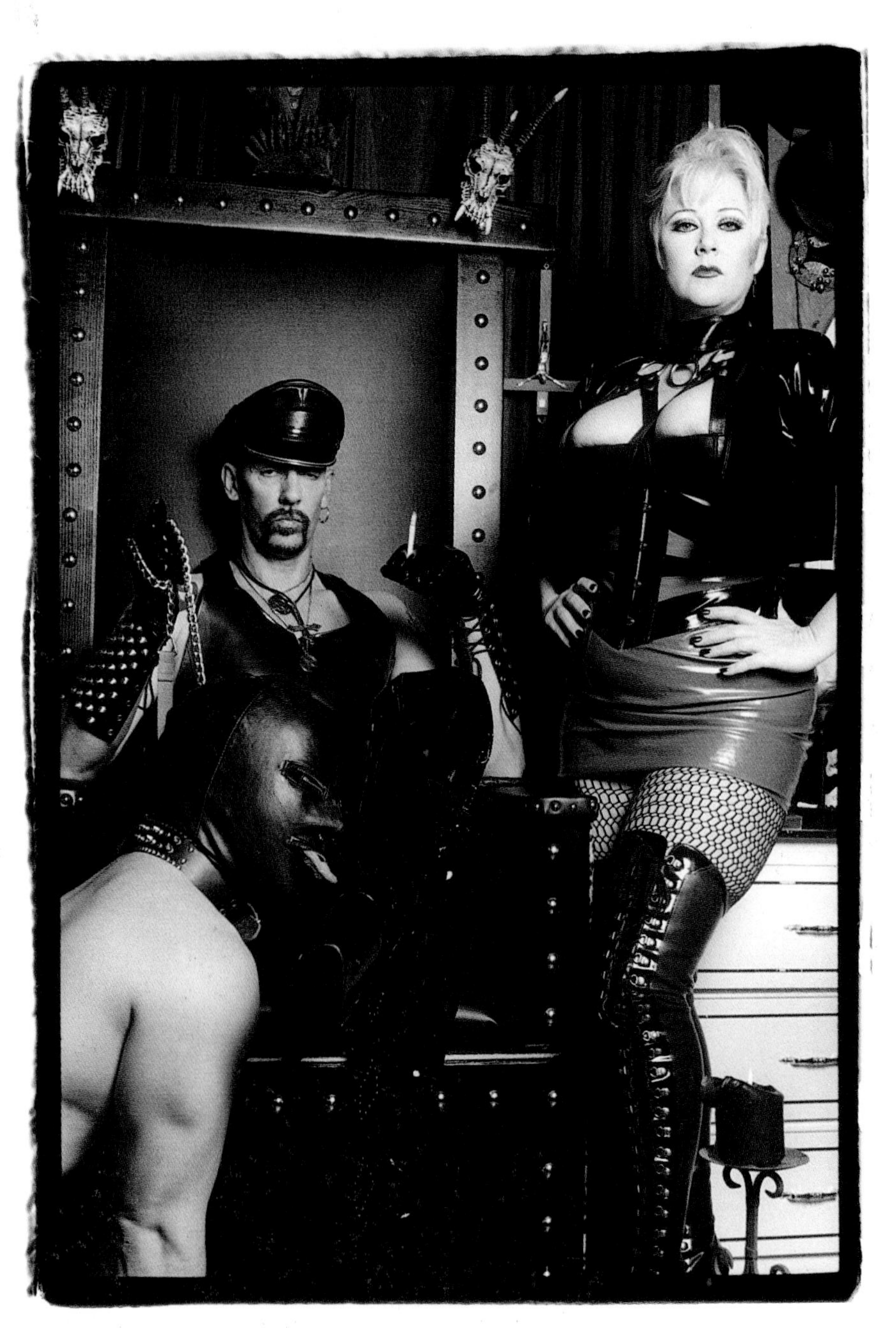

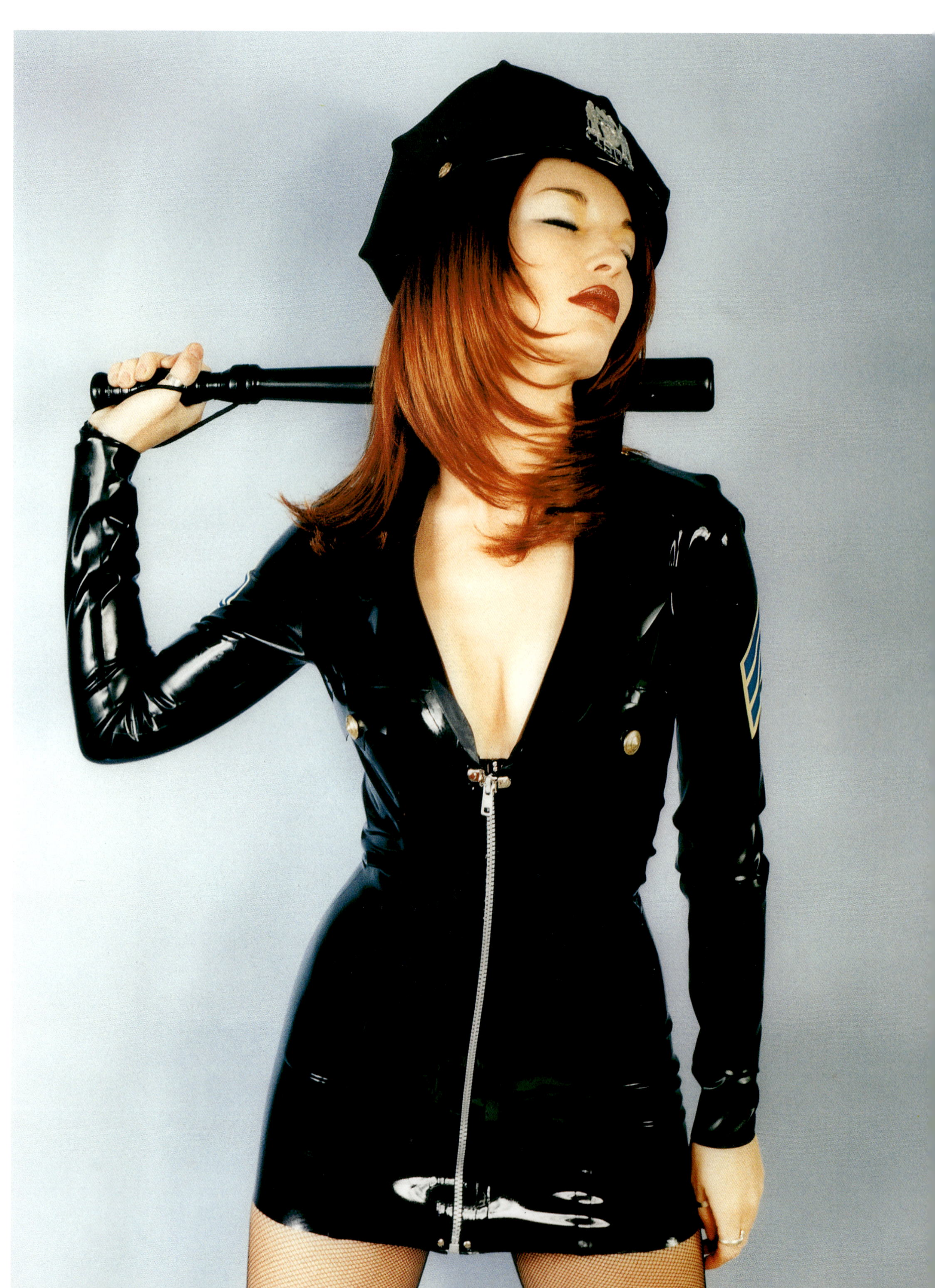

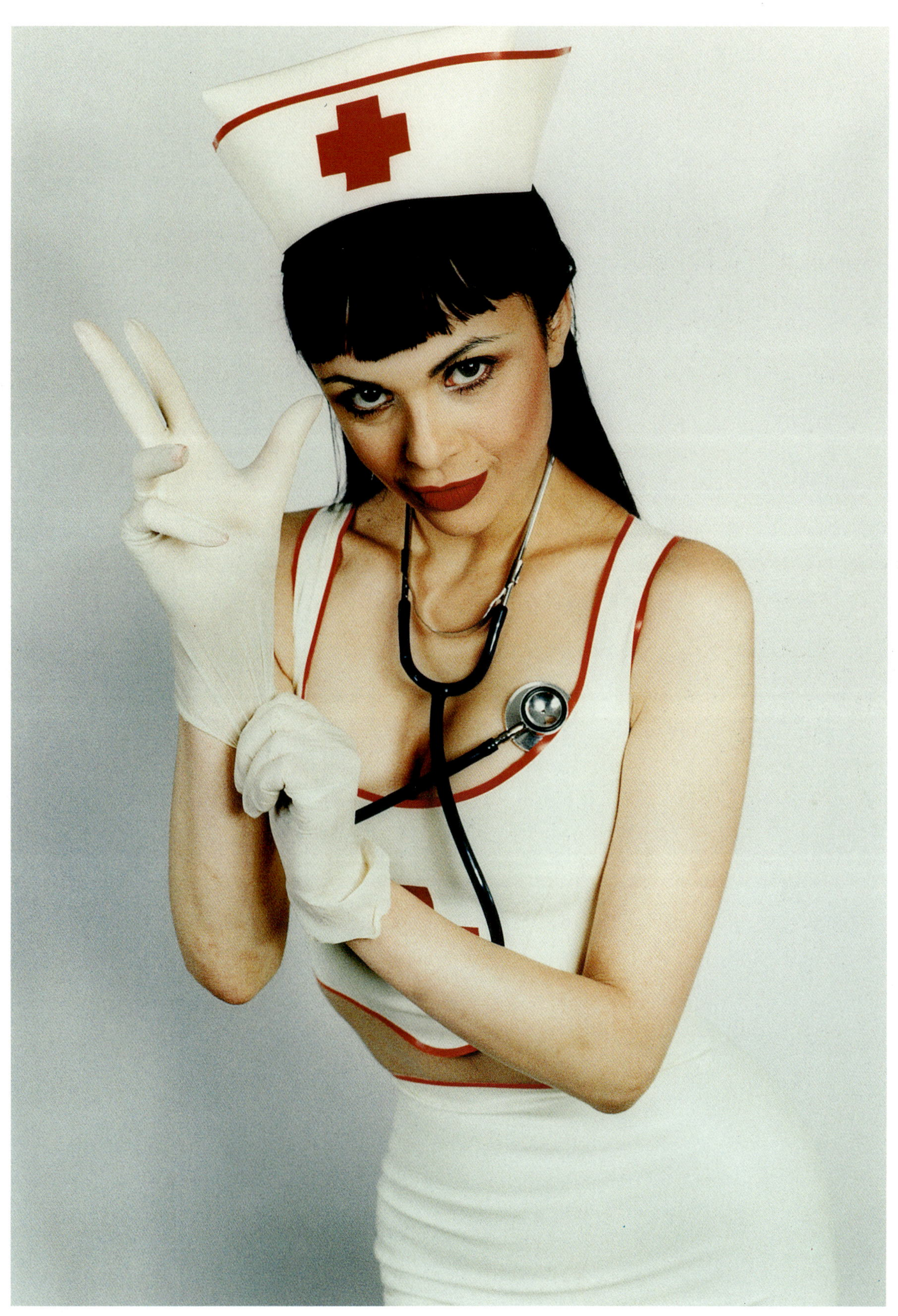



Doralba Picerno 85

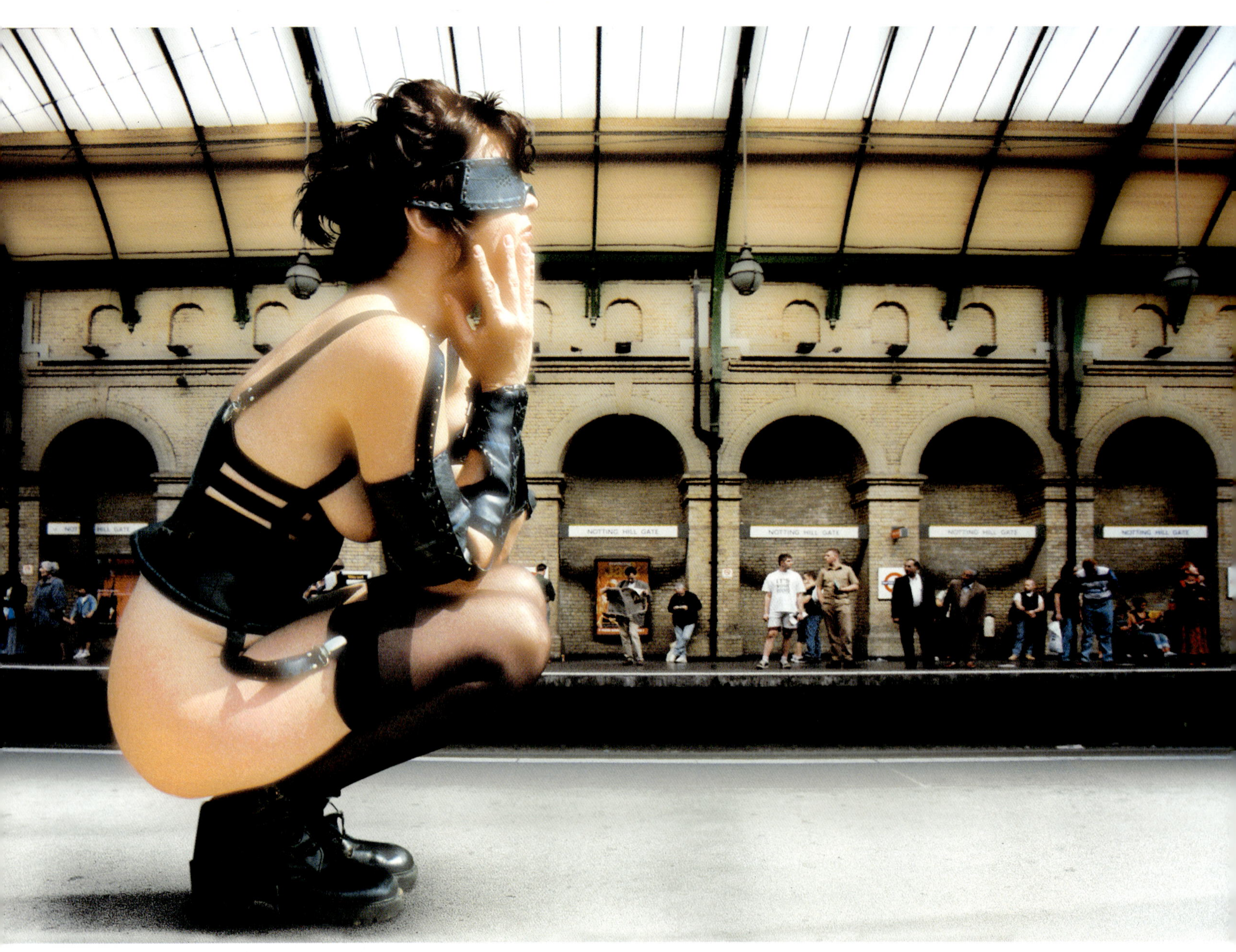
NOTTING HILL GATE
NOTTING HILL GATE
NOTTING HILL GATE
NOTTING HILL GATE

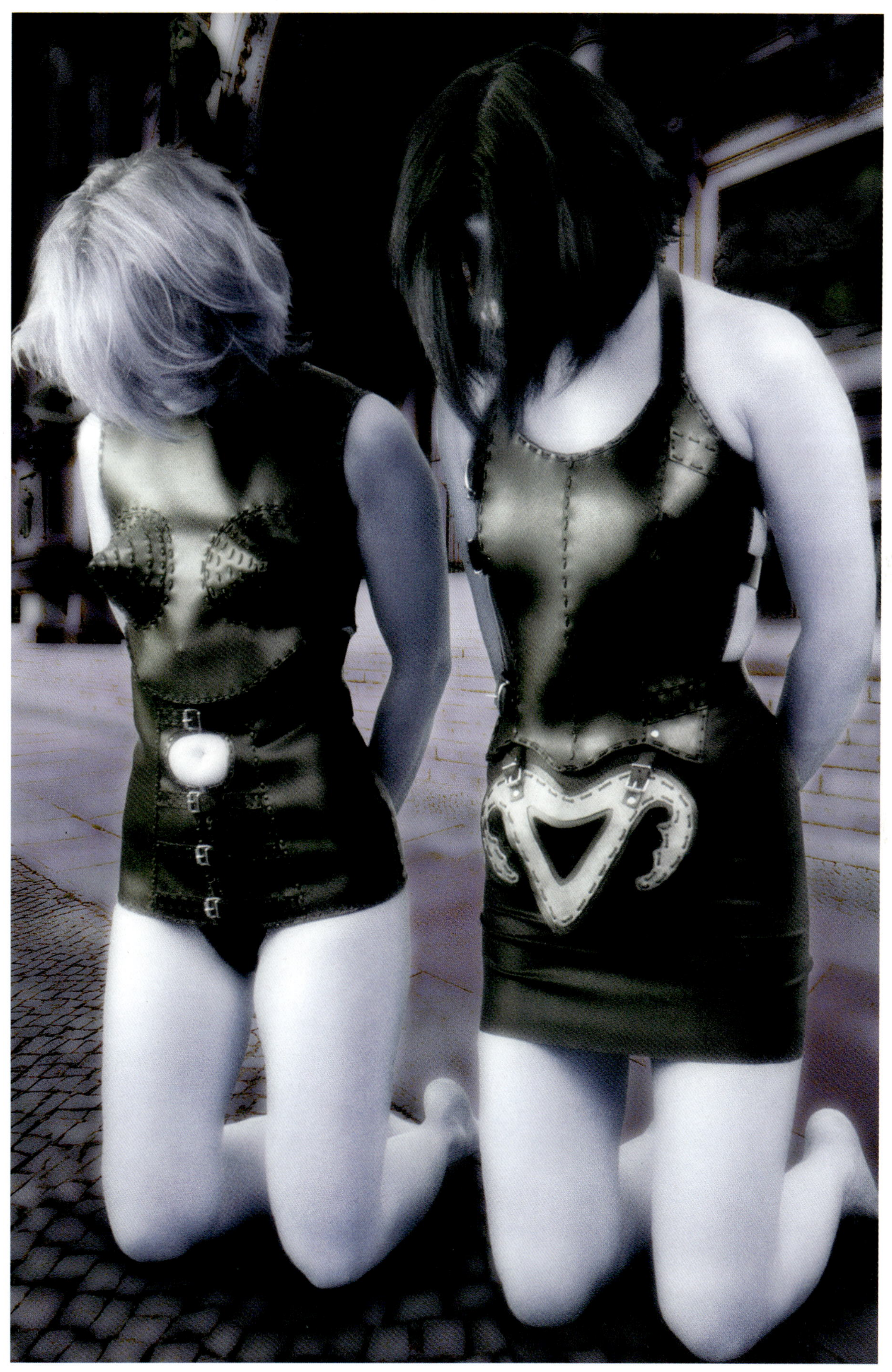

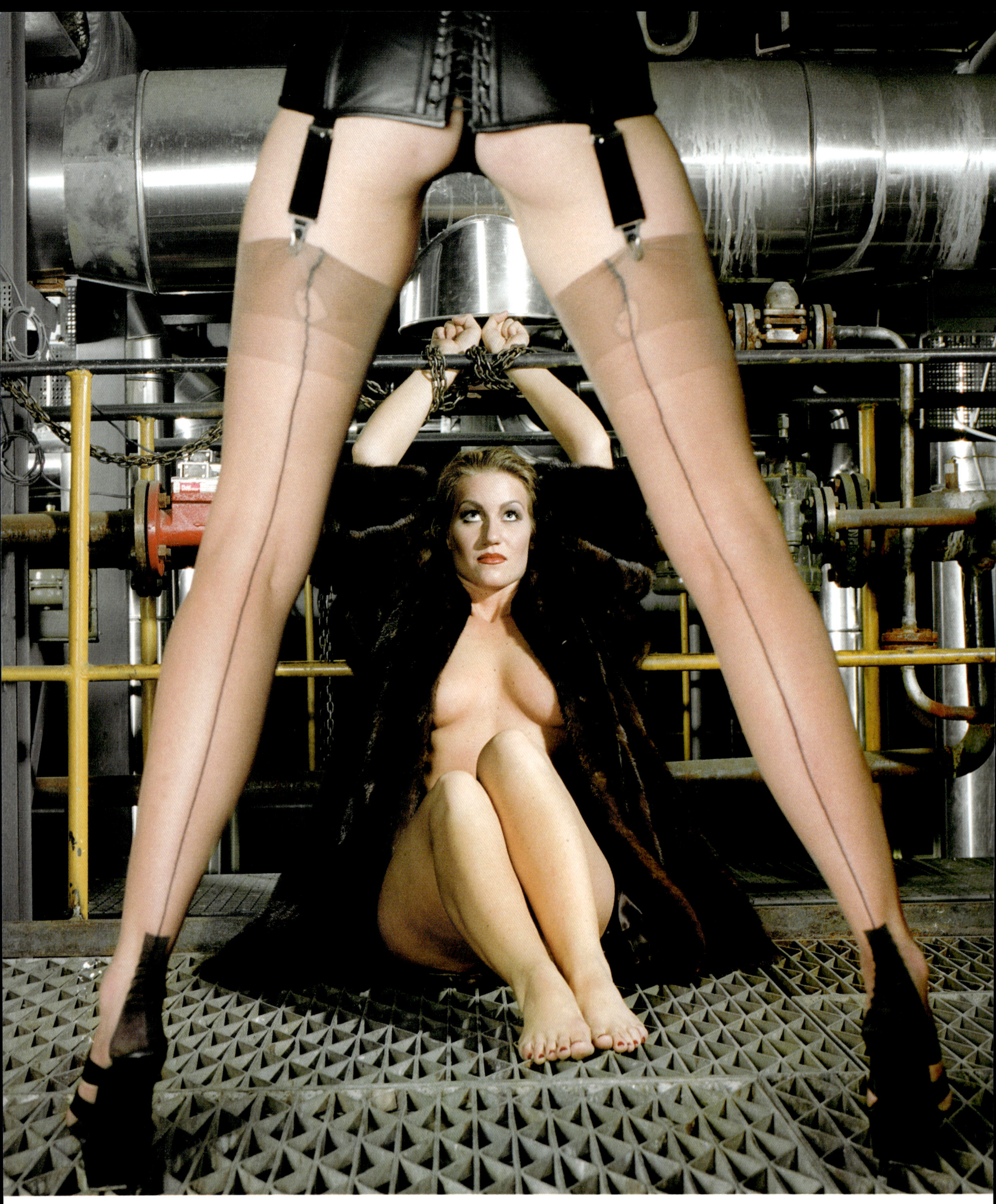

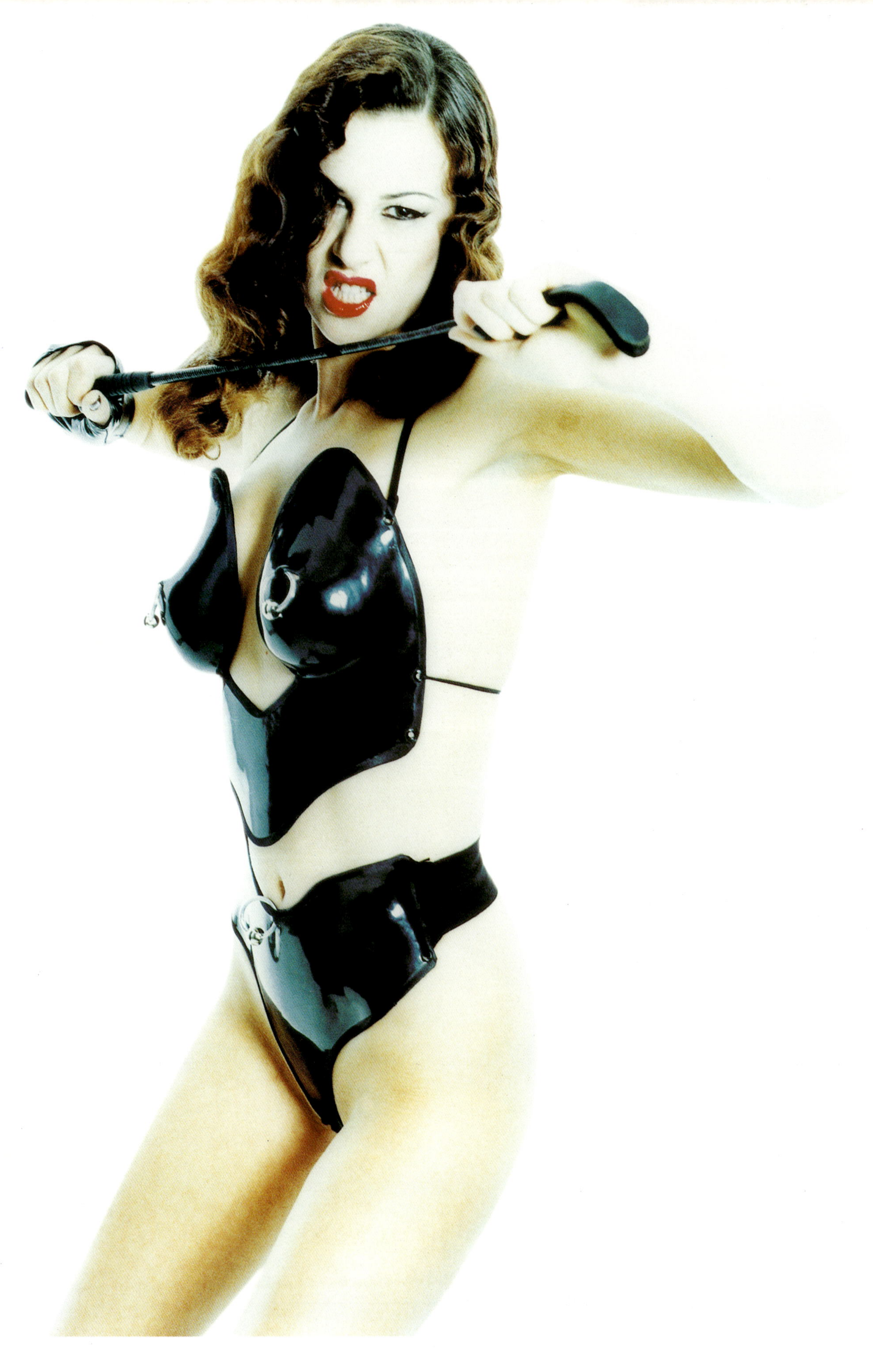

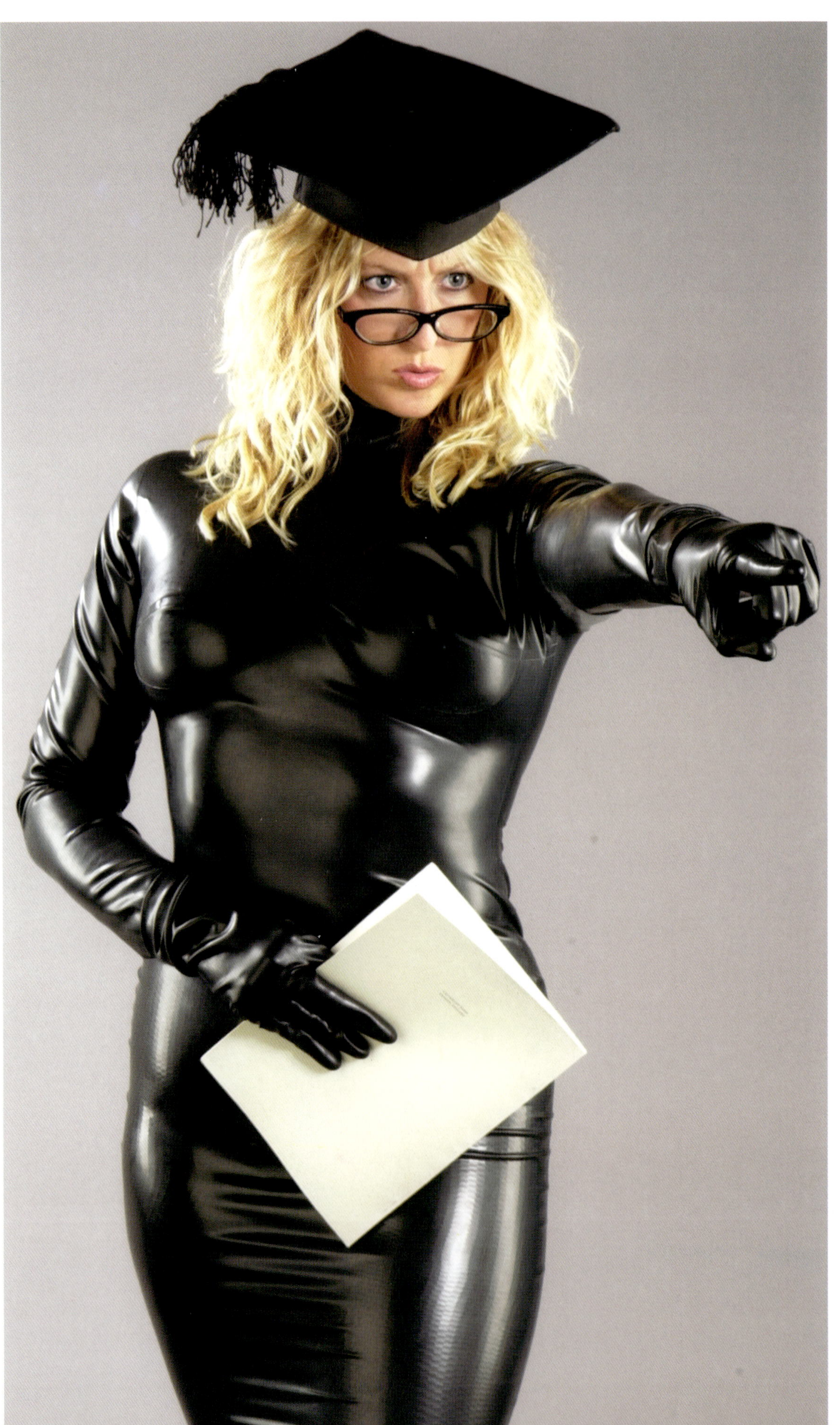

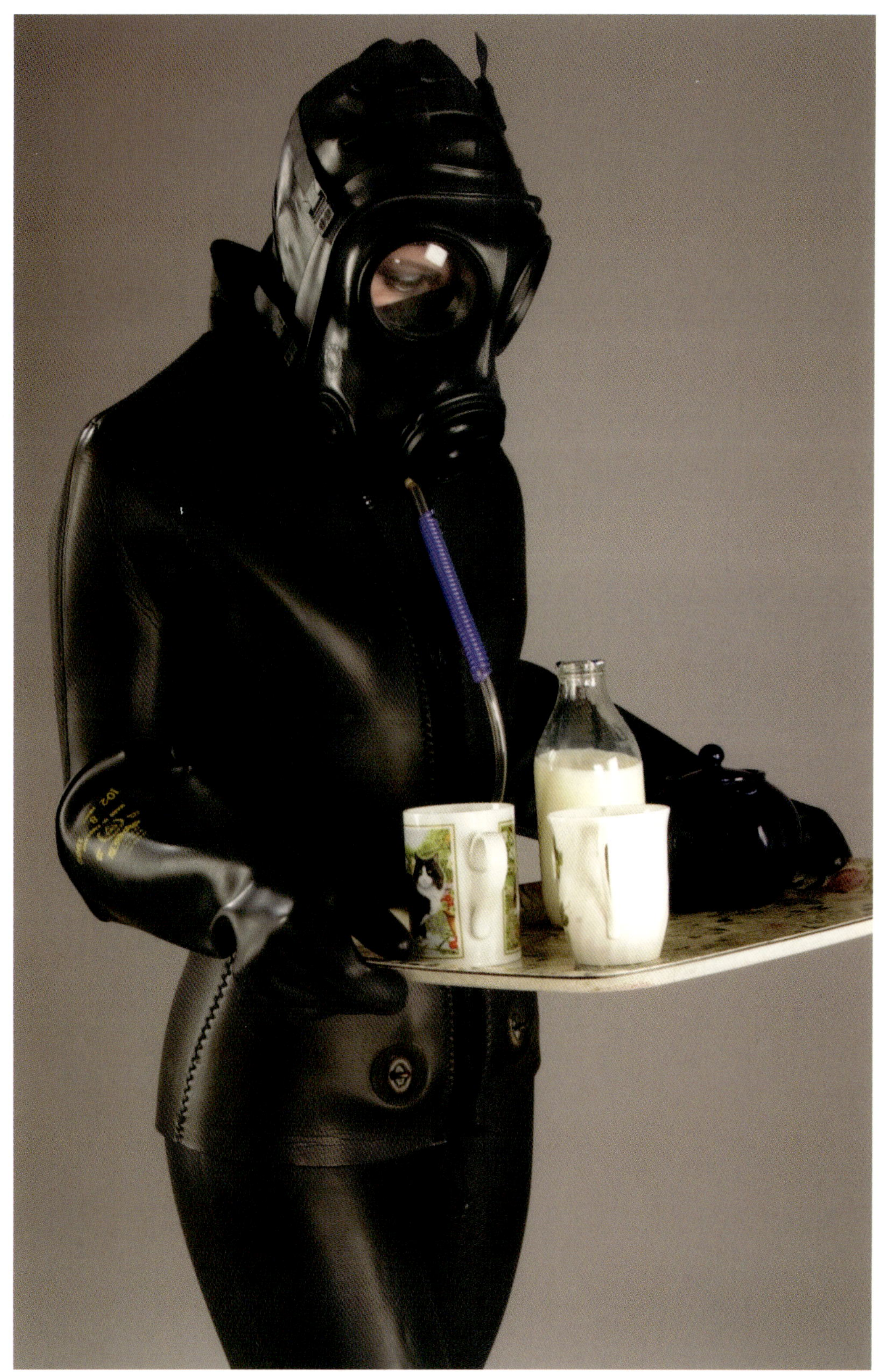

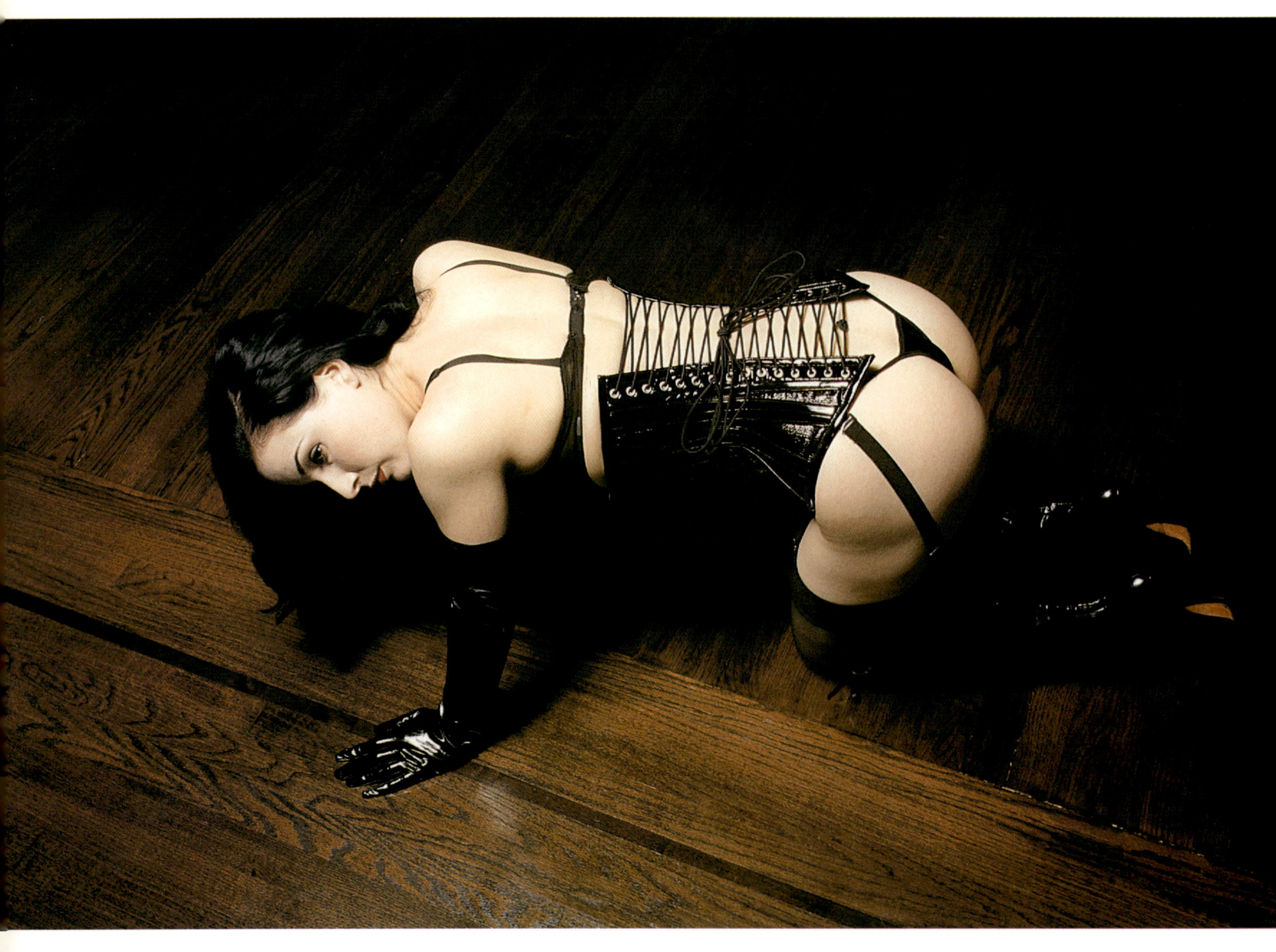

 Gary & Pierre Silva

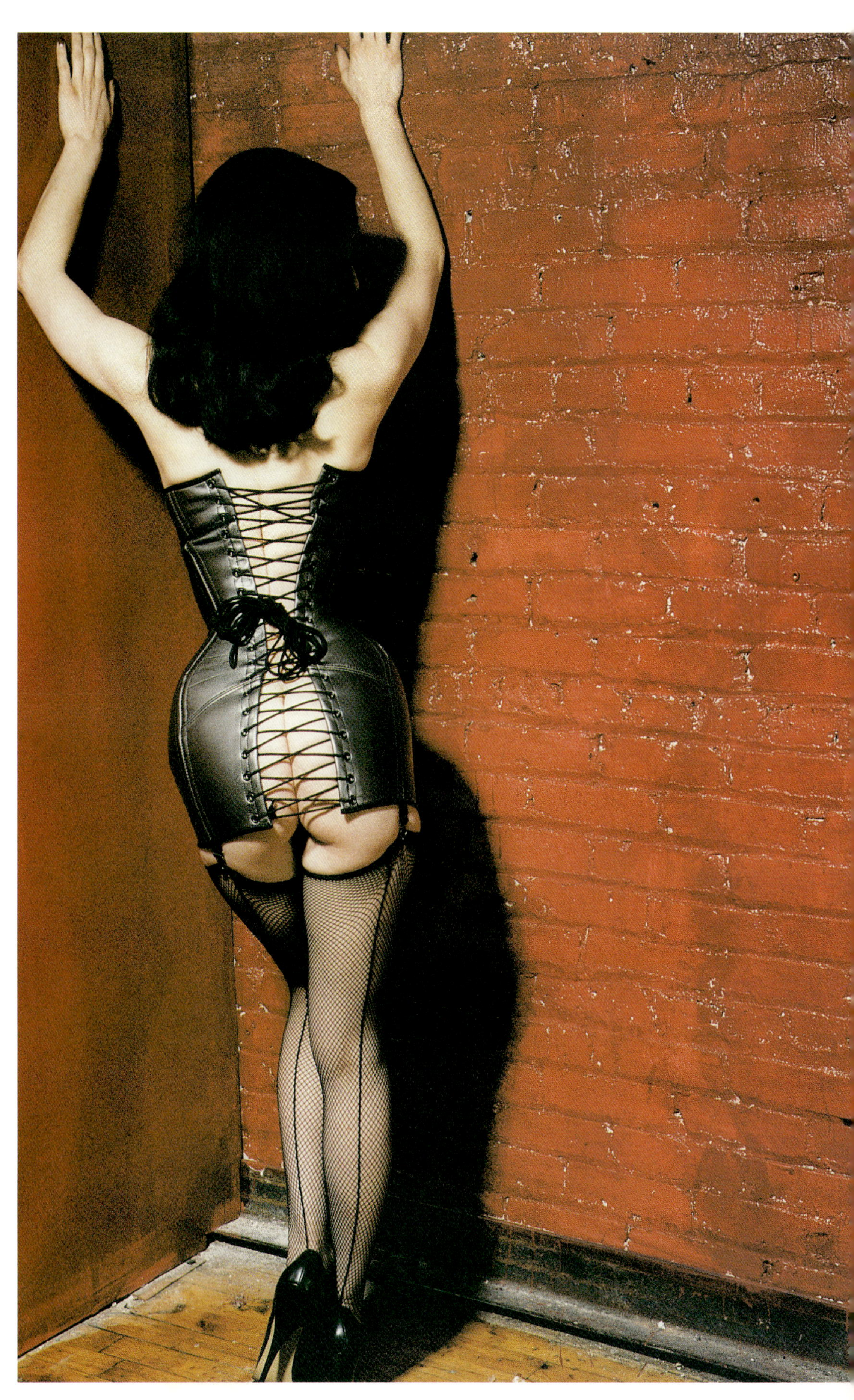

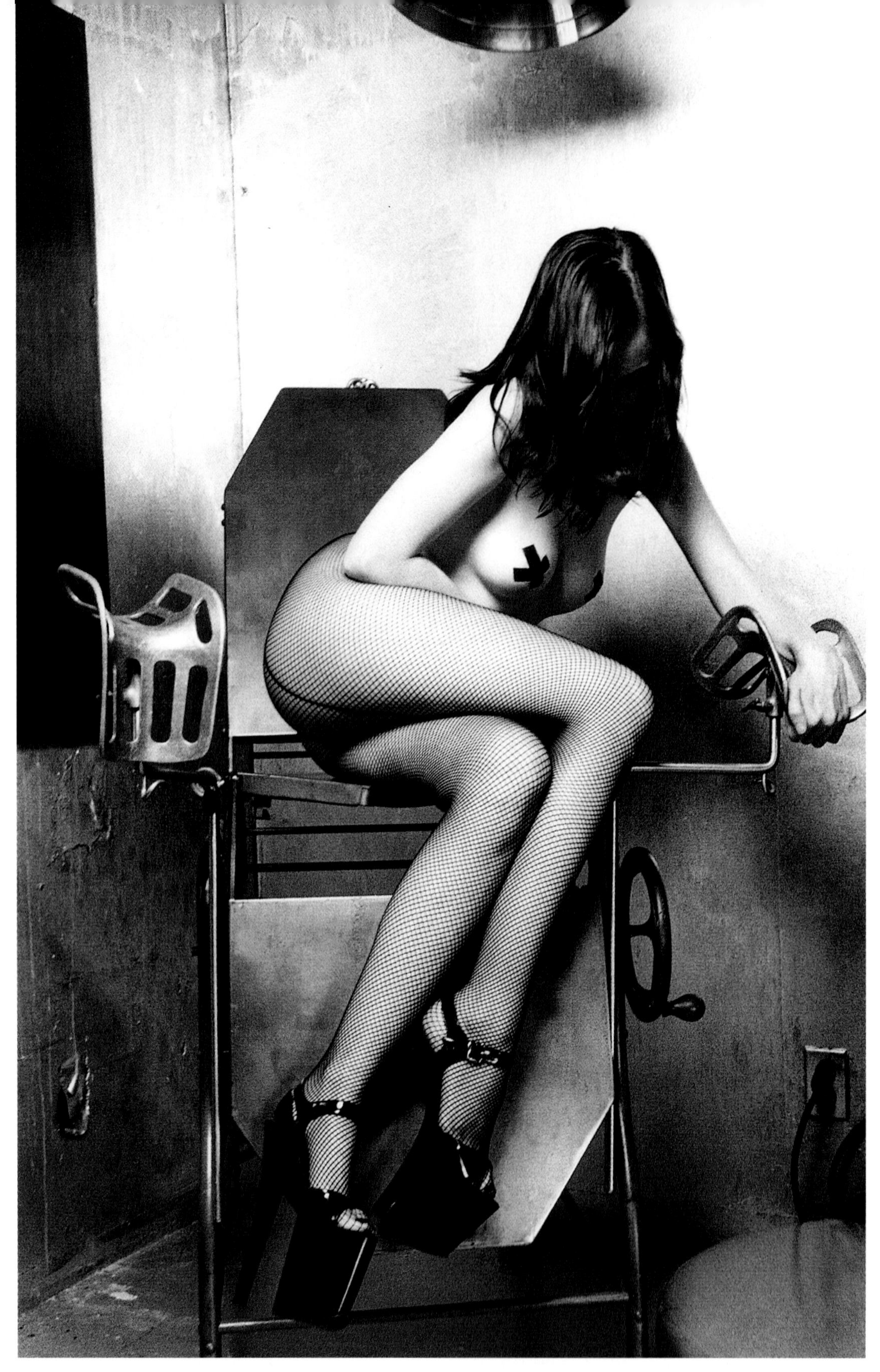



Opposite Gary & Pierre Silva

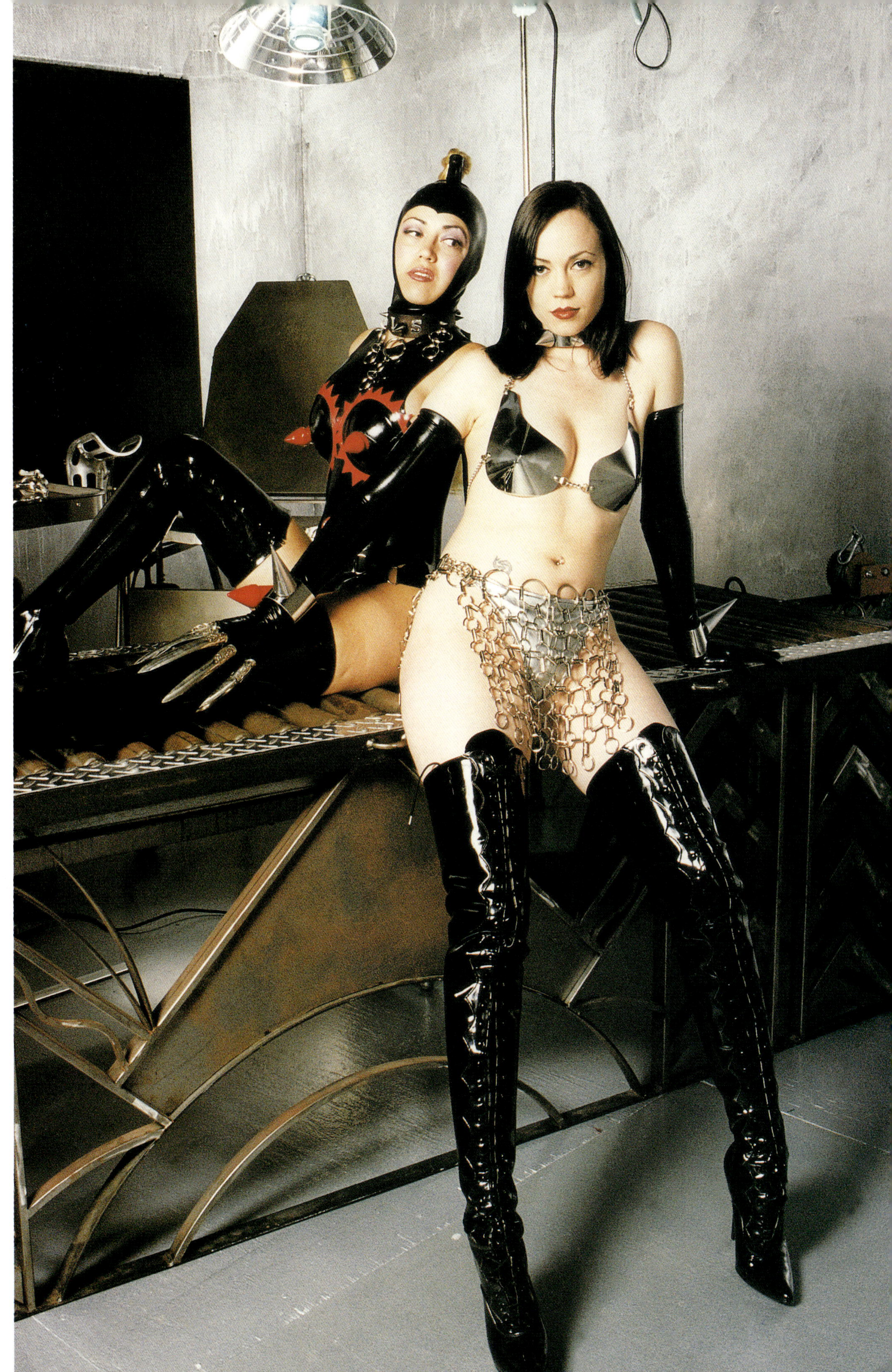

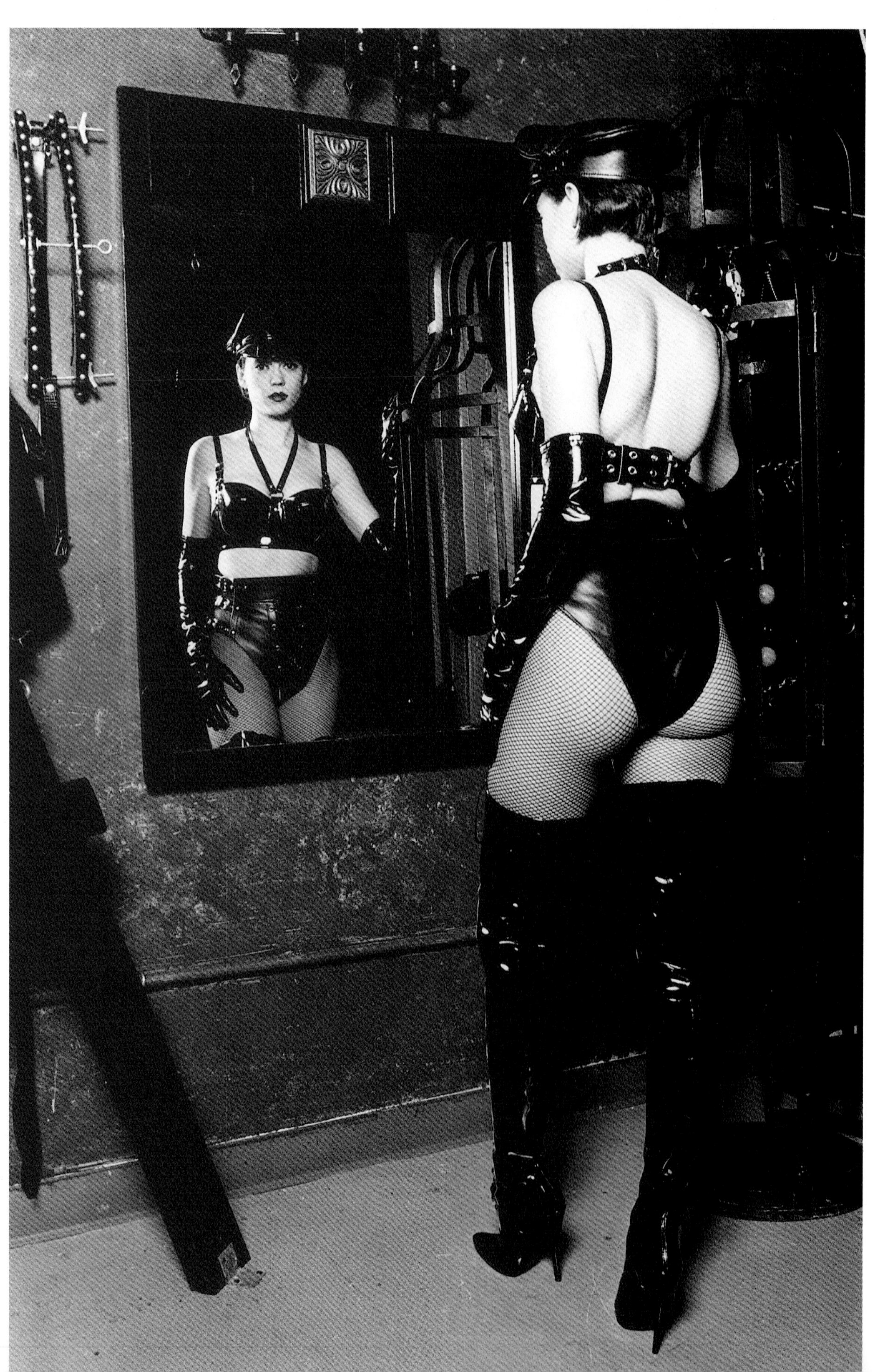

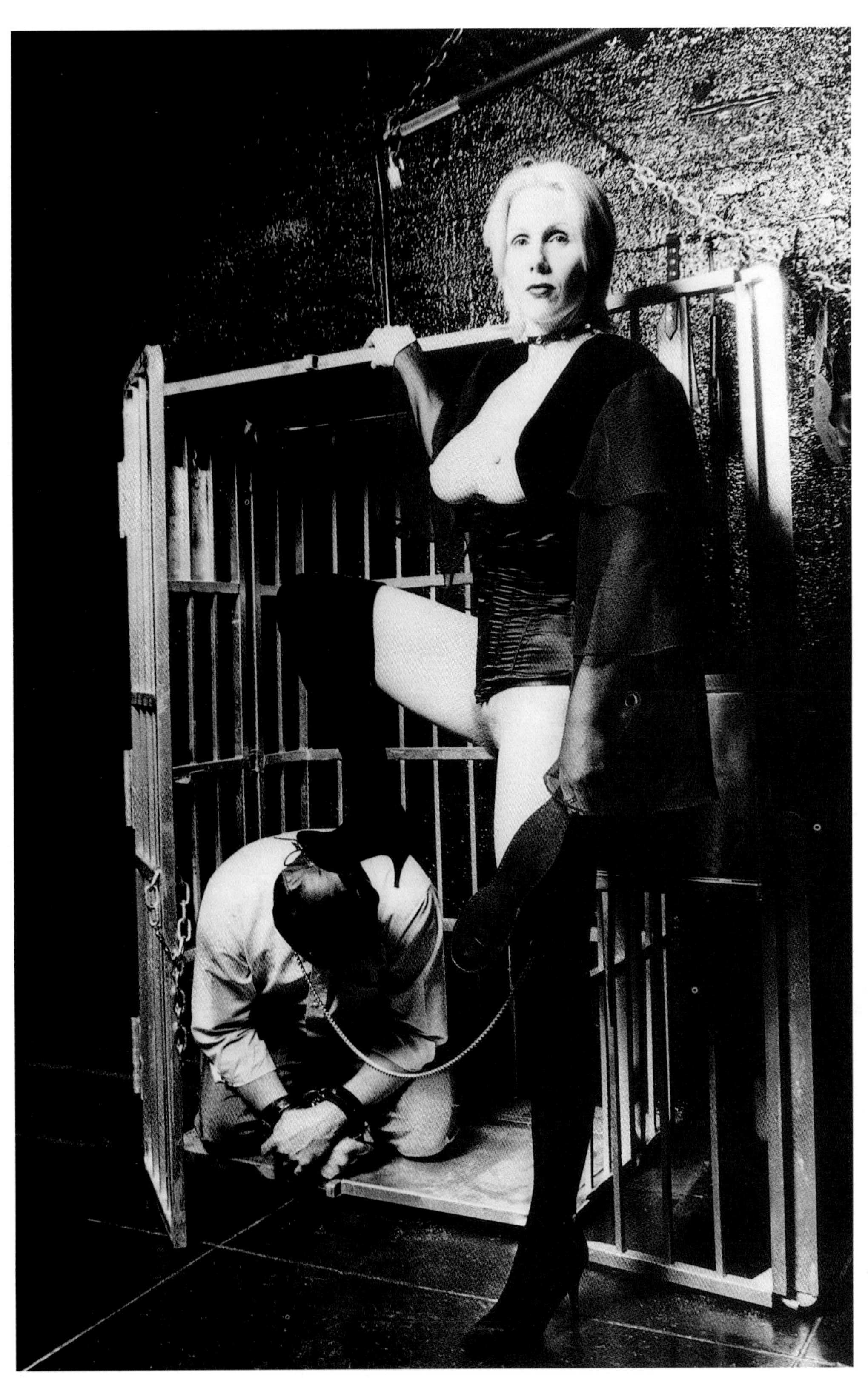



Gary & Pierre Silva 97

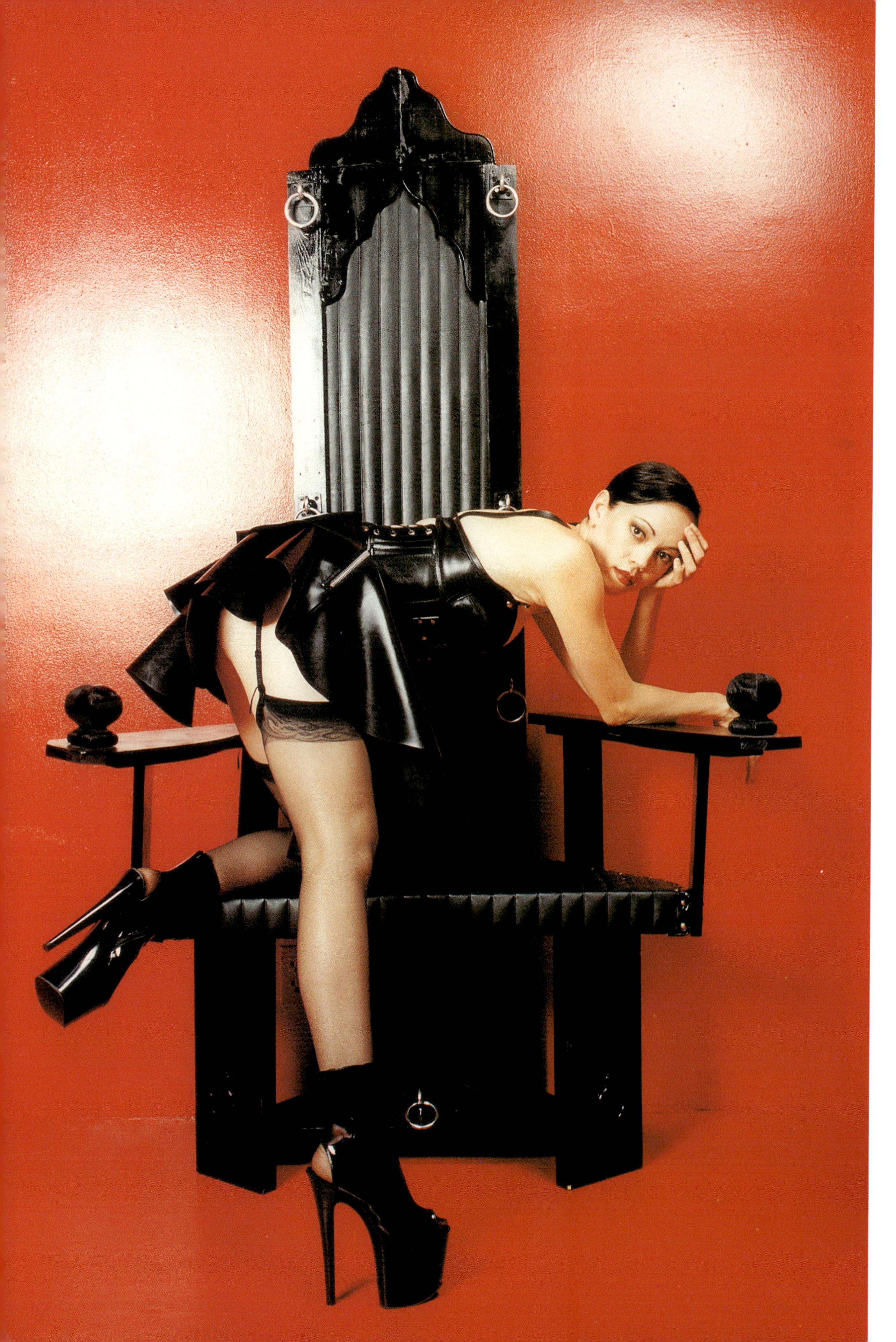

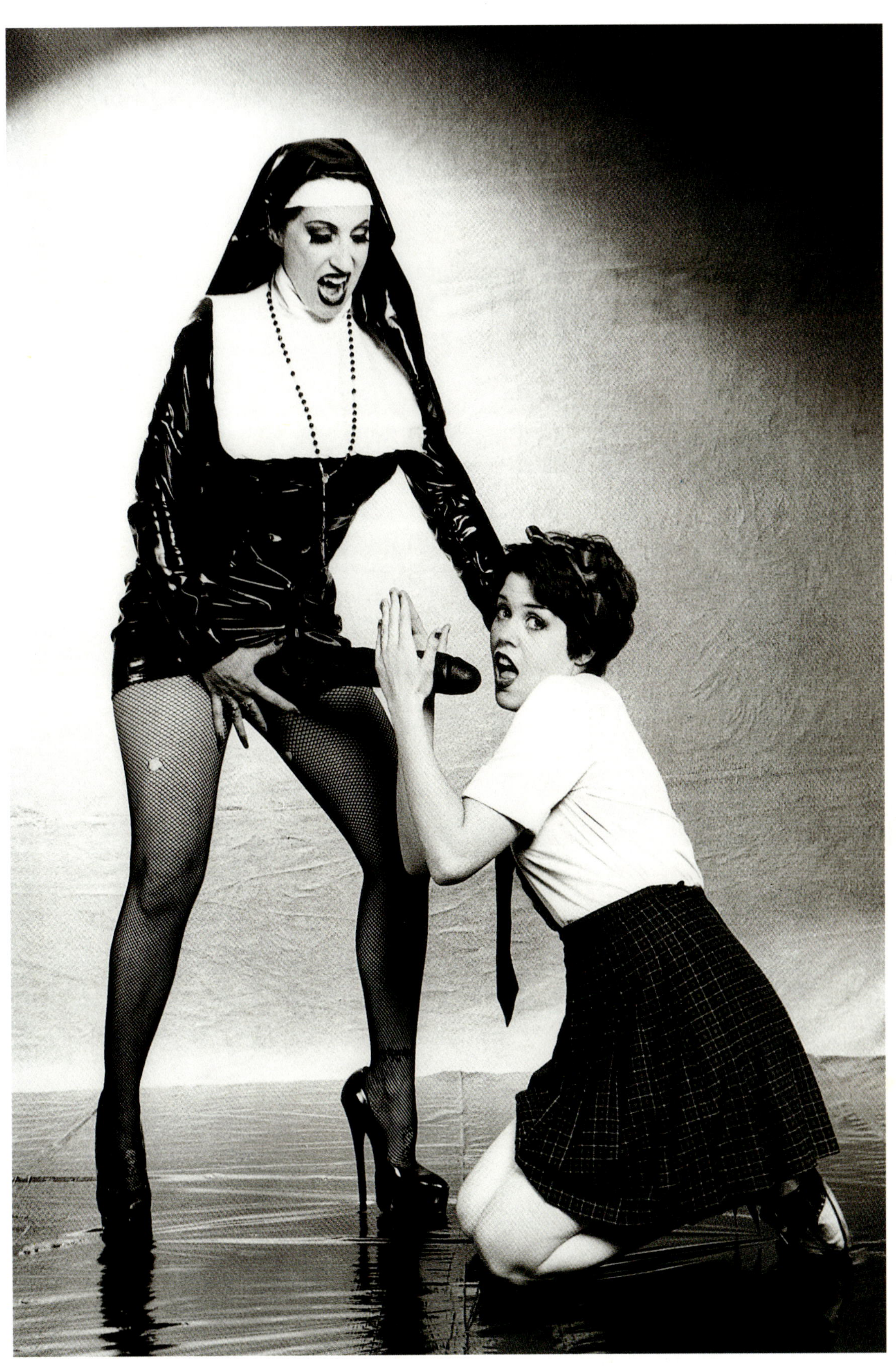

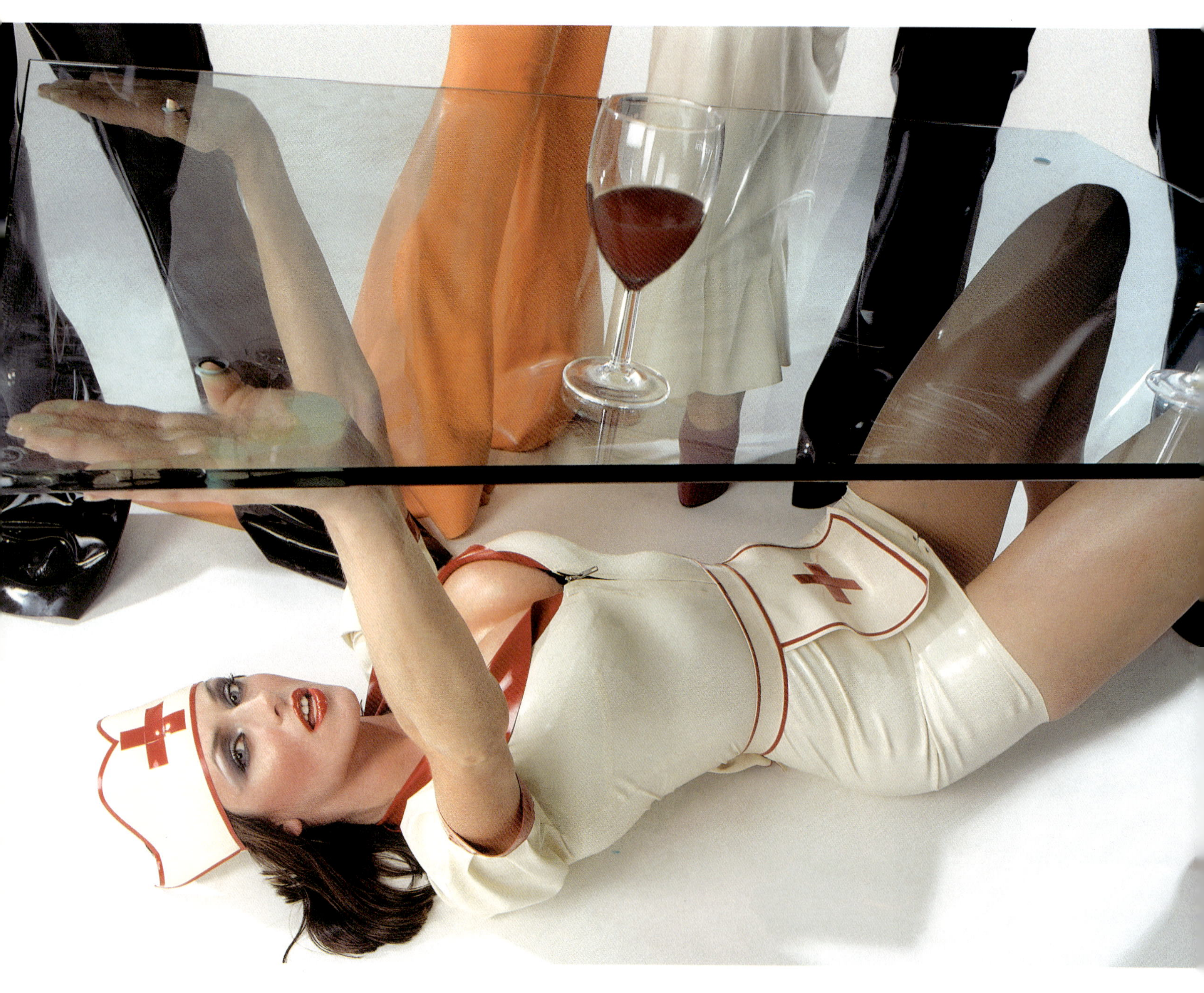



Opposite James & James

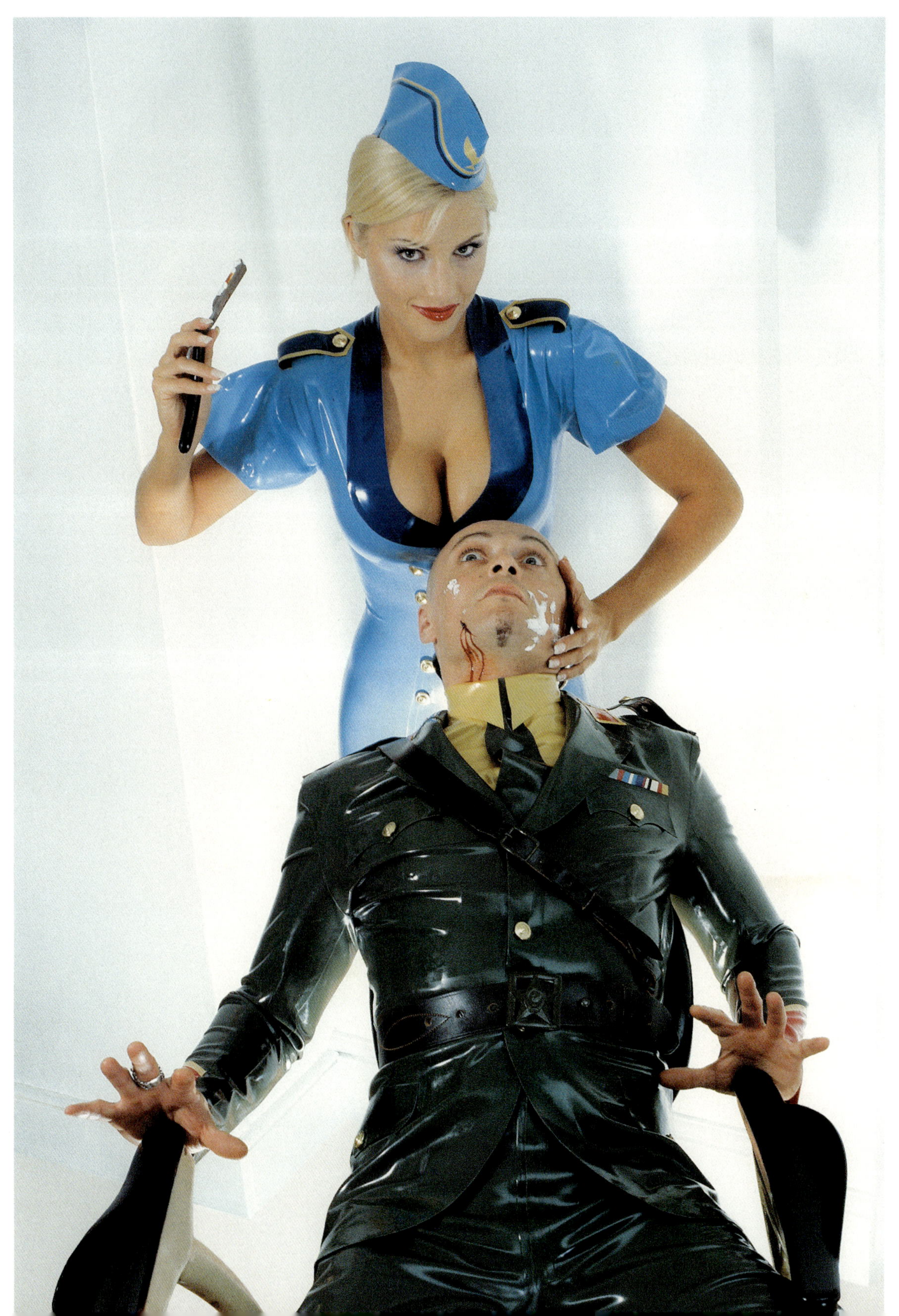

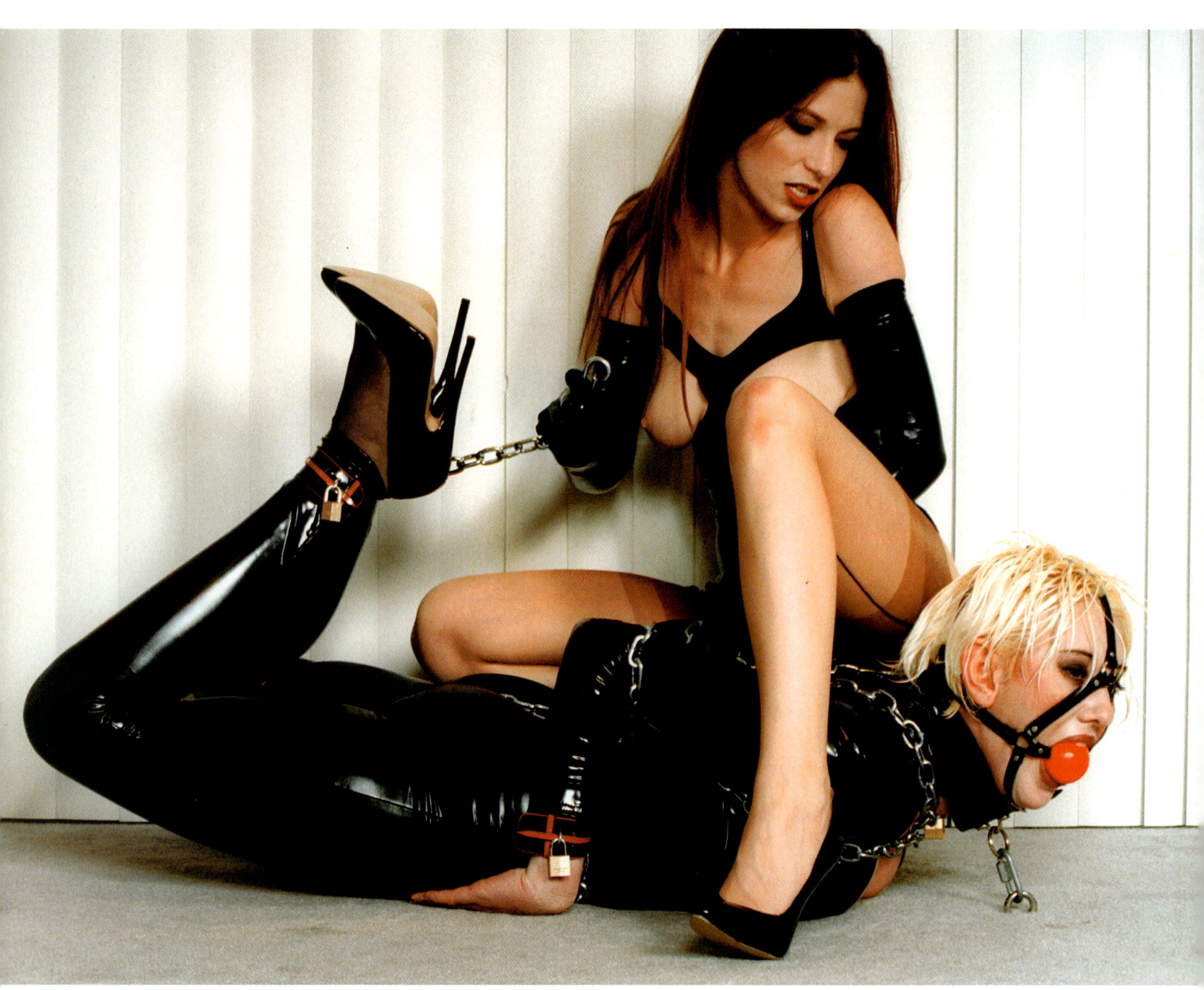

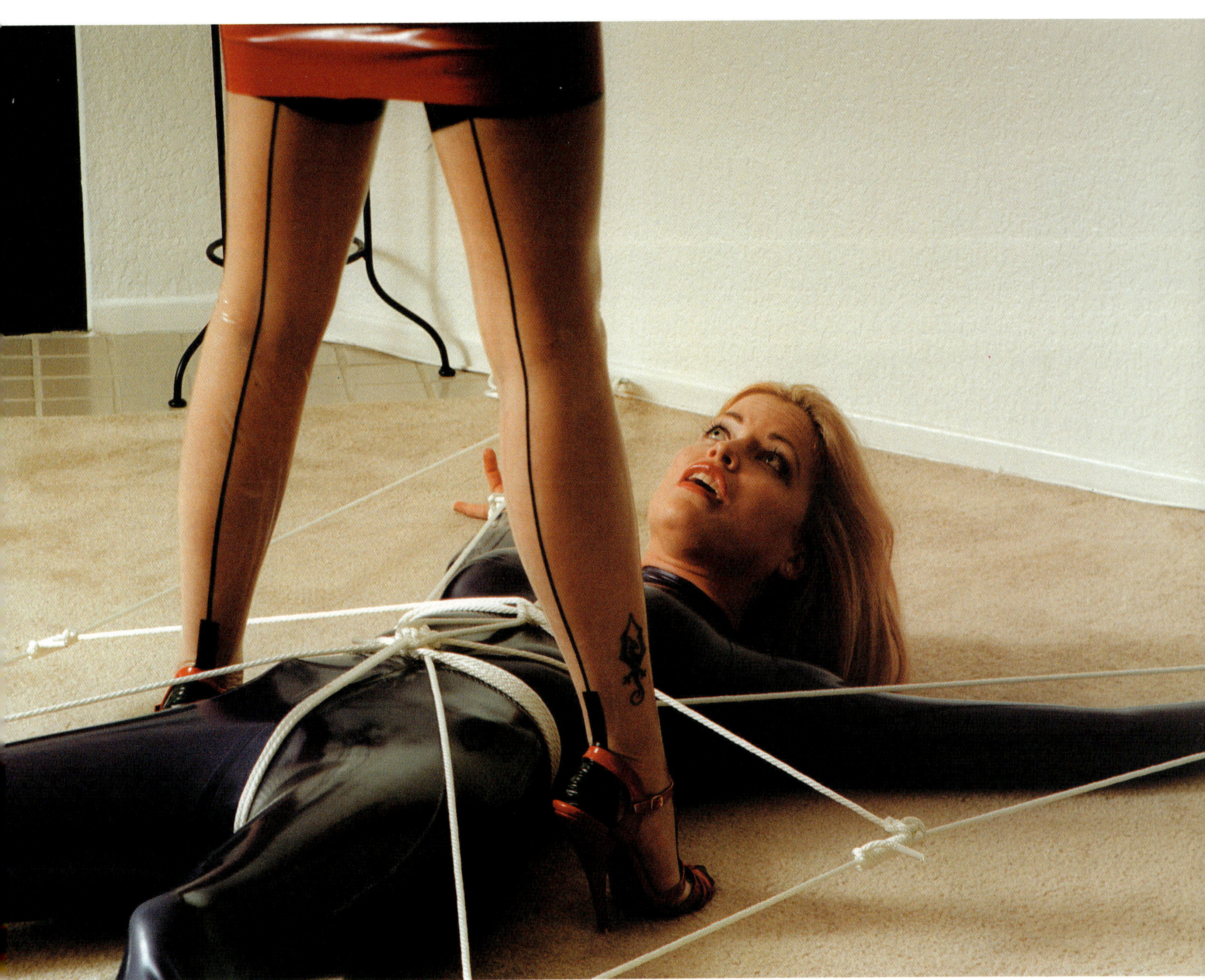

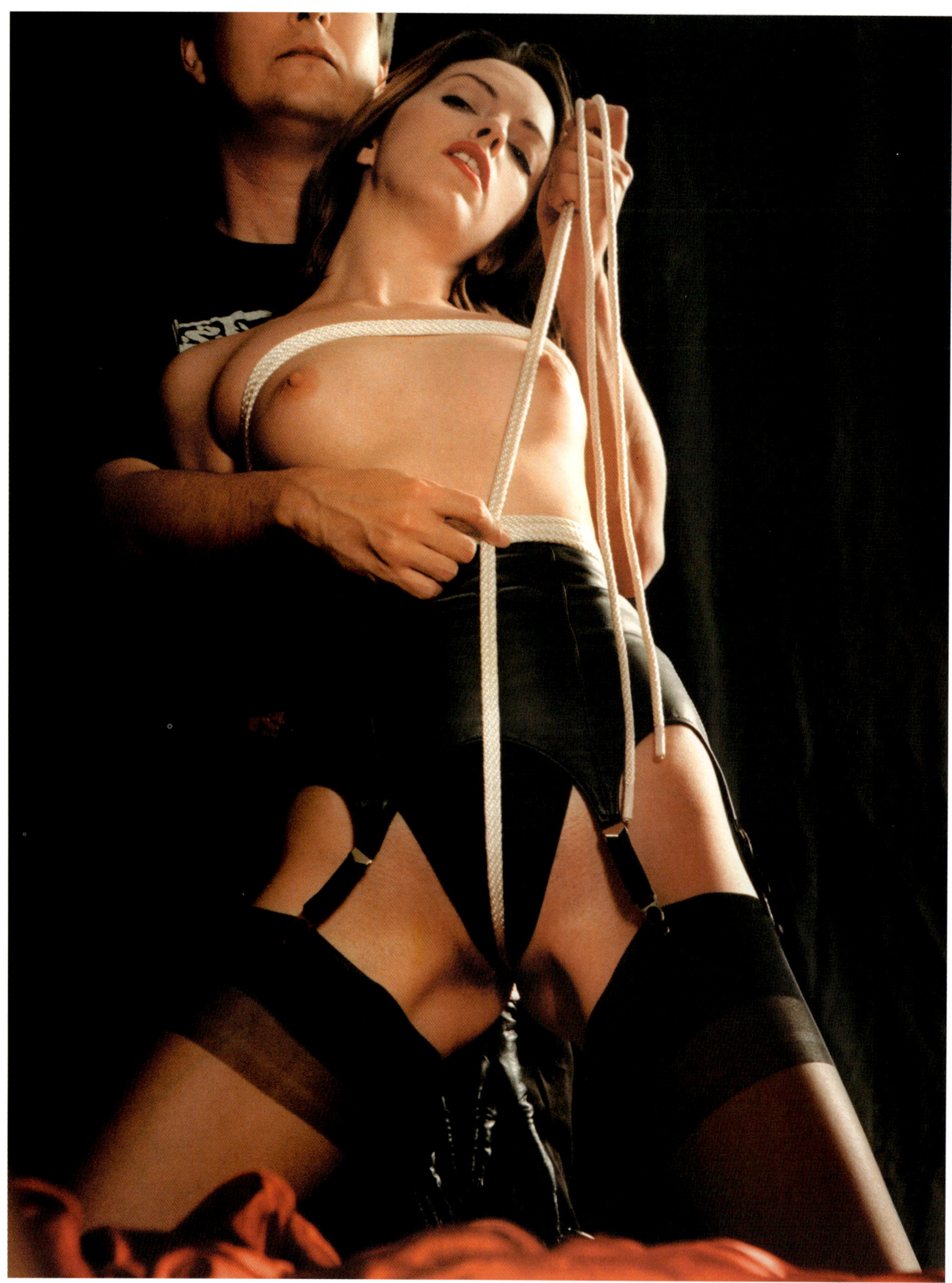

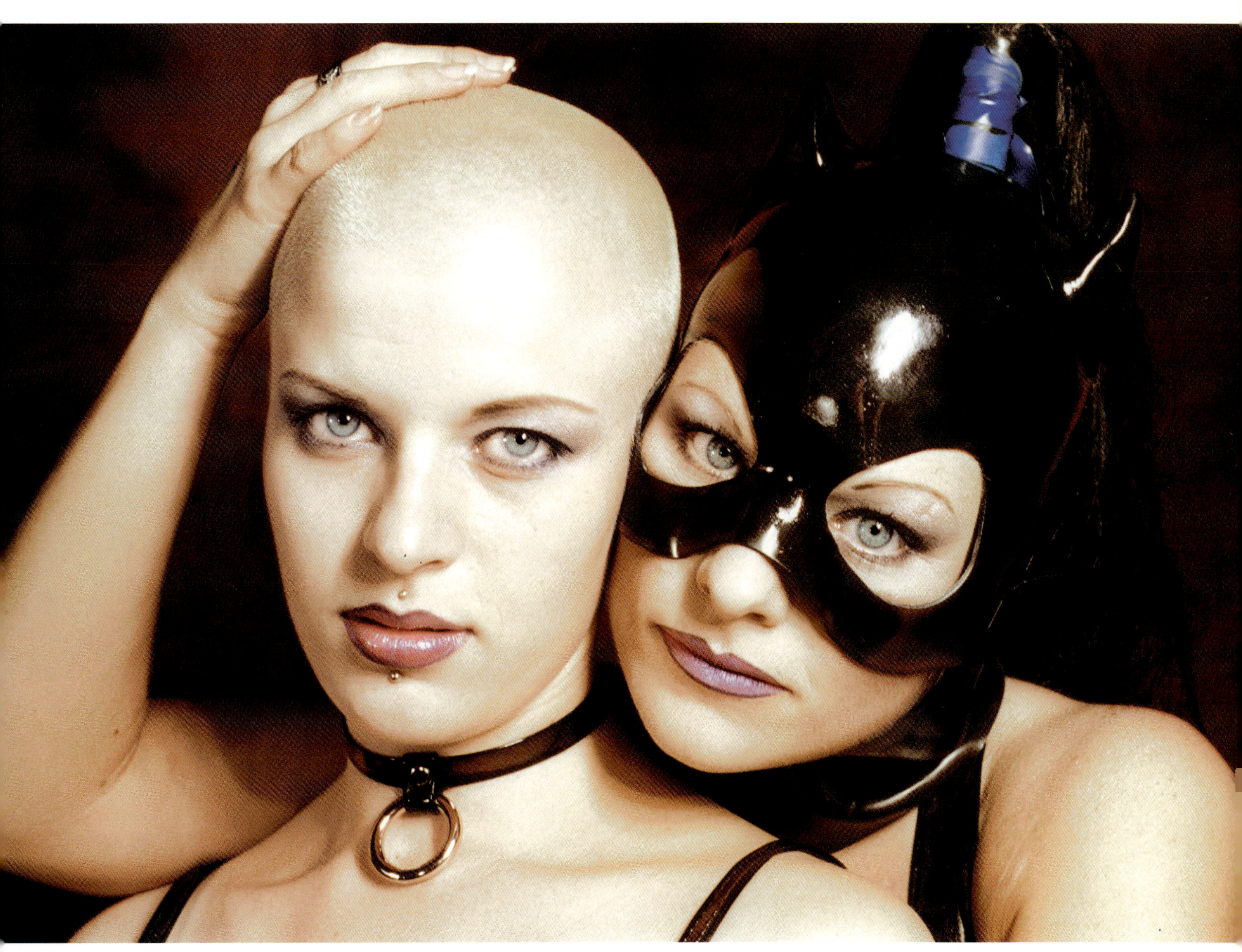

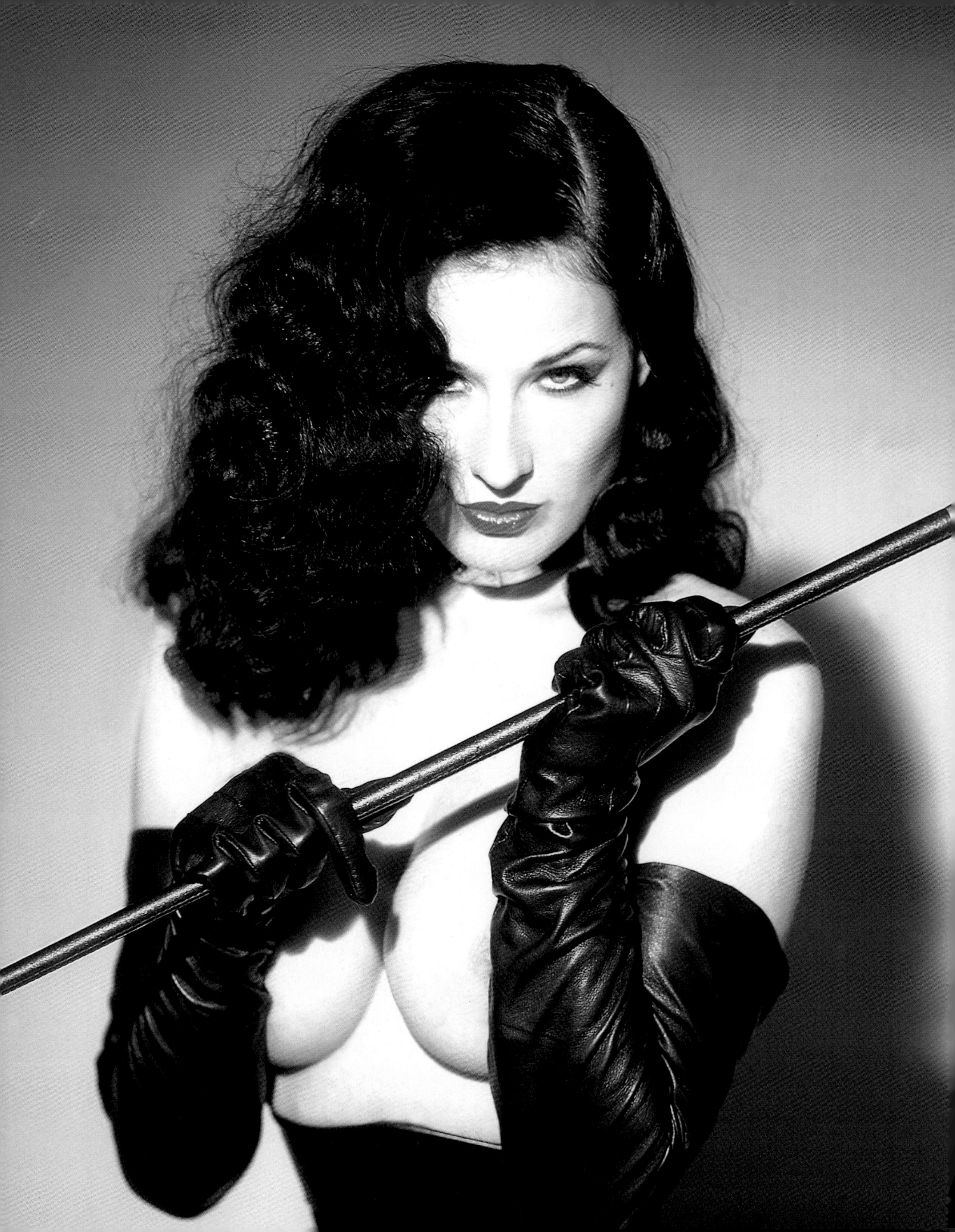

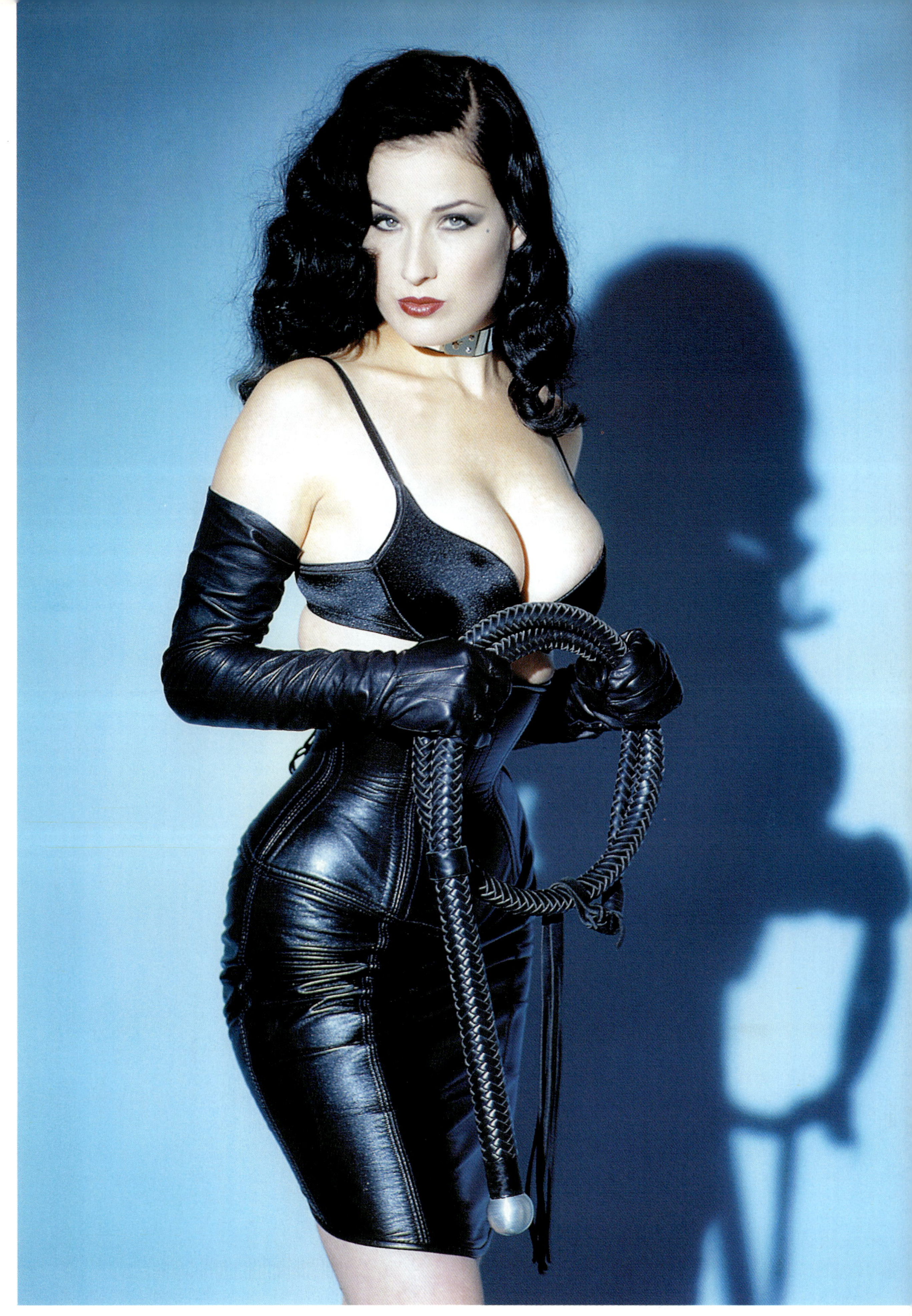

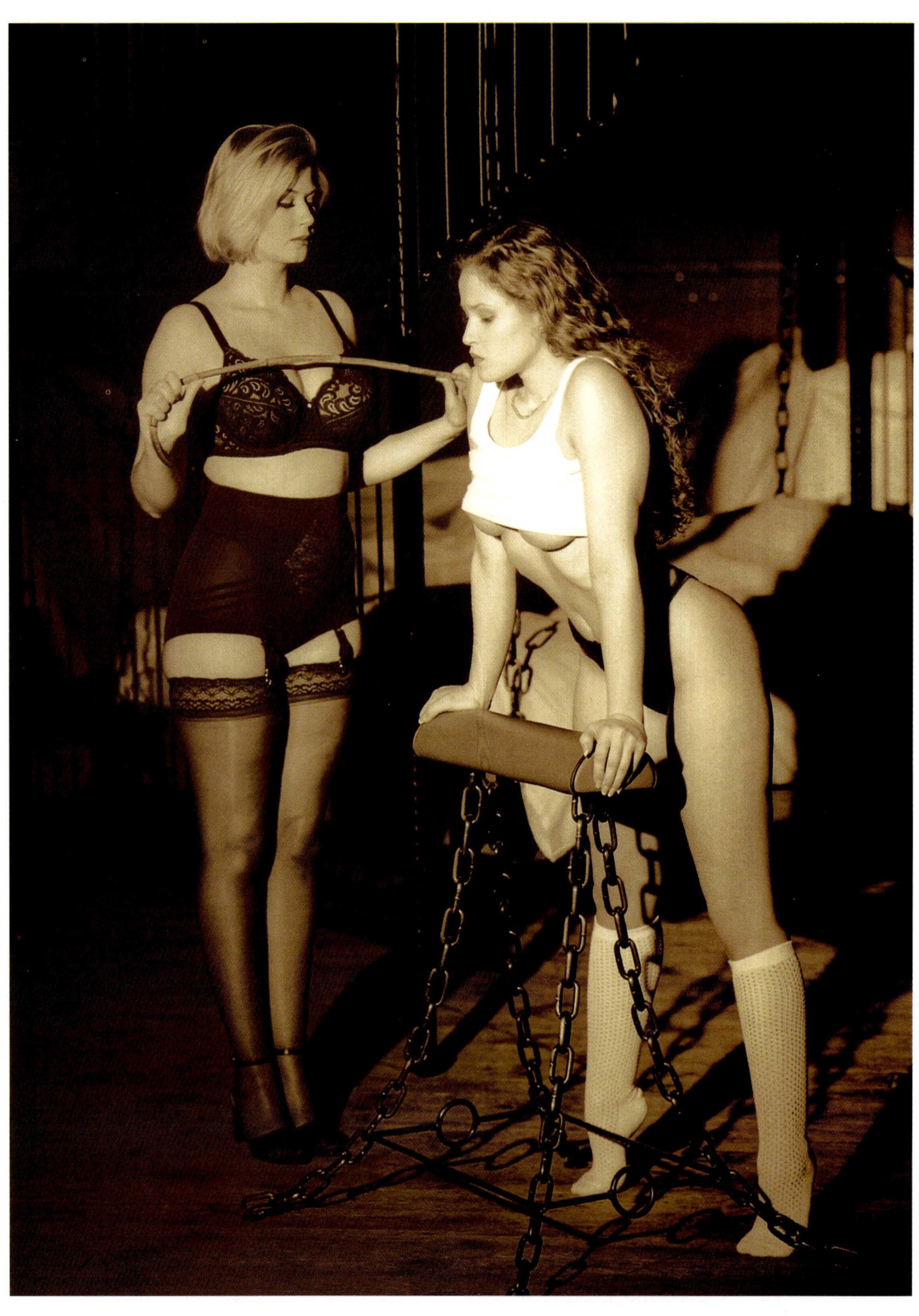

 John Dietrich

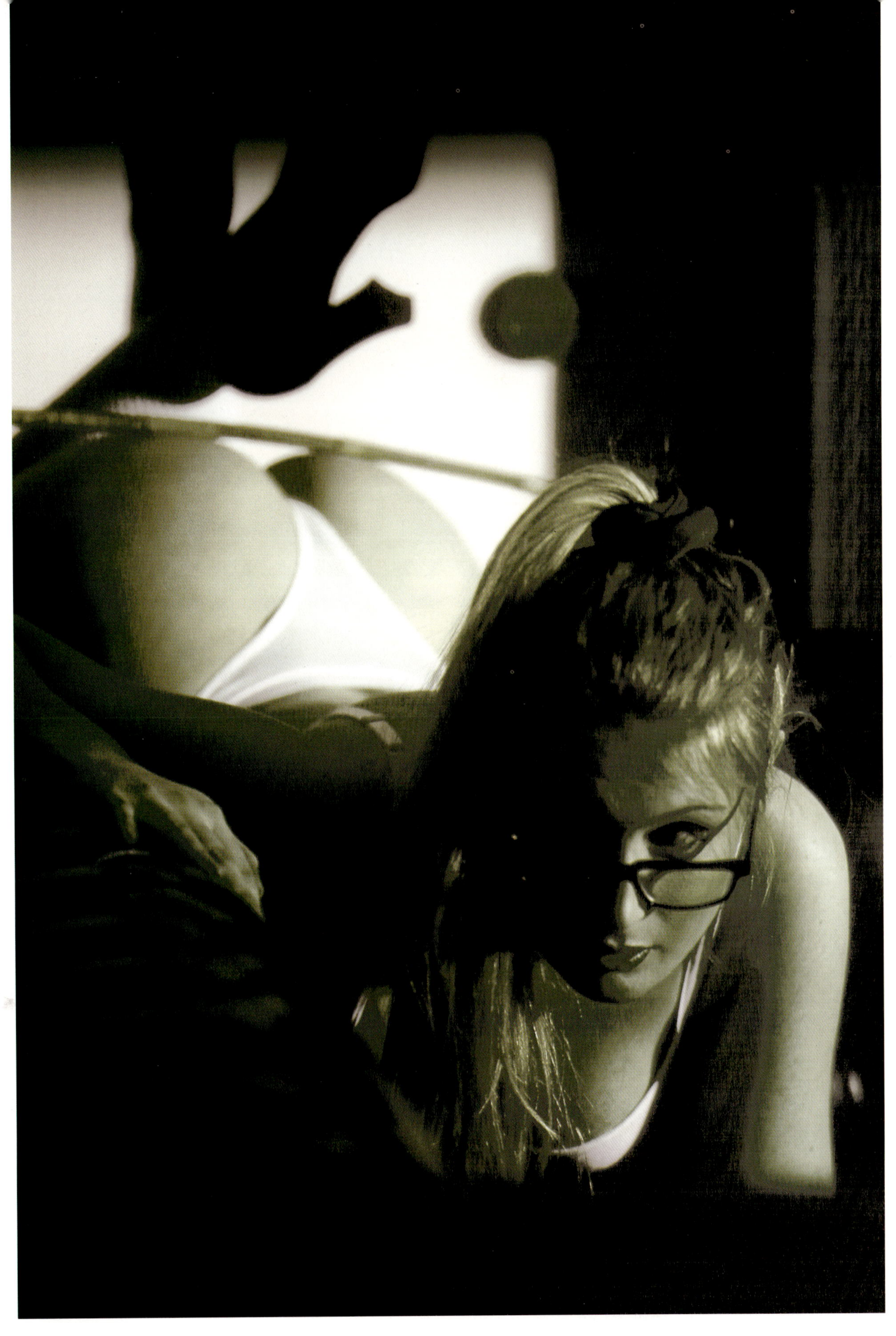

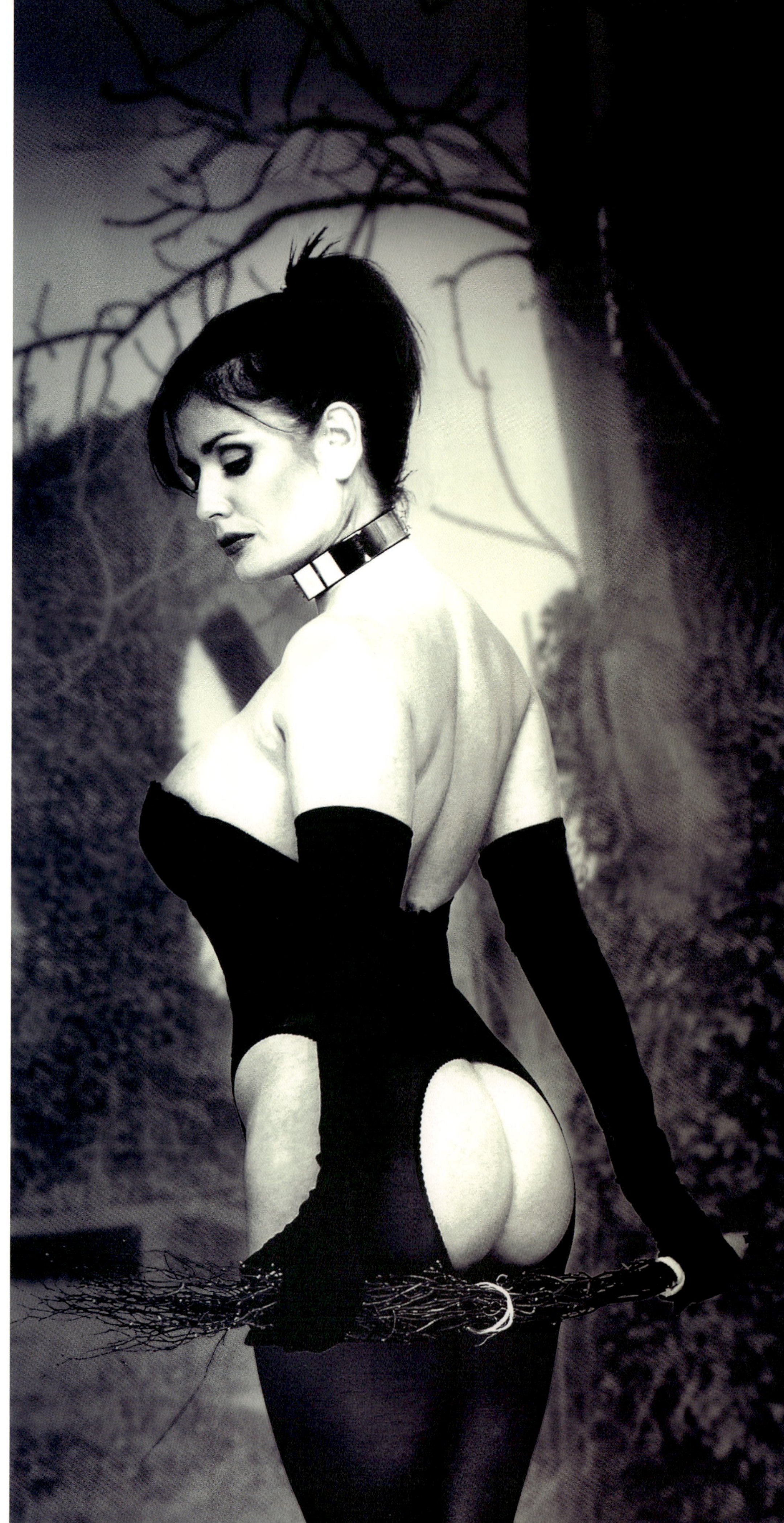

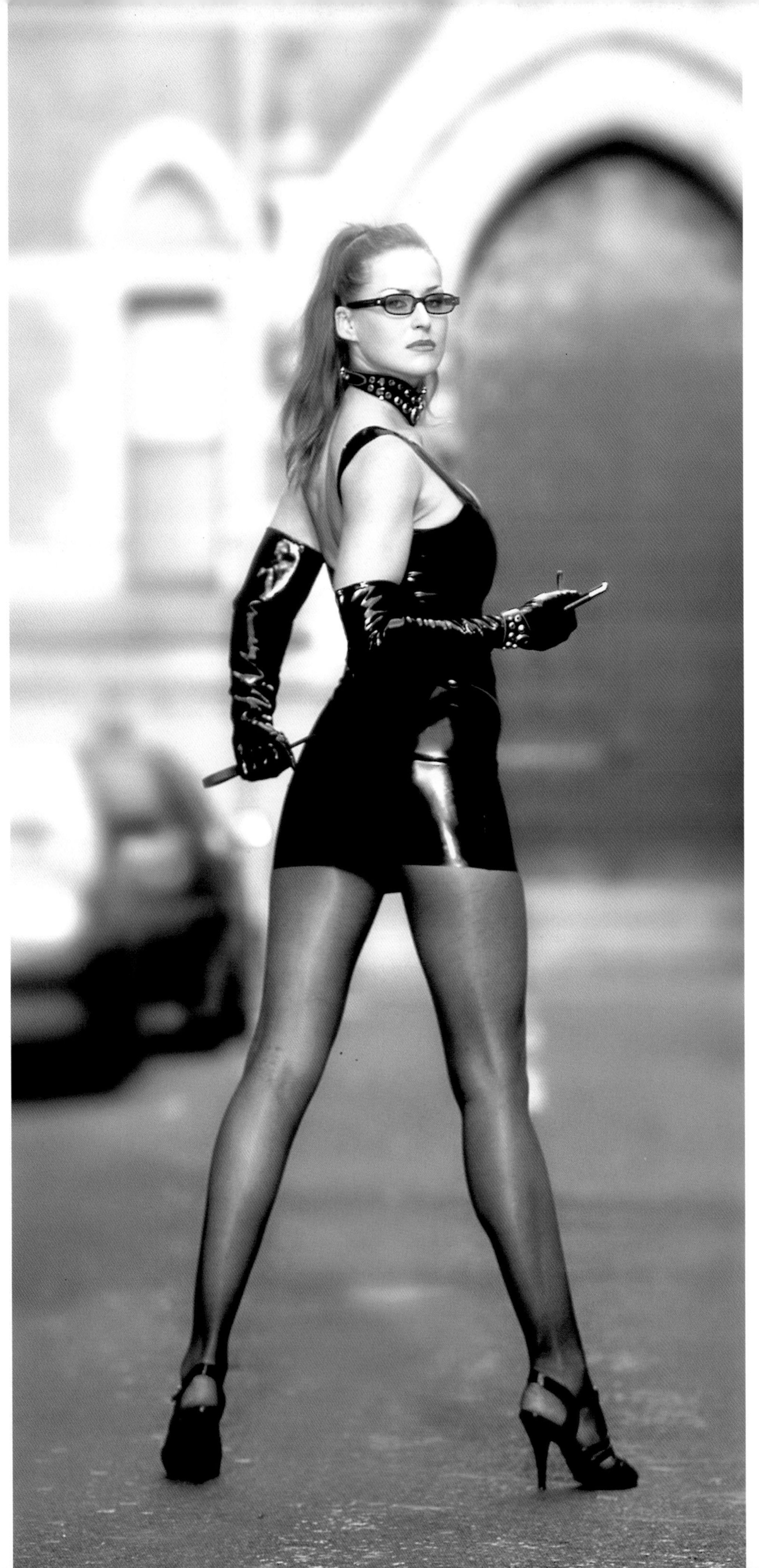

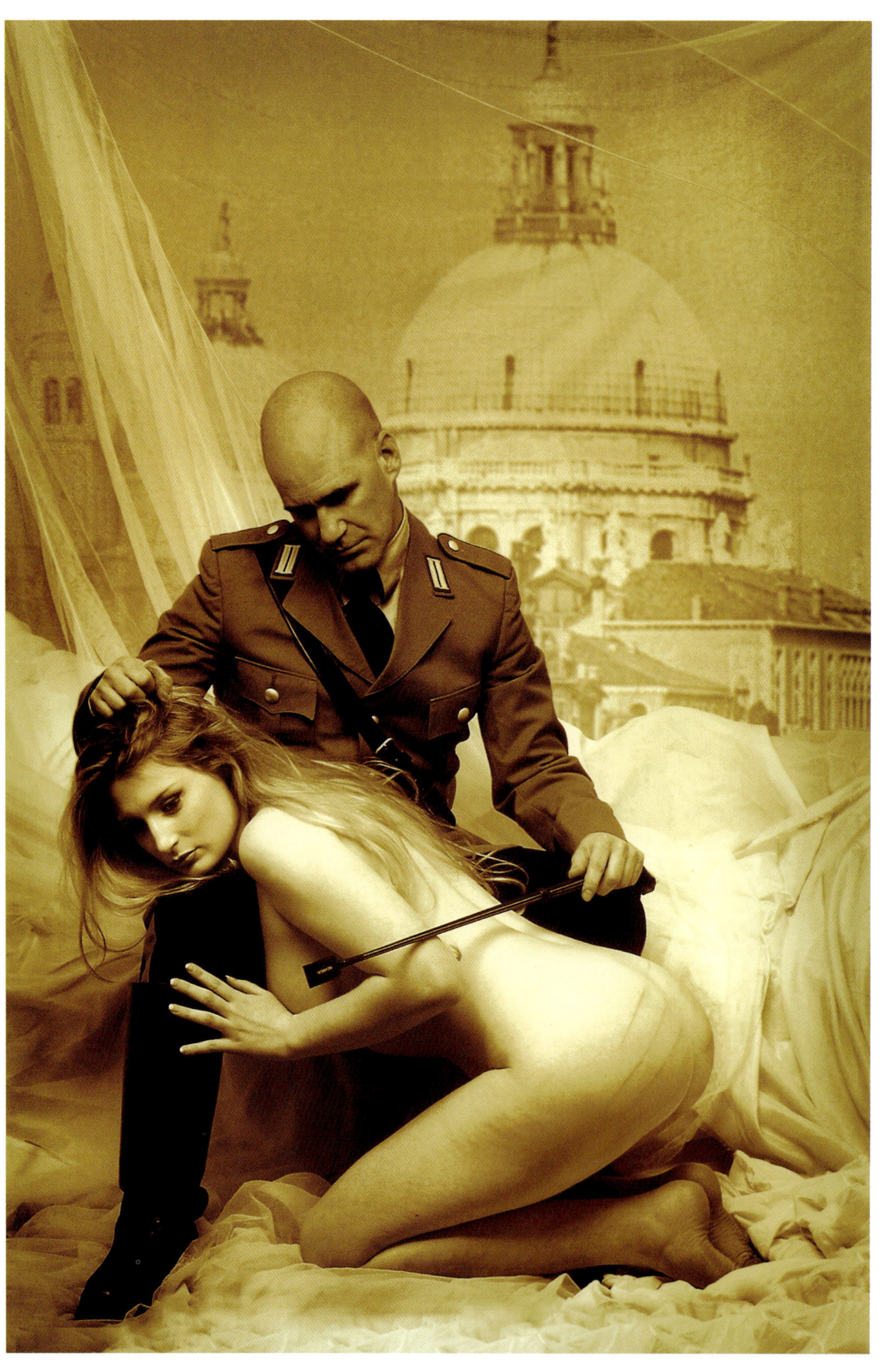

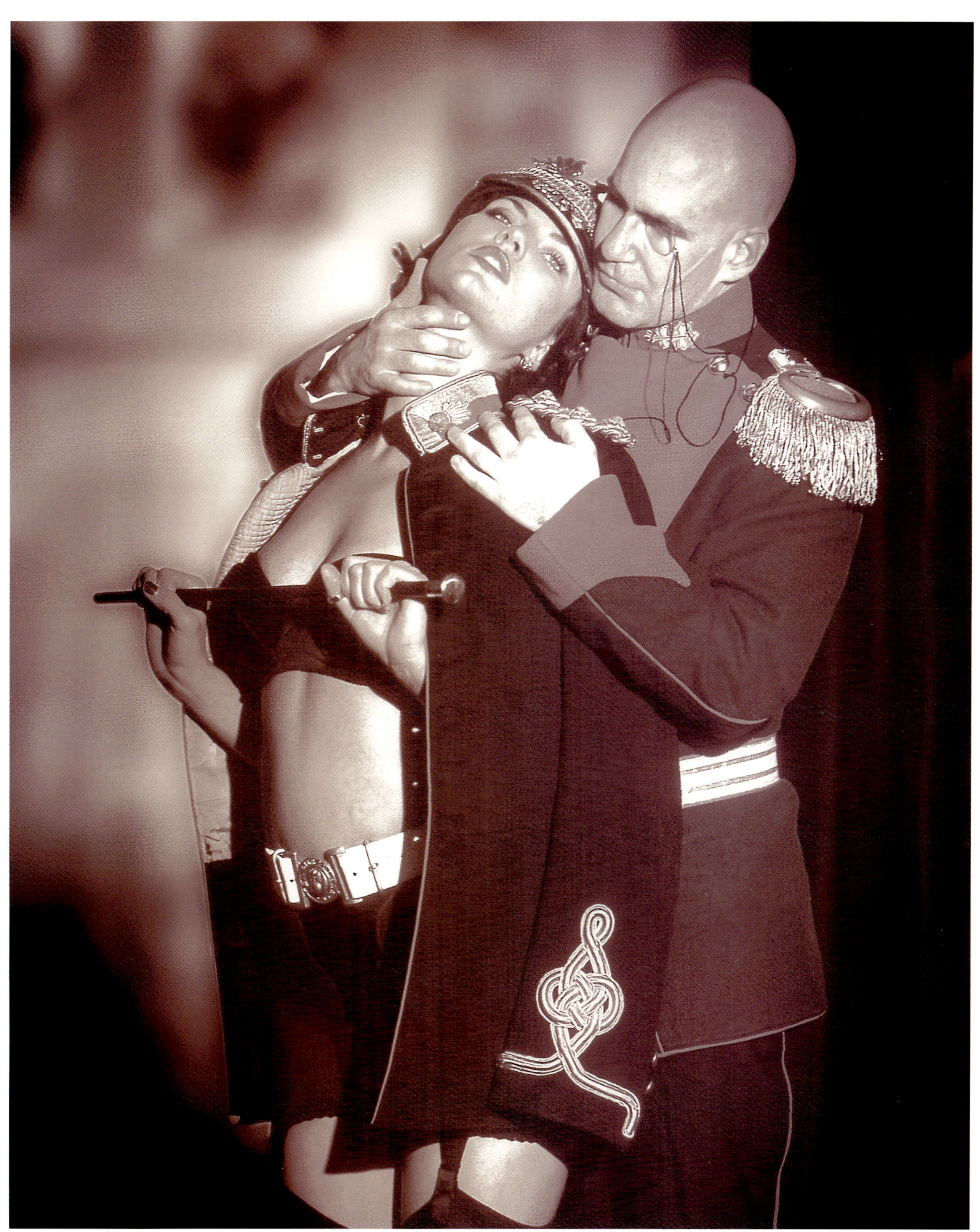

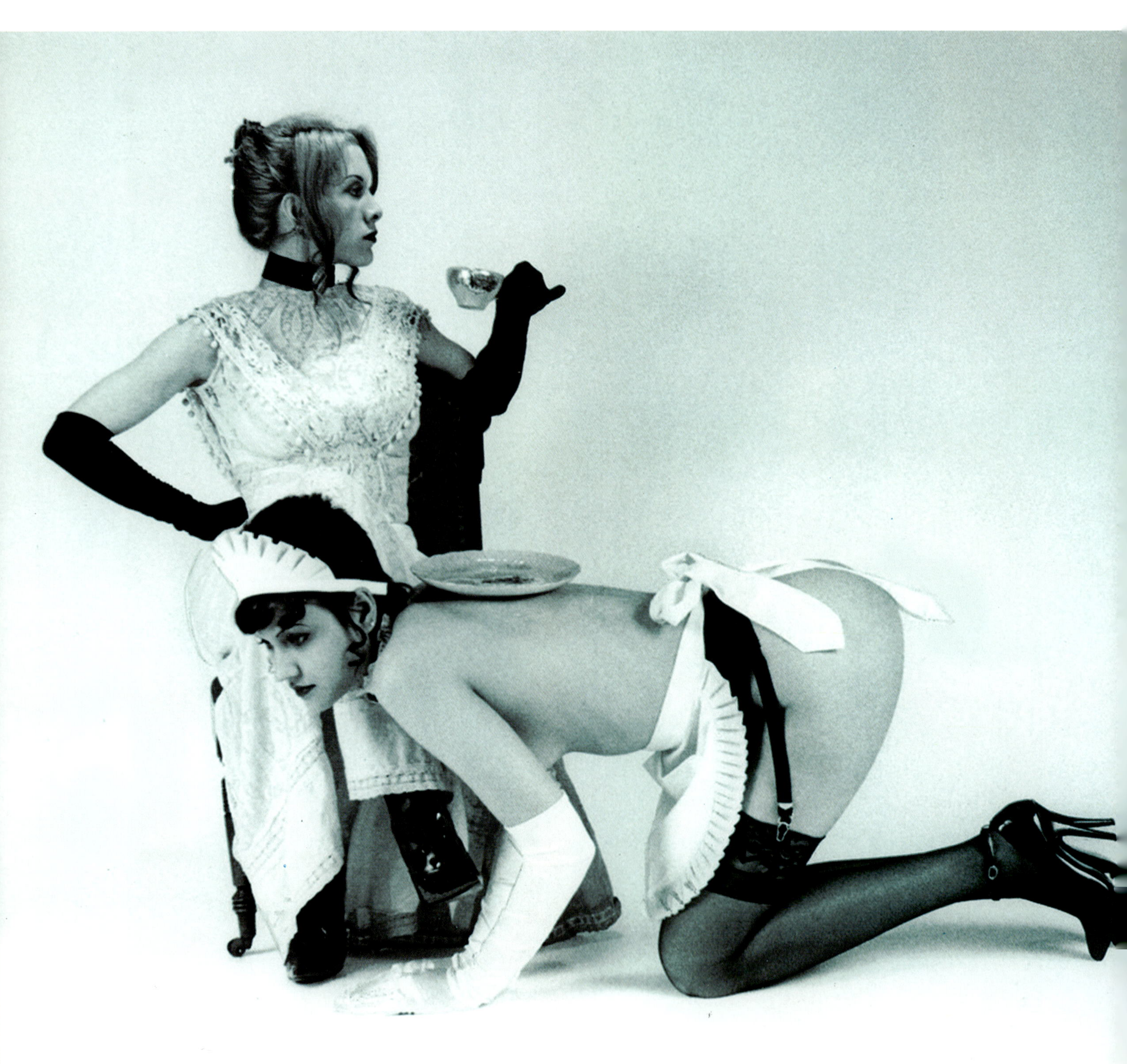

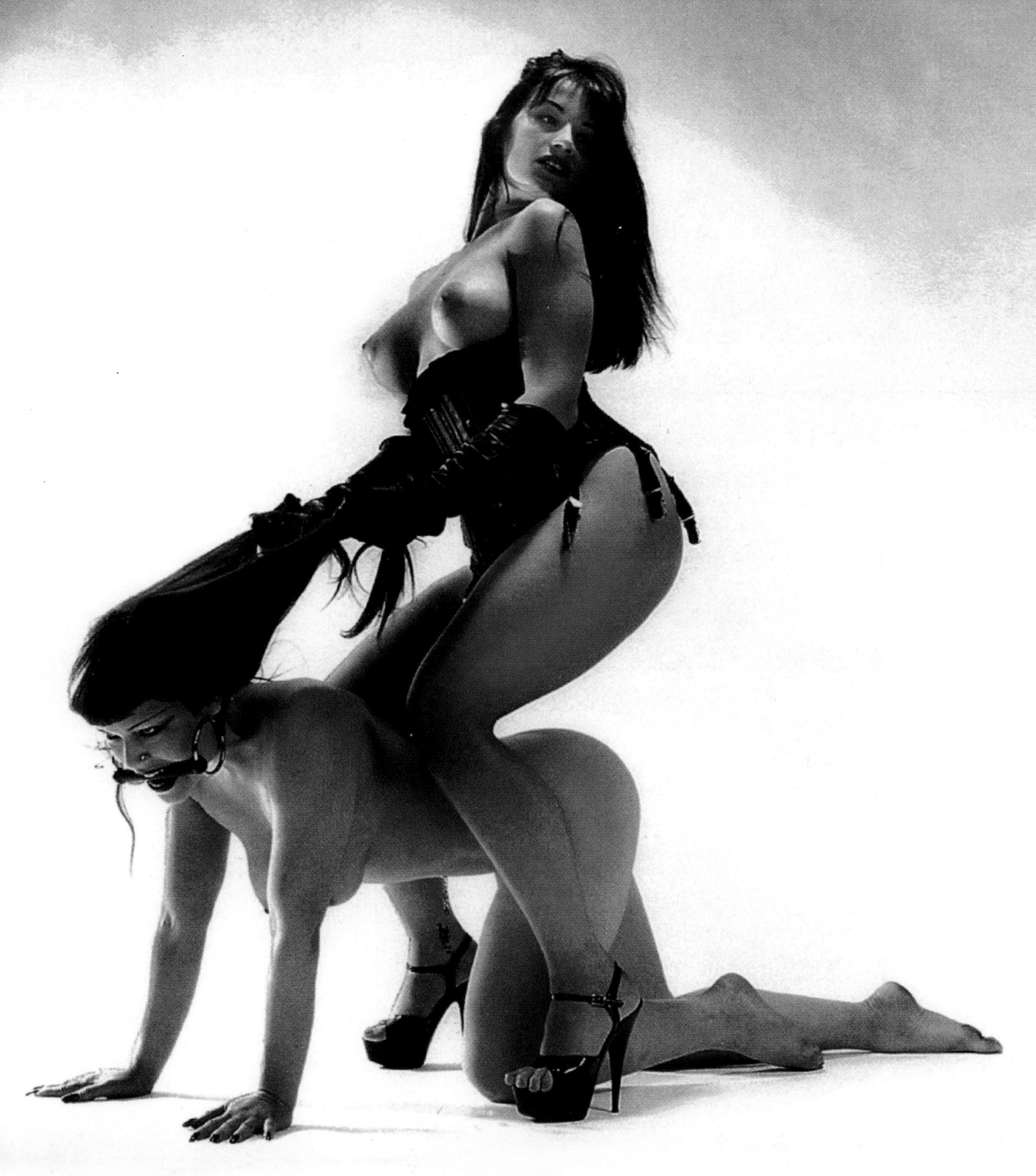

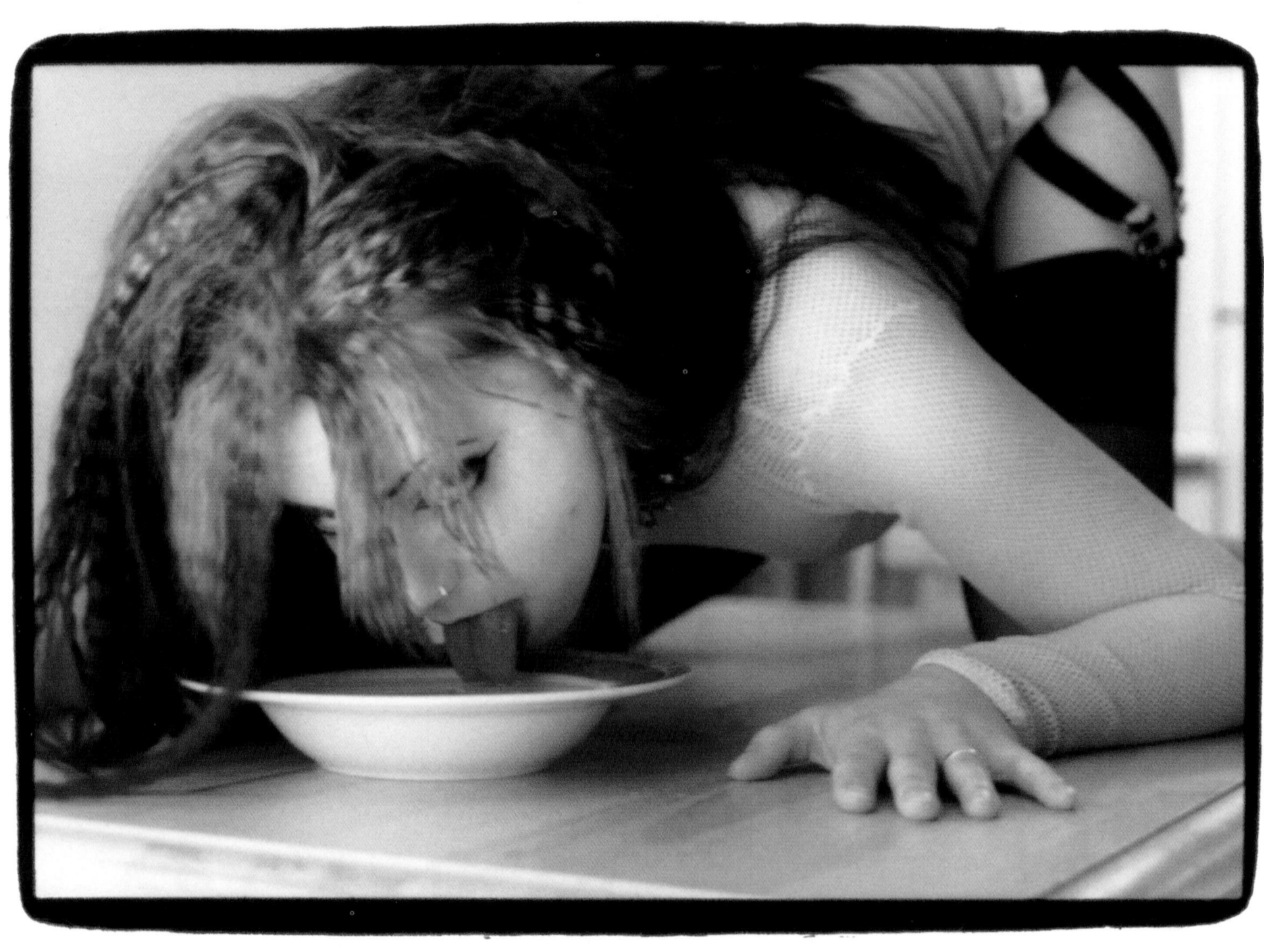

 Kevin Hundsnurcher

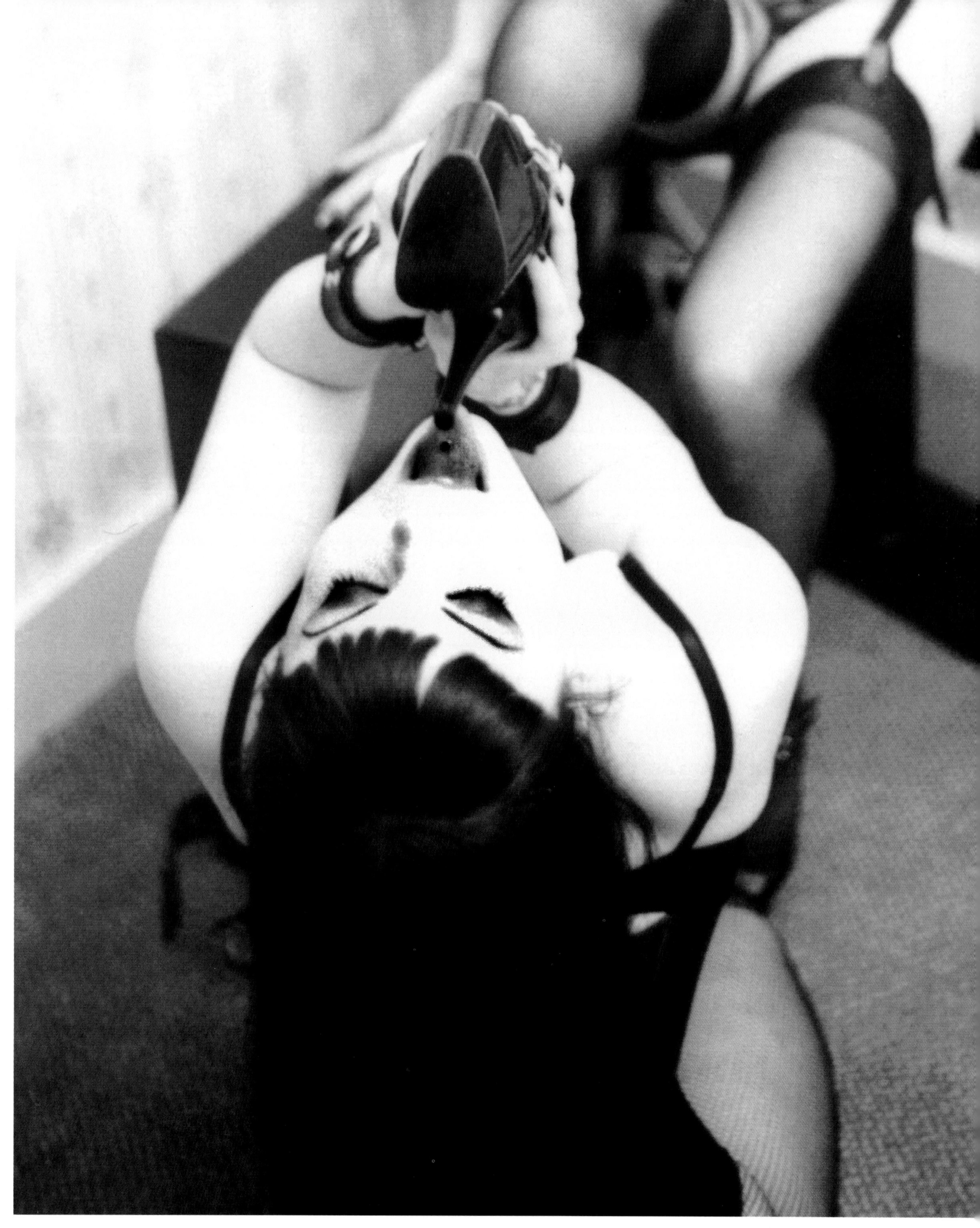

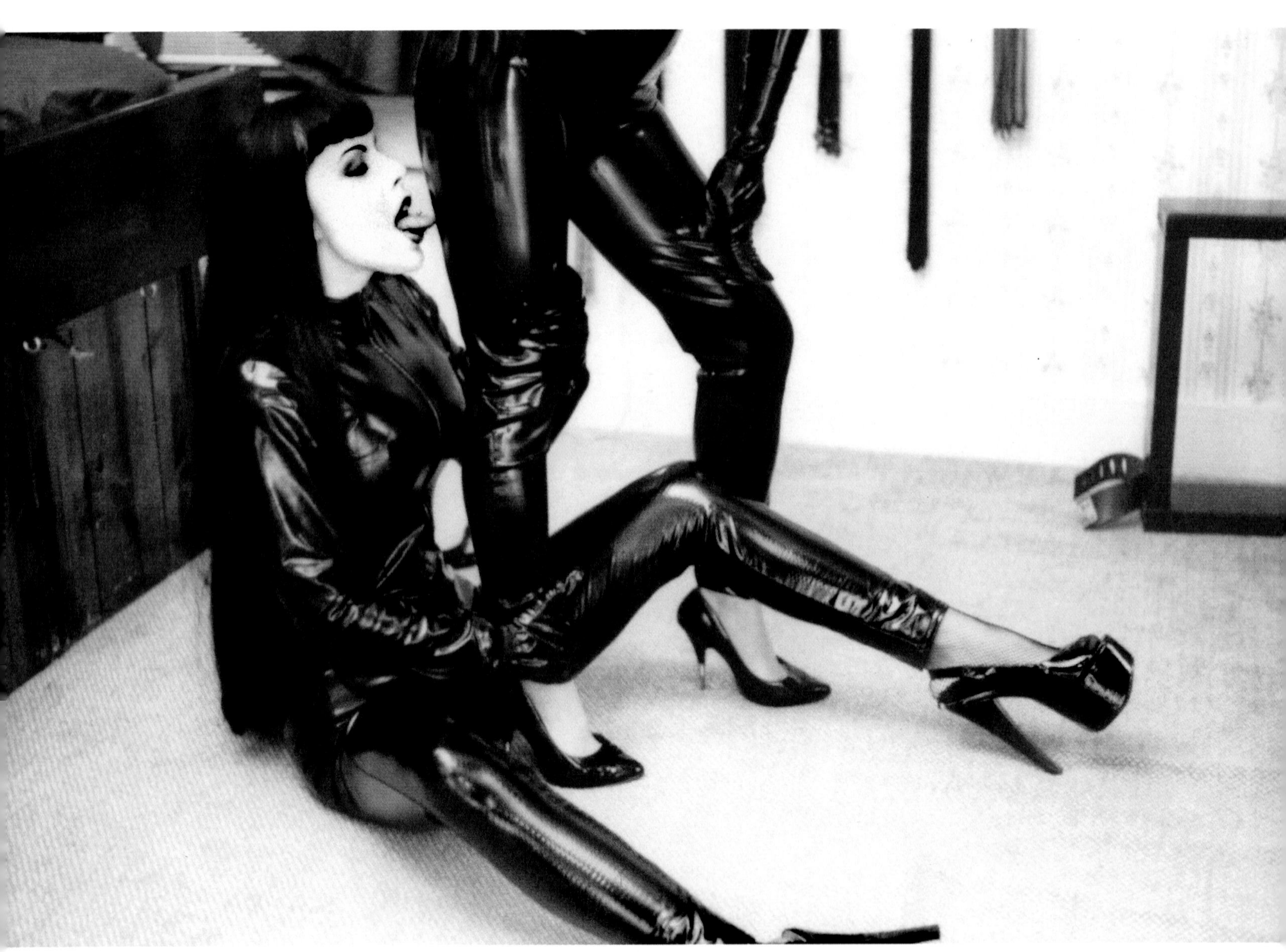

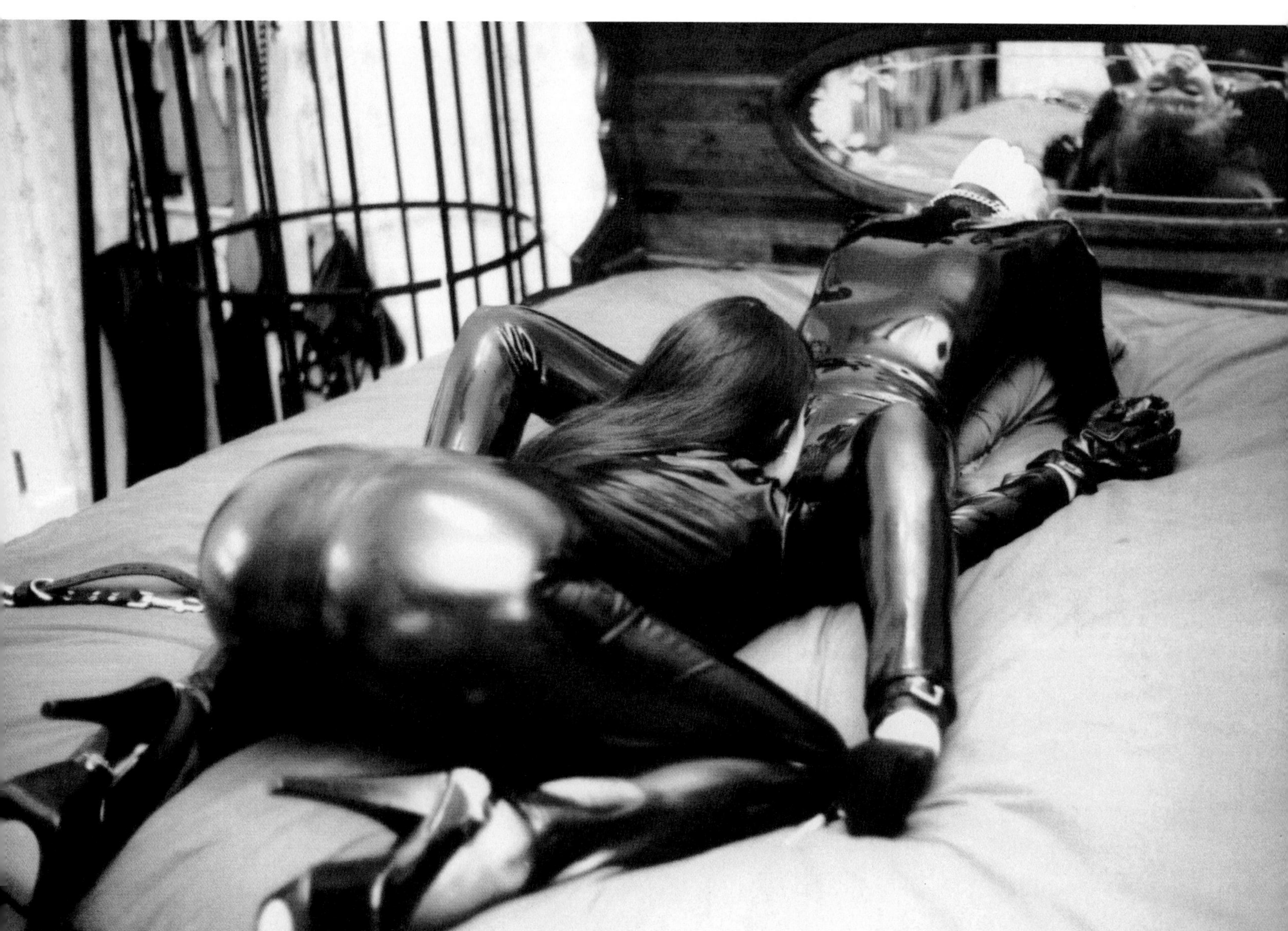

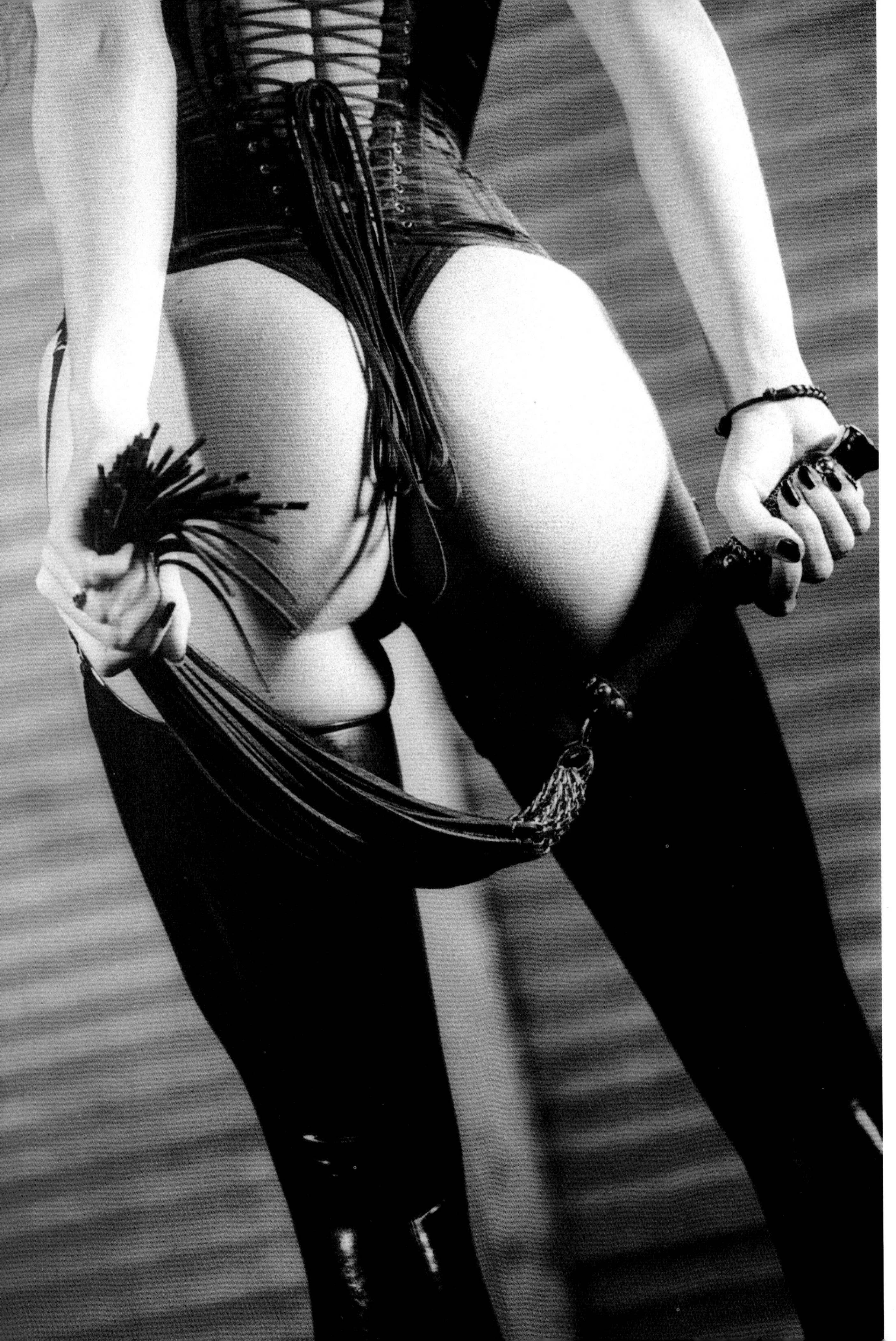

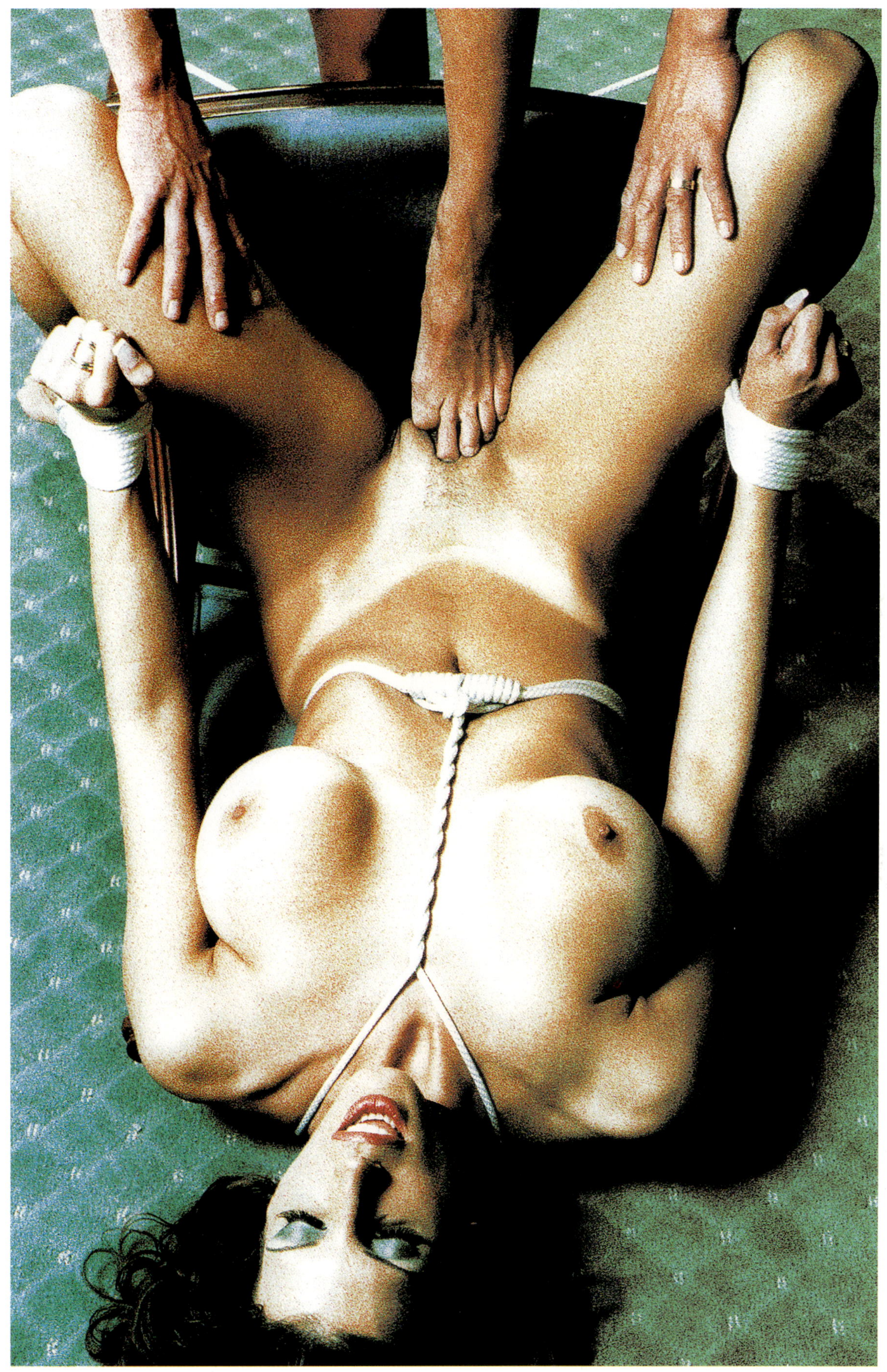

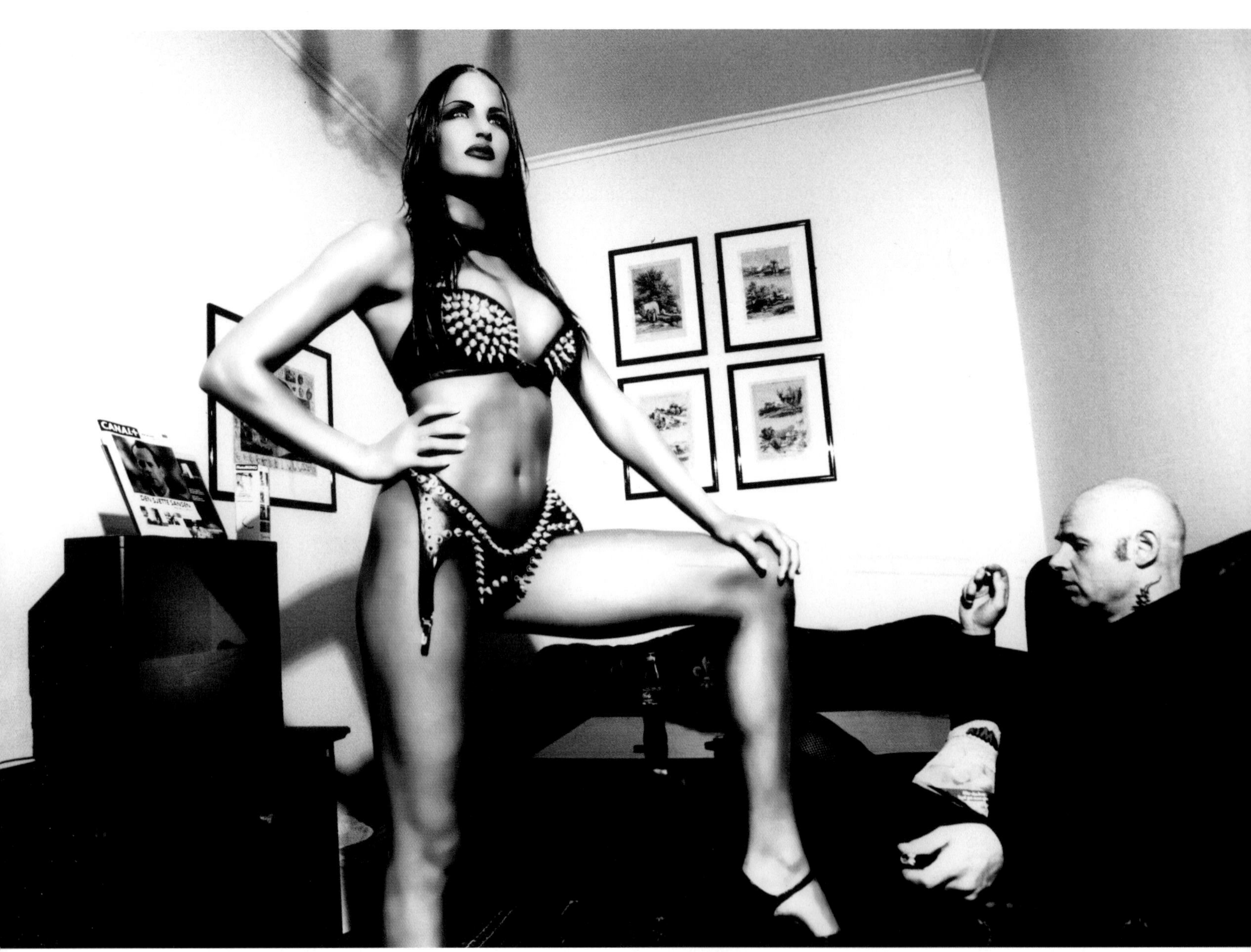

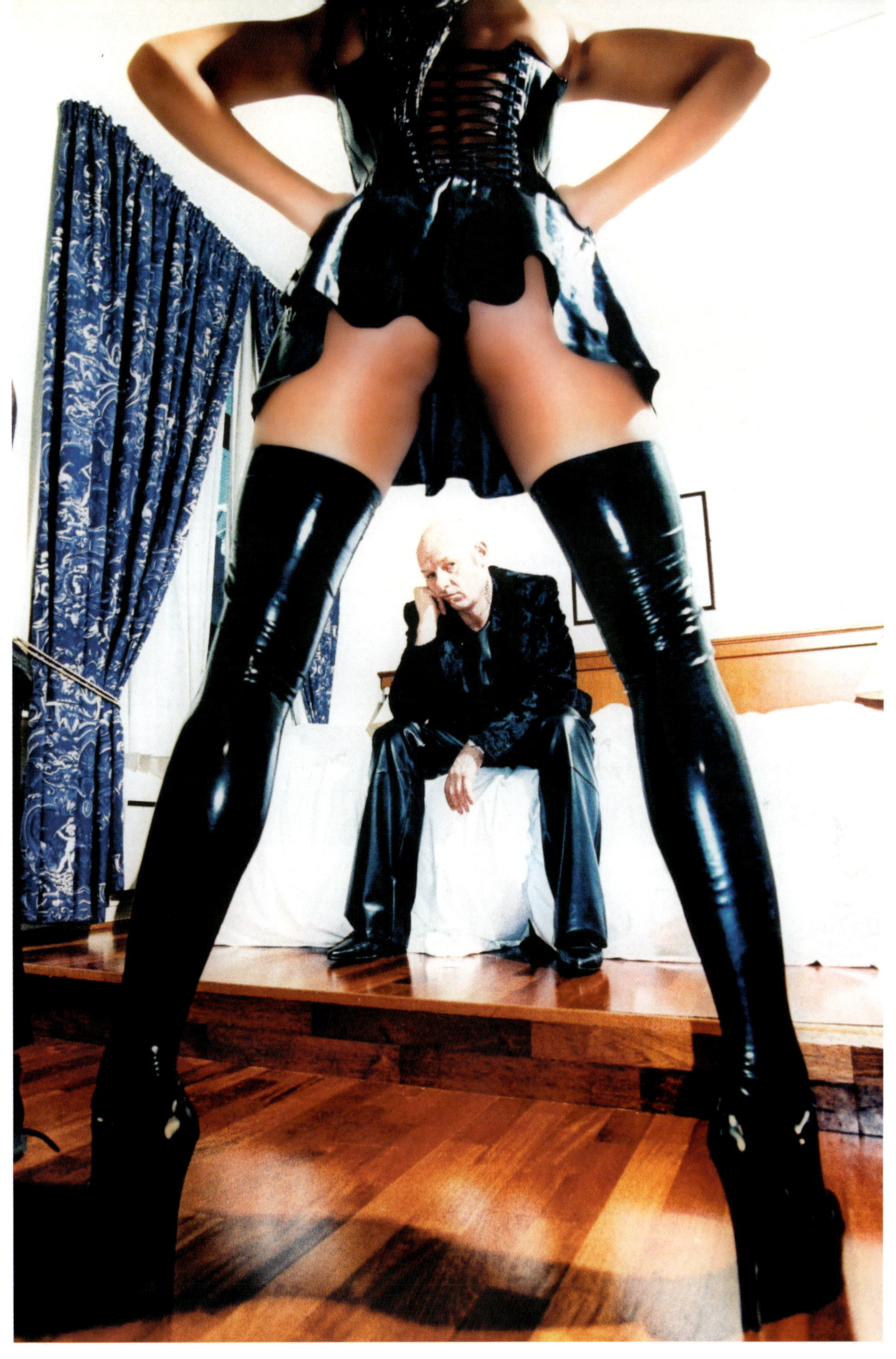

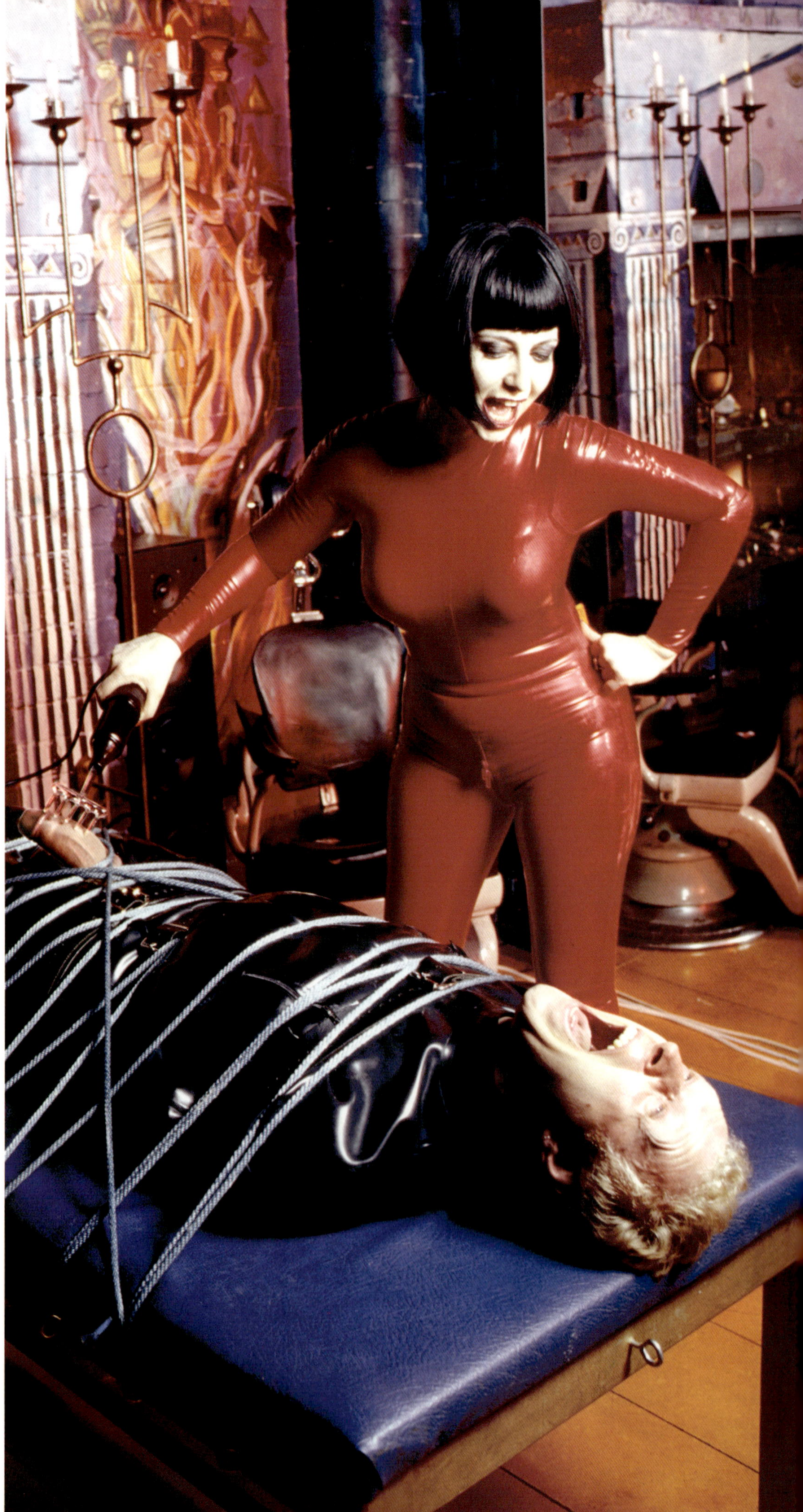

 Trevor Watson

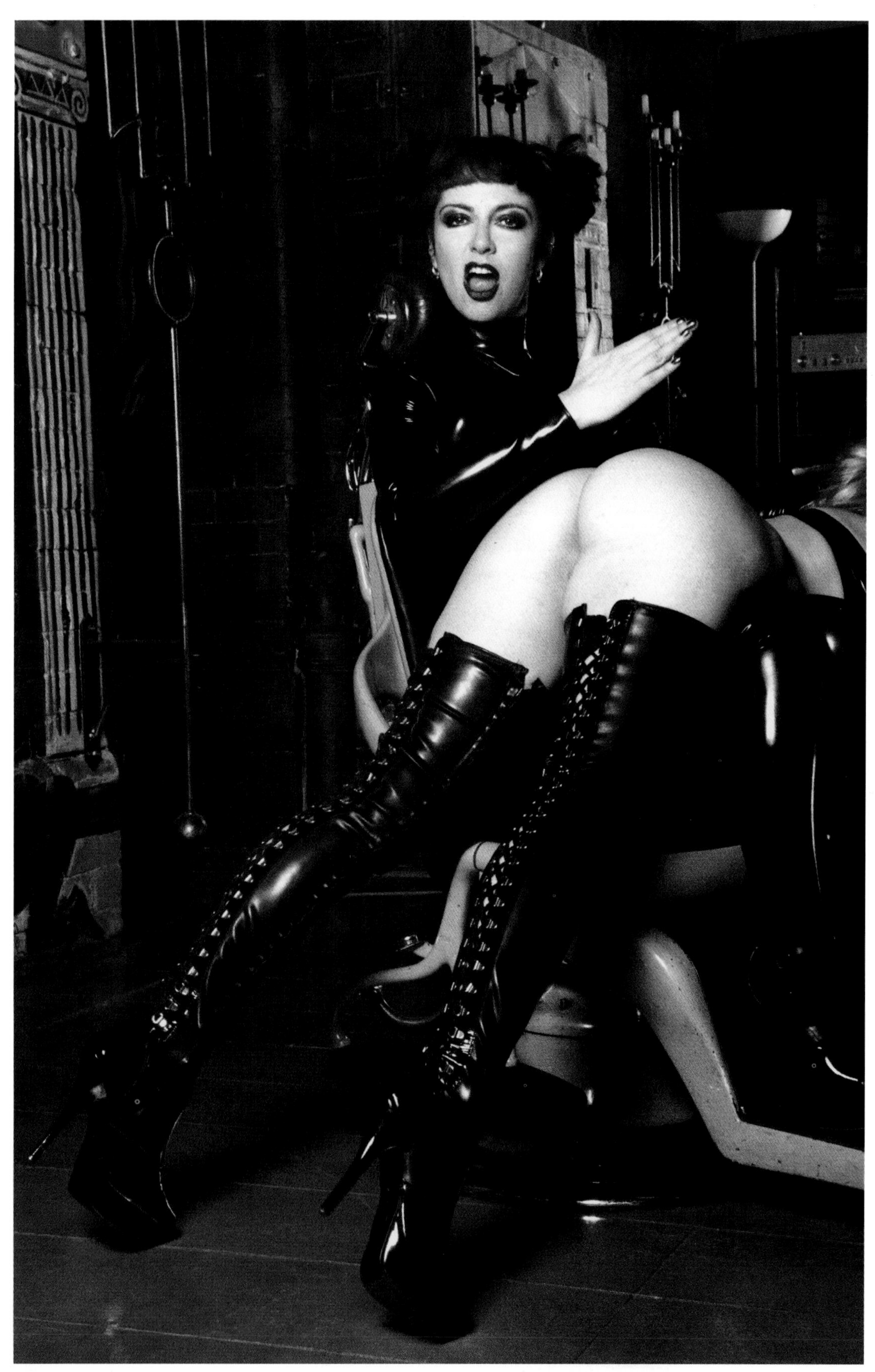

# BONDAG

Of all the fetishes, bondage has by far the biggest following. The number of magazines, books, videos, websites and newsgroups dedicated to this subject far outstrips those for any related area of interest. Whether it is enjoyed as a game that two can play or as a solitary pleasure, nothing seems to inspire greater enthusiasm than the fantasy of erotic restraint. It really is a consuming passion. It is, also, primarily a submissive passion: the desire to be tied up for erotic fun is far more common than the desire to do the tying!

People who enjoy being in bondage do so because of the powerful, complex combination of physical and mental stimuli they experience. As ropes, chains, straps or layers of restrictive clothing are applied, they undergo a gradual transformation from free individual to captive, and at the point of no return, control and, therefore, responsibility for what happens next, passes inexorably from them to their captor. Bondage enthusiasts often say that only through bondage can they be truly free: the realisation that they cannot escape is the very thing that allows their inhibitions to be fully released.

Bondage also provides enjoyable physical stimulation. Ropes or other restraints that stretch limbs or compress flesh provide powerful physical input to reinforce fantasising. A bit of light bedtime bondage, perhaps using scarves or stockings, may be all it takes to fulfil your dreams of helplessness and sexual vulnerability. But some people expect their restraints to look, feel and be authentically inescapable – which can sometimes take hours of delicious struggling to

establish! Bondage can be an occasional kinky extra to spice up lovemaking; a means of restraining someone for teasing, punishment or heavy SM play; or something akin to a tantric sex ritual whose objective is total catharsis.

Photography also uses bondage in different ways. In the hands of Victorian and Edwardian photographers, bondage was mainly a branch of "fladge" (flagellation) porn, although in the hands of a few serious European photographers of the female nude, it did receive more artistic interpretation. Among modern photographers who have kept this early fine art style alive are Craig Morey in the United States and Roman Kasperski in Europe.

For the last 50 years, however, America has been the major producer of bondage imagery, and the arrival of the internet has only increased American dominance of the genre. Modern American bondage photography owes its style very much to the work of Irving Klaw and John Willie in the 1950s. These pioneers and their contemporaries, working with models such as the legendary Bettie Page, established a pin-up genre featuring girls in their underwear tied up with white washing line. It was the foundation of what is now called classic American rope bondage.

In the 1970s and 1980s, this style was revived and modernised by a new breed of West Coast publishers, and of the American photographers working in the field today, none is more committed to keeping up standards than Jim Weathers, the man behind the website Bondage Café. Whether exploring the tightly-bound-and-gagged fetish look (*Double Cross*, p.151 and *Sweet Tangerine*, p.154), putting his own modern slant on lingerie bondage (*Anticipation*, p.156 and *Pink Kittens*, p.157) or evoking the vintage look of a John Willie ball-tie (*Homage to Sweet Gwendoline*, p.152 and *Perfect Teese*, p.153), Jim injects a sense of style that is unparalleled in current American work.

Britain, meanwhile, may boast fewer devotees of the vintage American genre, but the prolific output of Ben Westwood is some compensation. Westwood's fondness for vintage American bondage is obvious in images such as that on p.129 with its evocation of John Willie's bondage heroine Gwendoline – right down to the artist's trademark "painted lips" gag. It has been said that American bondage has it real roots in the country's cowboy traditions, and this would certainly help to explain why bondage imagery in Britain and, indeed, the rest of Europe, is more centred around the chains and fetters of the medieval dungeon. This spirit – albeit with the modern twist – is clearly evoked by the heavy slave irons of Emma Delves-Broughton's *Dungeon 2000* (p.147), the steel and wood restraints of Austrian duo No Mercy's images (pp.160–166) and the collar and cuffs worn by Roman Kasperski's models (pp.168–169).

Alongside the enthusiastic application of American rope and European steel, we have seen an emergence of Western appreciation for the low-tech, high-art bondage of the Far East. Japanese rope bondage is a highly deco-rative yet totally functional erotic technique that evolved from the rope torture techniques of medieval times. Although a subject of serious photographic interest in Japan for several decades, it has only recently become accessible to Western photographers, with France's Romain Slocombe among those making a contribution to our understanding of the phenomenon.

Western photographers also make much erotic use of modern institutional restraints. Police handcuffs, for example, have become a universal symbol of bondage, much fetishised by those who enjoy the idea of "official" restraint using dedicated equipment. However, simply slapping a pair of handcuffs on your model is considered an extremely lazy and clichéd way of creating a bondage image, so photographers often look for more imaginative ways to use them. In *Antonia 2001* (p.137) for example, Dave Naz demonstrates that what is fit for the wrists can also be fit for the ankles. And if hospital restraints strike you as an unlikely type of sex aid, then taking a look at what Carlos Batts can do with a pretty girl in a straightjacket (pp.133–135) may well change your mind.

Enthusiasm for dedicated bondage equipment does not stop at devices such as these, borrowed from the "real world". Beyond lies a whole universe of specialist clothing and apparatus made in leather, rubber and steel. Hoods, harnesses, gags, single arm gloves, leg-spreaders, inflatable suits, vacuum sheets – if you can envisage it, somebody has probably already made it, and somebody else is probably struggling helplessly in it for a photographer right now.

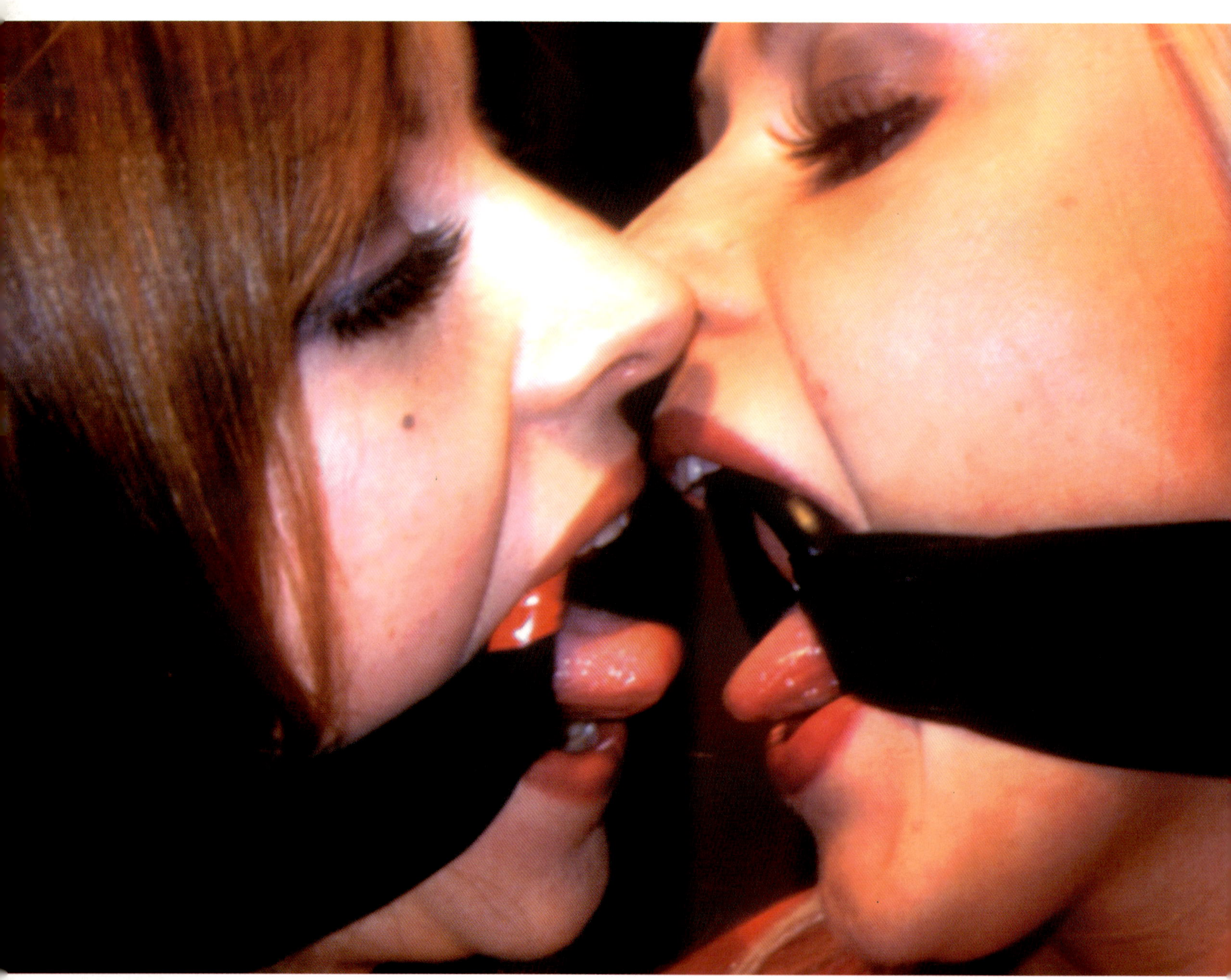



Opposite **Ben Westwood**

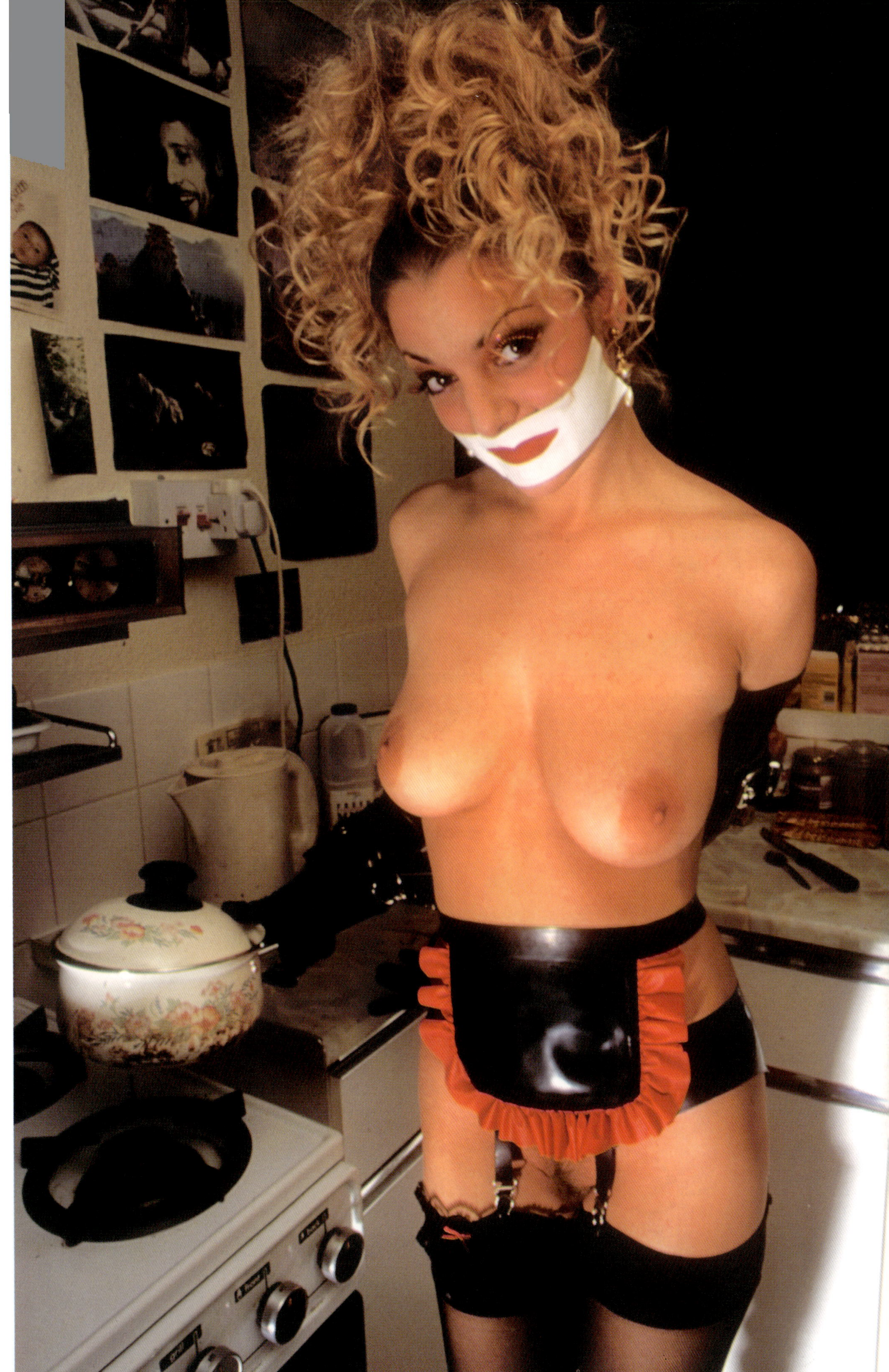

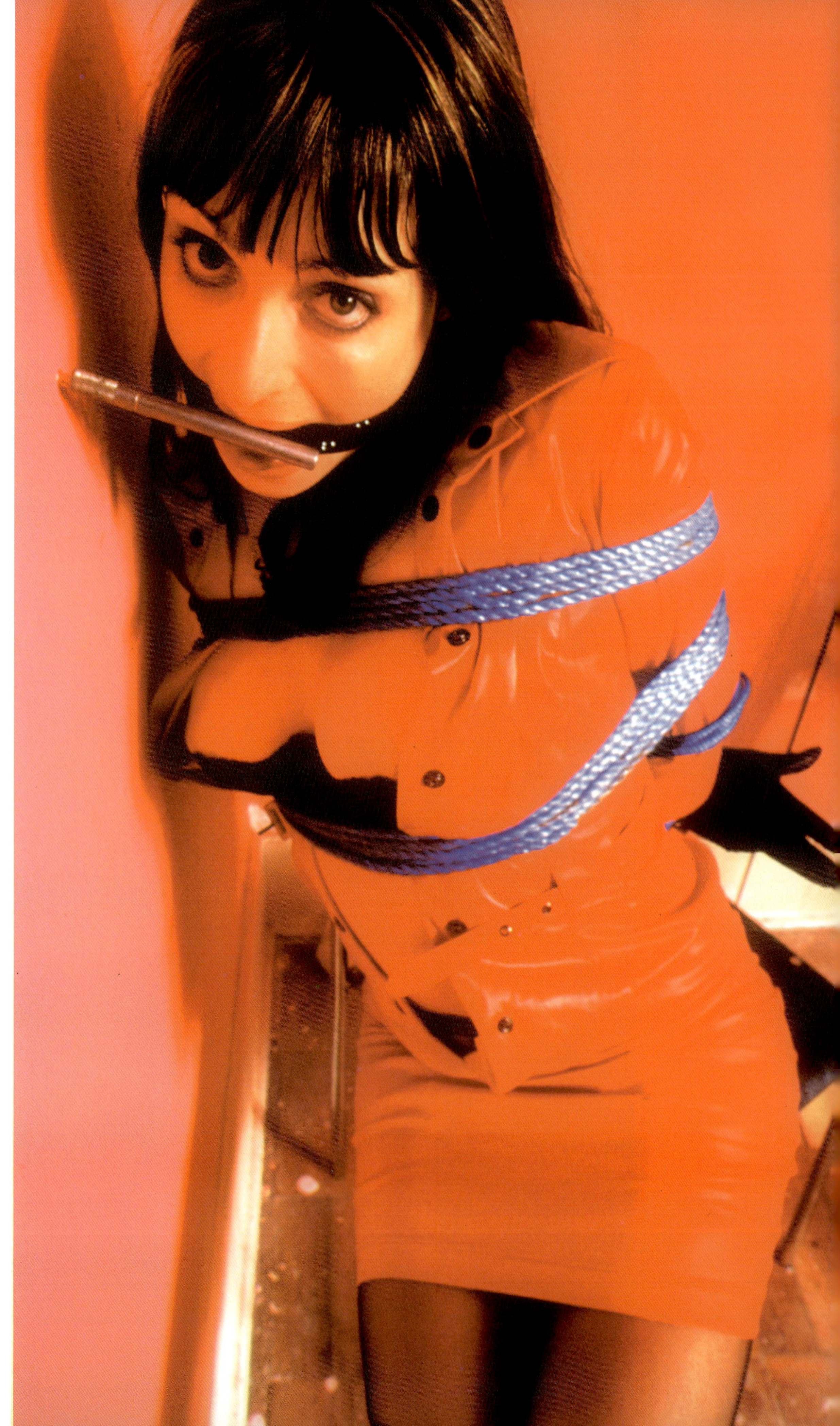

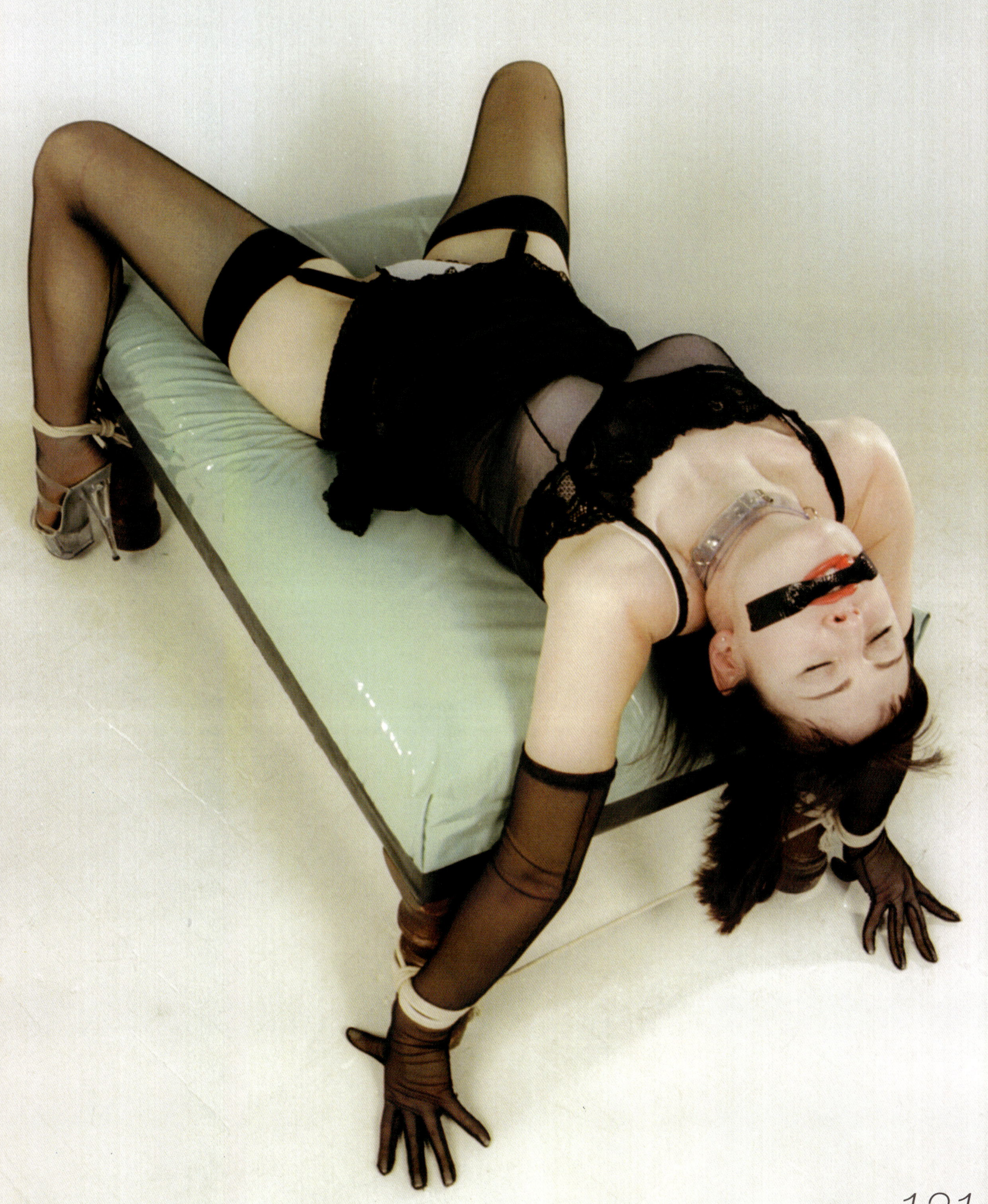

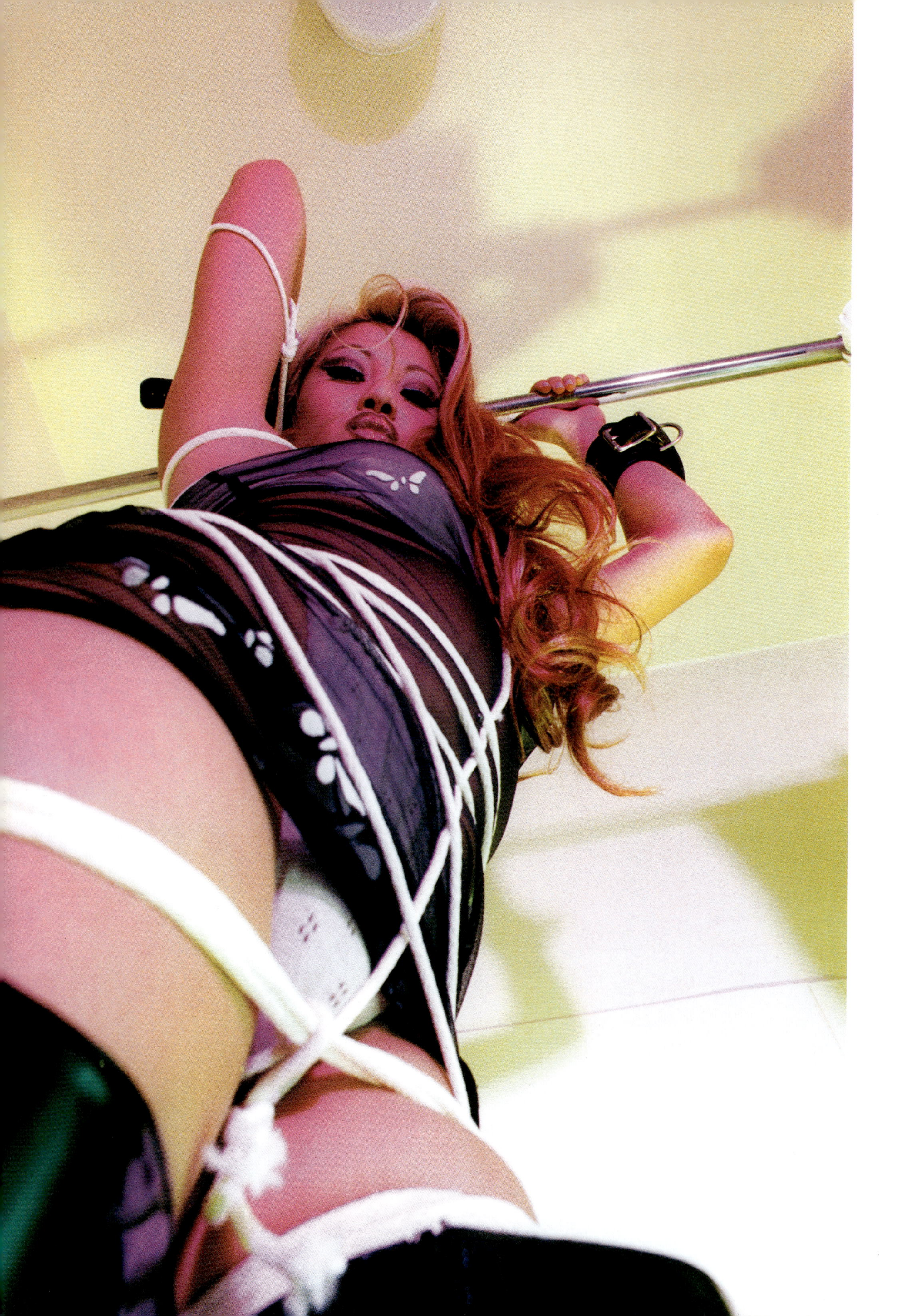

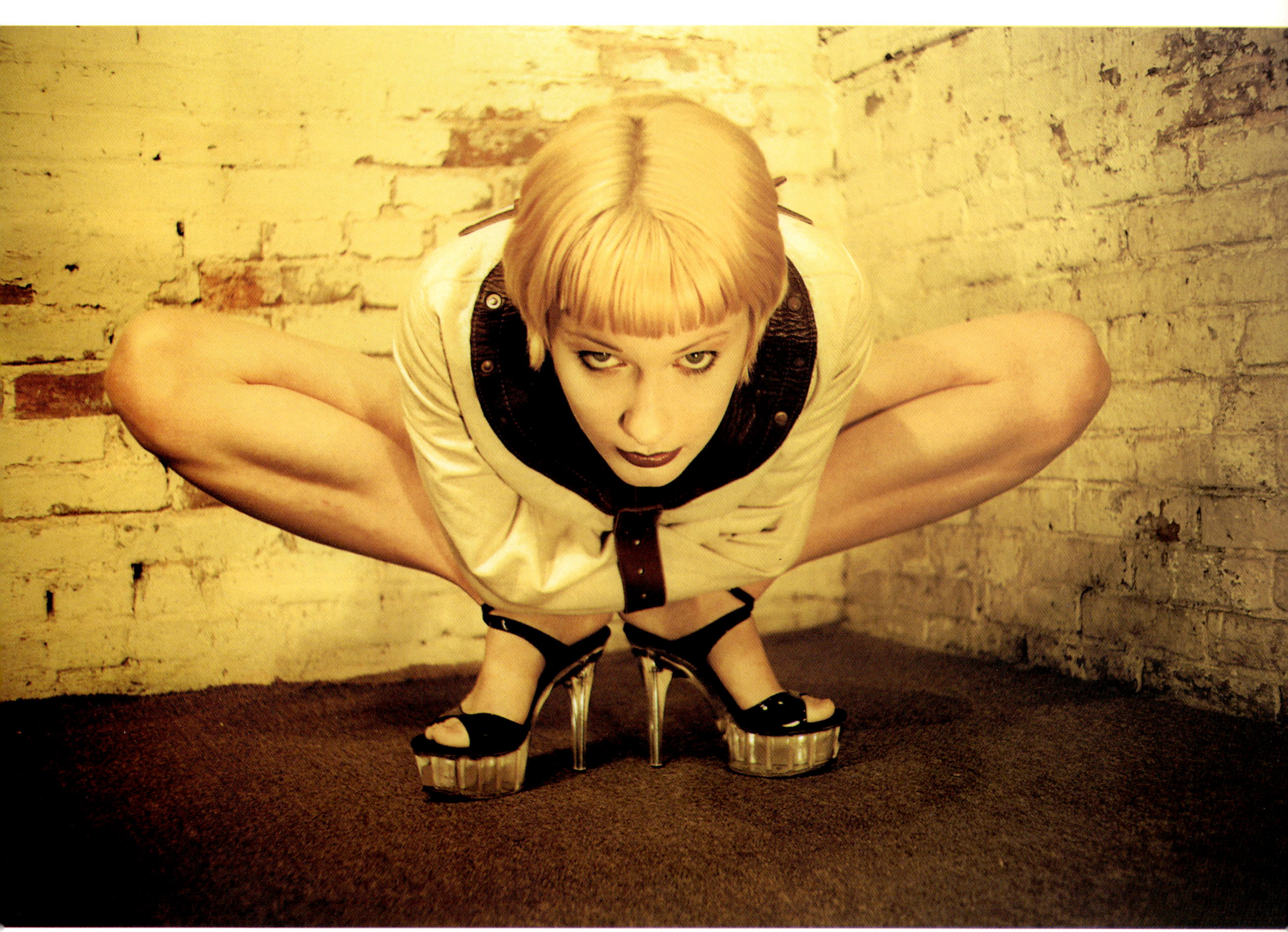

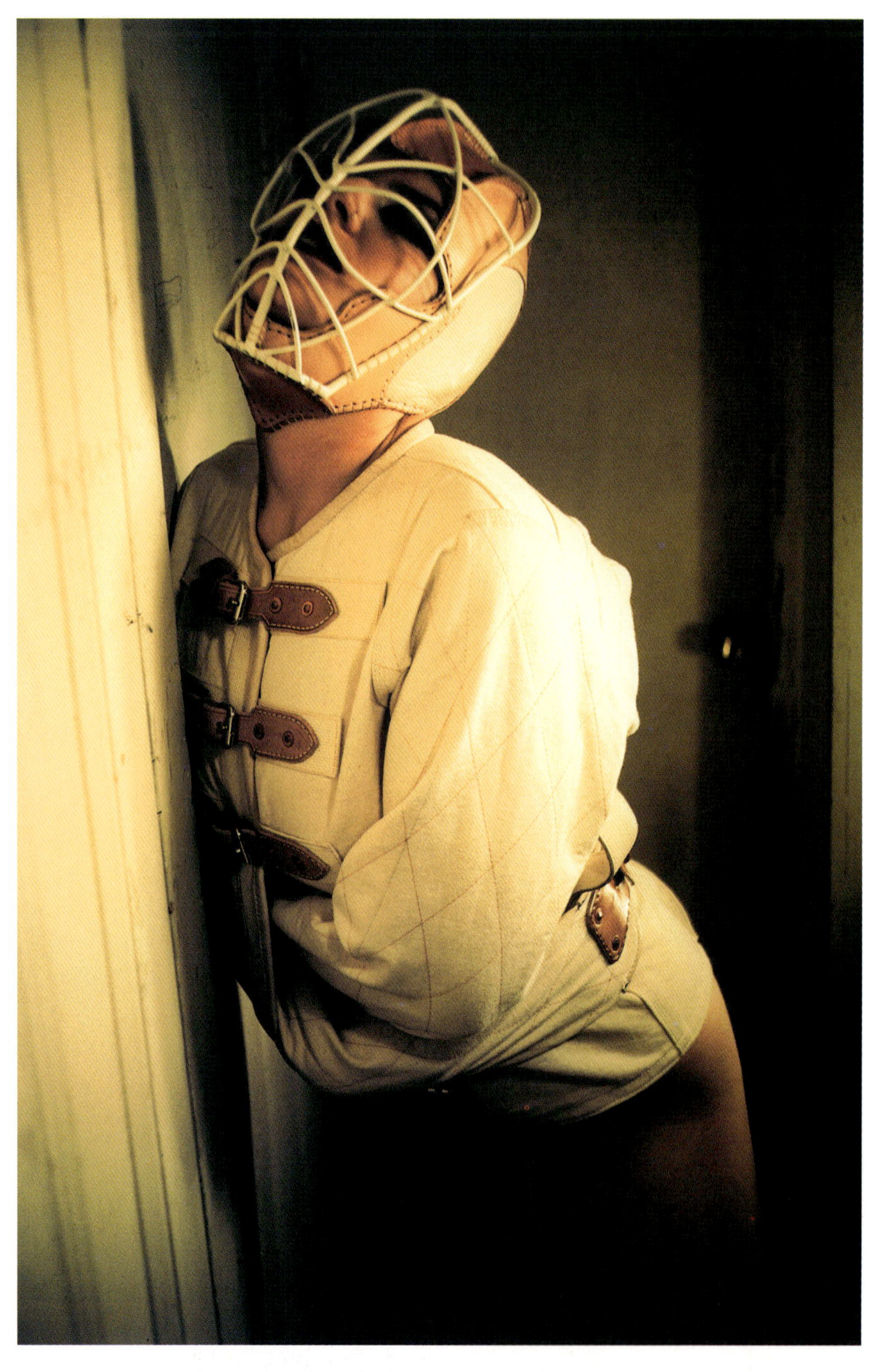



Opposite **Carlos Batts**

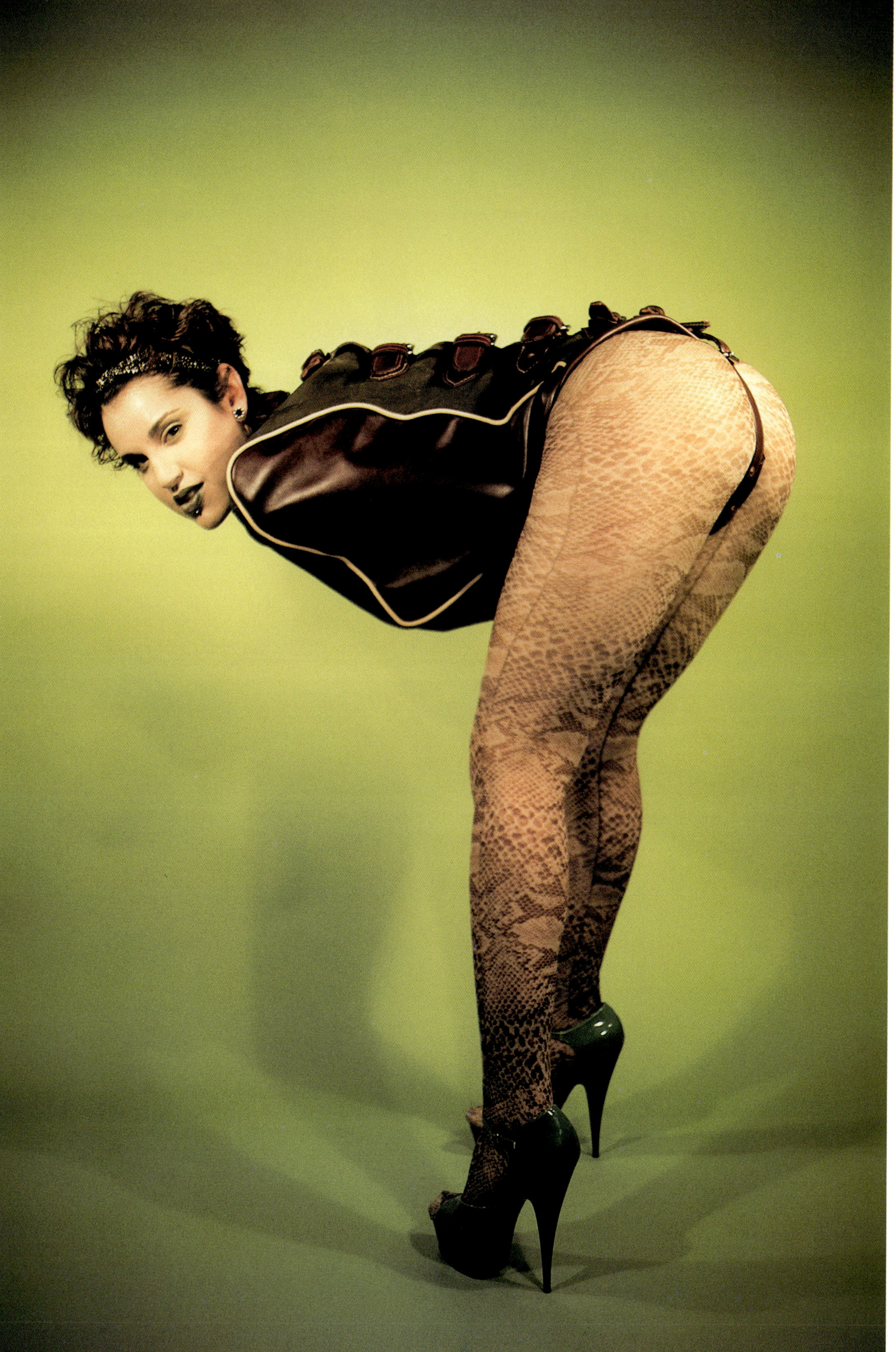

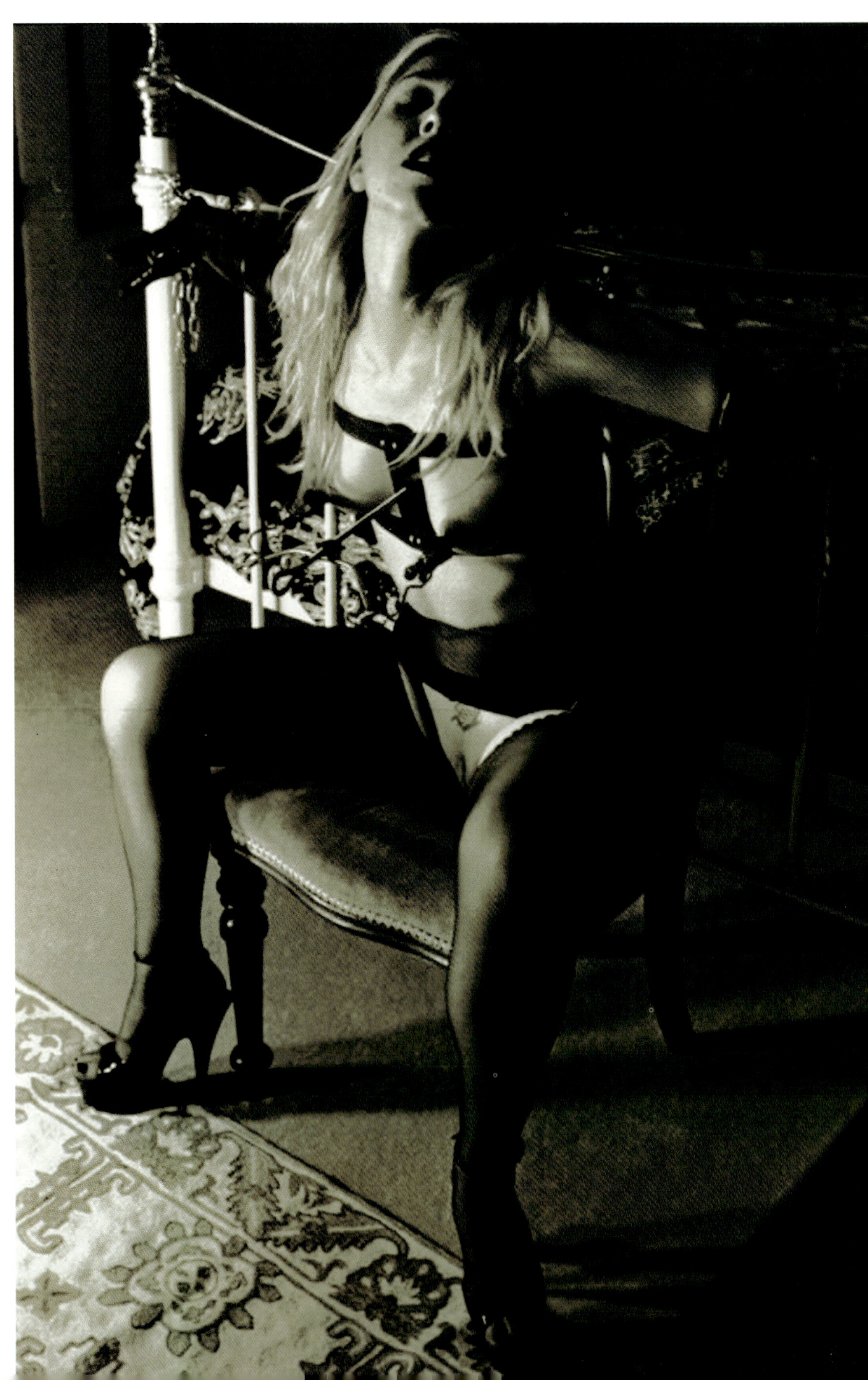

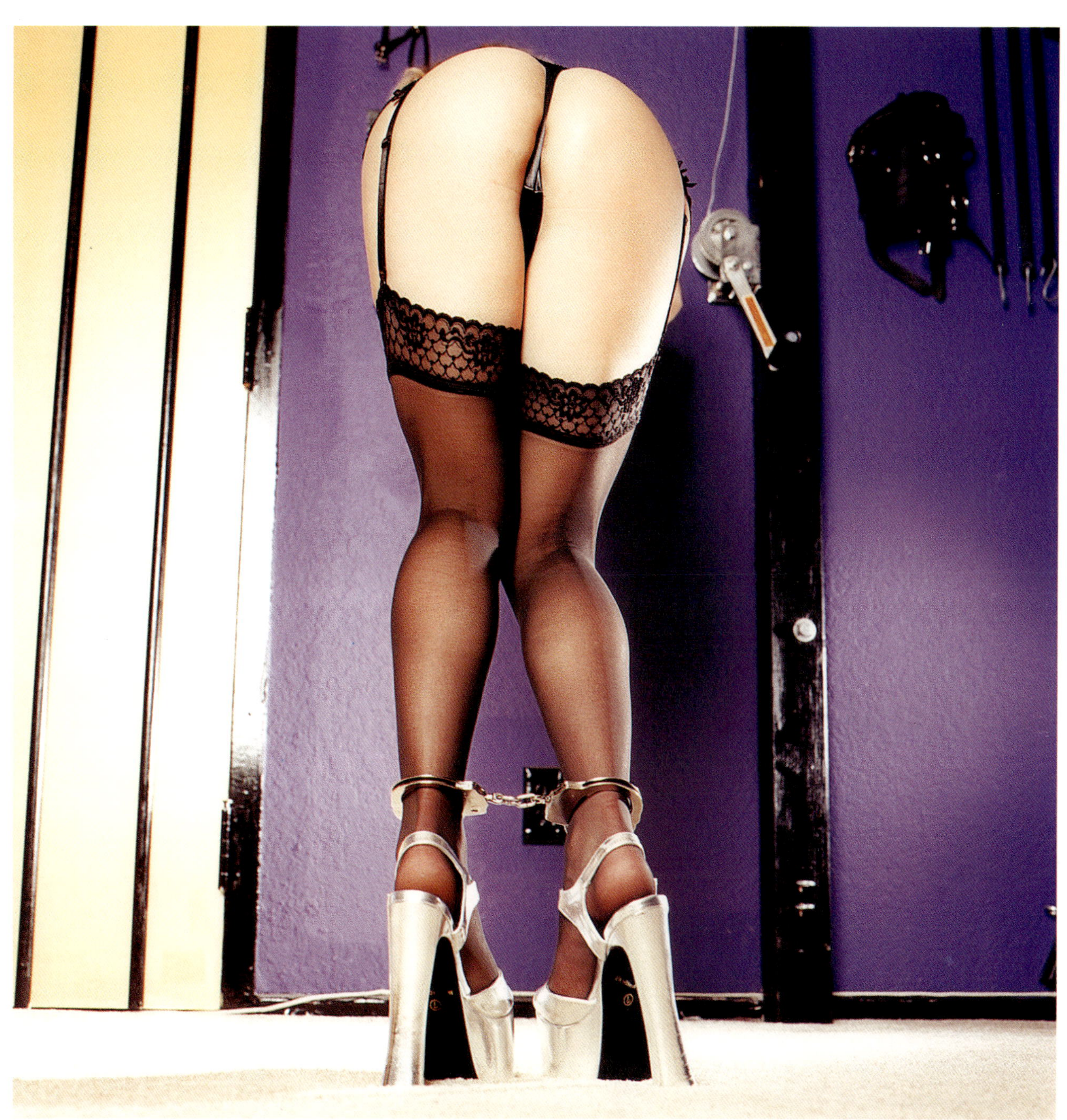

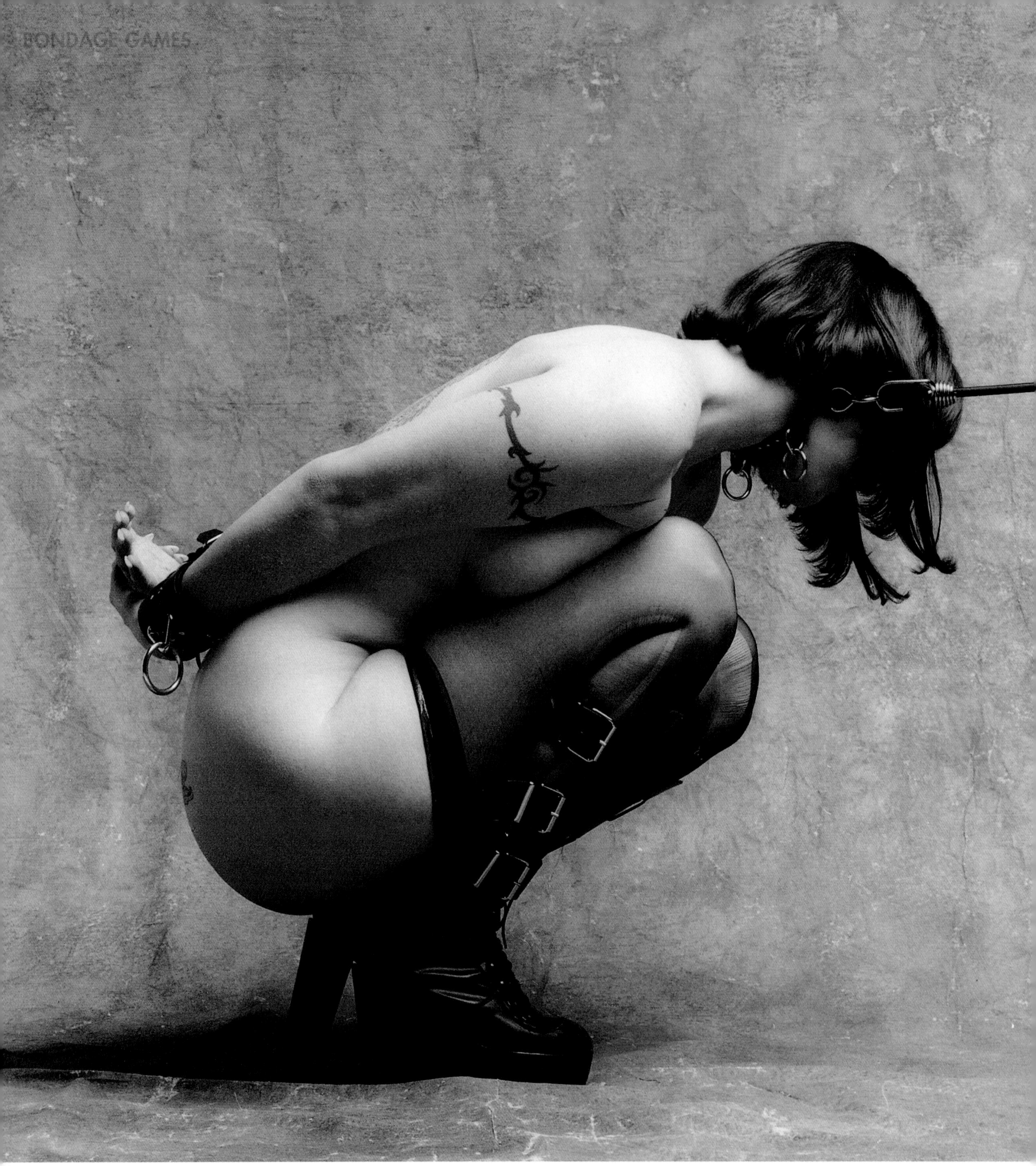



138 Craig Morey

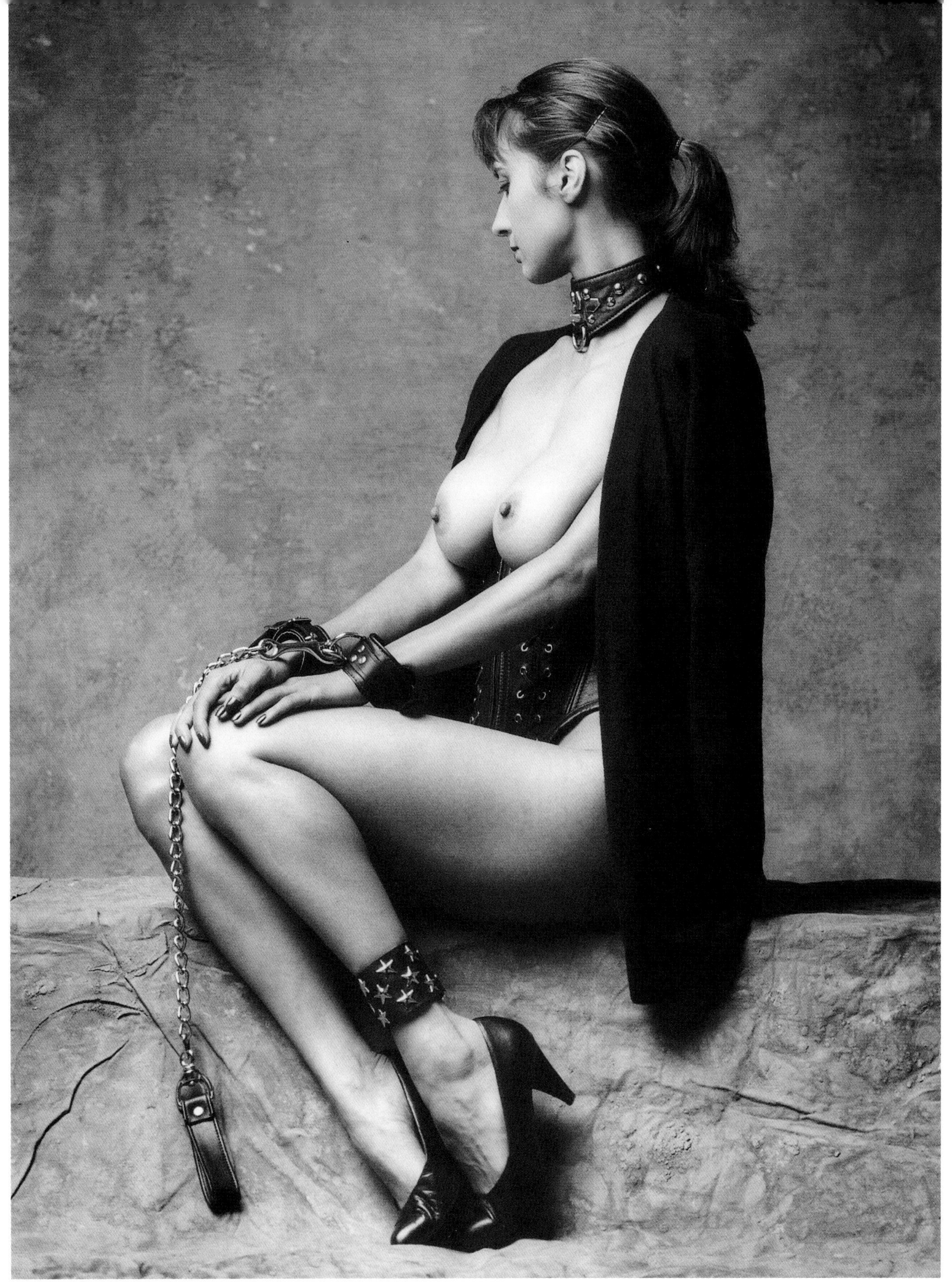

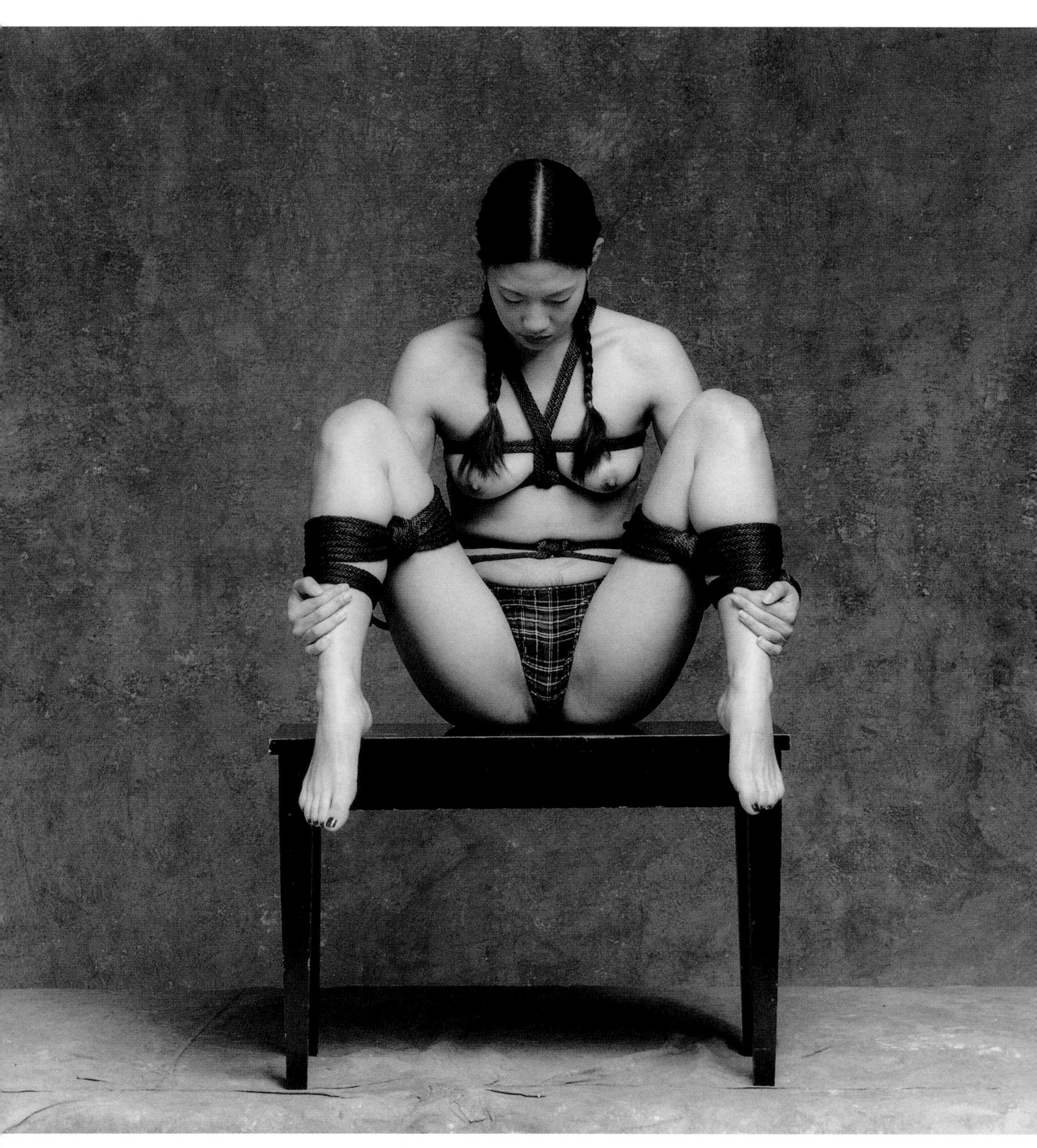

 Craig Morey

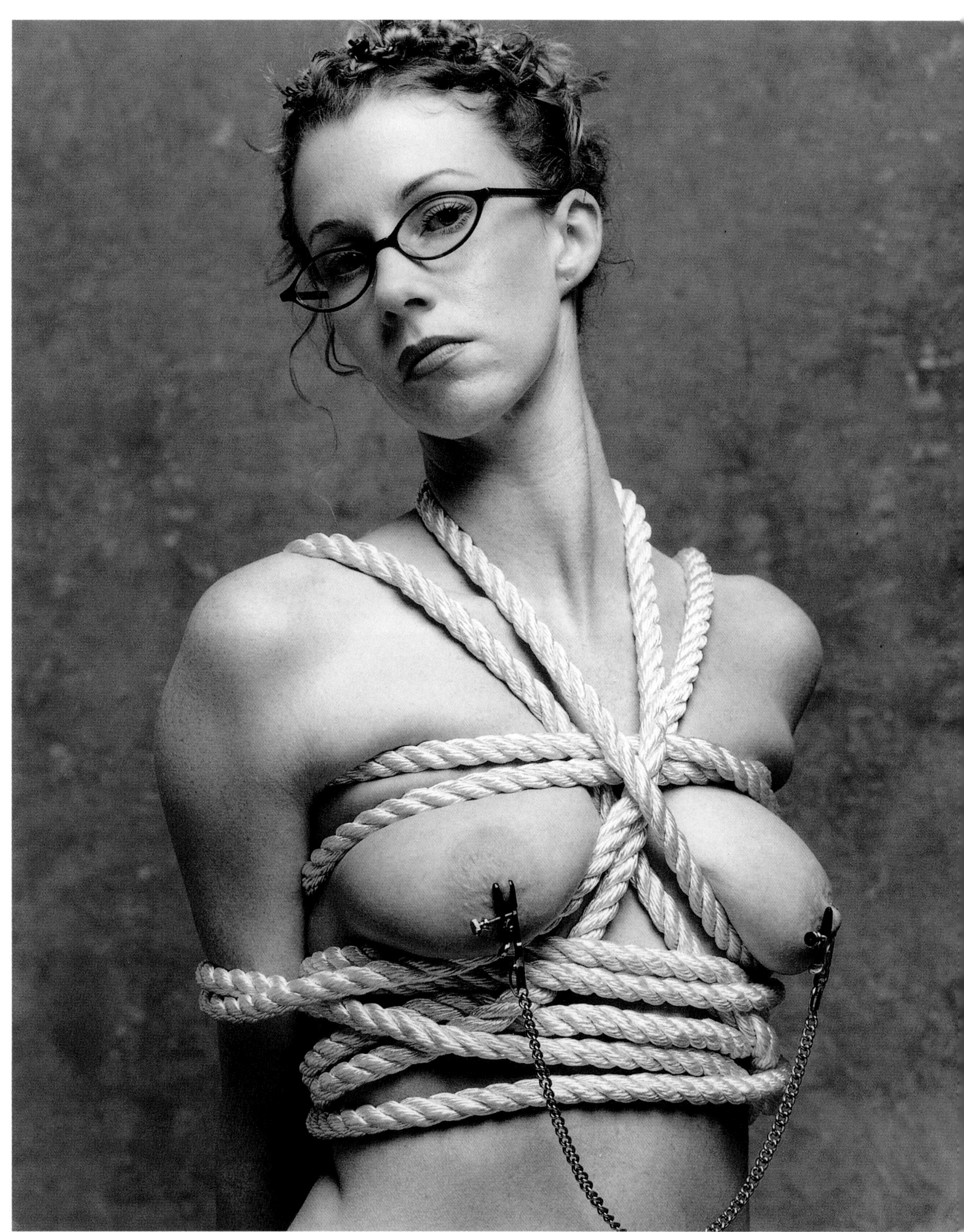

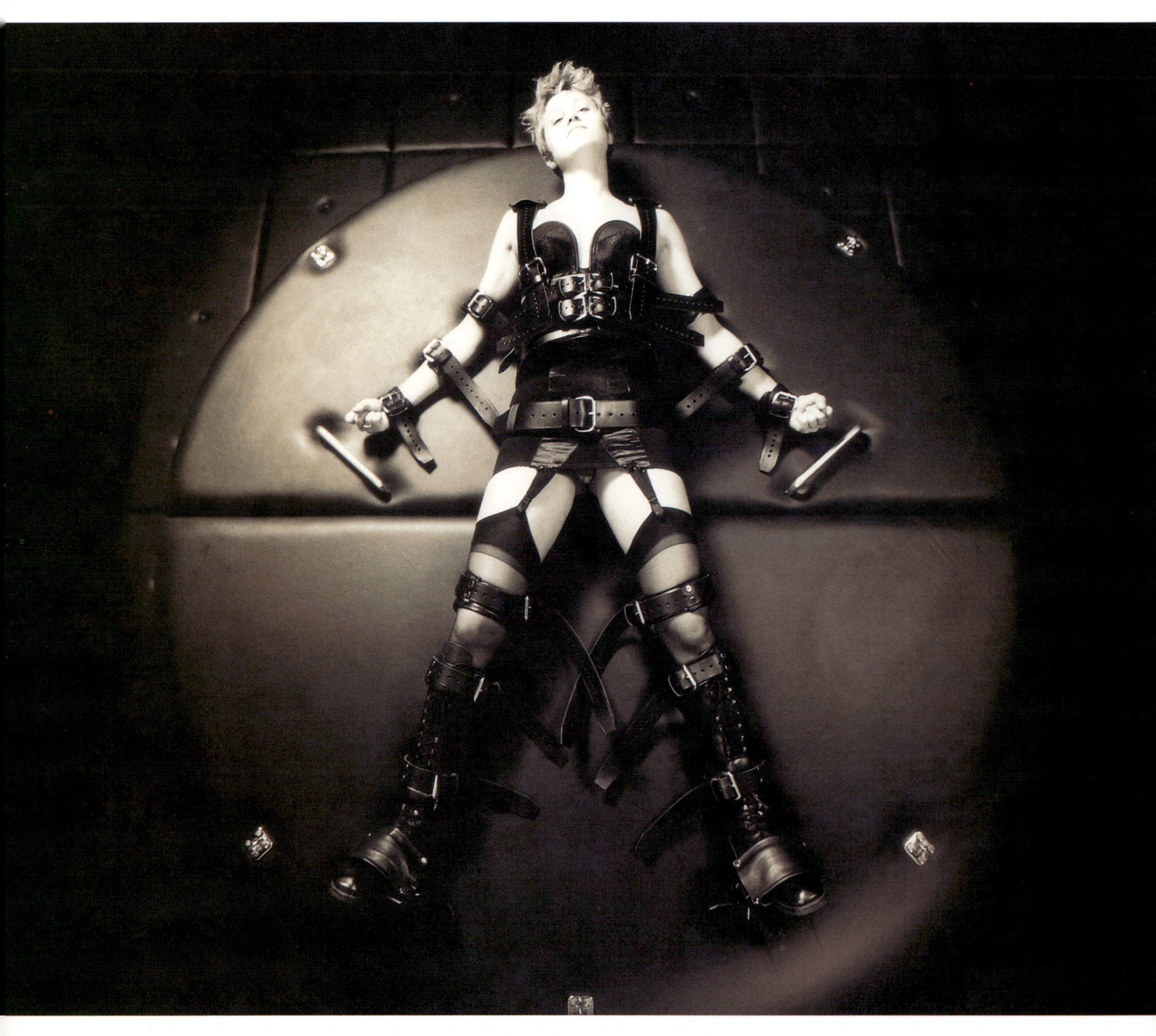

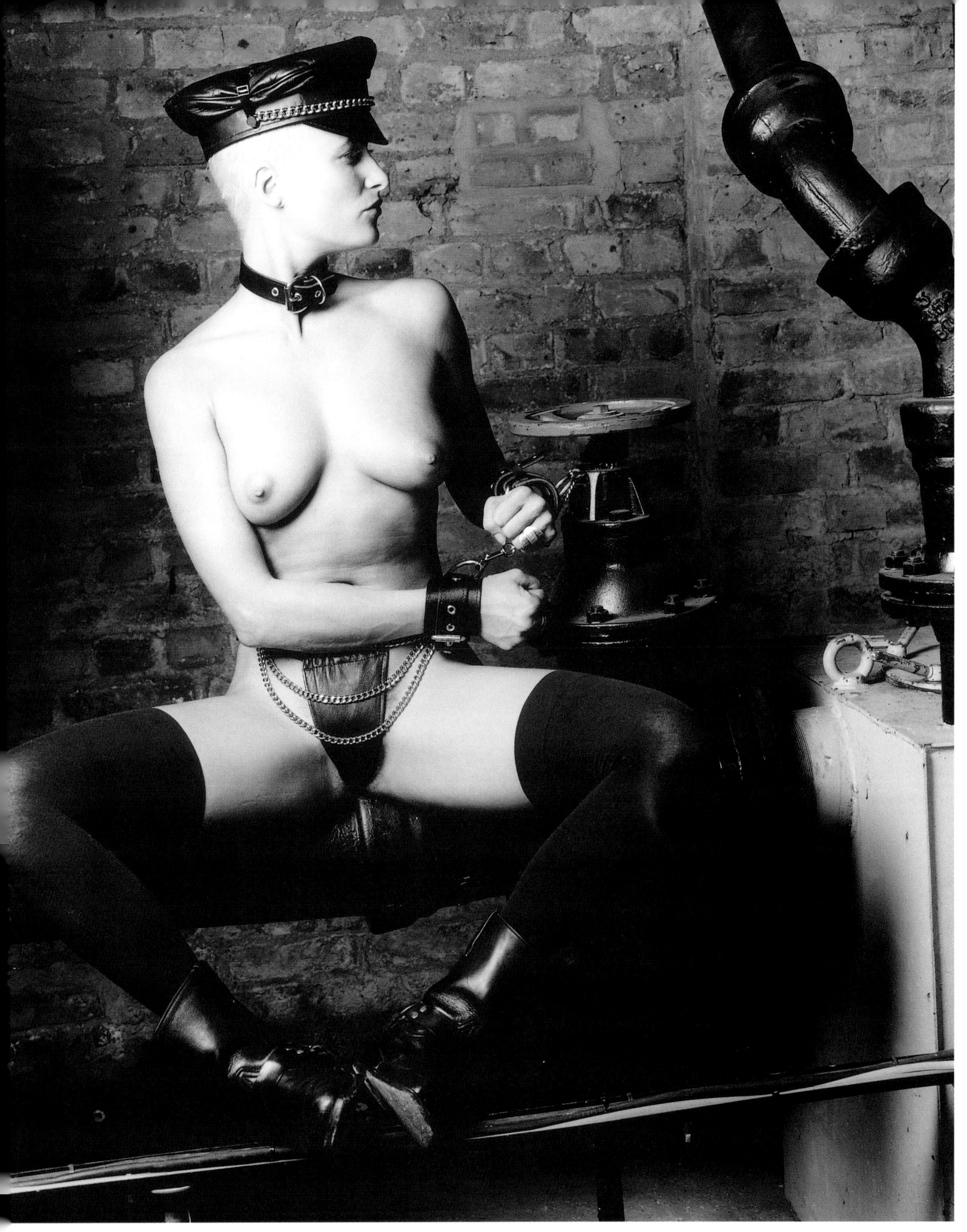

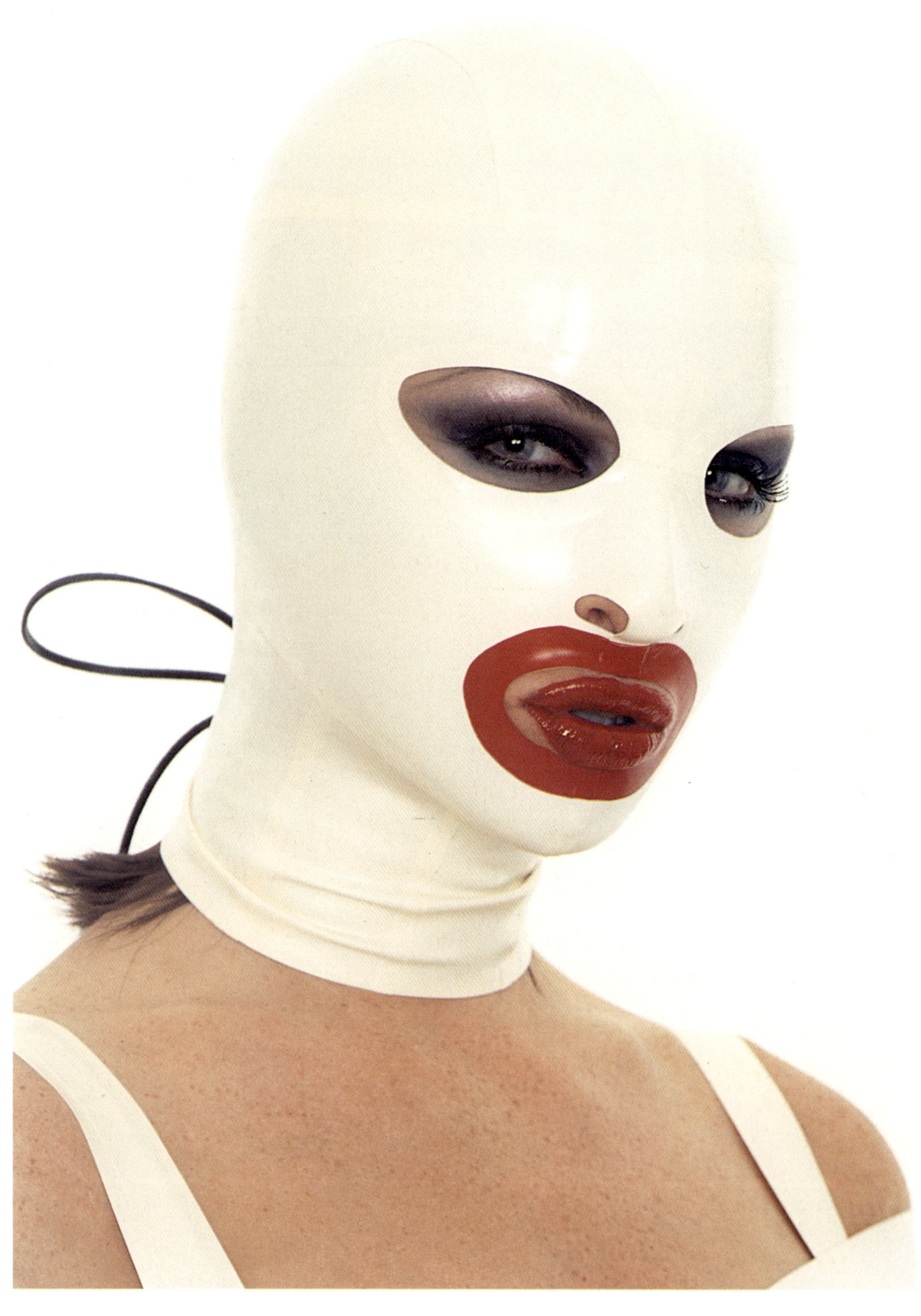

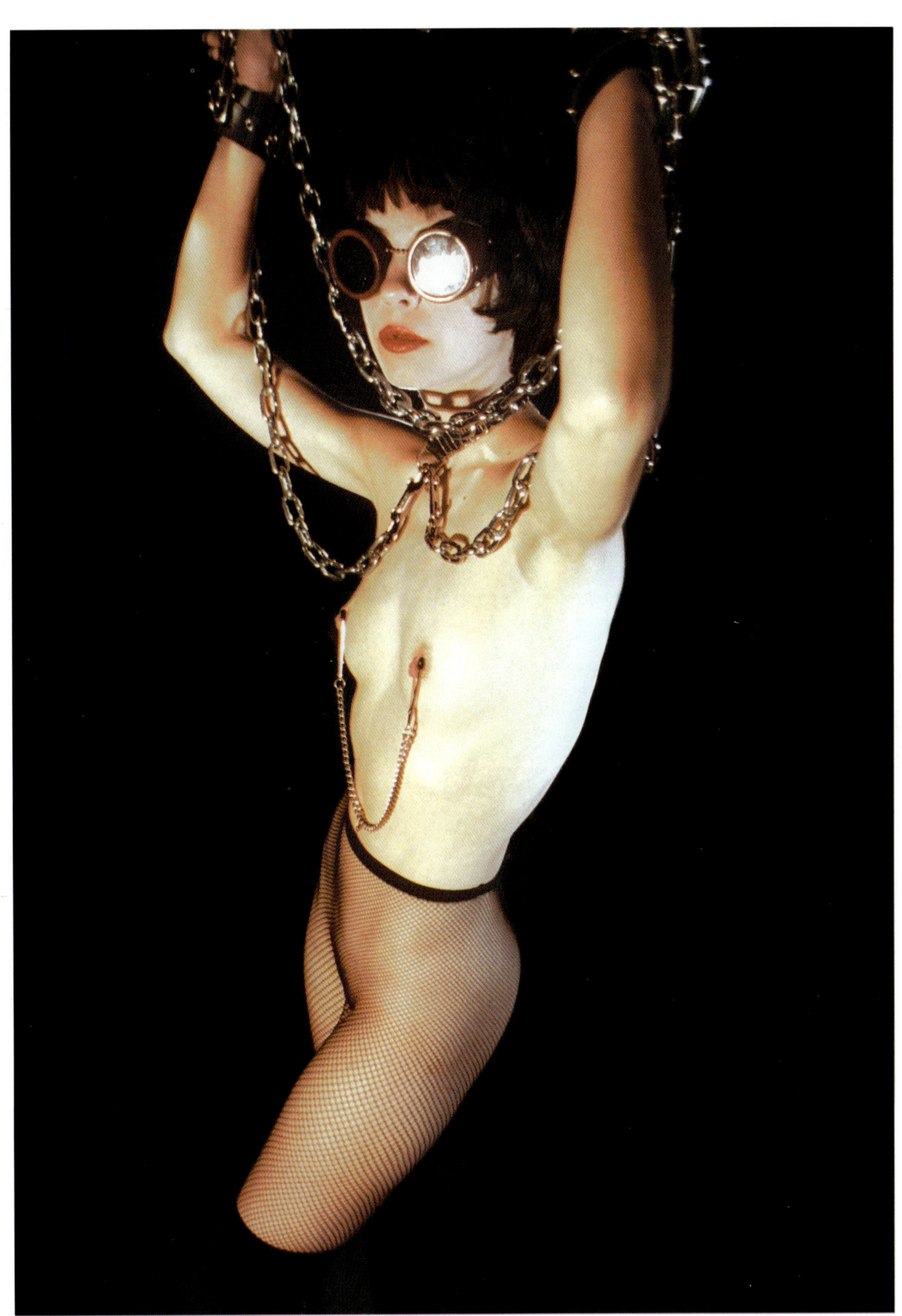

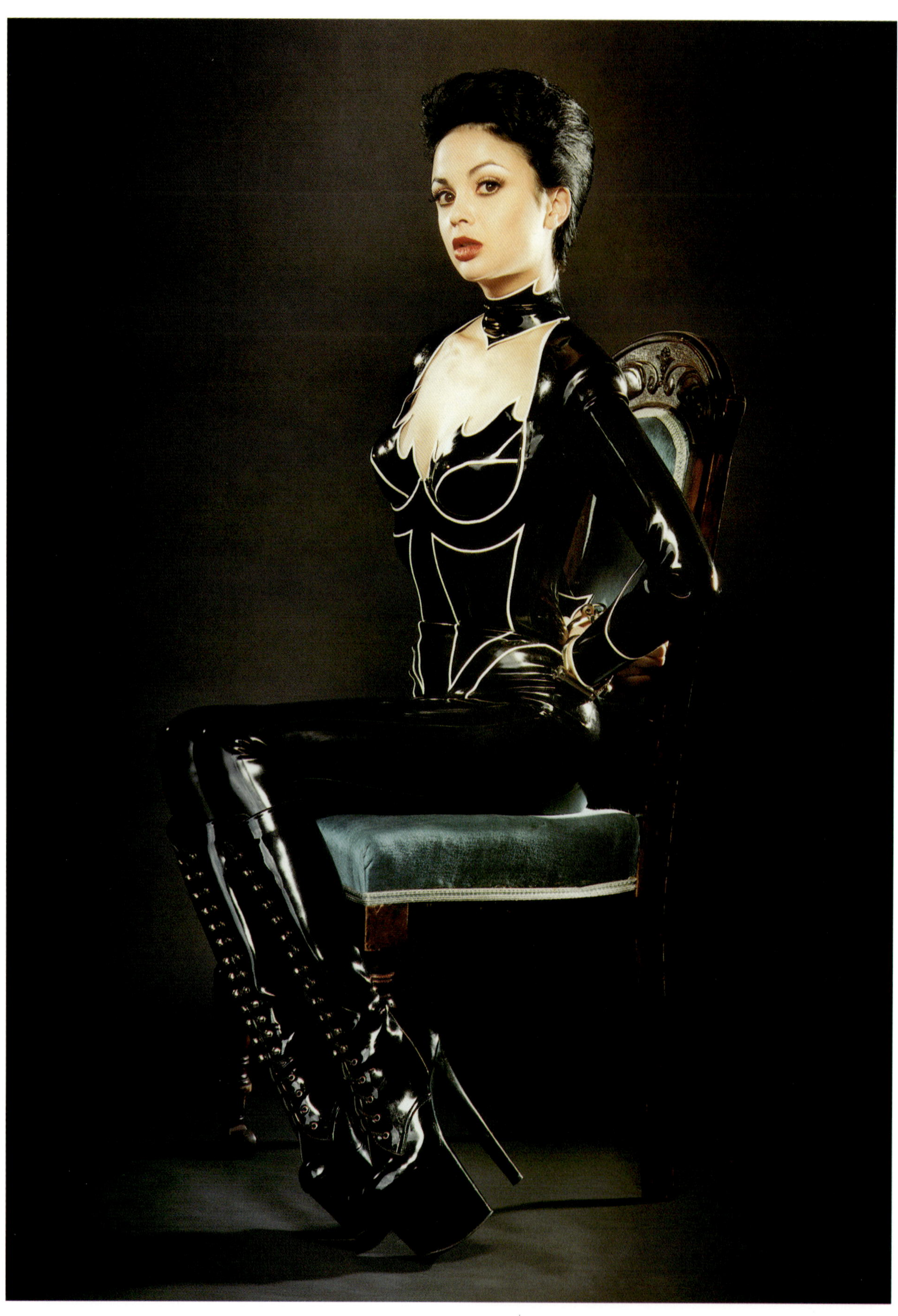

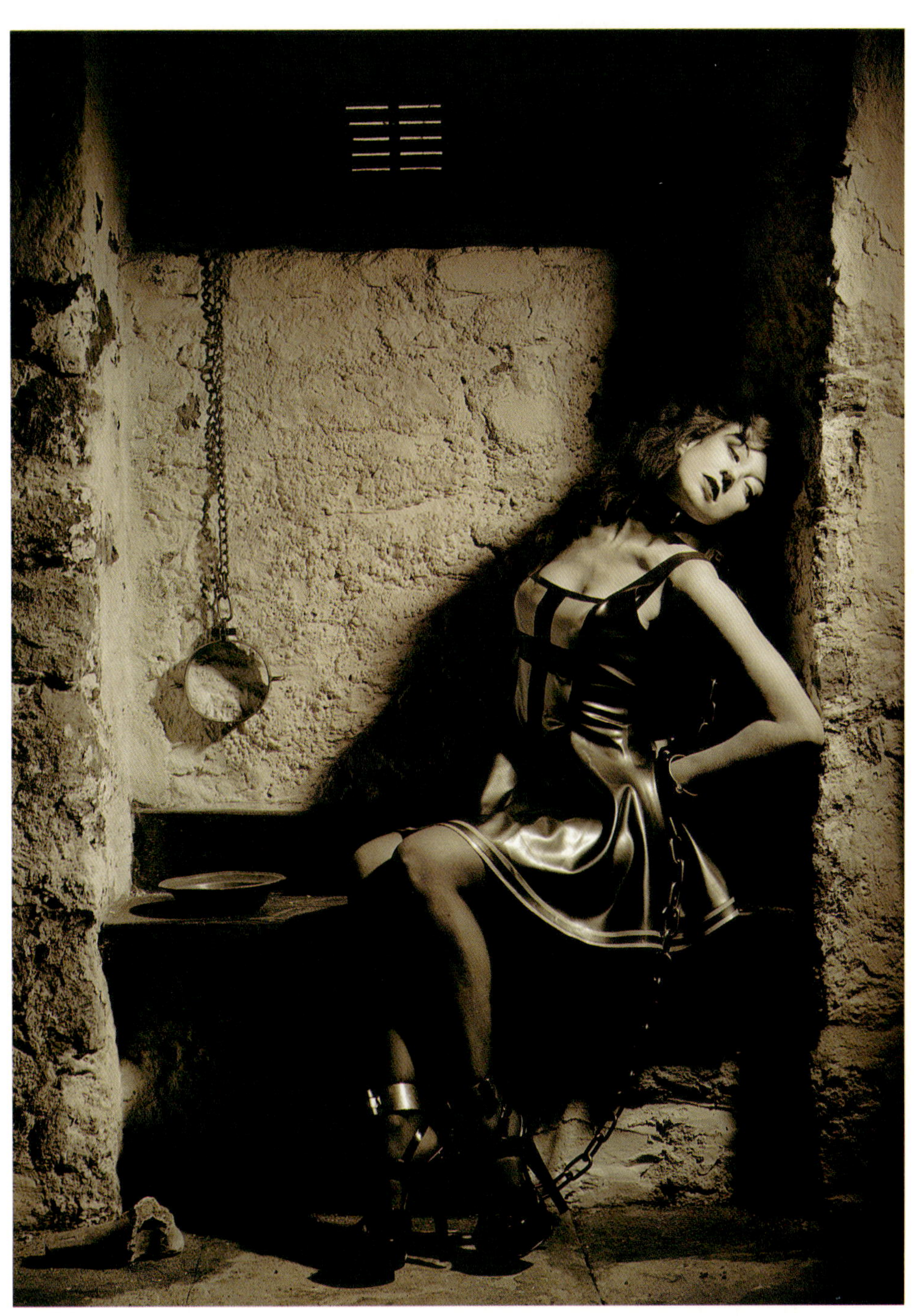

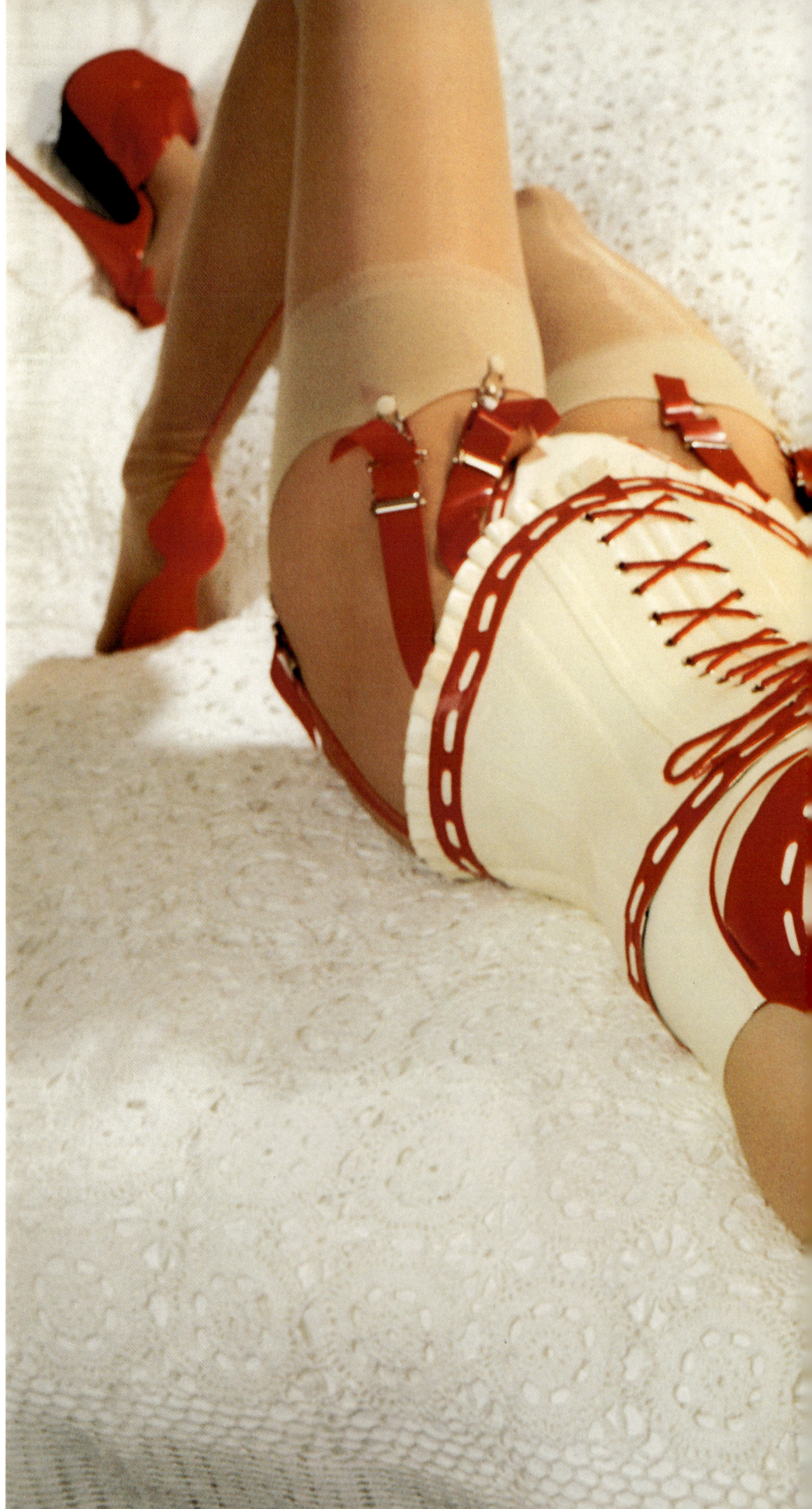

 Emma Delves-Broughton

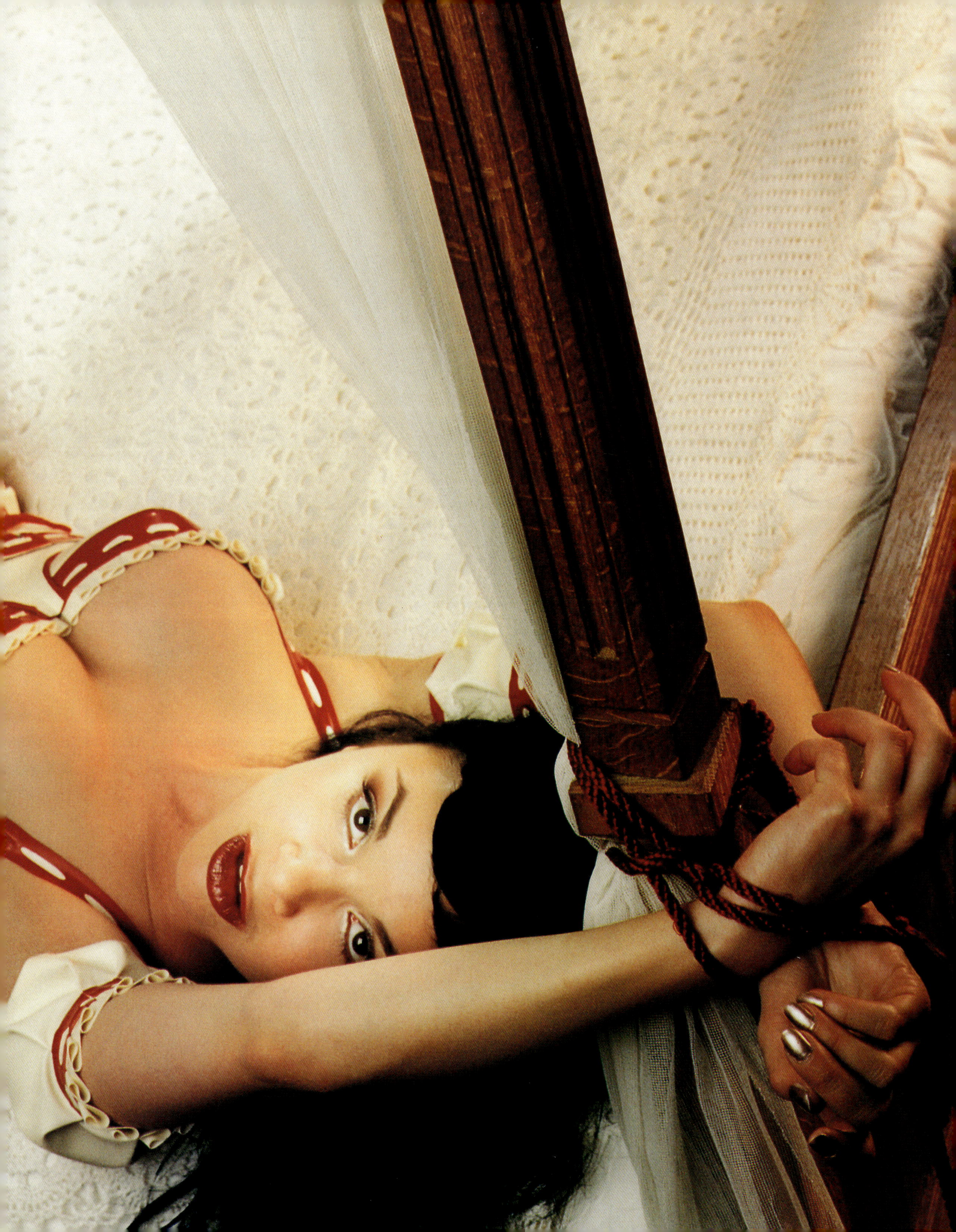

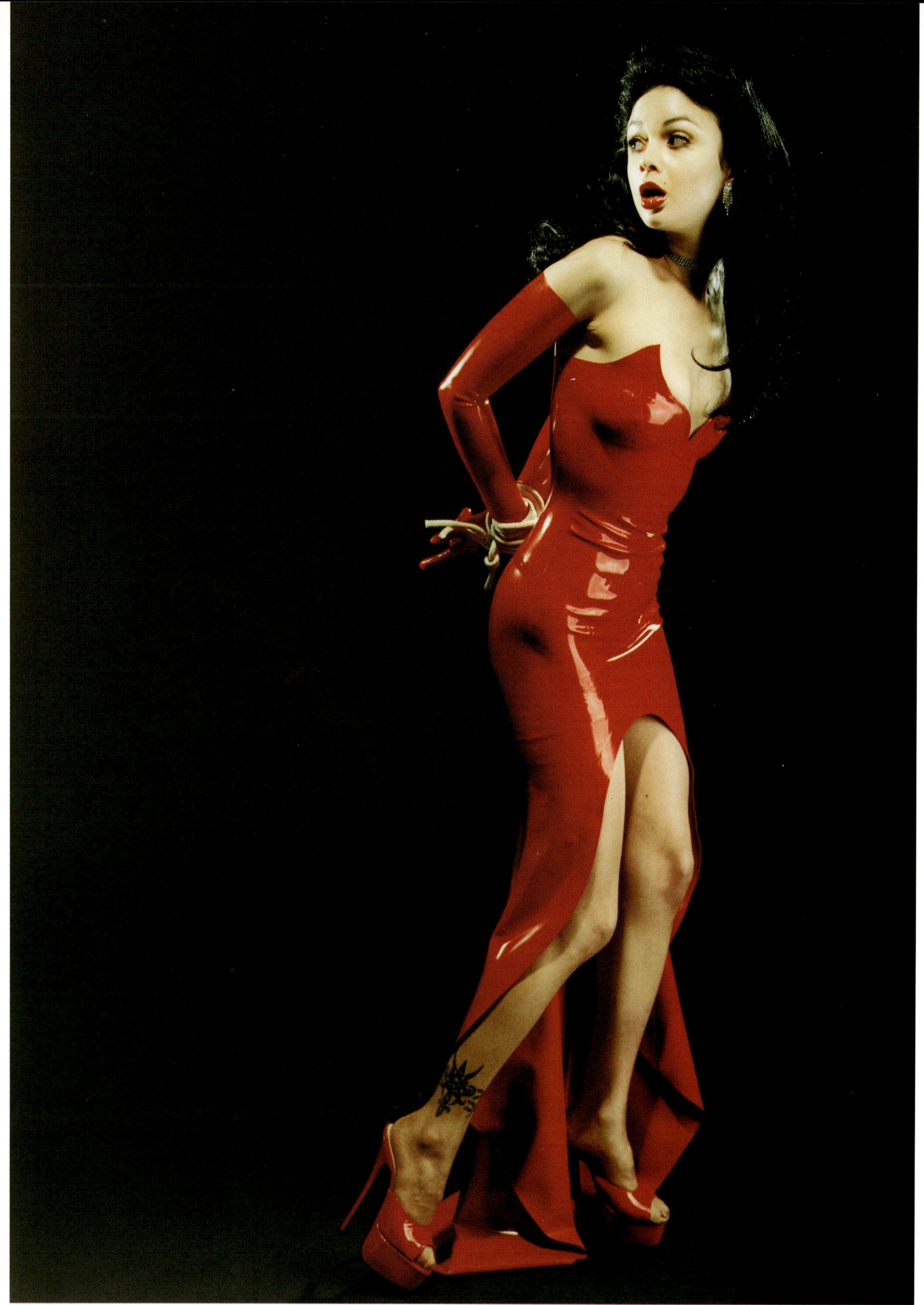

 Emma Delves-Broughton

Opposite Jim Weathers

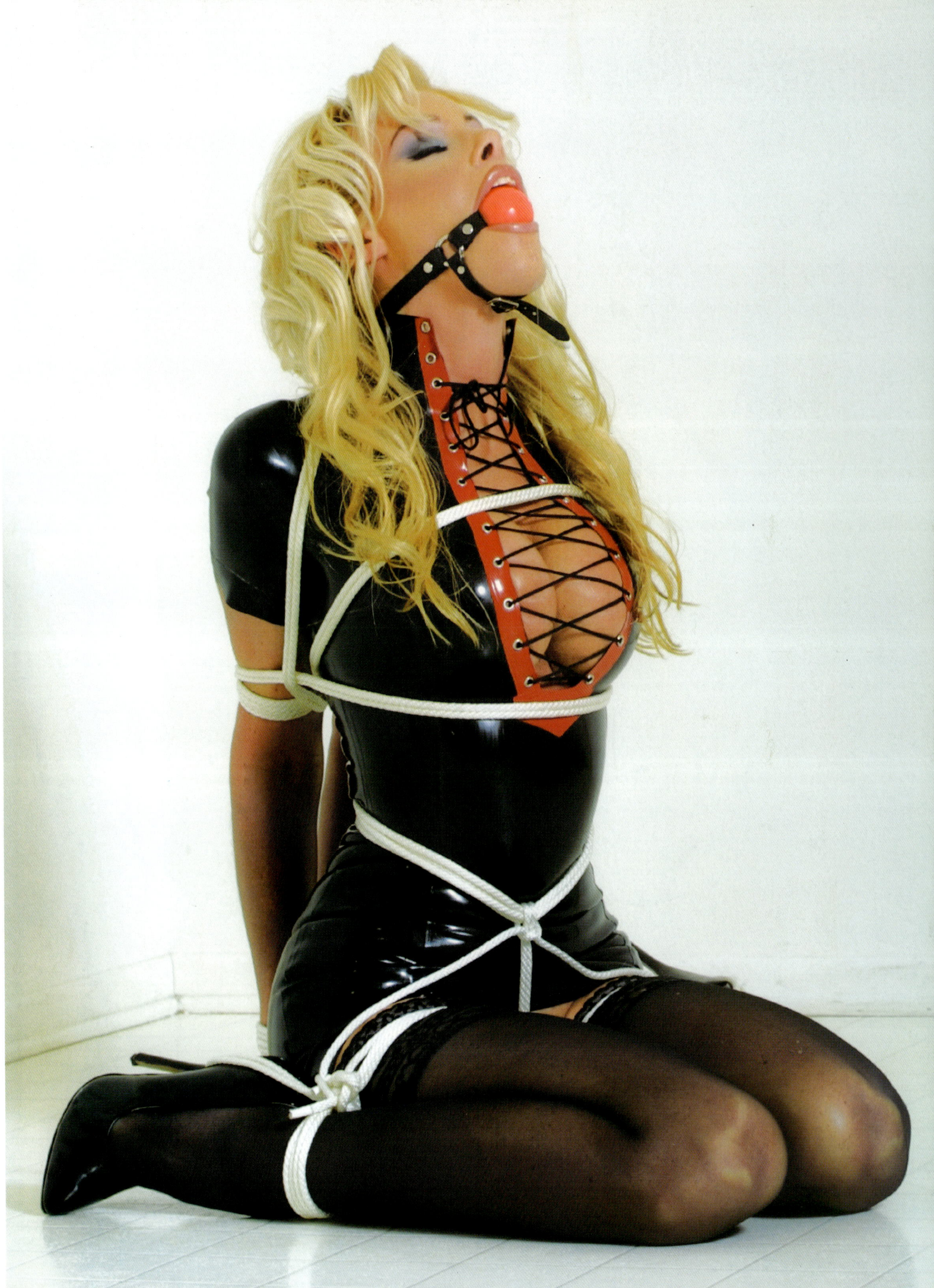

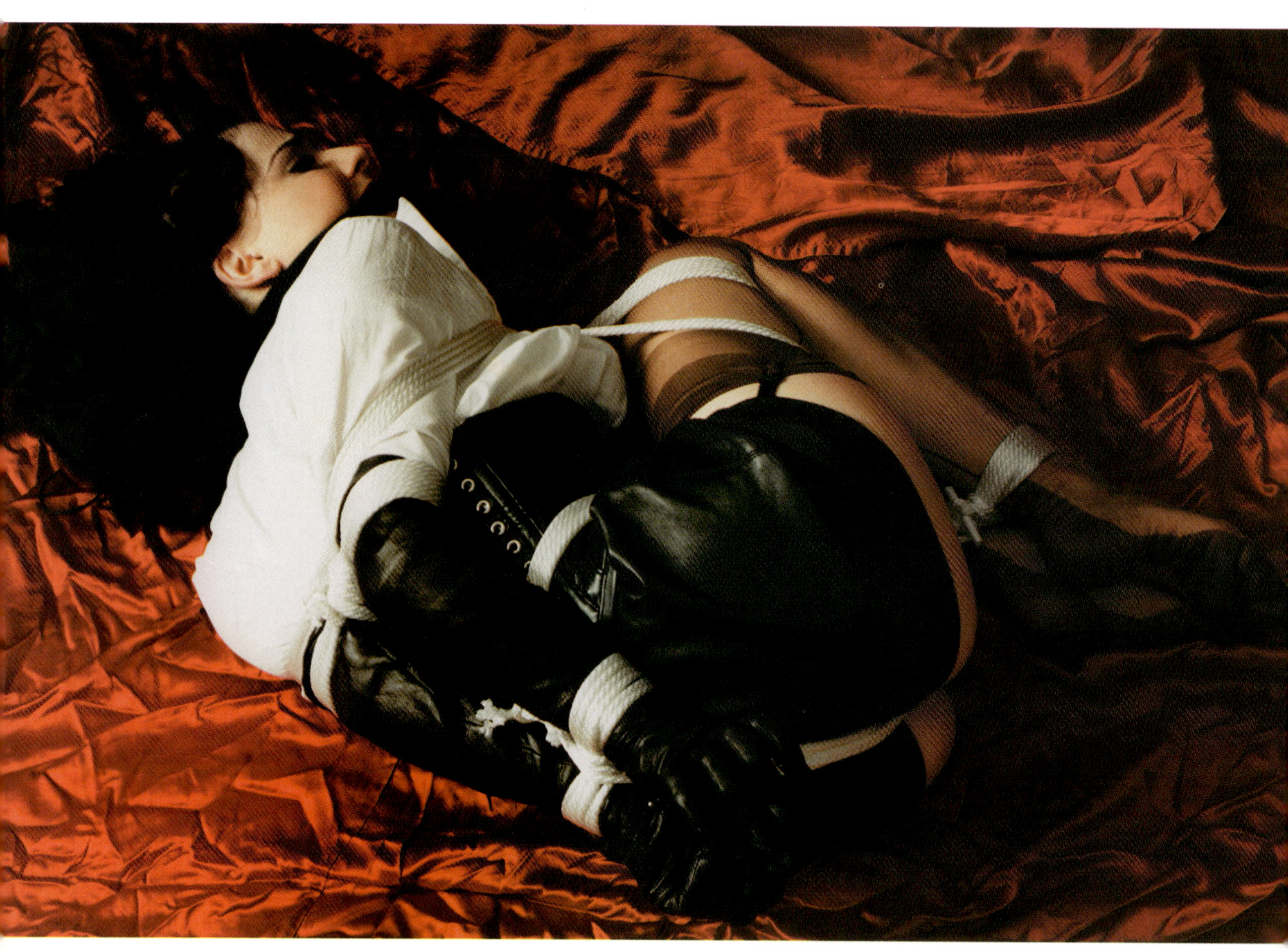

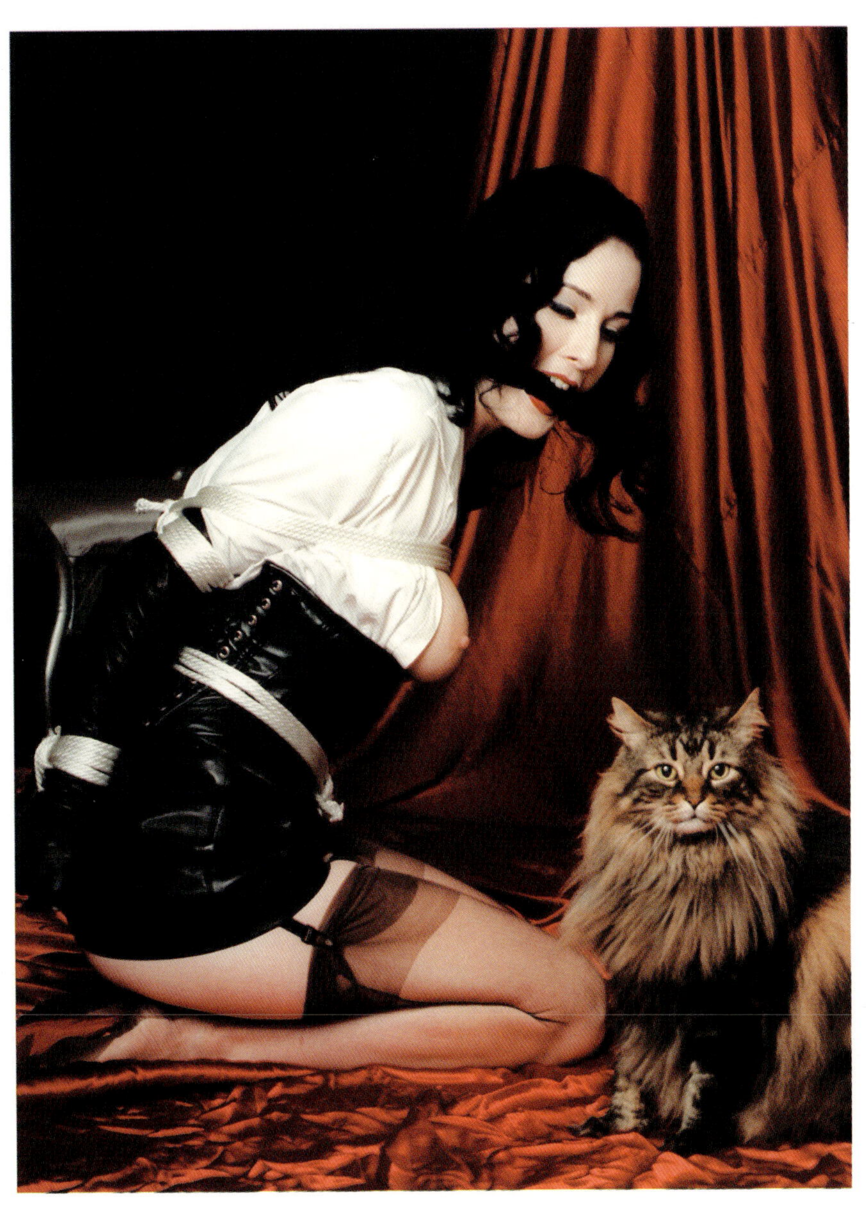

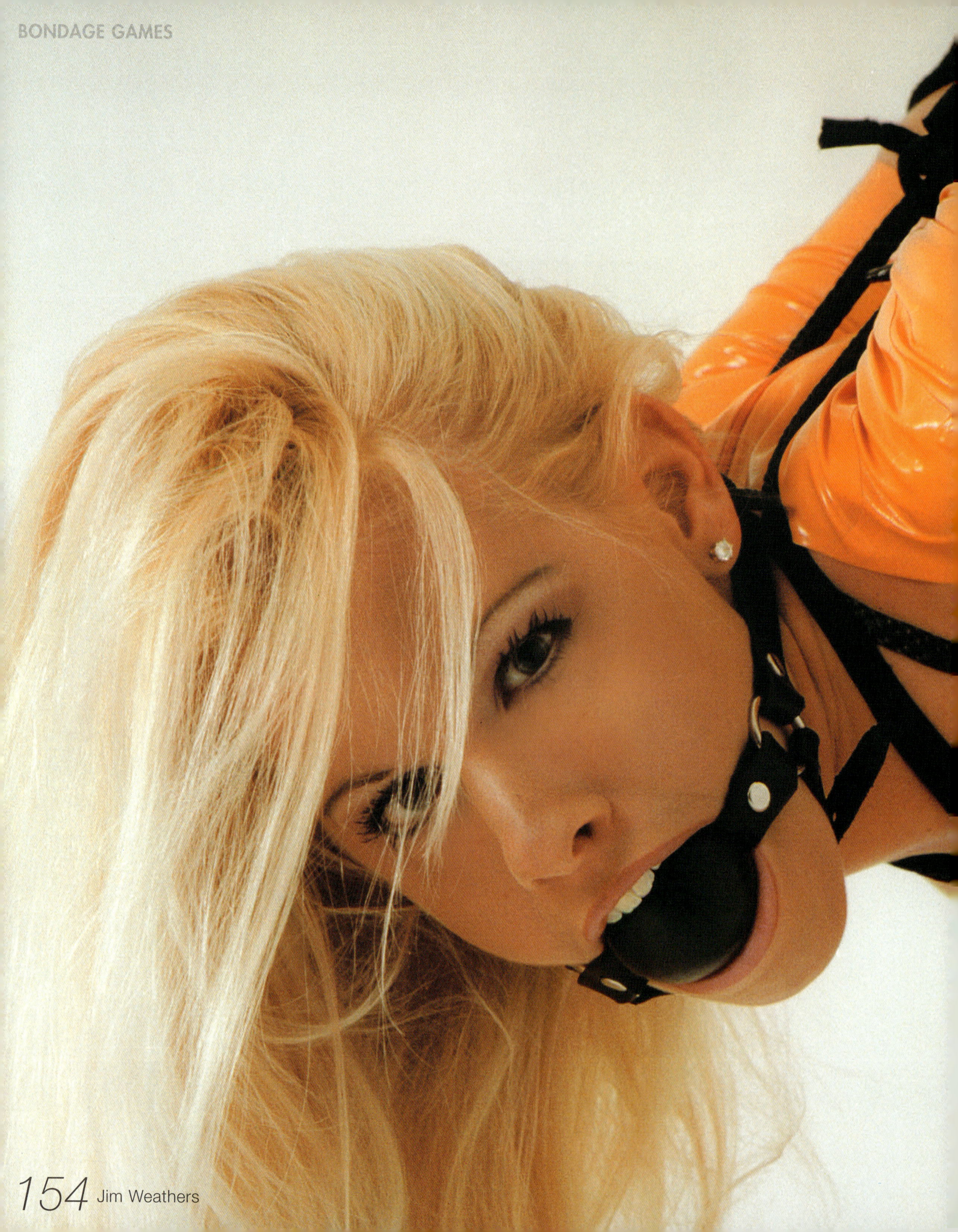

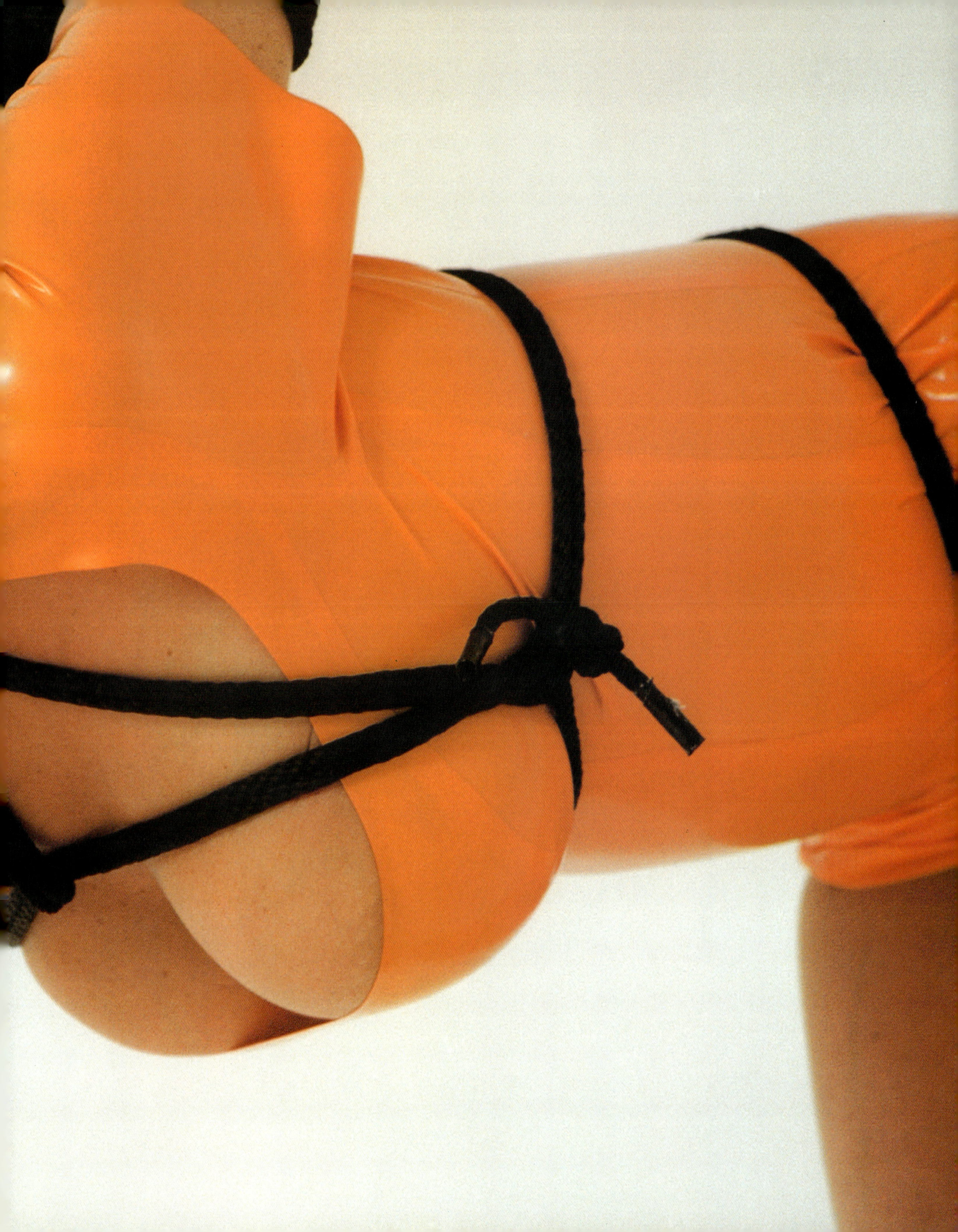

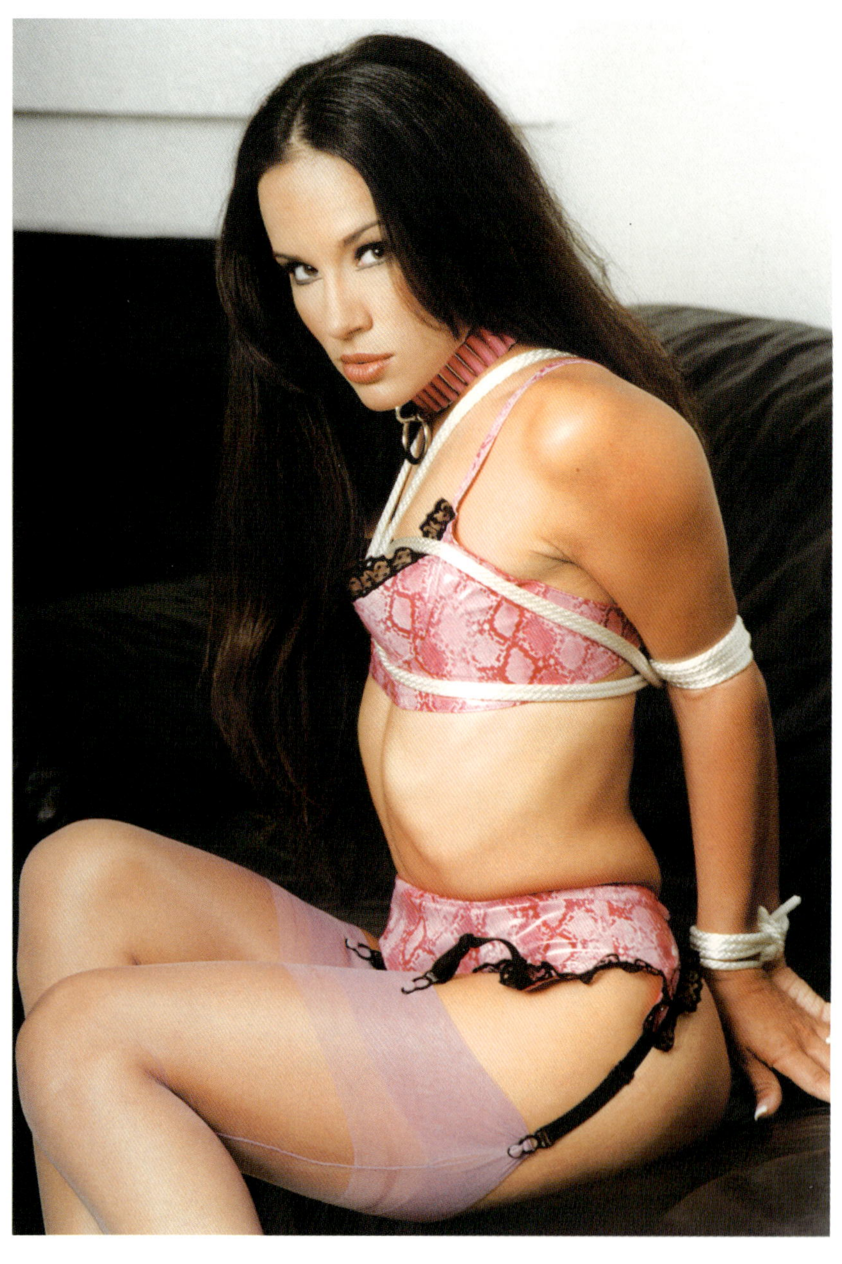

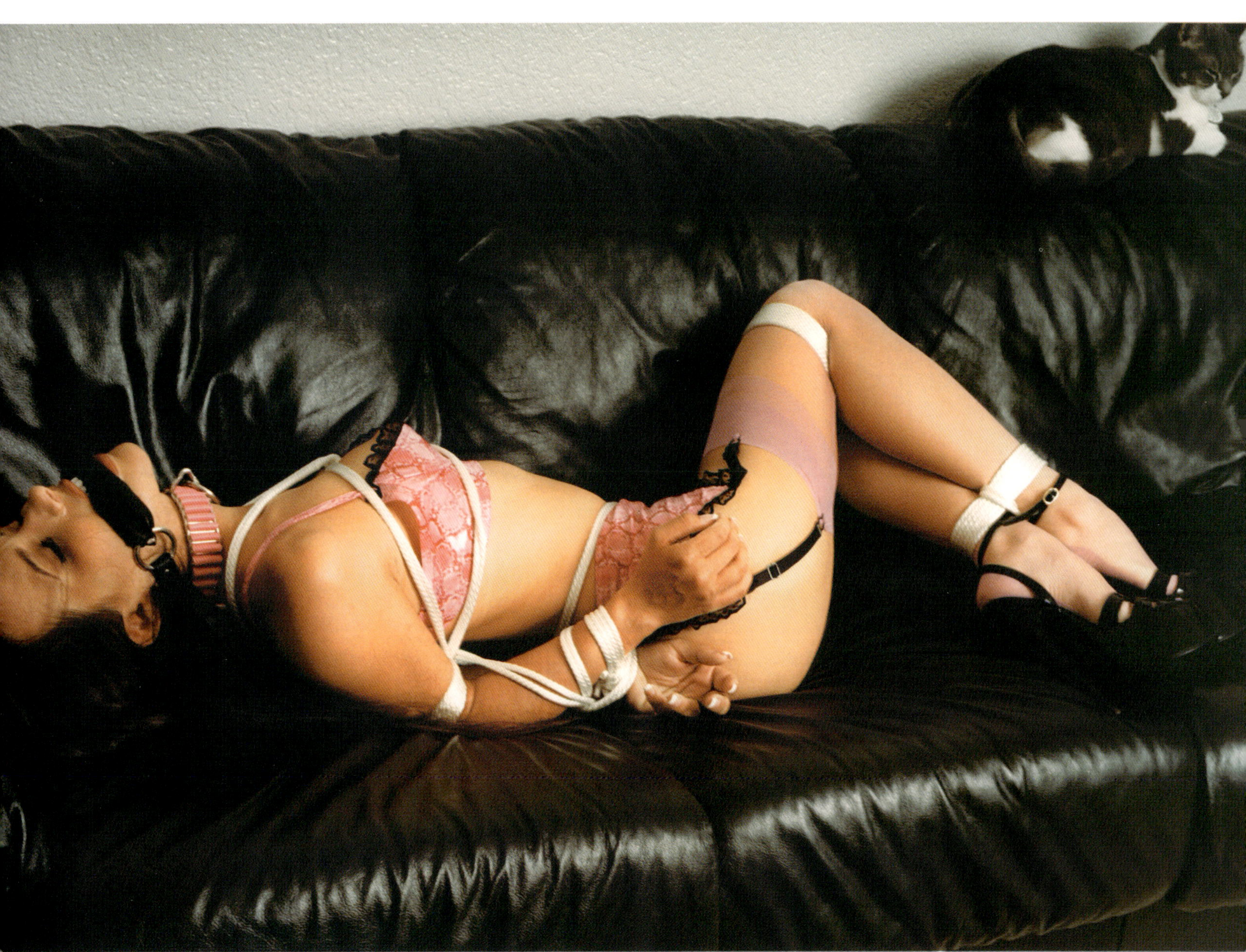

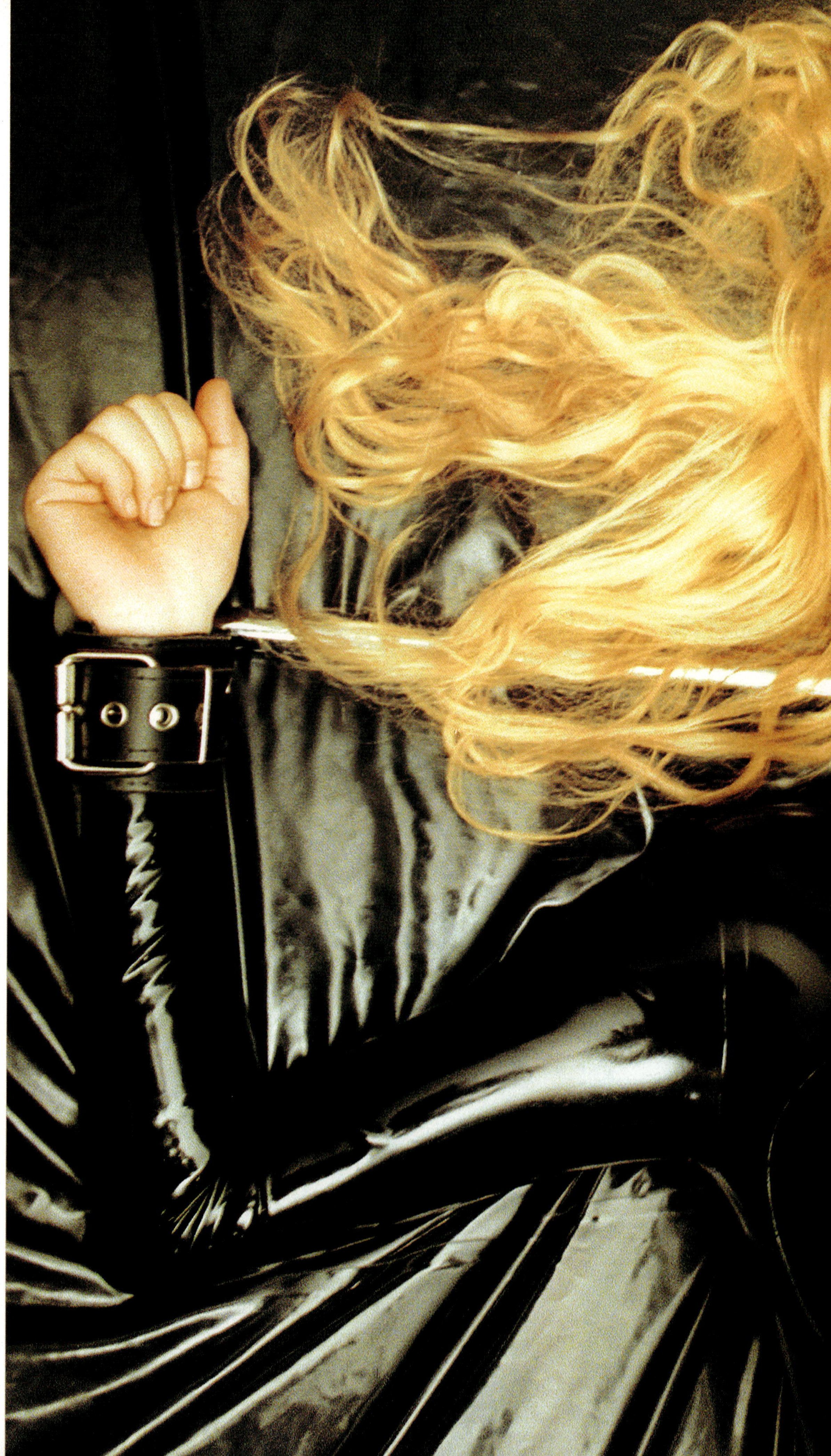

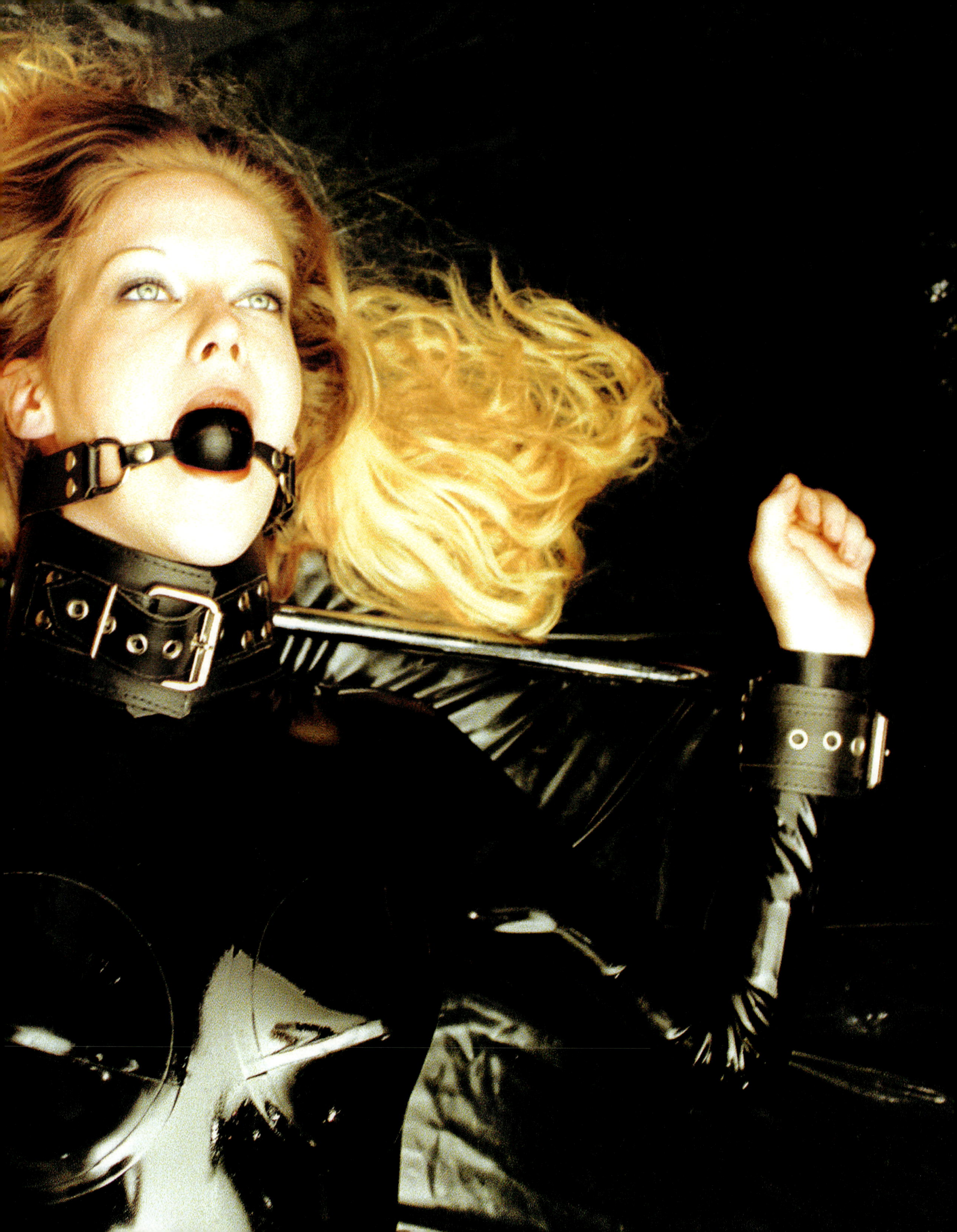

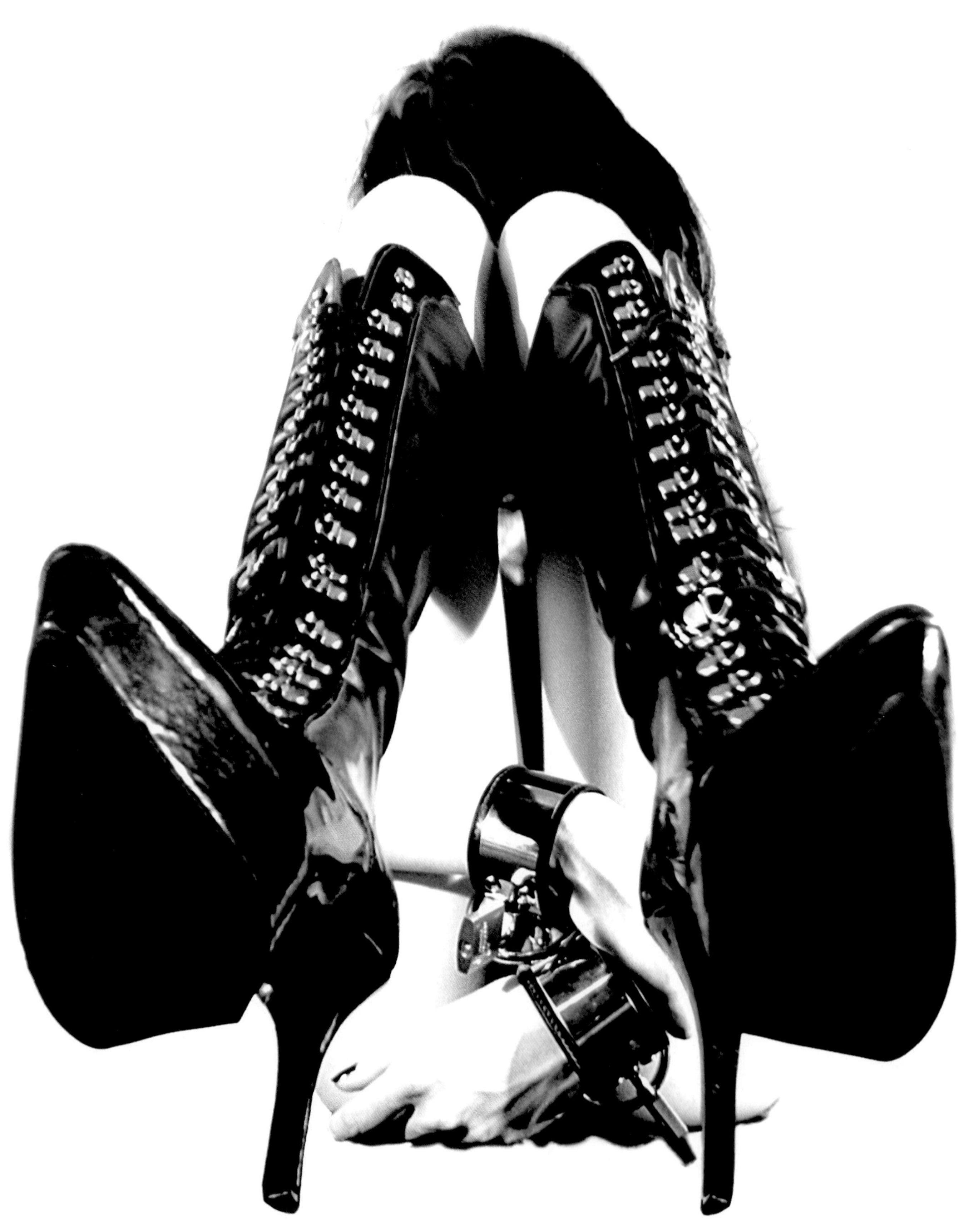



Opposite No Mercy

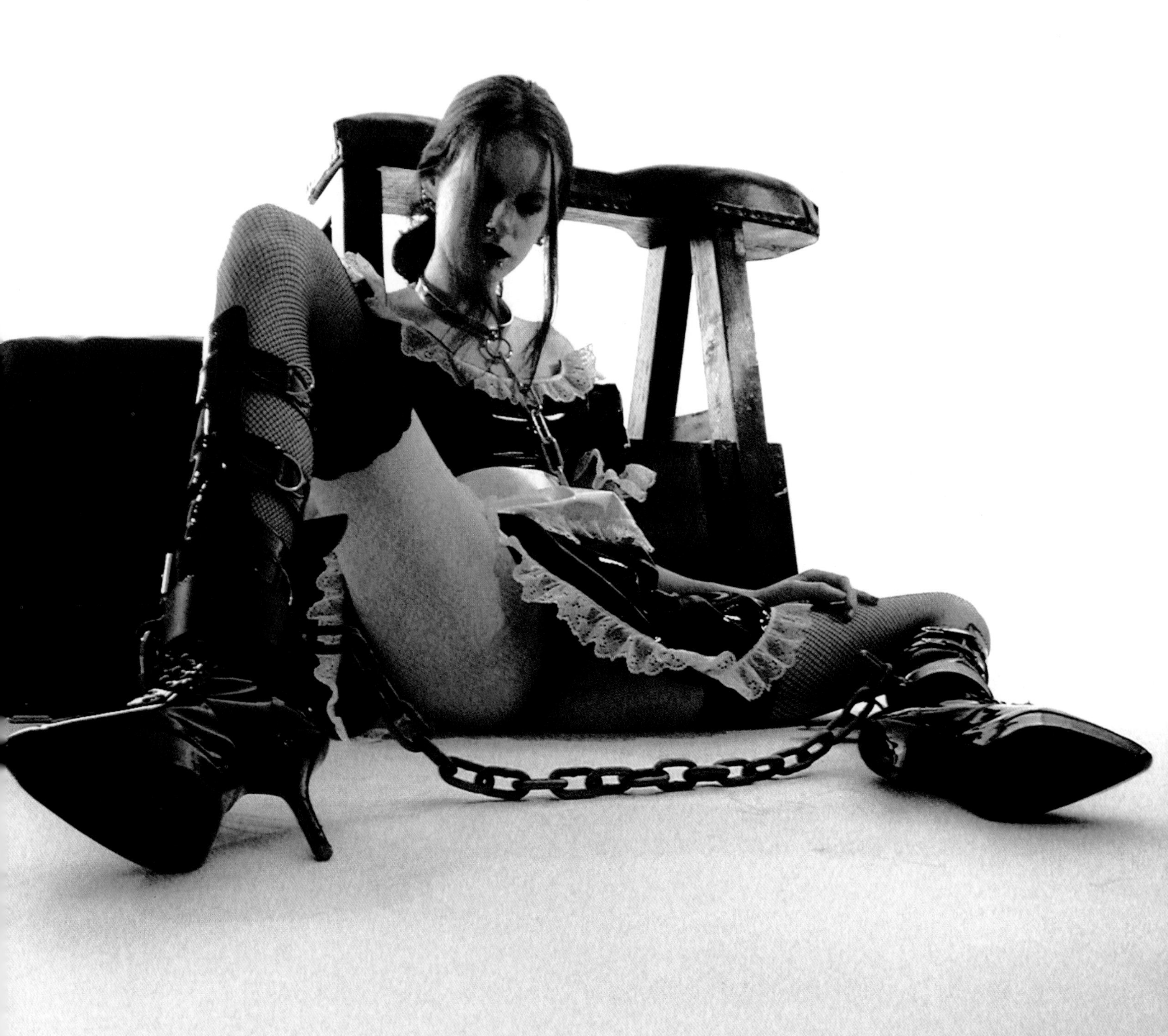

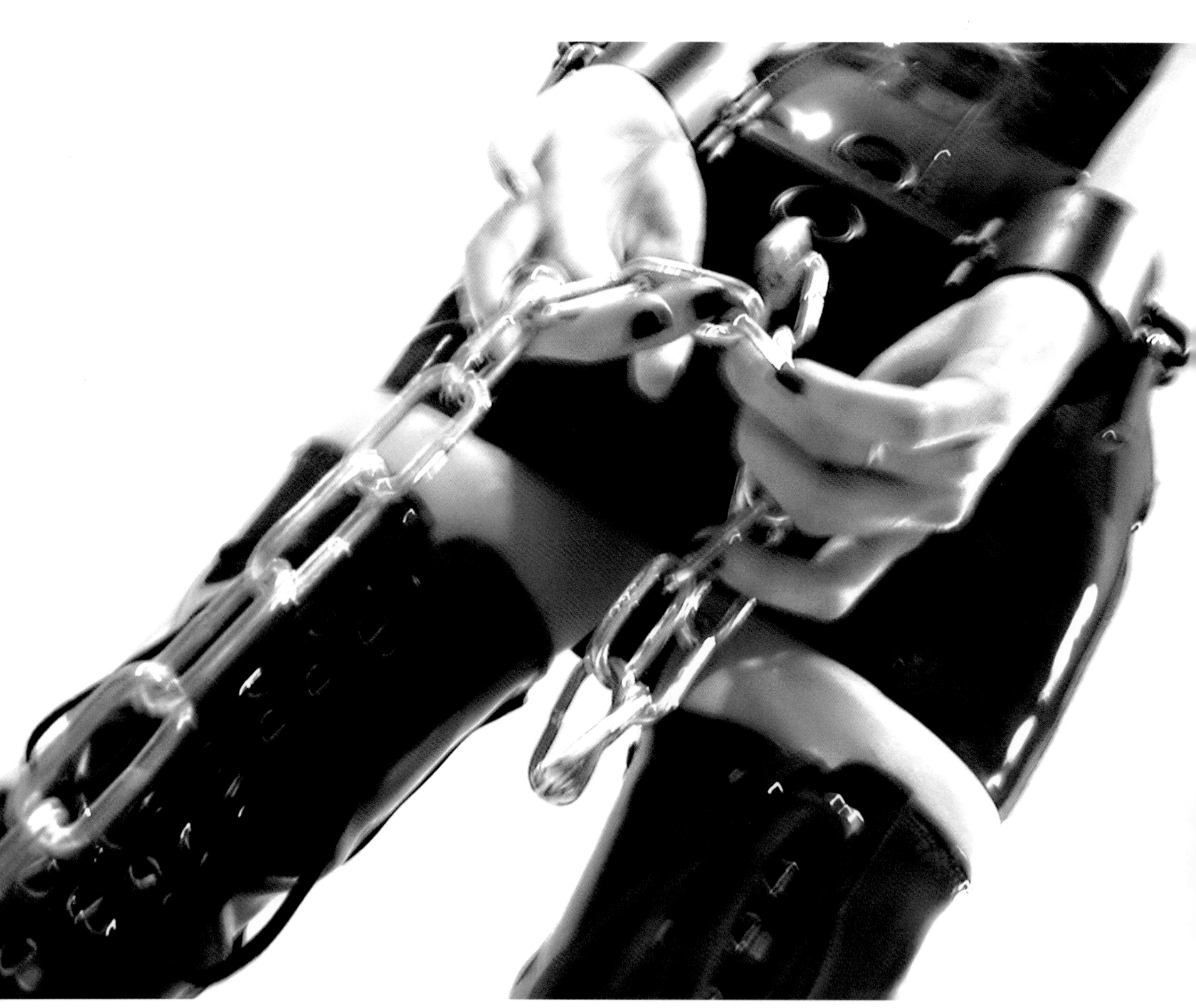

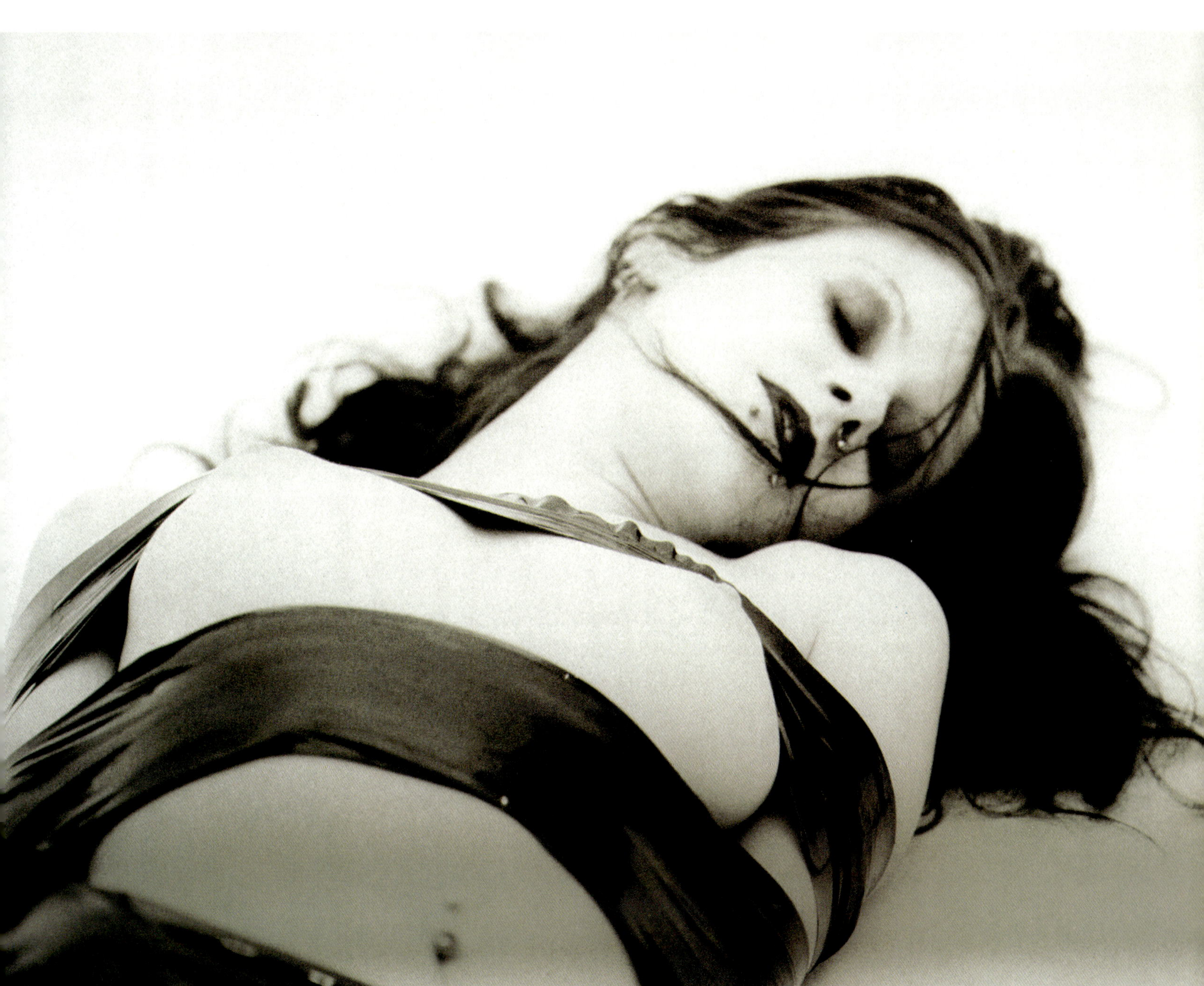

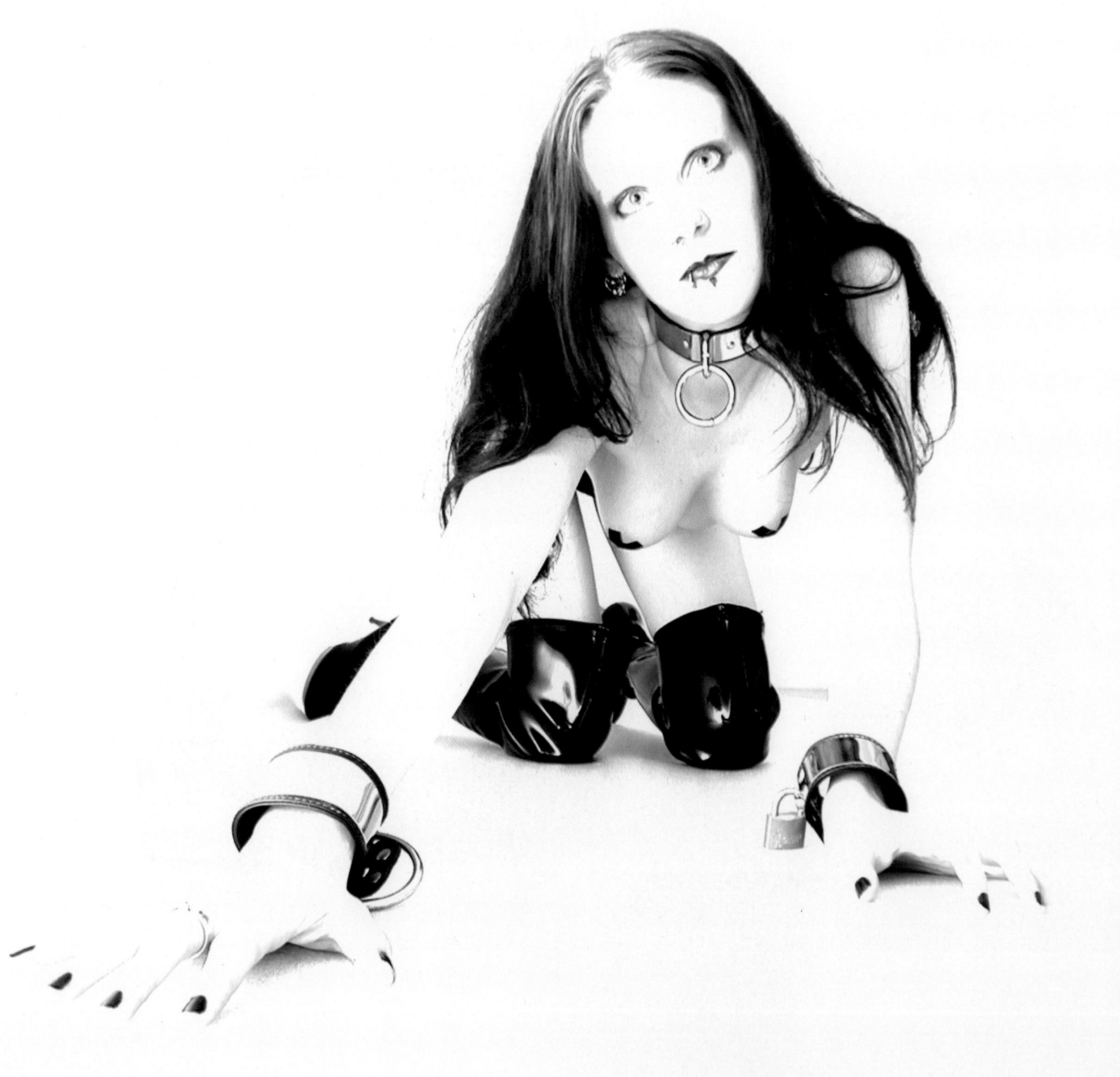

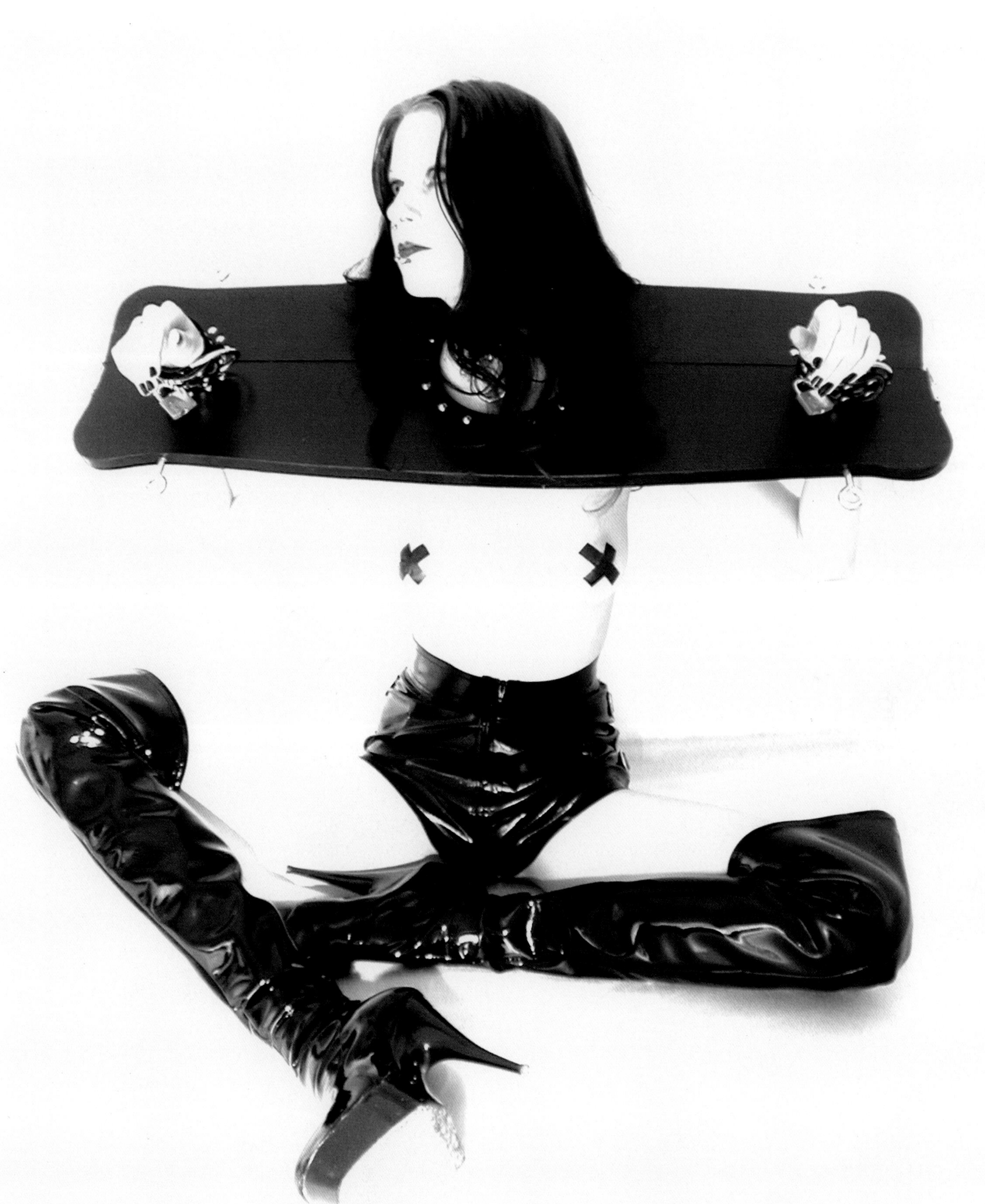

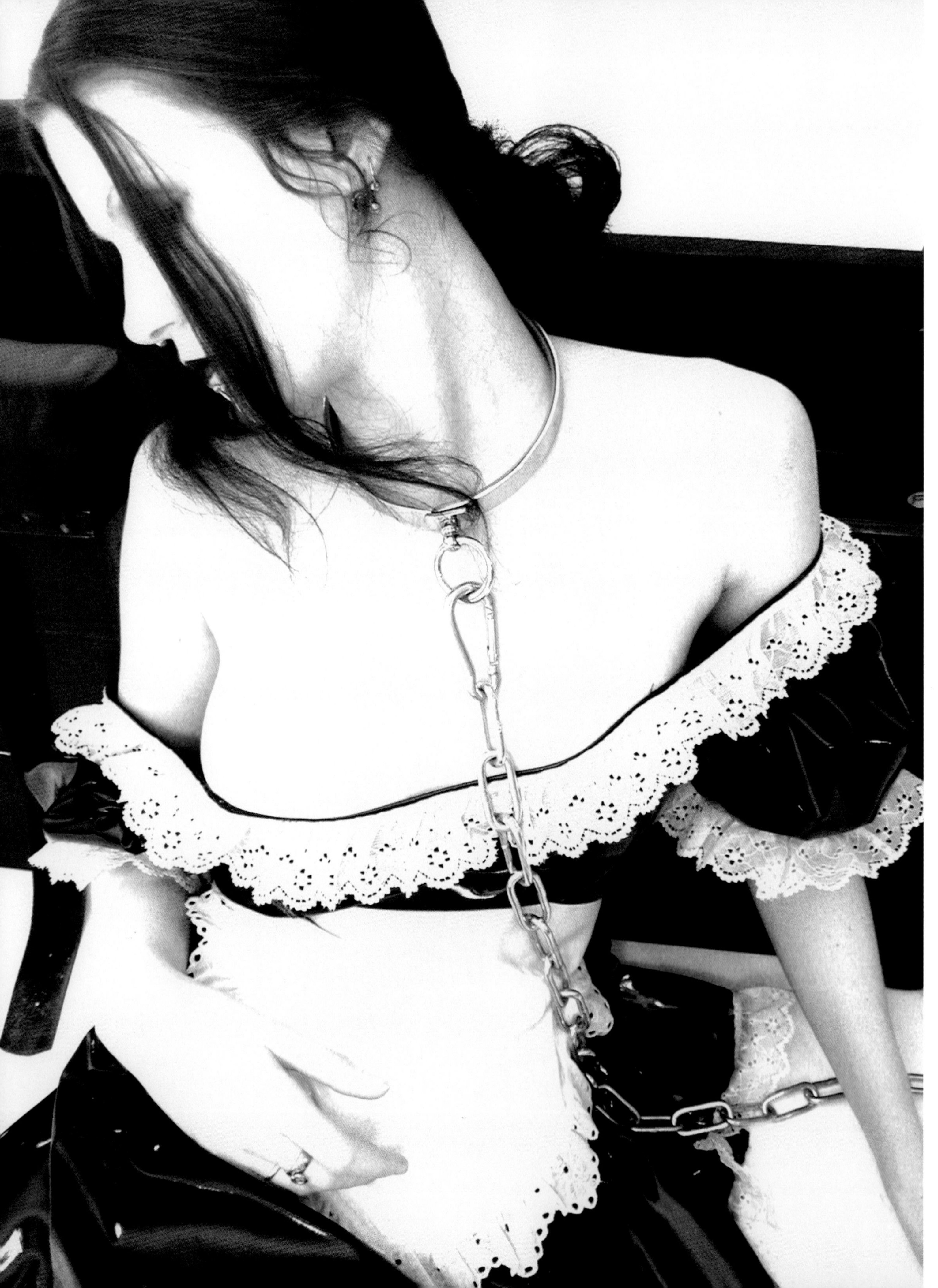

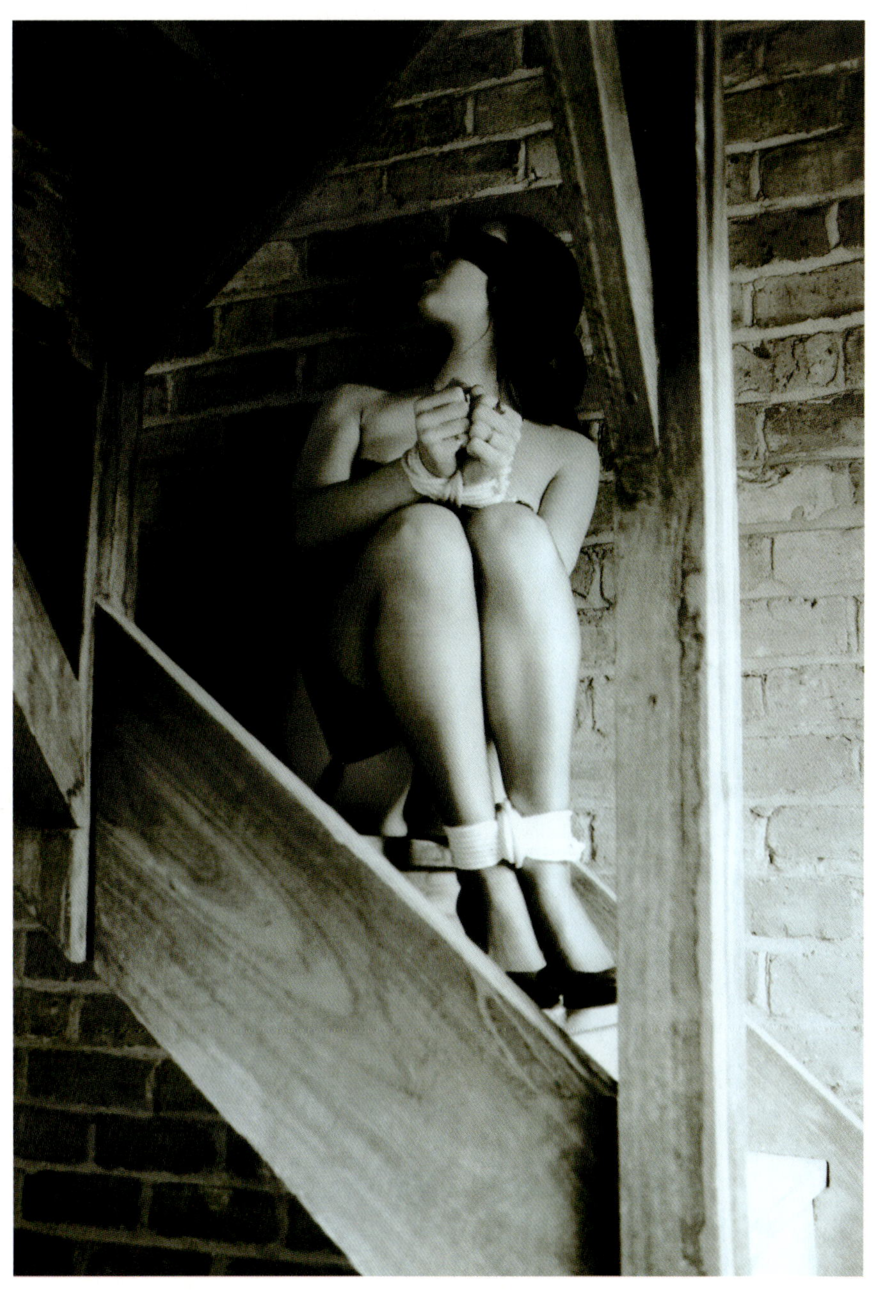

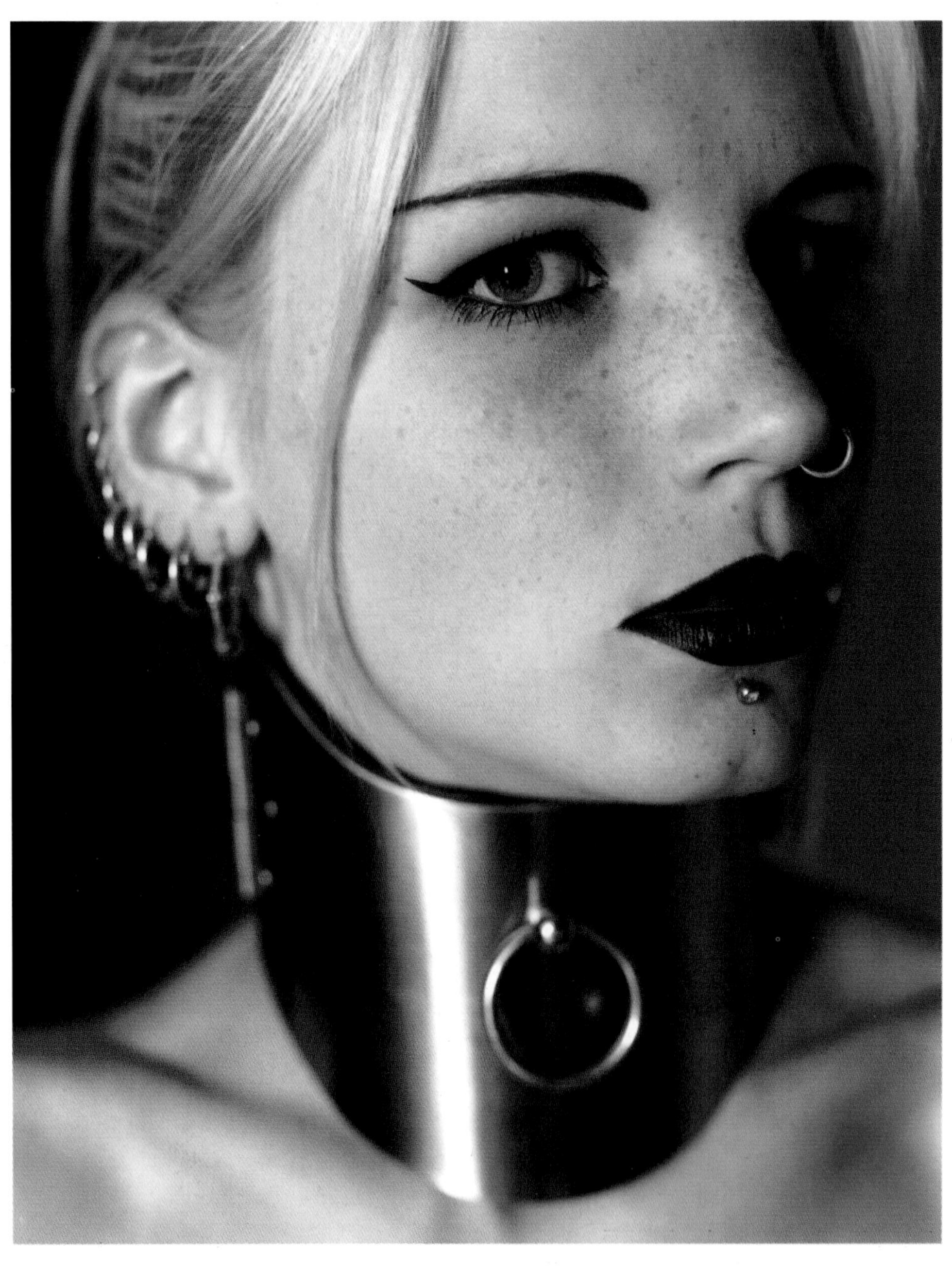

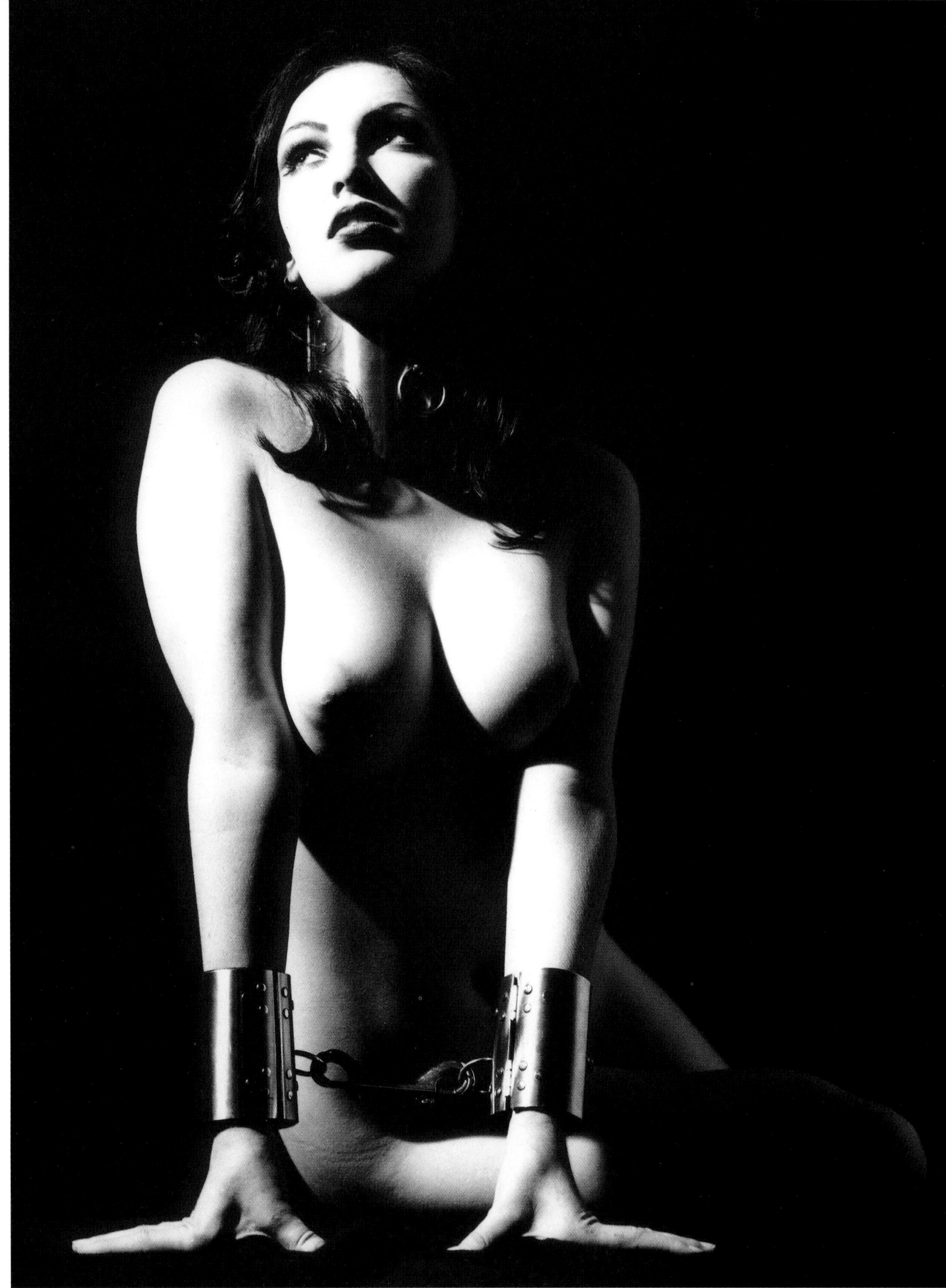

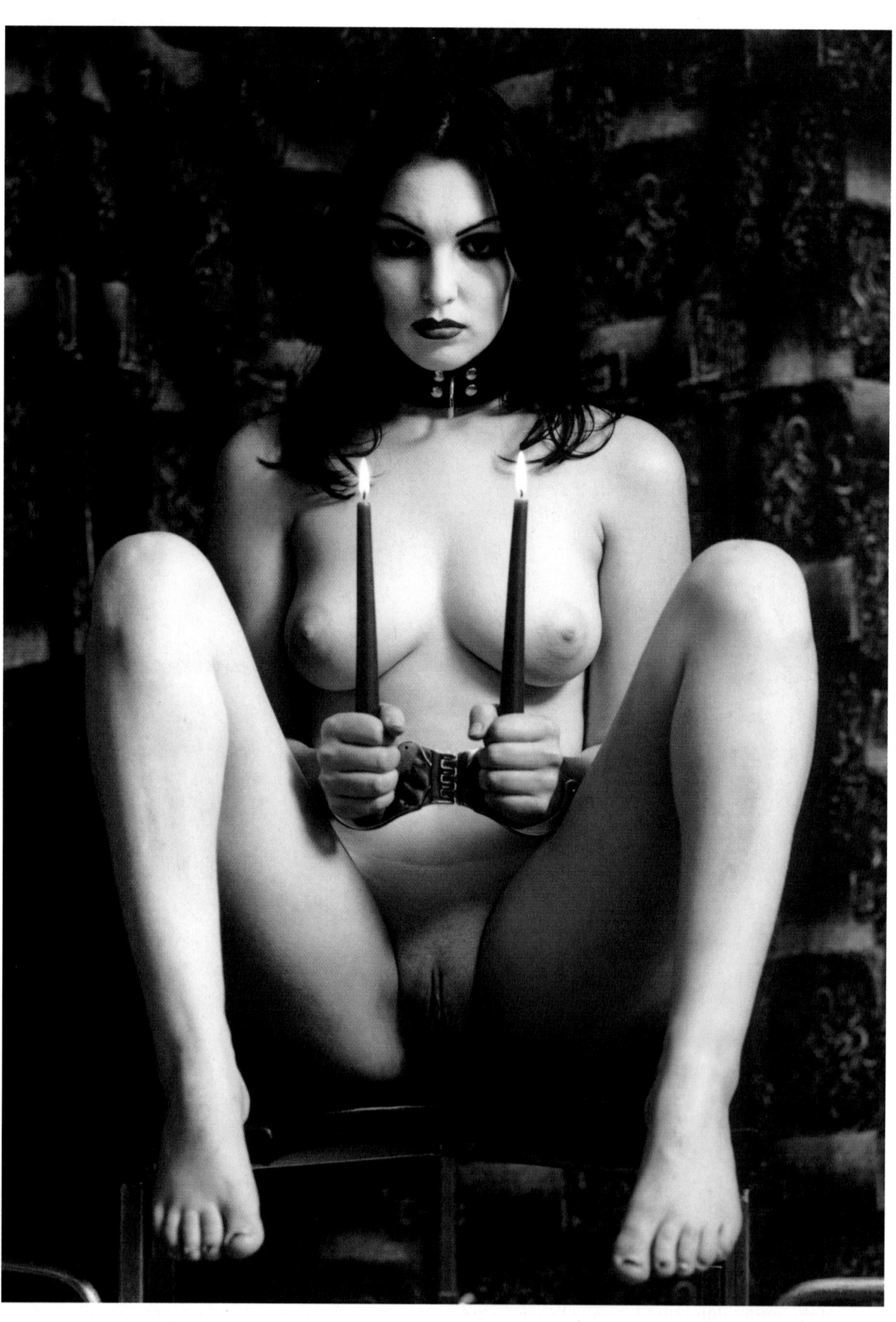



Opposite Roman Kasperski

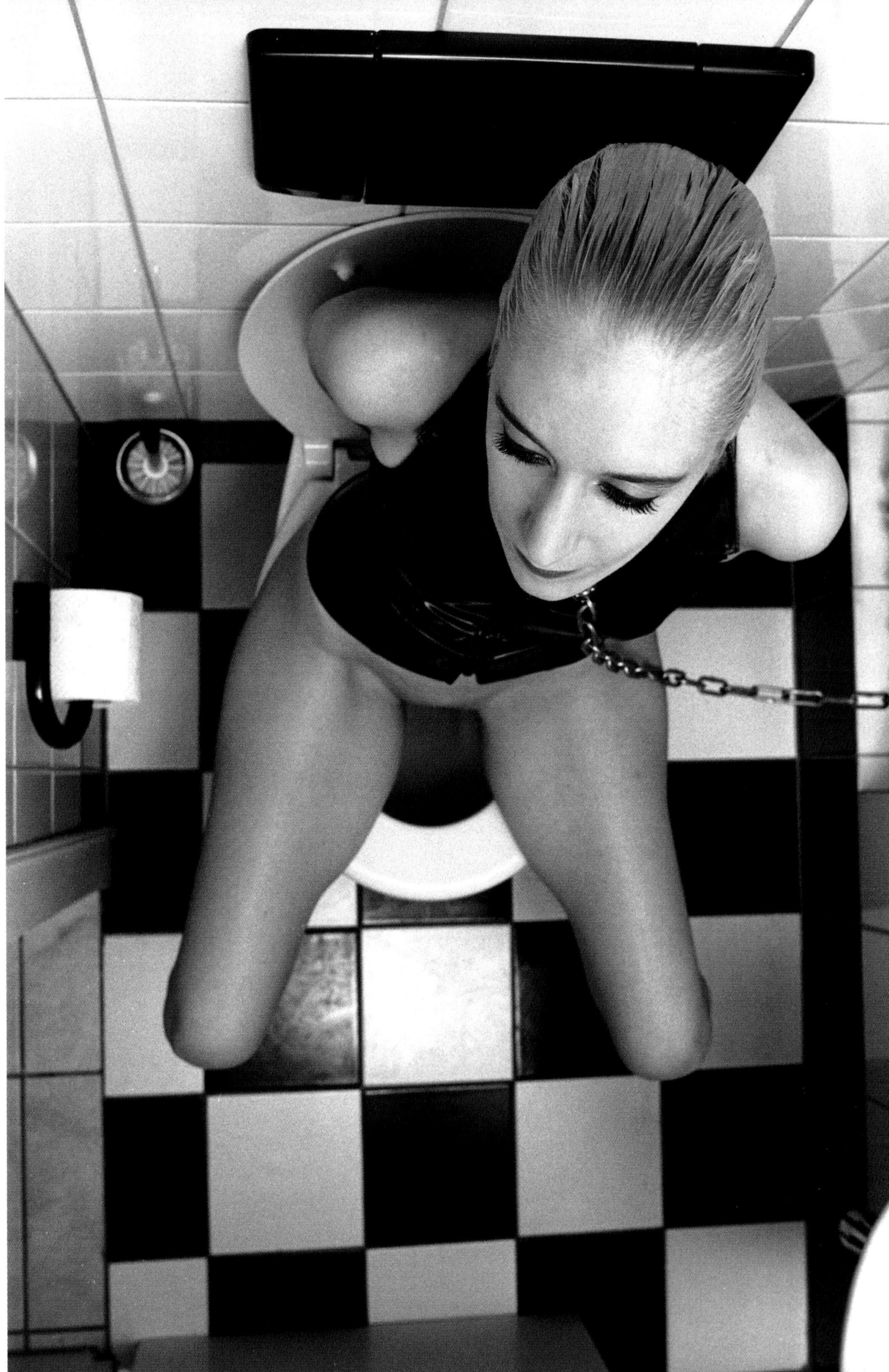

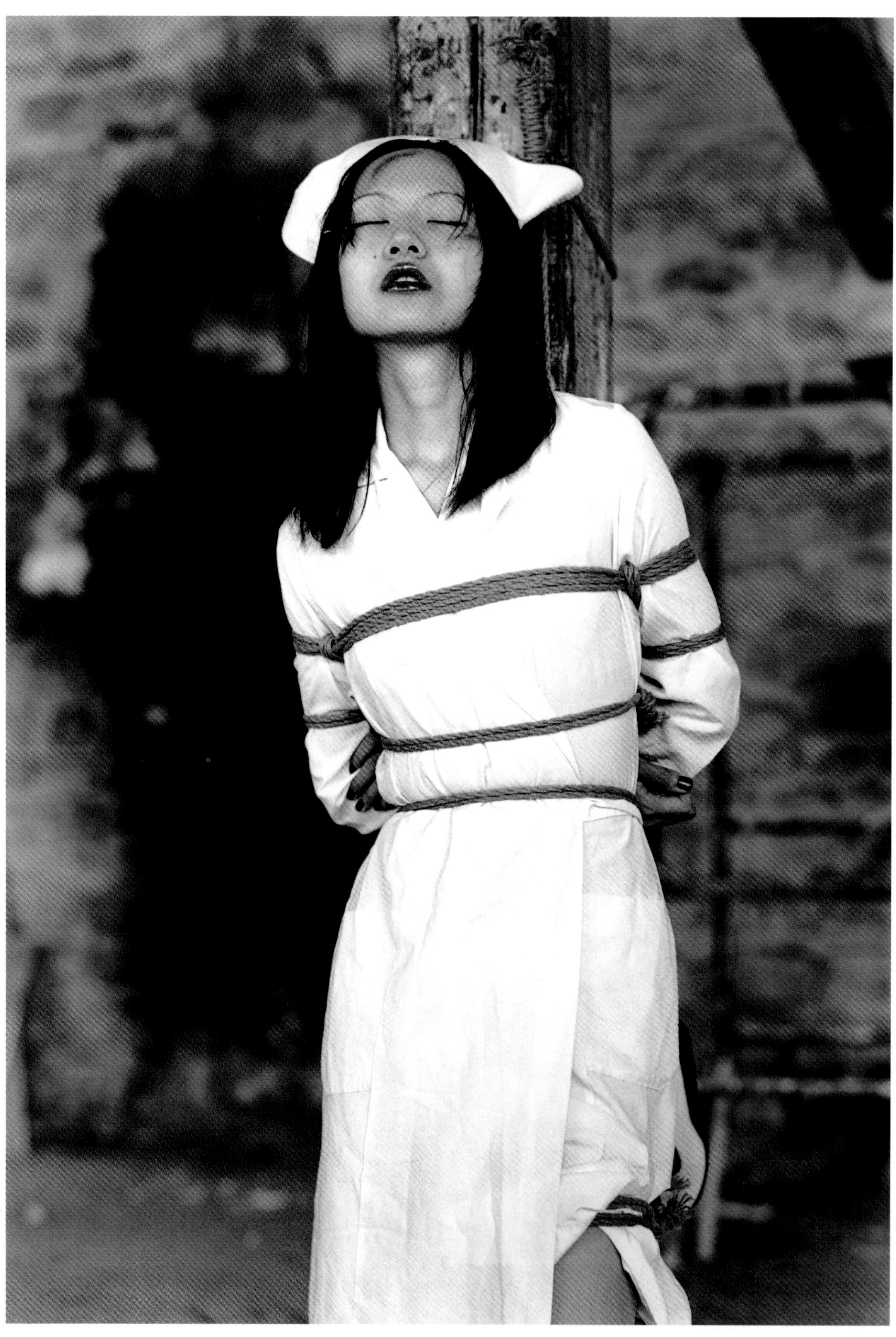

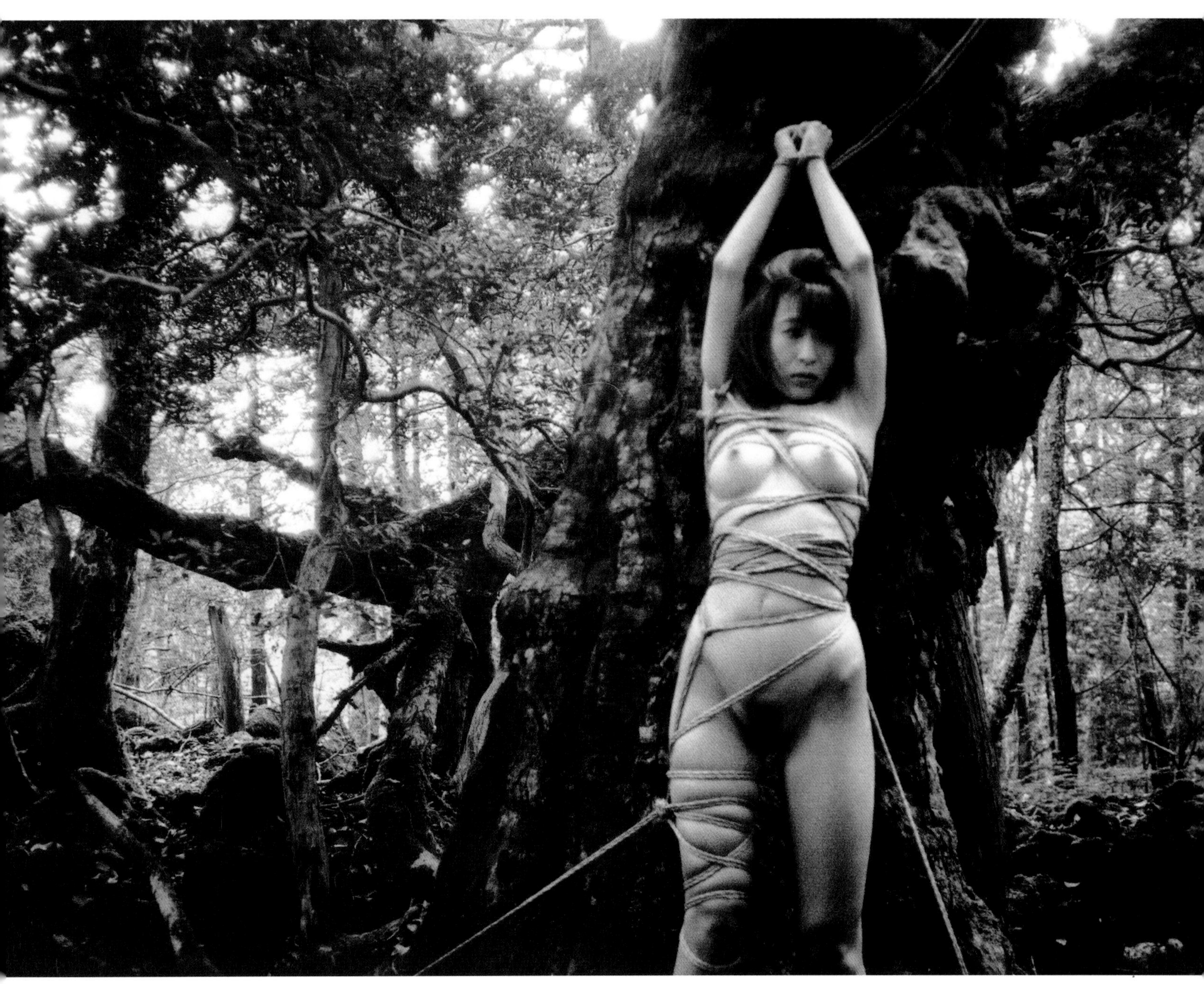

# EXTREME MEA

Unfortunately, there is no completely reliable way of defining what constitutes extreme behaviour in the pervy world. To say that one person's meat is another's poison is as true here as anywhere else, and it is a fact that in the world of fetishism and BDSM, one person's everyday kink can be another's dangerous edge-play and yet another's total turn-off. It would be unrealistic, therefore, to imagine that every reader will consider every image in this chapter "extreme". But, given what is "out there" and also what is publishable in a legitimate photography book, the hope is that at least some of the images that follow will satisfy your curiosity about what happens on the outer fringes of kinky photography.

In the realm of fetish imagery, relatively subtle alterations or additions can push an outfit beyond the "normal" into the bizarre. Familiarity today with fetish fashions in black or brightly-coloured rubber is probably the reason that transparent and semi-transparent latex, previously the main preserve of medical fetishism, is increasingly used in mainstream fetish design. However, the subversive potential of this unnervingly cutaneous material remains undiminished. Used for a multi-layered and hooded second-skin outfit such as that in Peter W. Czernich's *I C through U* (p.209), it transforms a conventional fetish pin-up pose into something altogether more intriguing and disturbing.

Hoods are one of the simplest and most effective ways of introducing a discomforting visual aspect to any fetish outfit. Replacing the human face with the psuedo-face of a hood can distort, disguise, exaggerate or obscure not only the wearer's identity but also the way they communicate with the outside world. So it should be no surprise that fetish photographers enjoy exploiting this potential. Hoods can be used to create total anonymity, as with Steve Diet Goedde's *Zentai Girl* (p.197) or reduce a whole face to just cartoon features as with Alexander Horn's *Masked Greta* (p.200). Moulded "lifelike" hoods such as that sported in Horn's *Mirrored Rubberdoll* (p.201) introduce yet another twist, transforming wearers into mannequin-like versions of themselves.

In the world of extreme rubber fetishism, however, this is just the beginning. Occlusion enthusiasts revel in the pleasures of gasmasks, enjoying them as an extension of traditional mackintosh fetishism (*Fetish Eyes*, pp.186 and 187), with modern fetish fashion (Rubber Brain's *Nun with Cross*, *Rubber Cyborg* and *Melt Down* pp.214–216), or just on their own (Tony Ward's *Oxygen*, p.217). And rubber's air-tight properties are exploited in all manner of strange inflatable designs – yin and yang inflatable hoods (John Fitzgerald, p.190), inflatable suits (Whiplash!, p.194) … even an inflatable "apple" capable of accommodating its own rubber-suited, hooded and masked human "worm" (Whiplash! p.196).

Such designs as these clearly overlap into the world of bondage fantasy, but they are by no means the only way photographers push bondage imagery past traditional notions of "romantic restraint". Beyond the stylised posing of the bondage pin-up lies the altogether scarier world of the SM dungeon – a place

# SURES

where, so fantasy has it, the restraint is unforgiving, the humiliation unending and the punishment unrelenting. In the imagery of this world, the vanities of fetish glamour are often stripped away to expose the raw dynamics of SM.

Nevertheless, photographers find many different ways of portraying this most intimate and personal side of the fetish psyche. With *Simone Kross & Slave* (p.176), Dave Naz offers us the torture chamber scene at its most minimalist and anonymous, with dominatrix, victim and room all stripped of anything not absolutely essential to the action. China Hamilton's *Metal Hell* (p.179) allows for more props, suggesting that a room can become an inescapable prison by adding a sturdy iron cage. But the same photographer's *Within My Chains* (p.180) and *Soft Entity* (p.181) tend to confirm that, for a really authentic dungeon atmosphere, nothing beats a bare brick wall, stone floor and naked flesh fettered by cold steel.

Like Naz and Hamilton, Lee Higgs produces some of his most striking photography in dungeon locations. Higgs distorts both perspective and colour to add a layer of acid-tinged surrealism to his images, and his particular fascination with distorting the human face finds him exploring such devices as tight rope bondage (p.191) and a steel dental gag (p.203) to create some truly unusual pervy portraiture. By contrast, John Fitzgerald creates dungeon scenes (p.192) that combine glamour and high fetish style with fiendish hi-tech "predicament bondage". But the most extensively equipped dungeons can still occasionally provide comic relief. Gary & Pierre Silva, who do many of their shoots in West Coast domination establishments, can find room for a little humour in the most exacting situations. Even that dreaded dungeon device, the rack, can provide us with a smile, as the duo show in *Torture Table* (p.189).

Some of the most provocative imagery of fetishism and BDSM results from photographers working outside the familiar territory of the genre. Transgender artist Del LaGrace Volcano's image of Ariane (p.184) as a girdle-and-stocking-clad, crop-brandishing magician complete with white rabbit is a good example. What throws the spanner into the works is Ariane's drag-king moustache: one element too many, perhaps, for the brain to assimilate unquestioningly. Like Volcano, Romain Slocombe specialises in an area that few other photographers touch upon. In Slocombe's case it is a very specific kind of medical fetishism: he is fascinated by Japanese girls dressed as nurses and/or wearing bandages, plaster casts or other types of hospital restraint. His pictures of "bandage bondage" on pp.212 and 213 are striking examples of a unique contribution to the imagery of the bizarre.

Perhaps it is fitting though that the last thought on the subject goes to Trevor Watson, whose pictures on pp.222 and 223 close this chapter. Given that no two pervs agree on what is "extreme", it may come as no surprise that the photographer himself had not considered that either of these images might fit that description. Presumably, then, *chez* Watson, this kind of thing goes on every day.

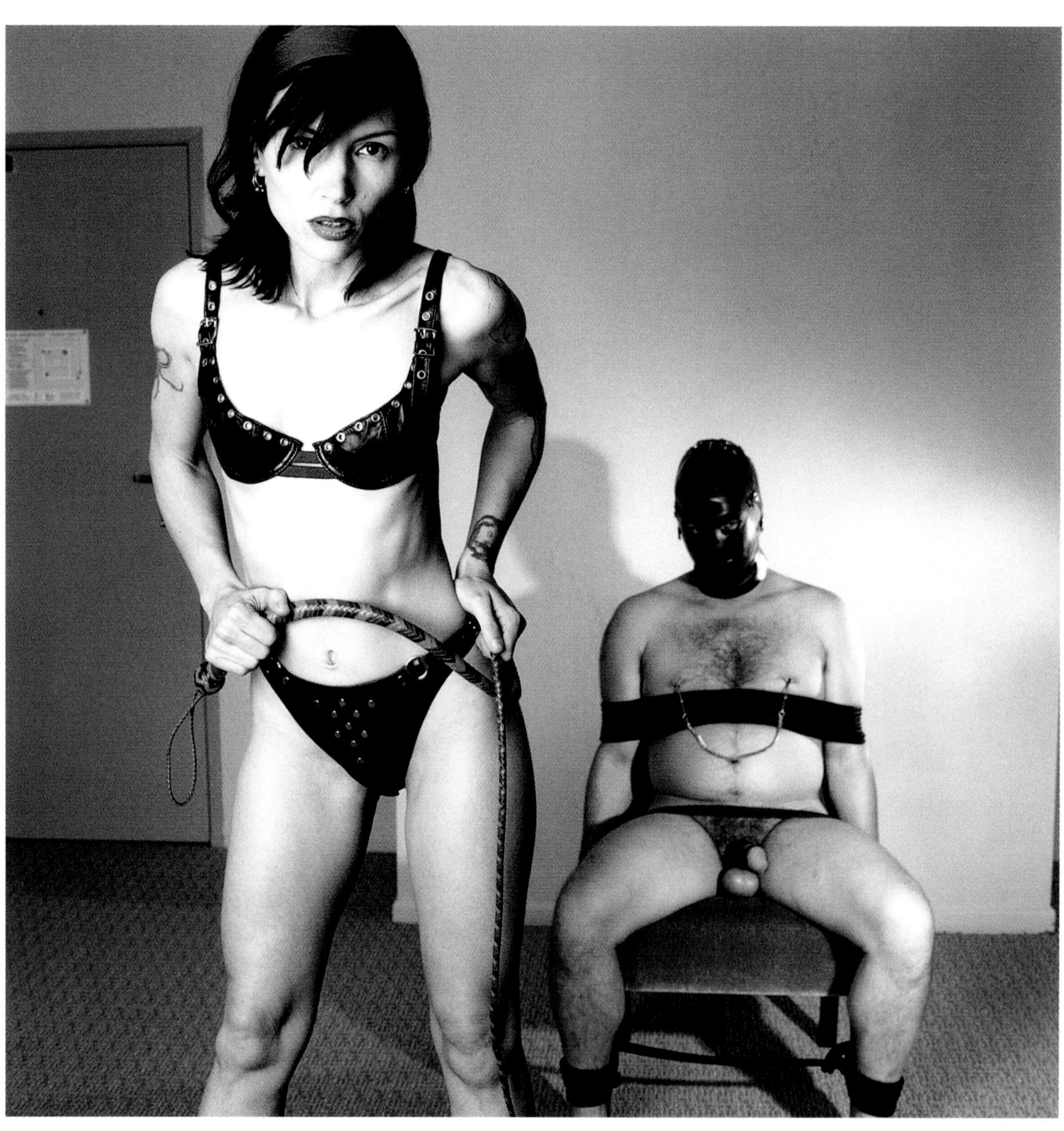

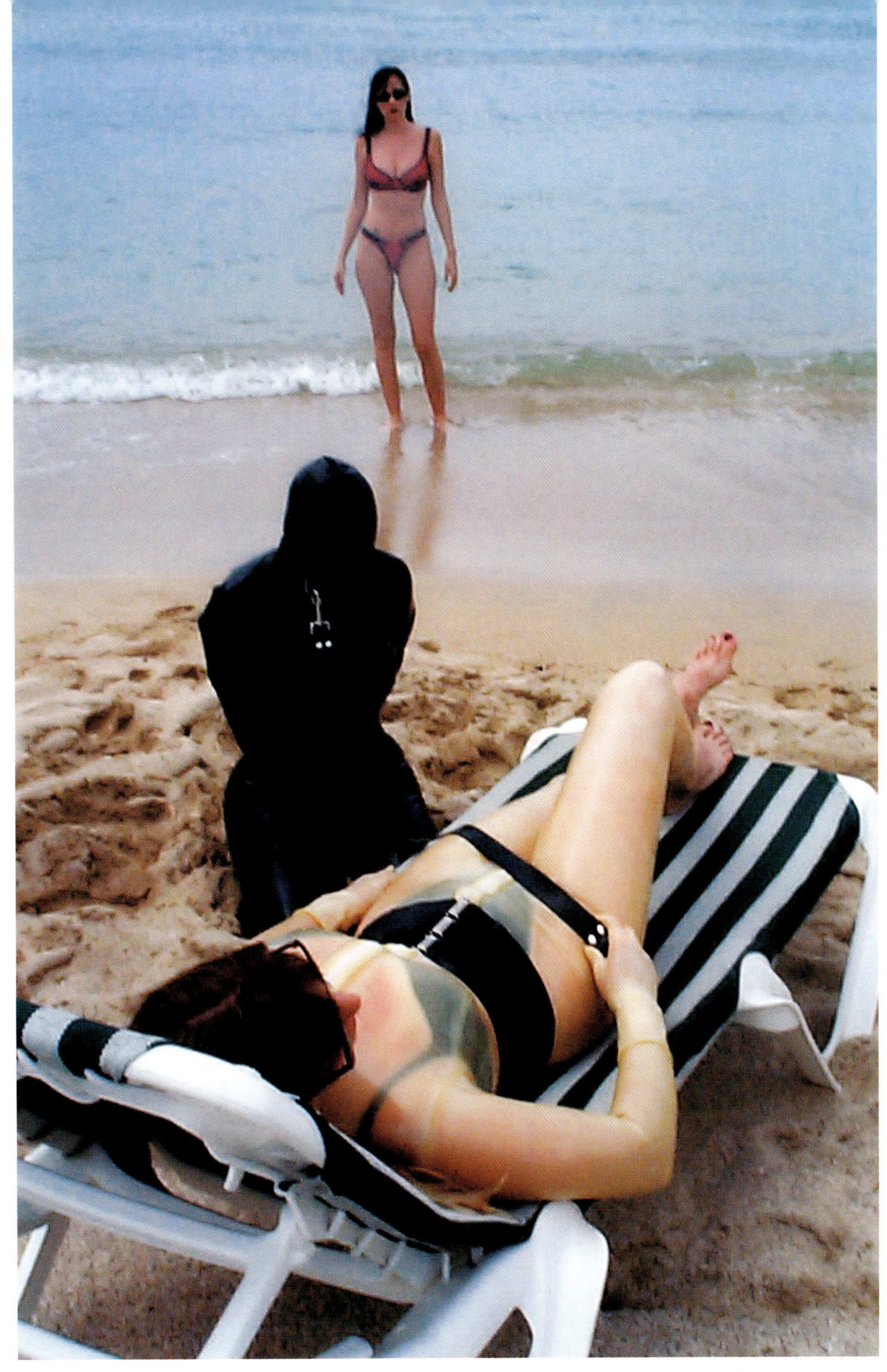

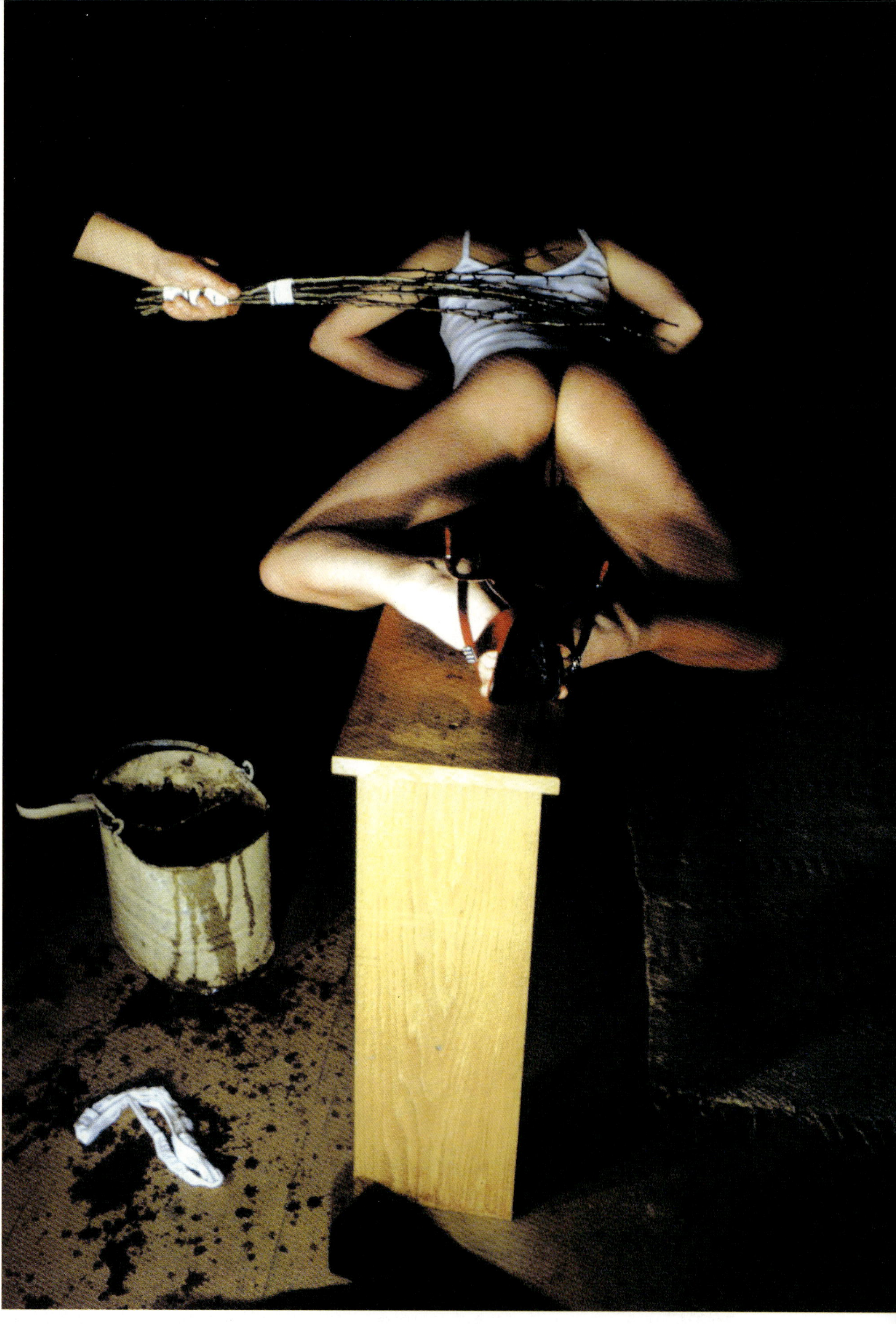

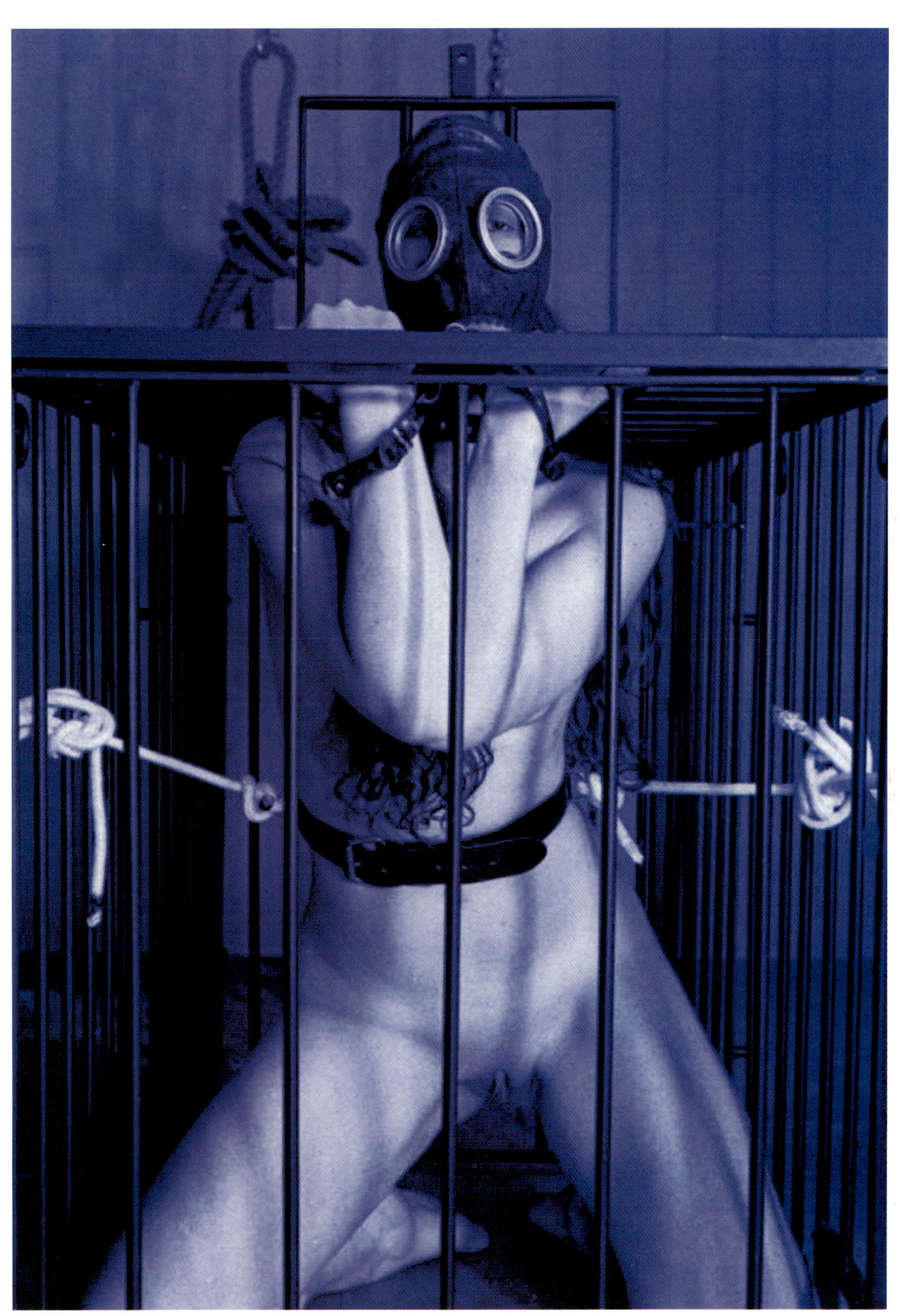

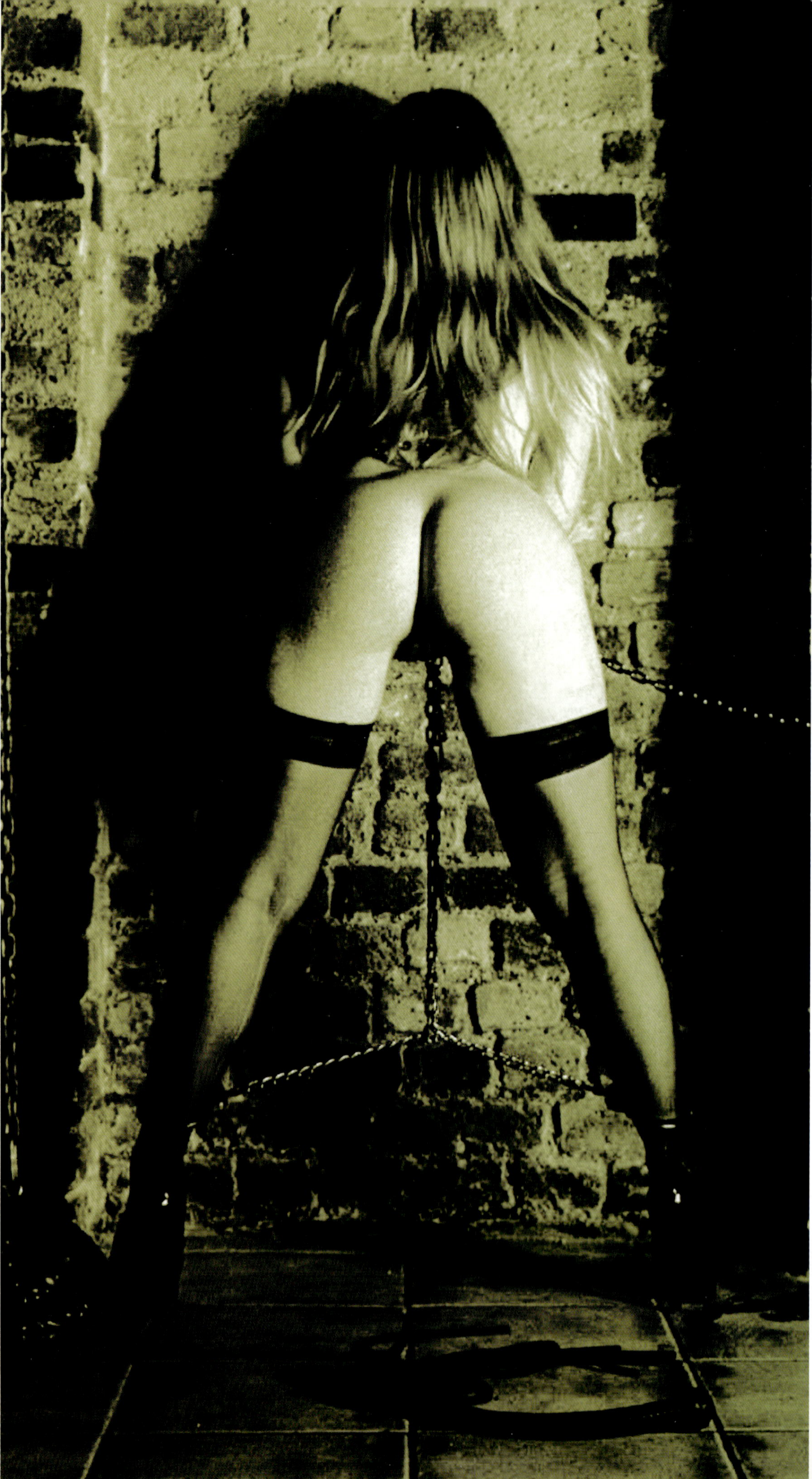

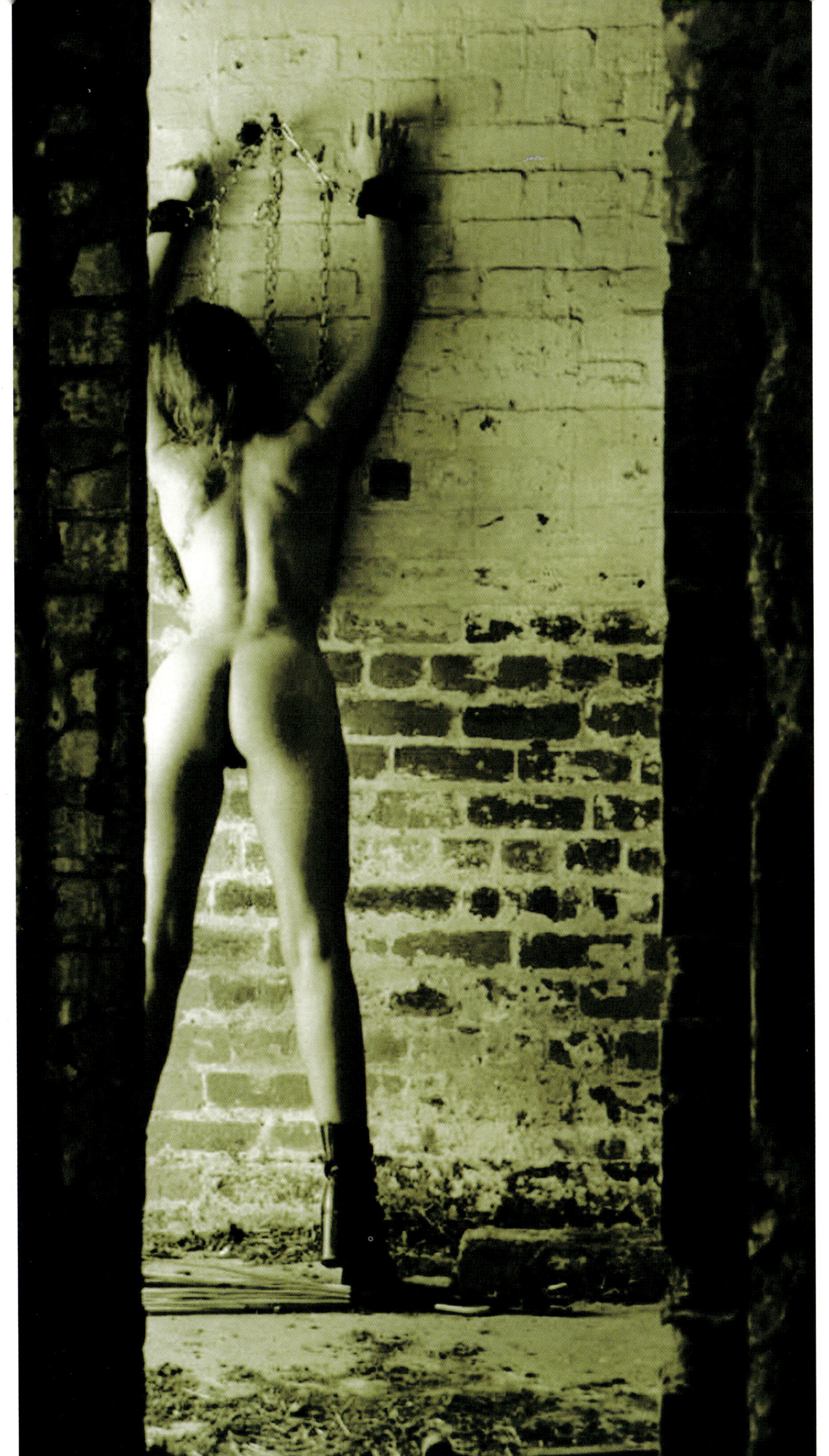

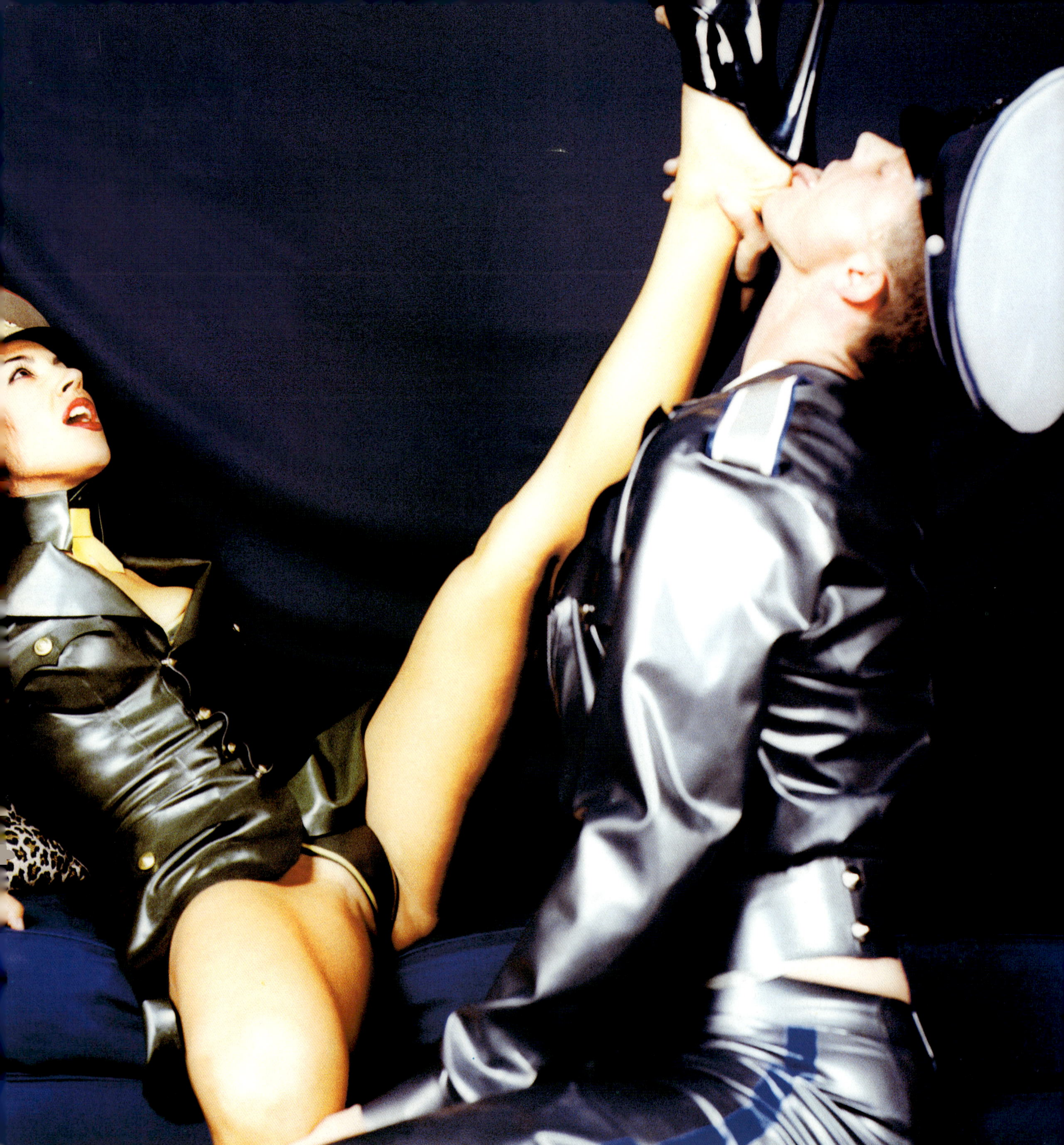

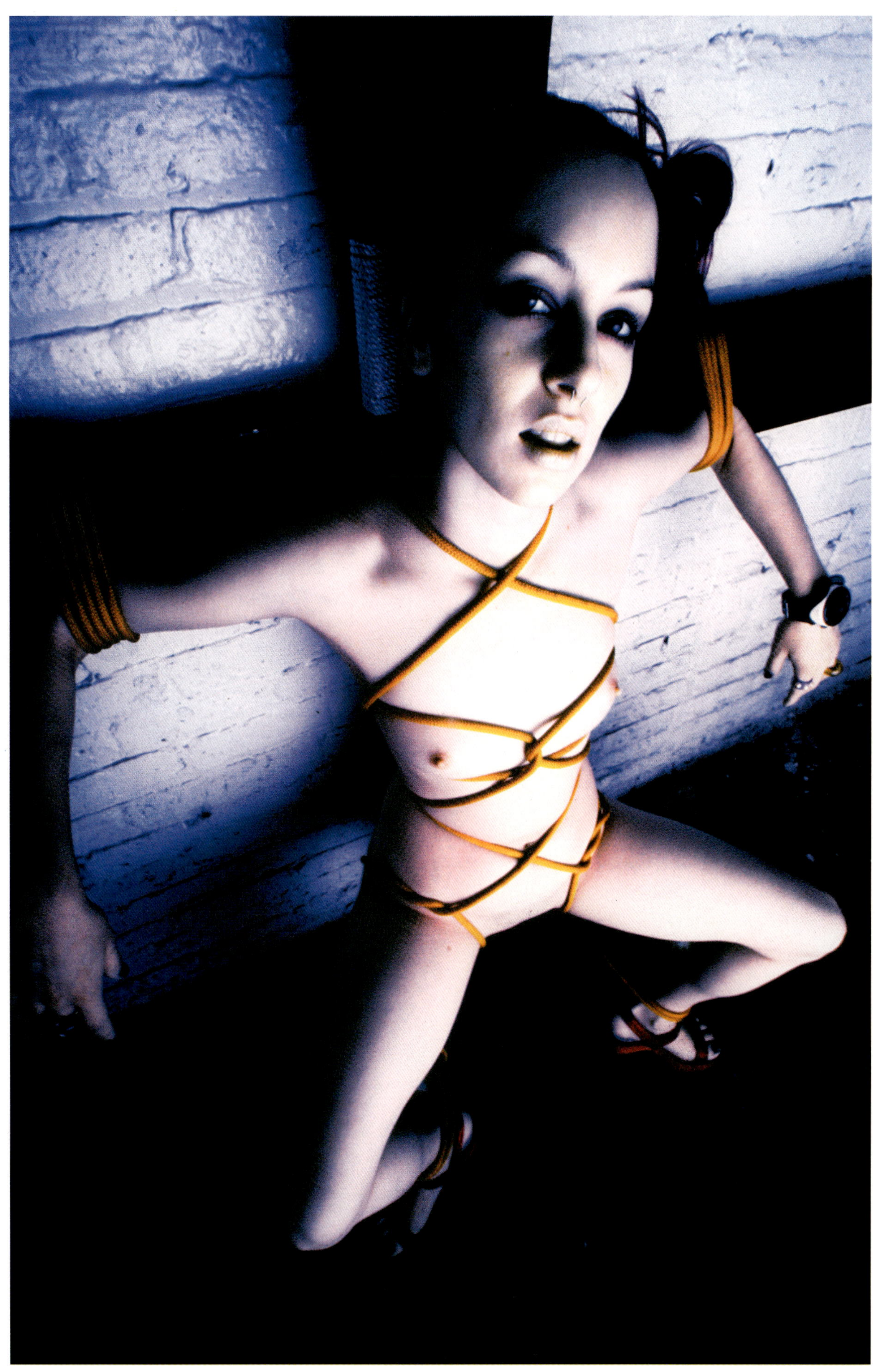

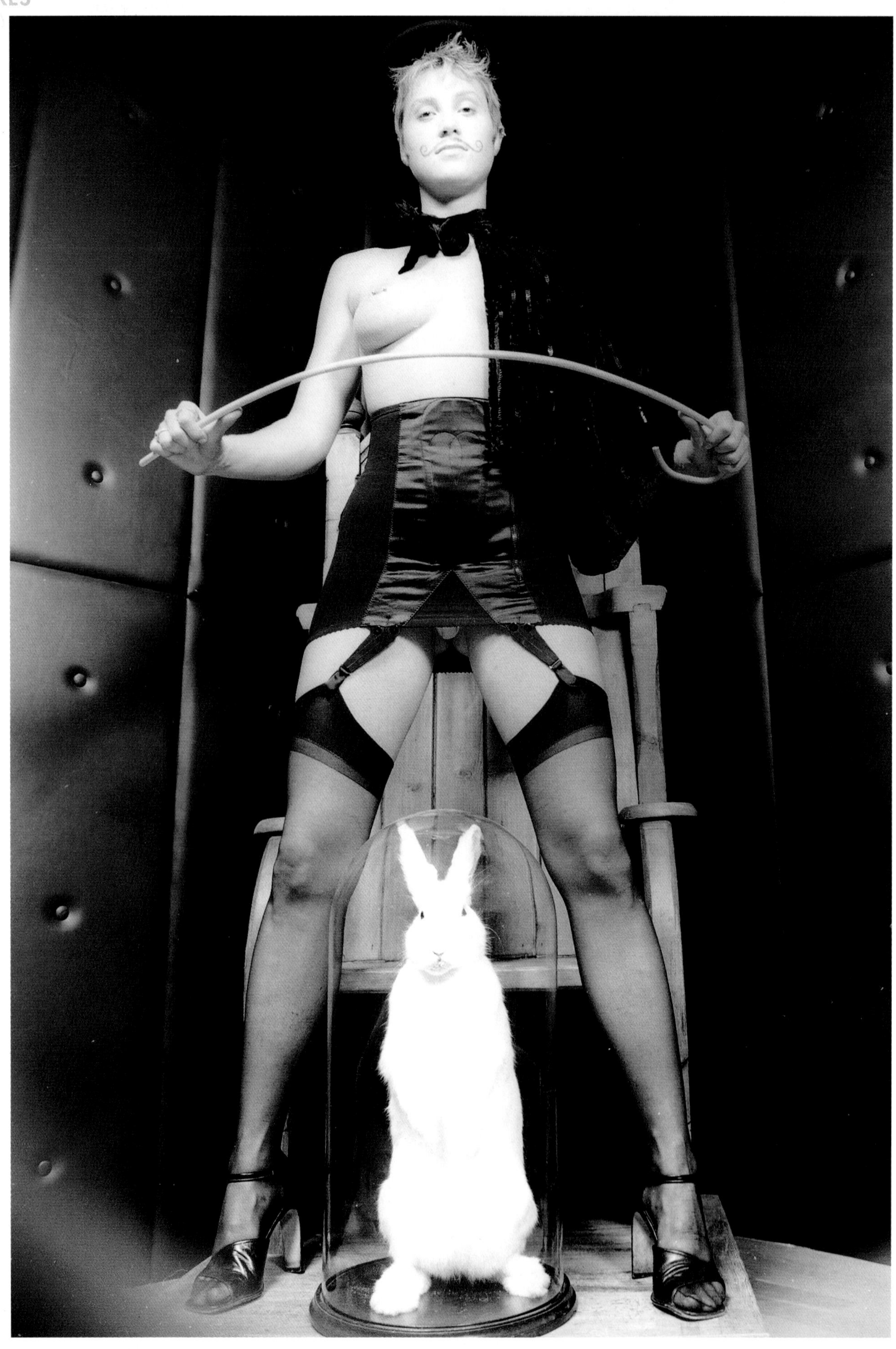

184 Del LaGrace Volcano

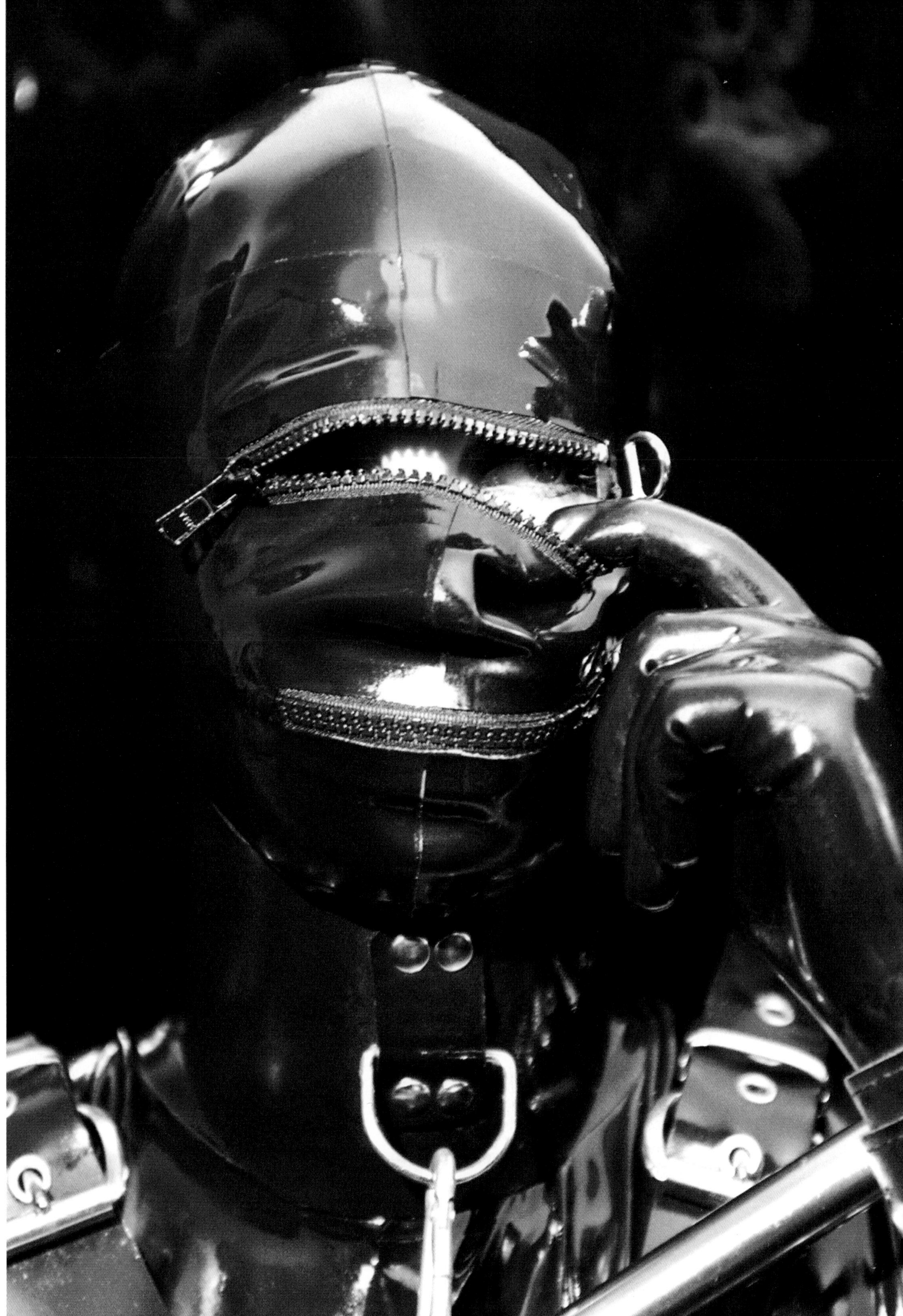

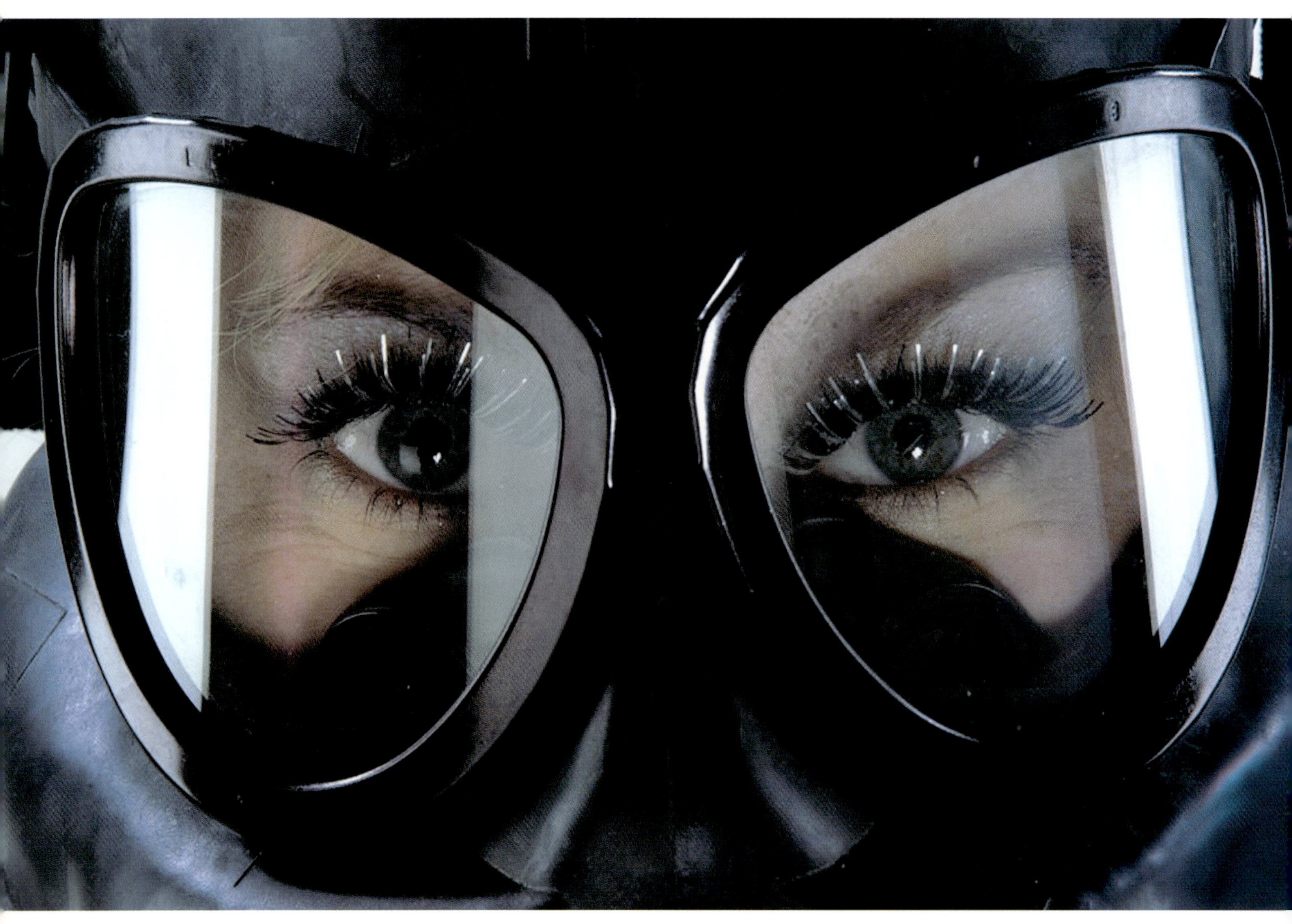

186 Fetish Eyes/Keital

Opposite Fetish Eyes/Keital

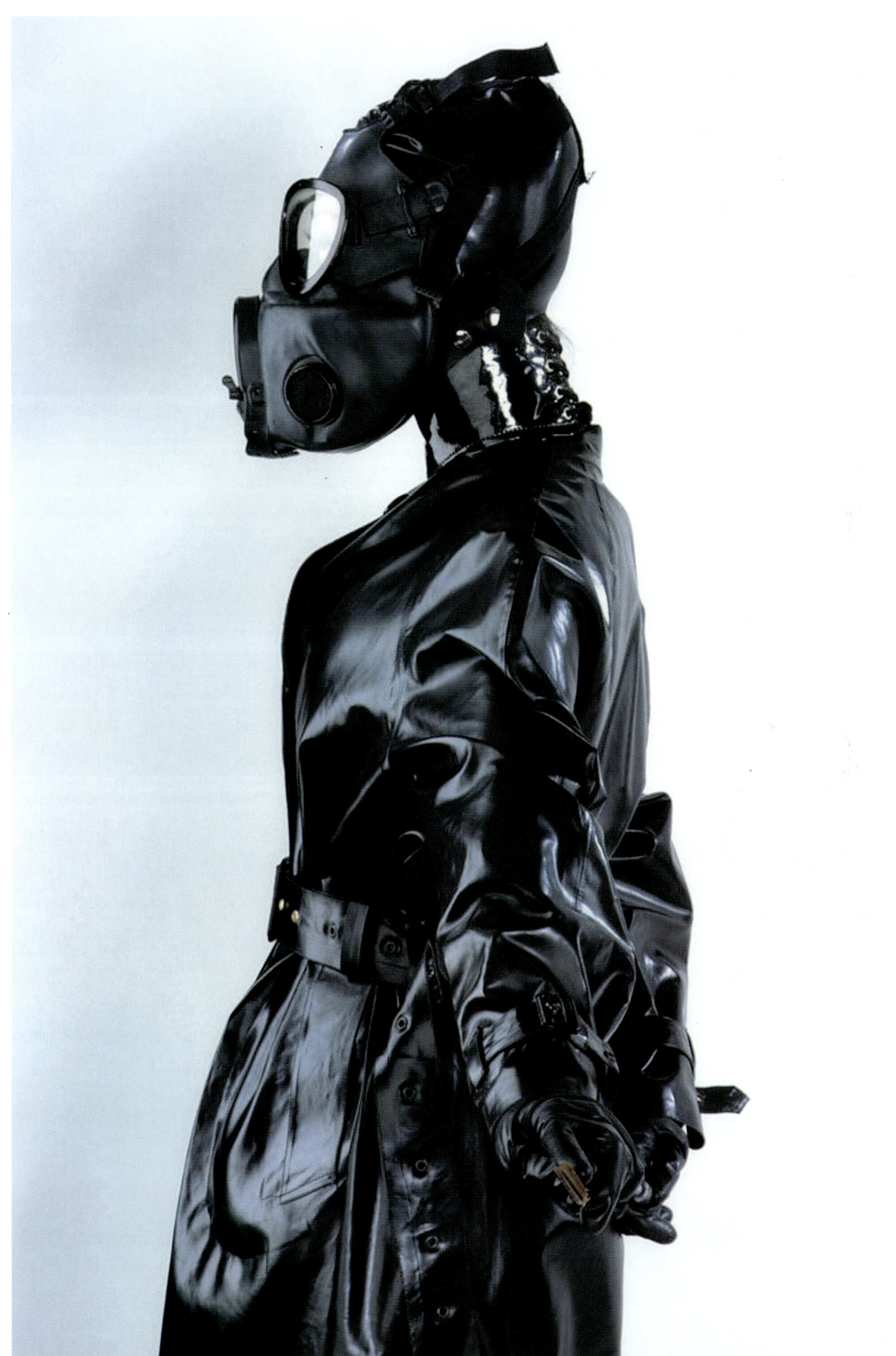

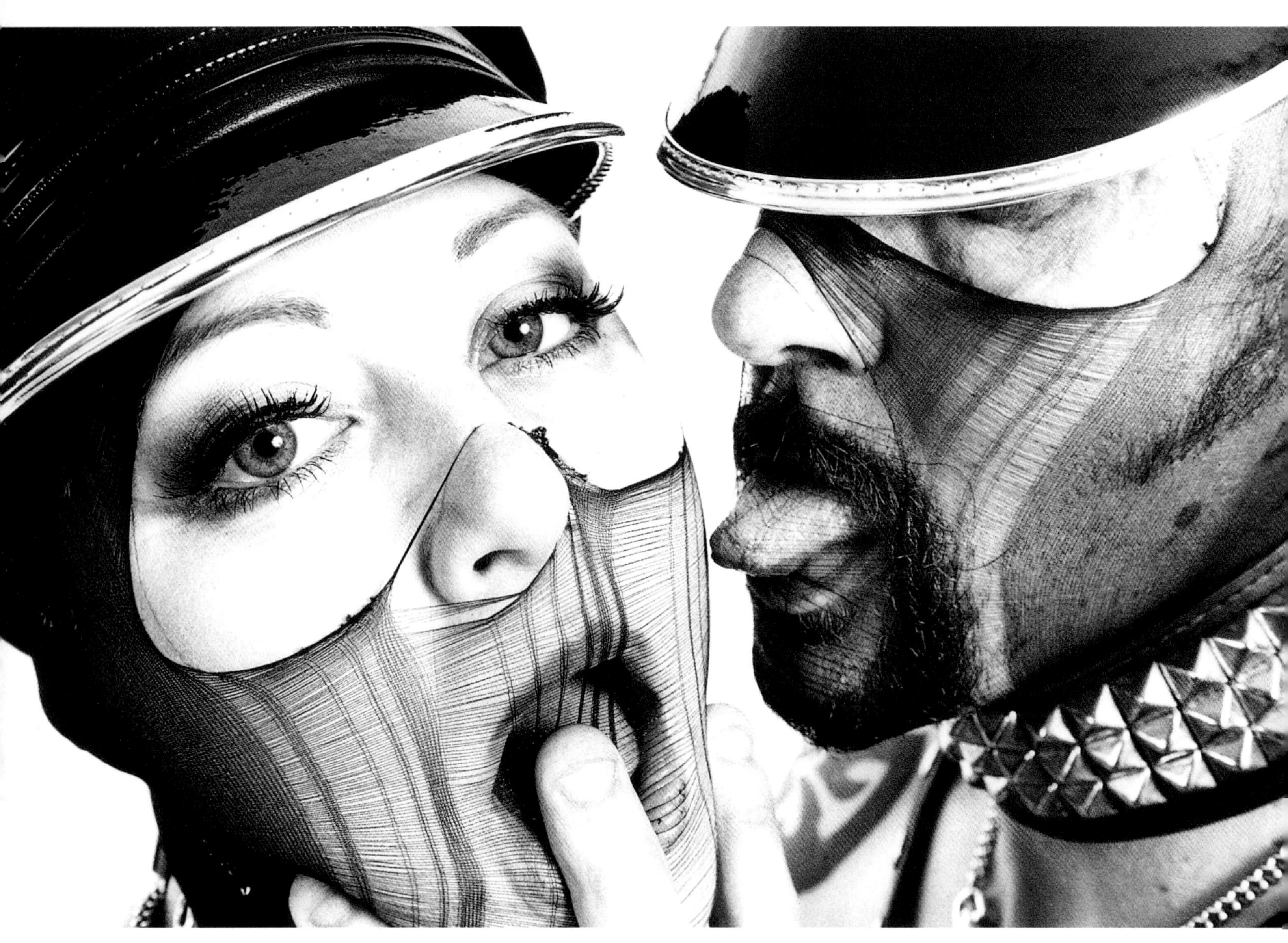

 Gary & Pierre Silva

Opposite Gary & Pierre Silva

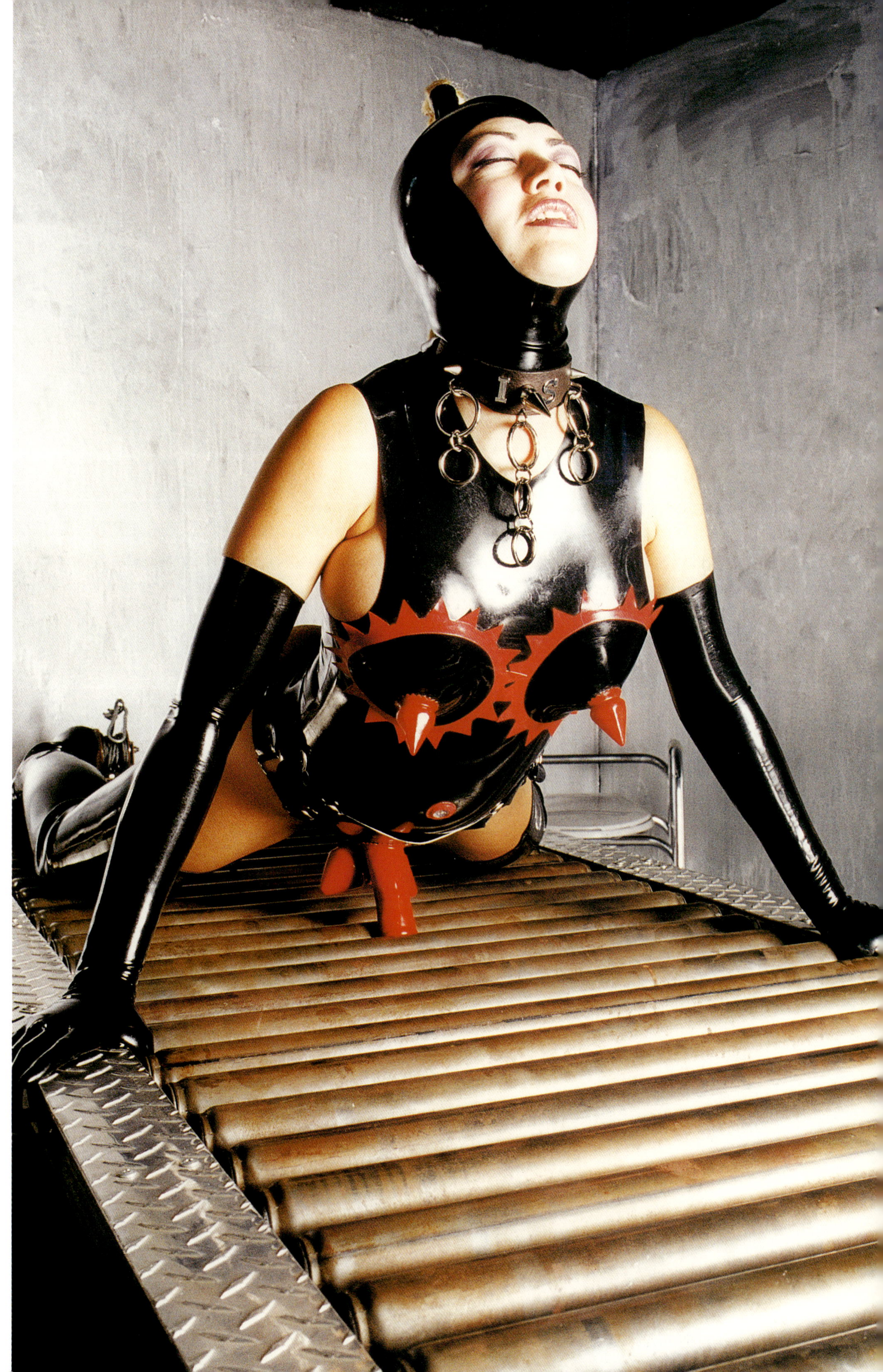

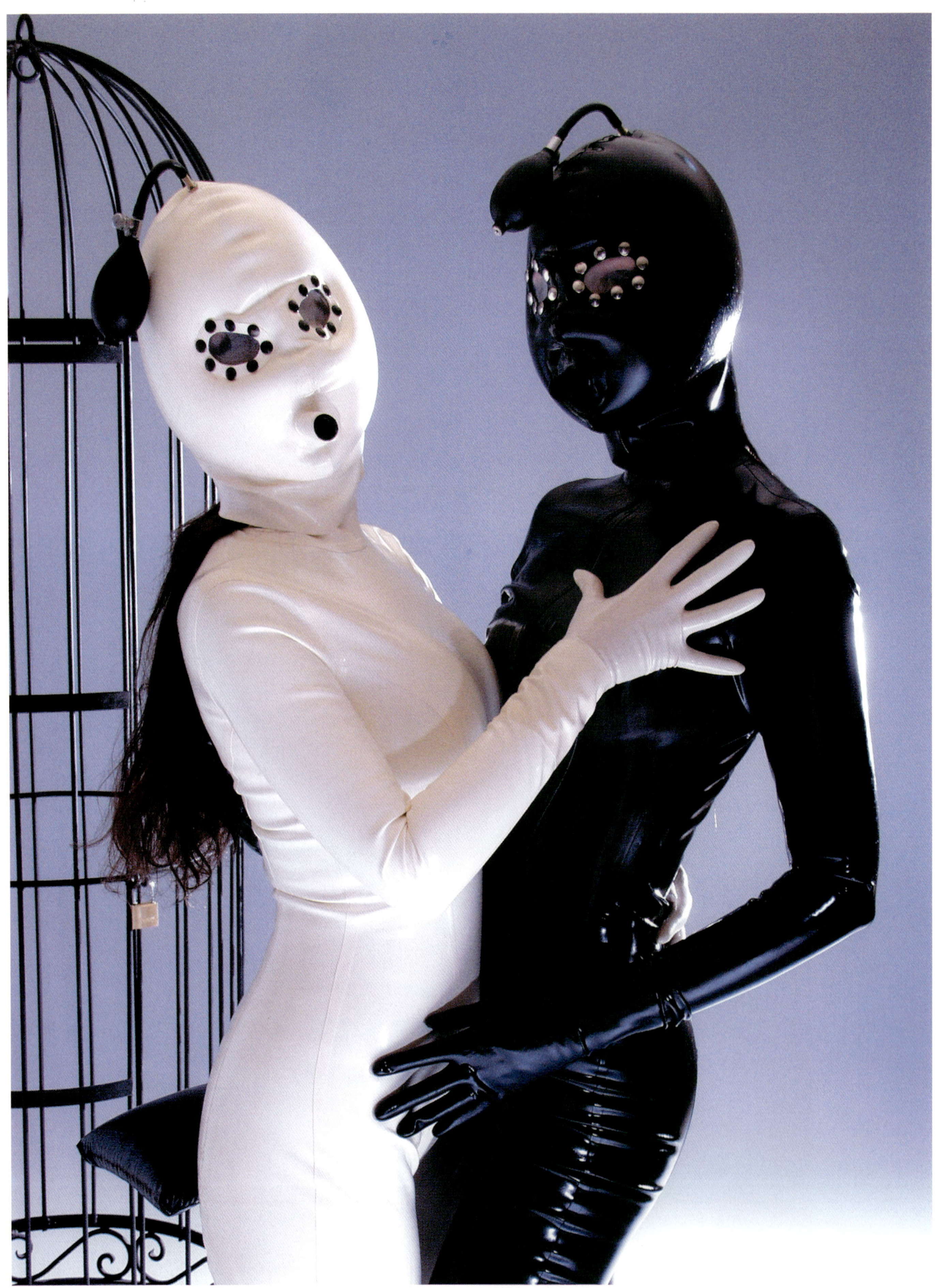

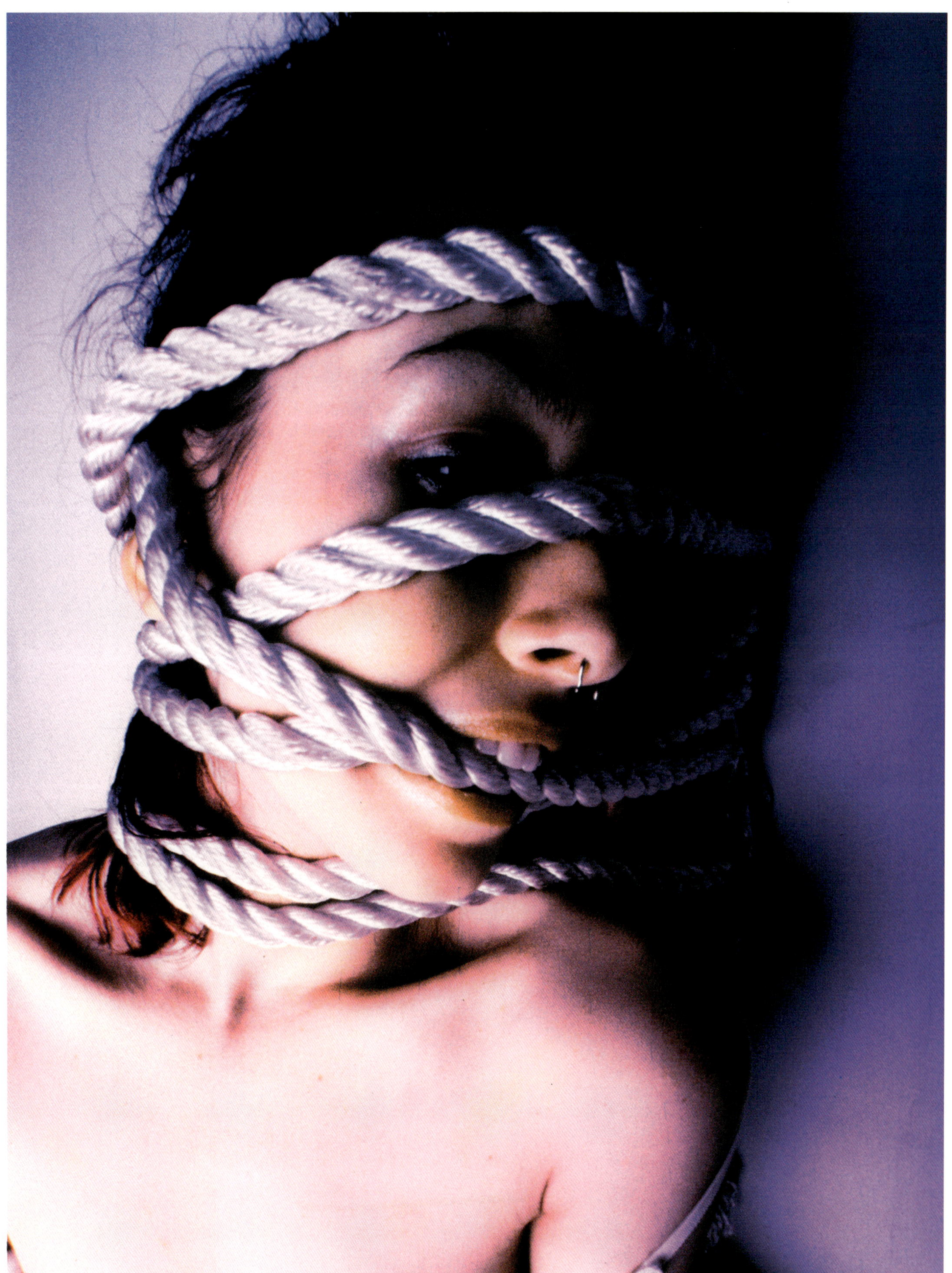

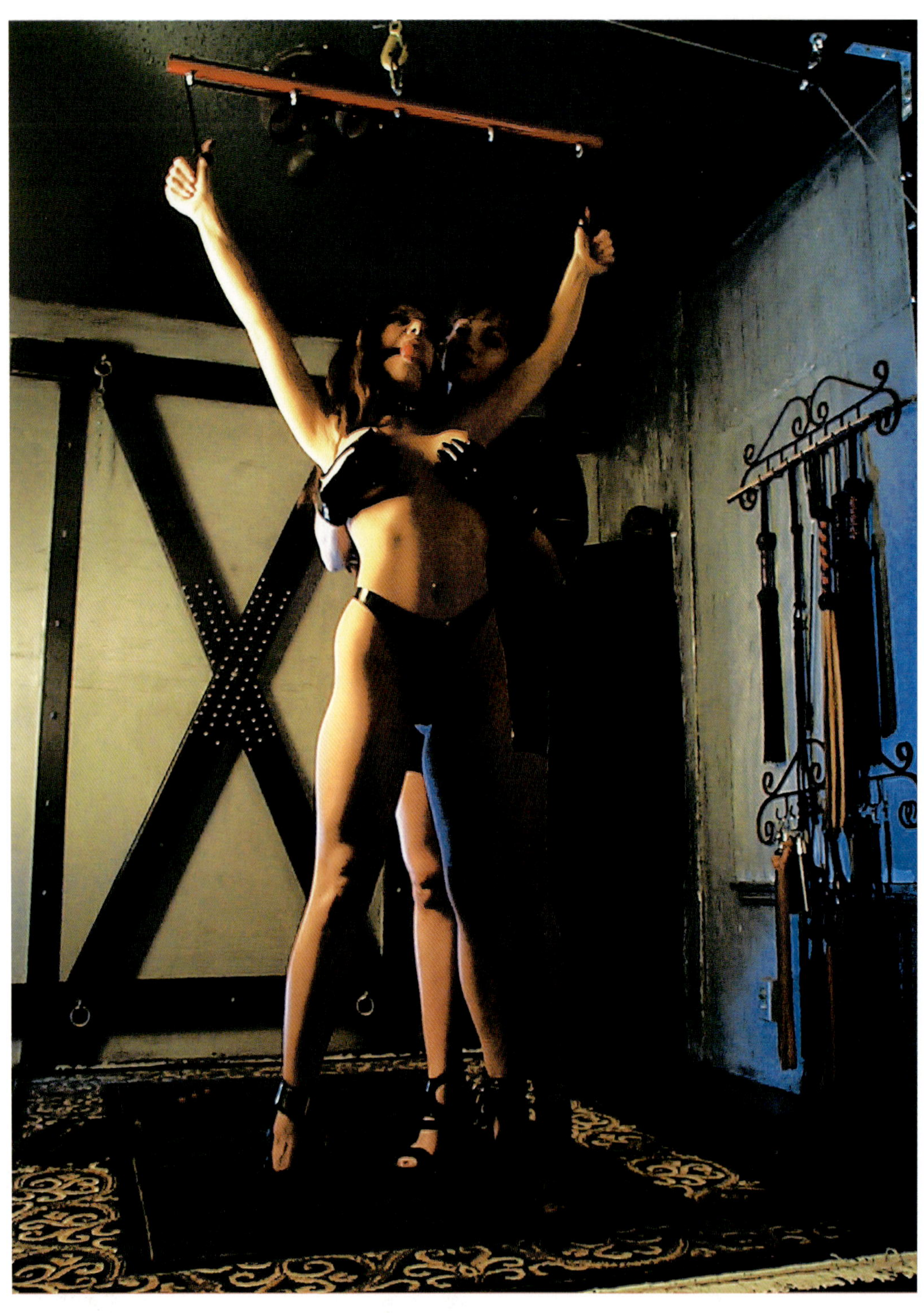

 John Fitzgerald

Opposite John Fitzgerald

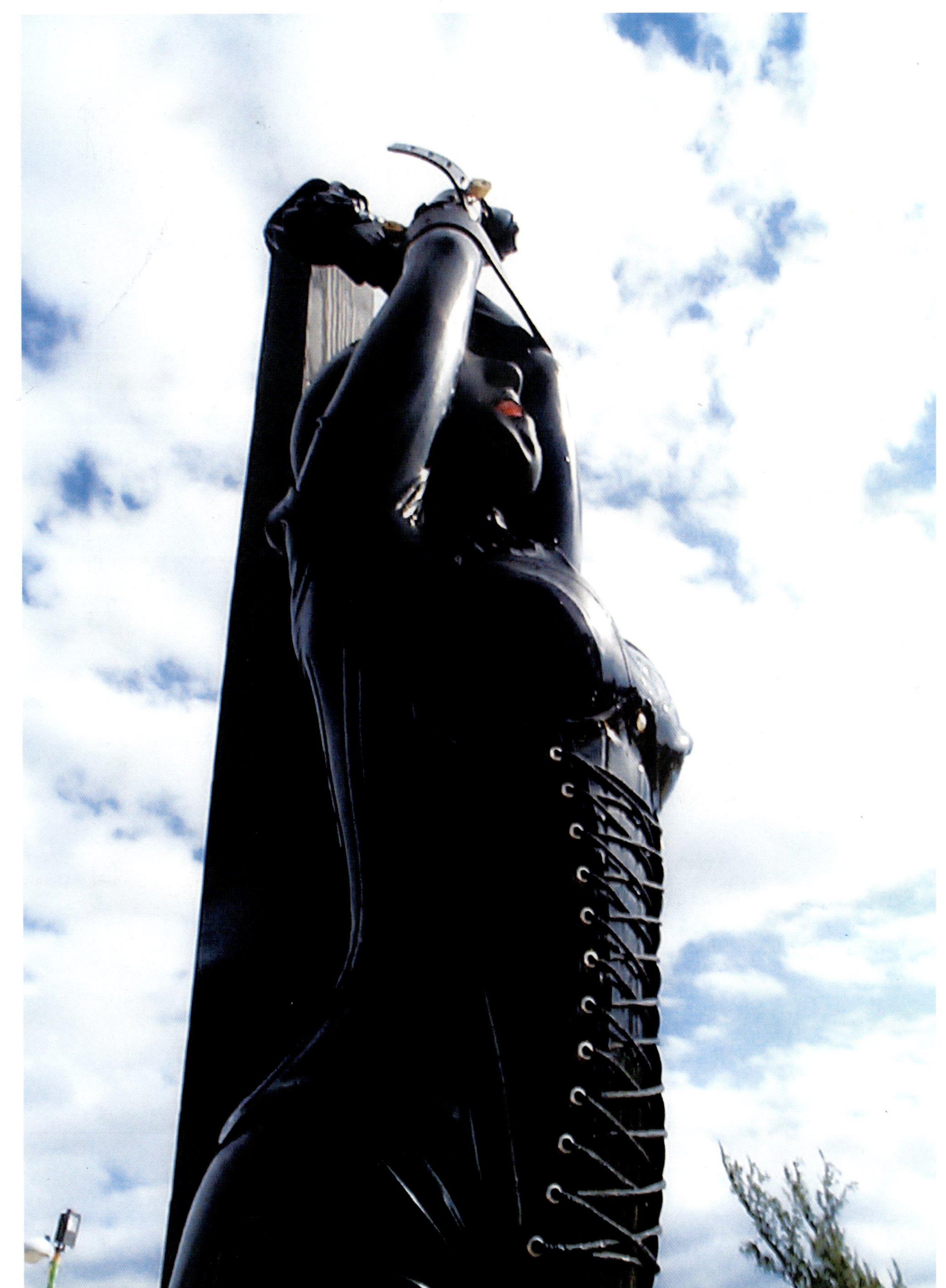

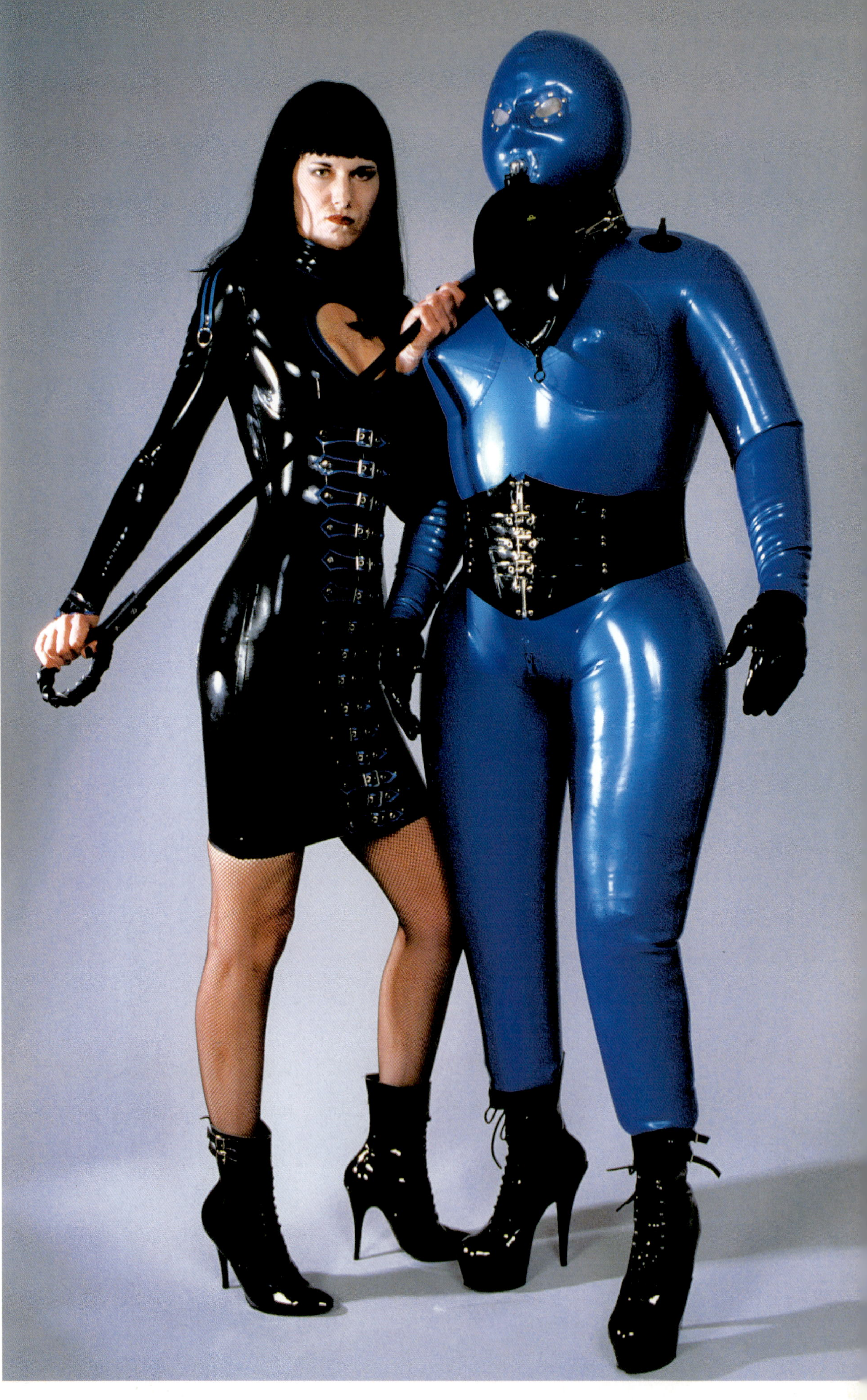



Opposite Whiplash!

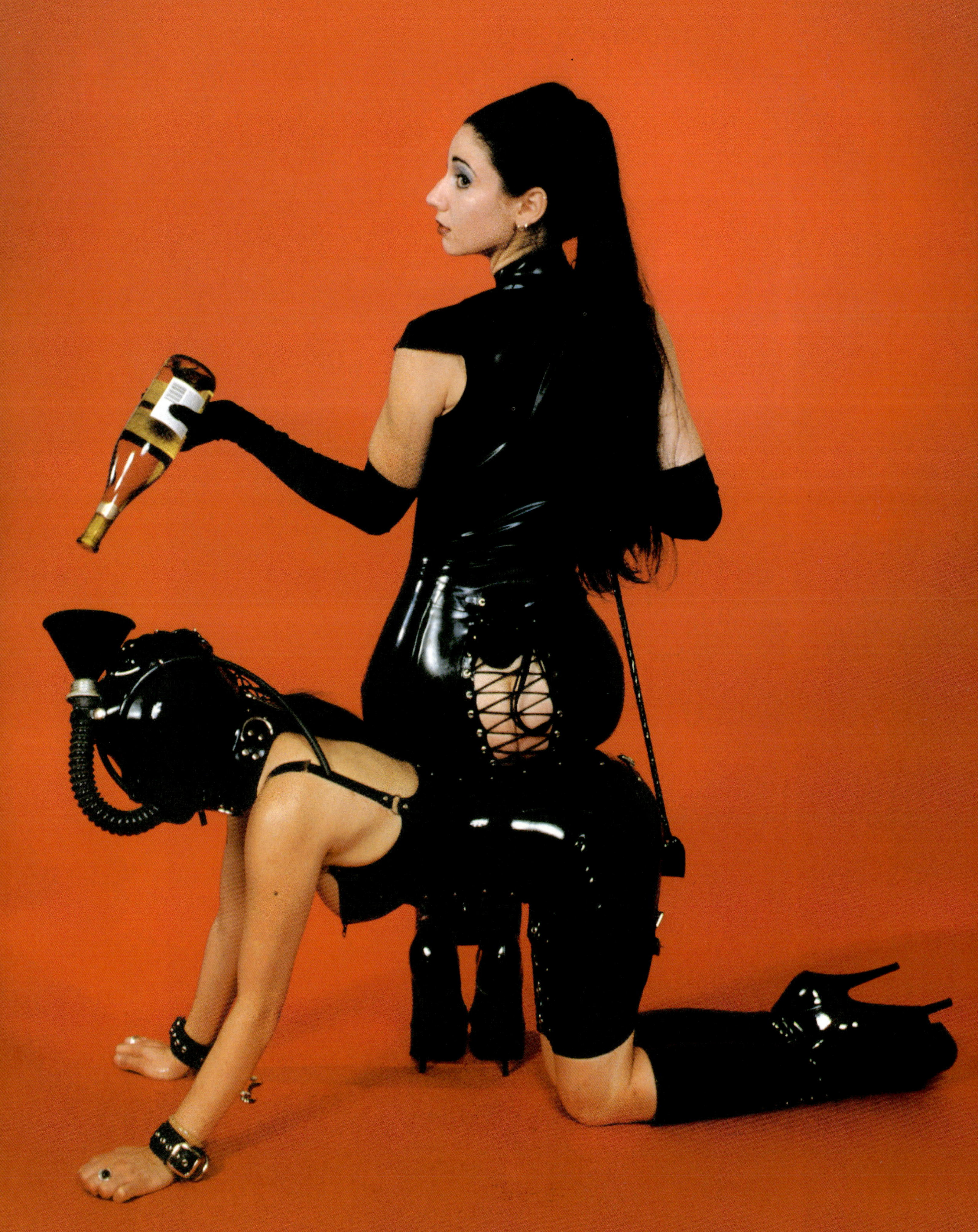

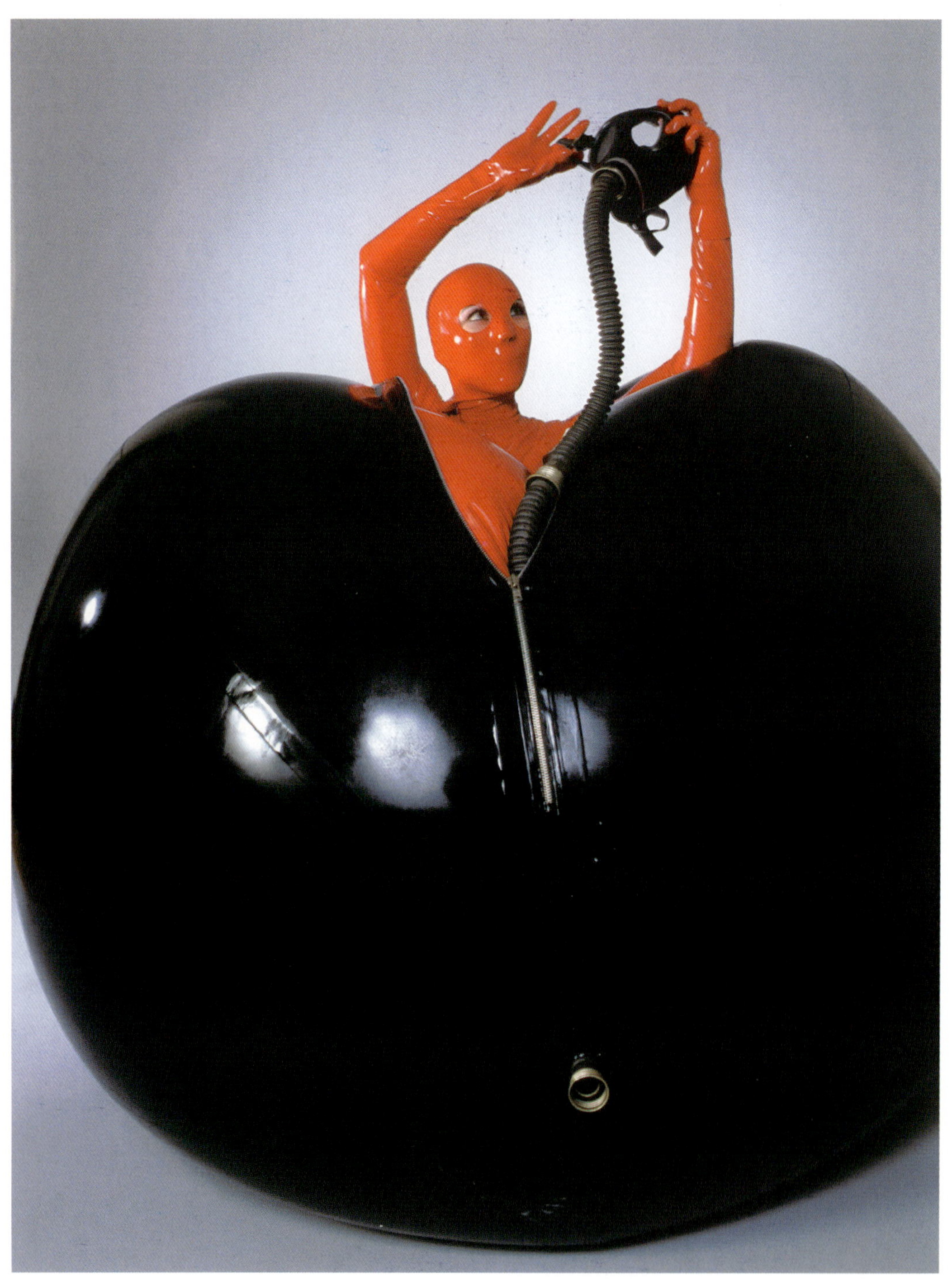

 Whiplash!

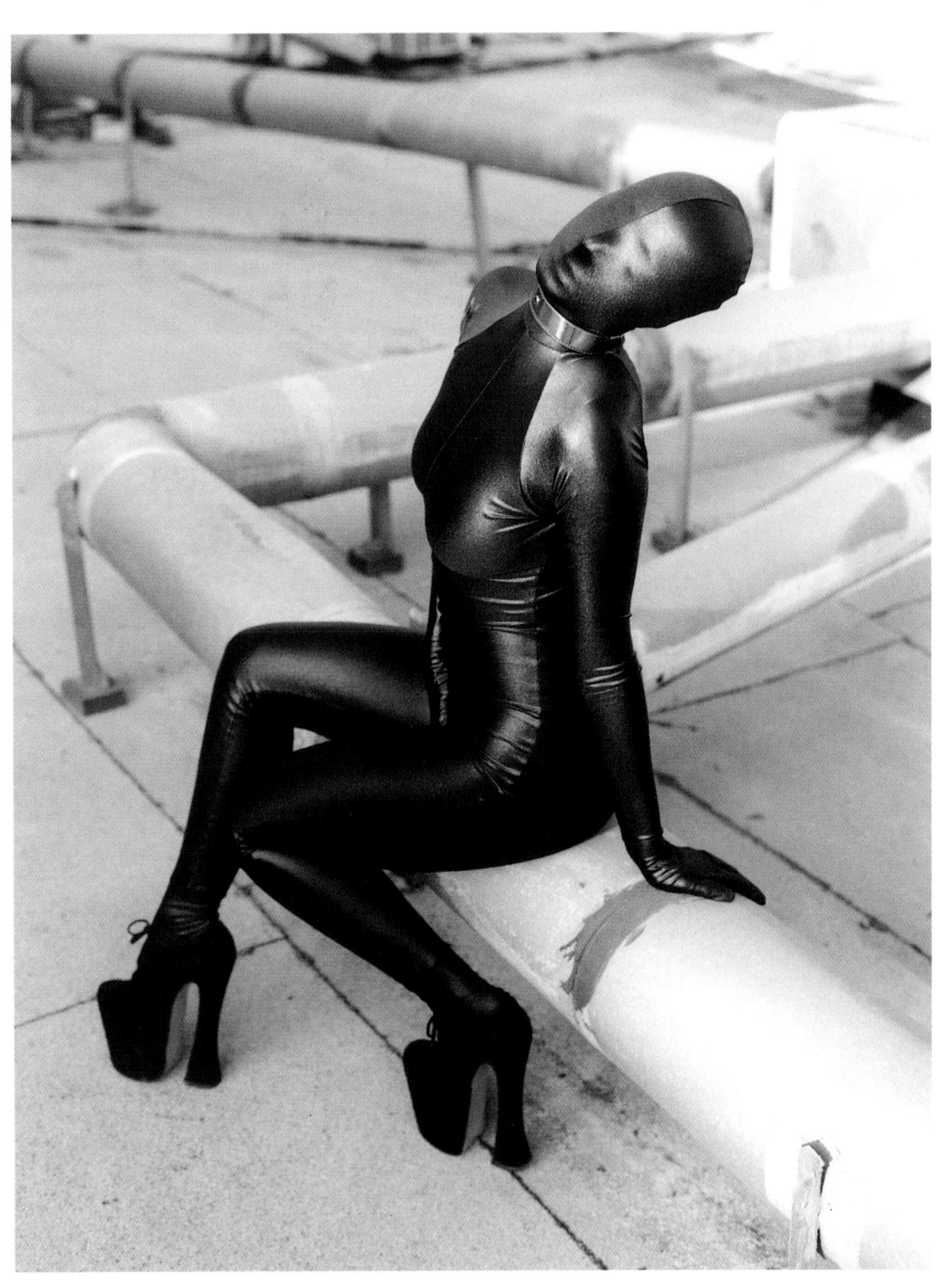

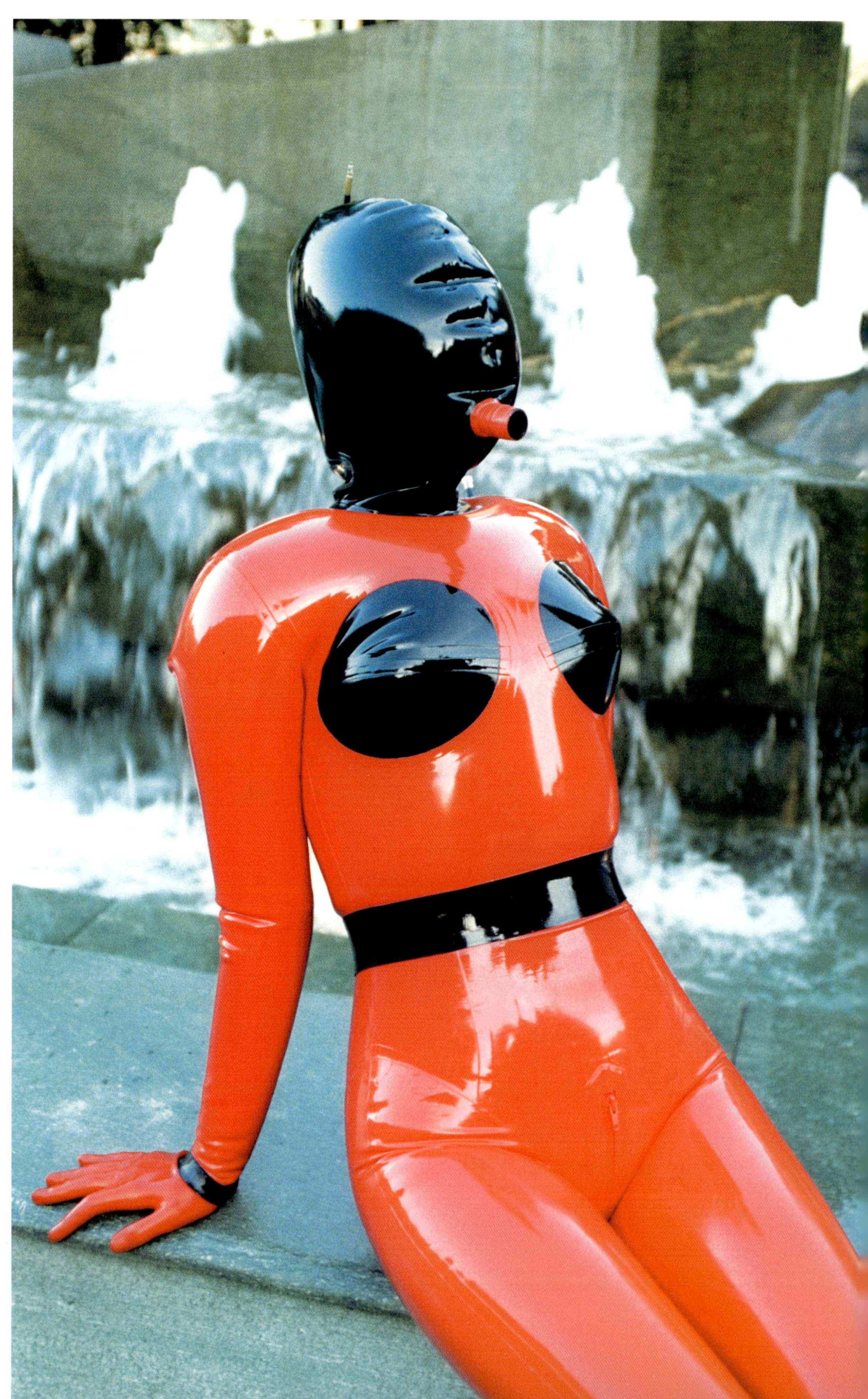

 Alexander Horn

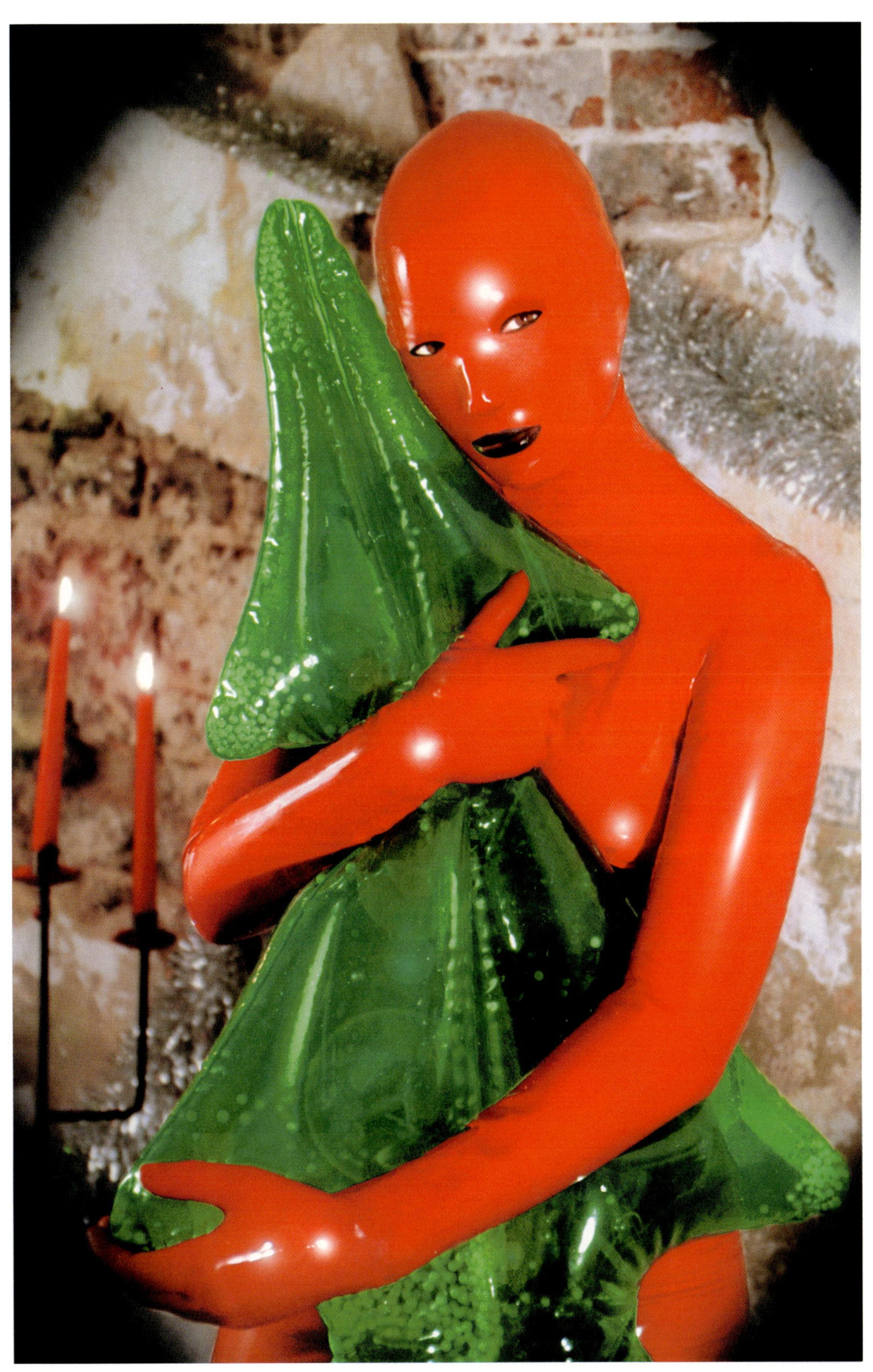

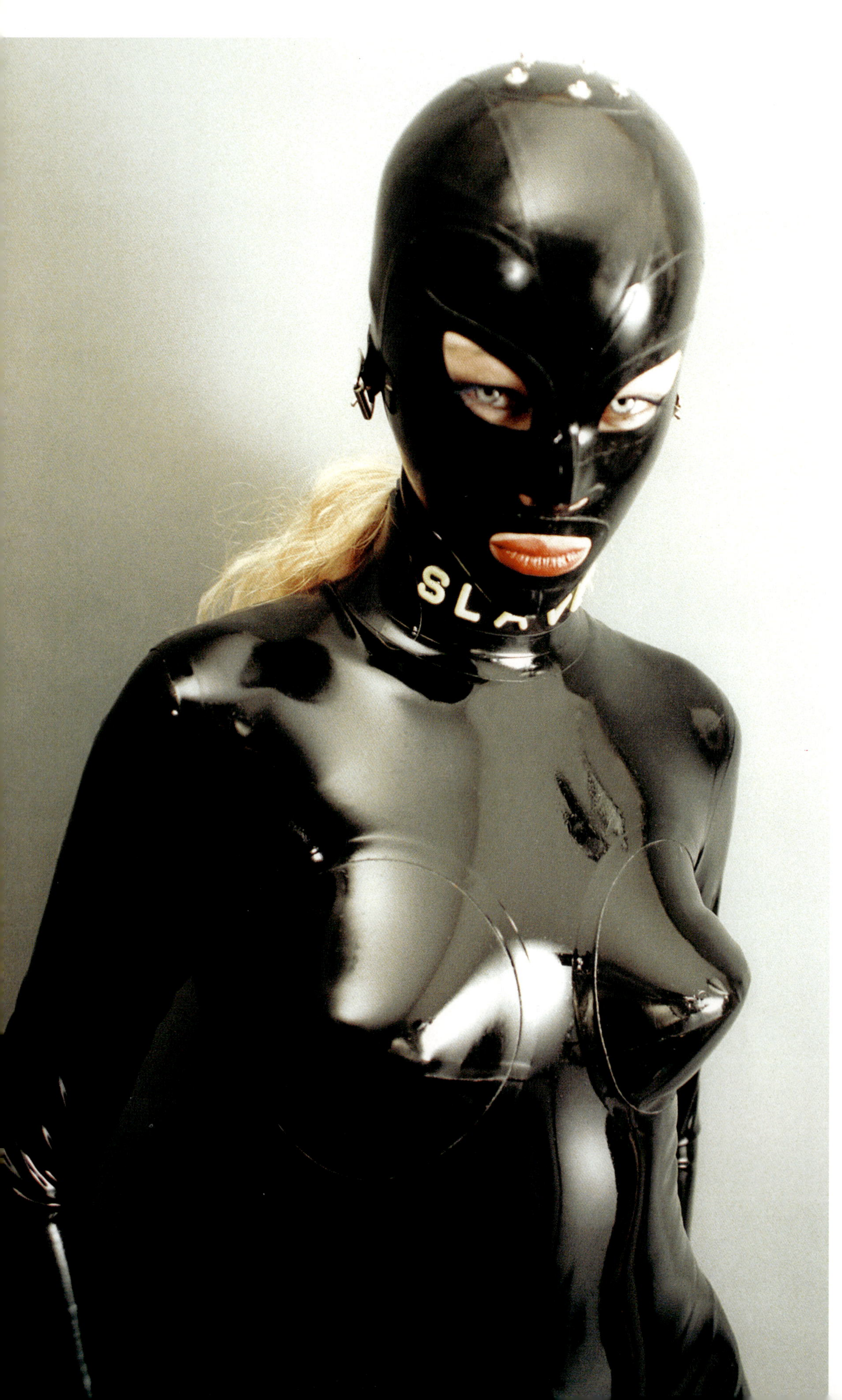

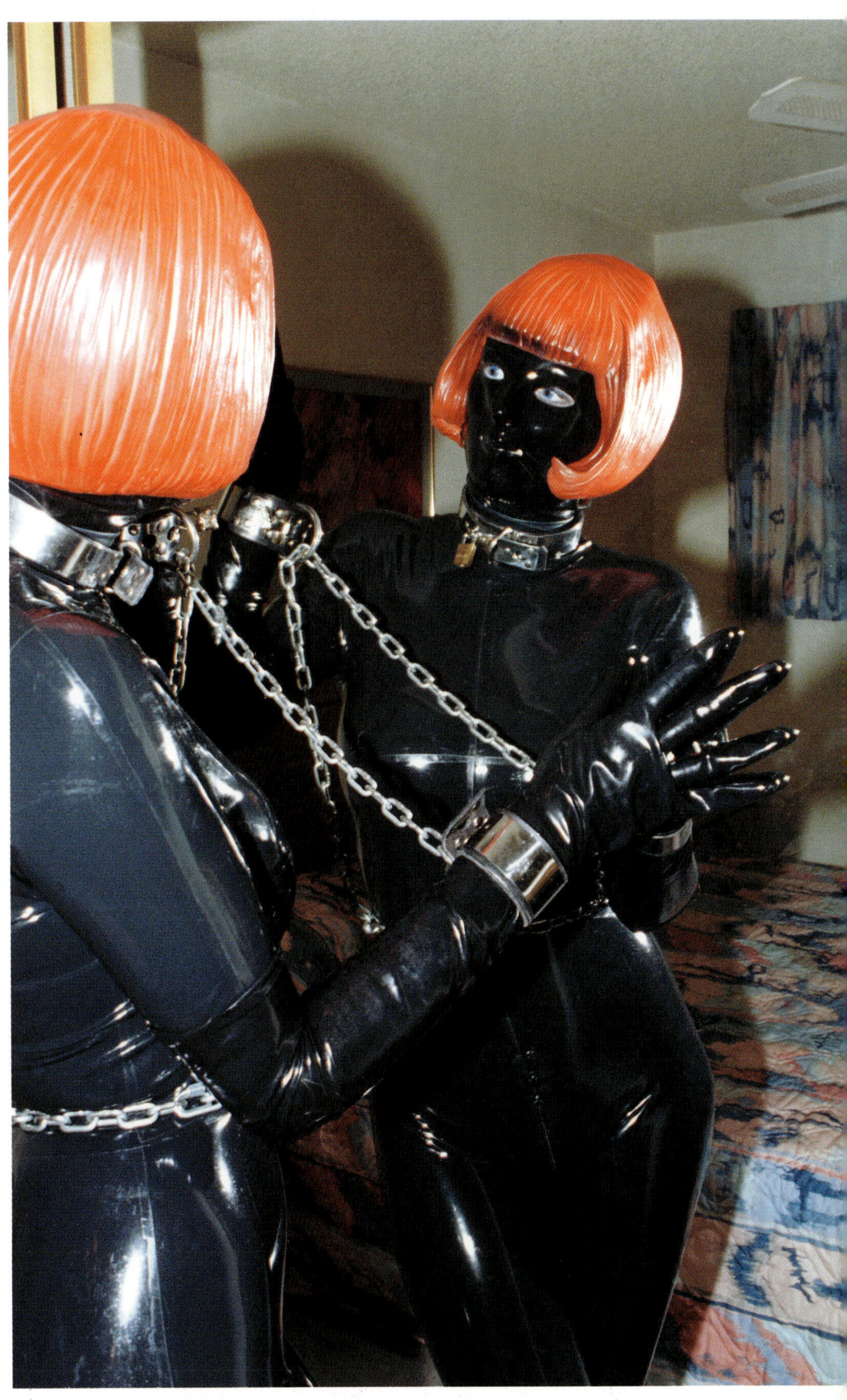

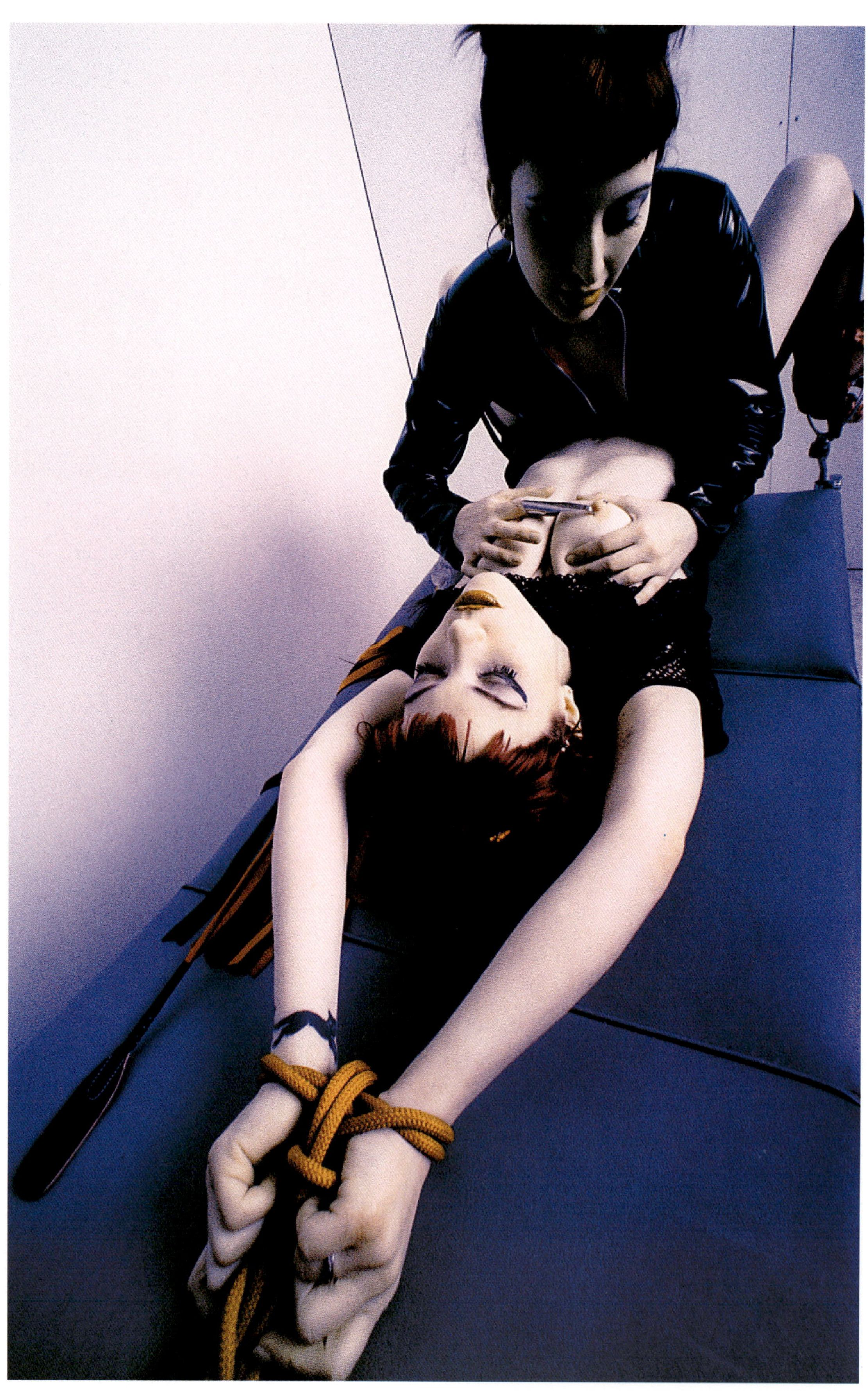

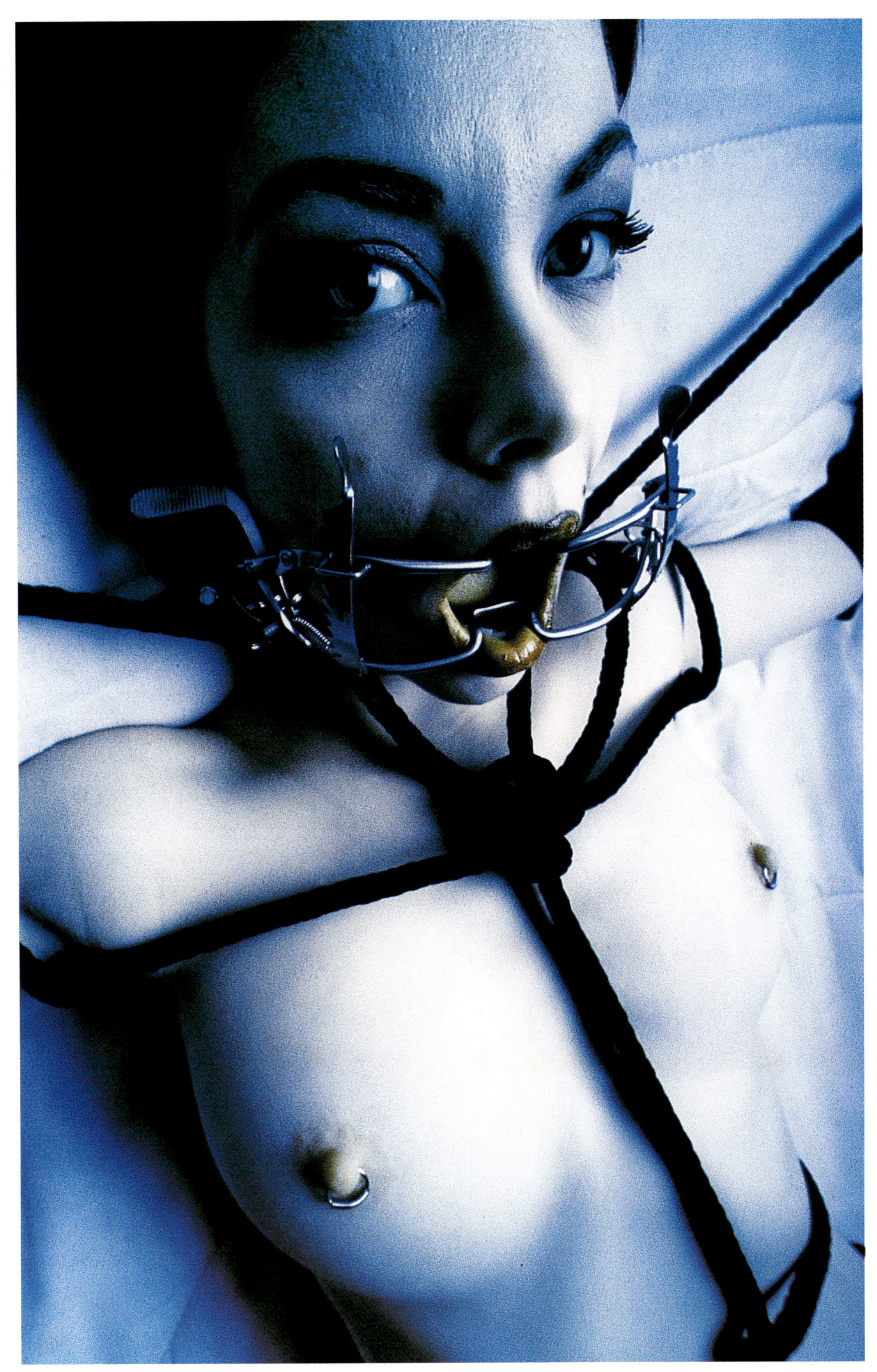

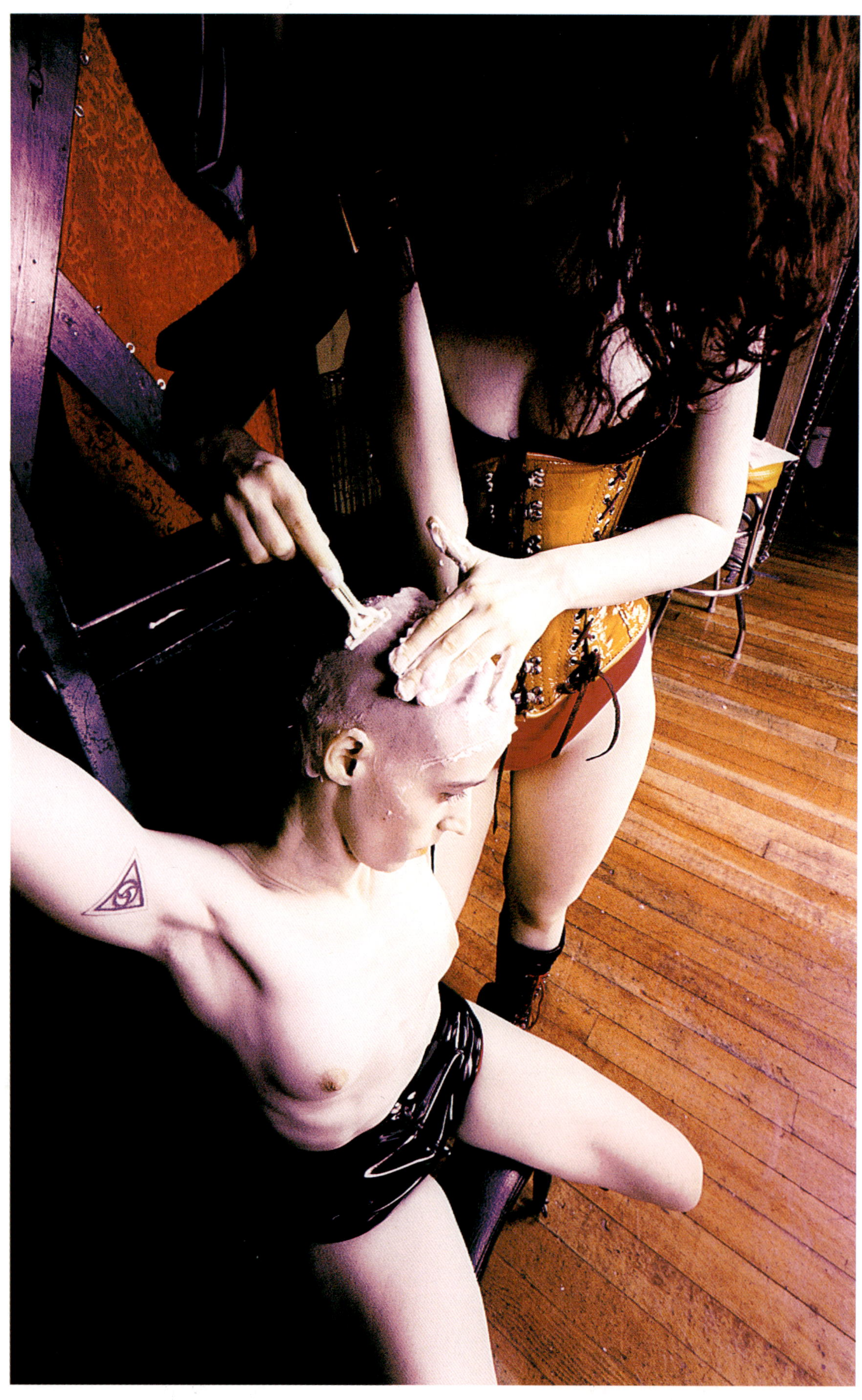

 Lee Higgs

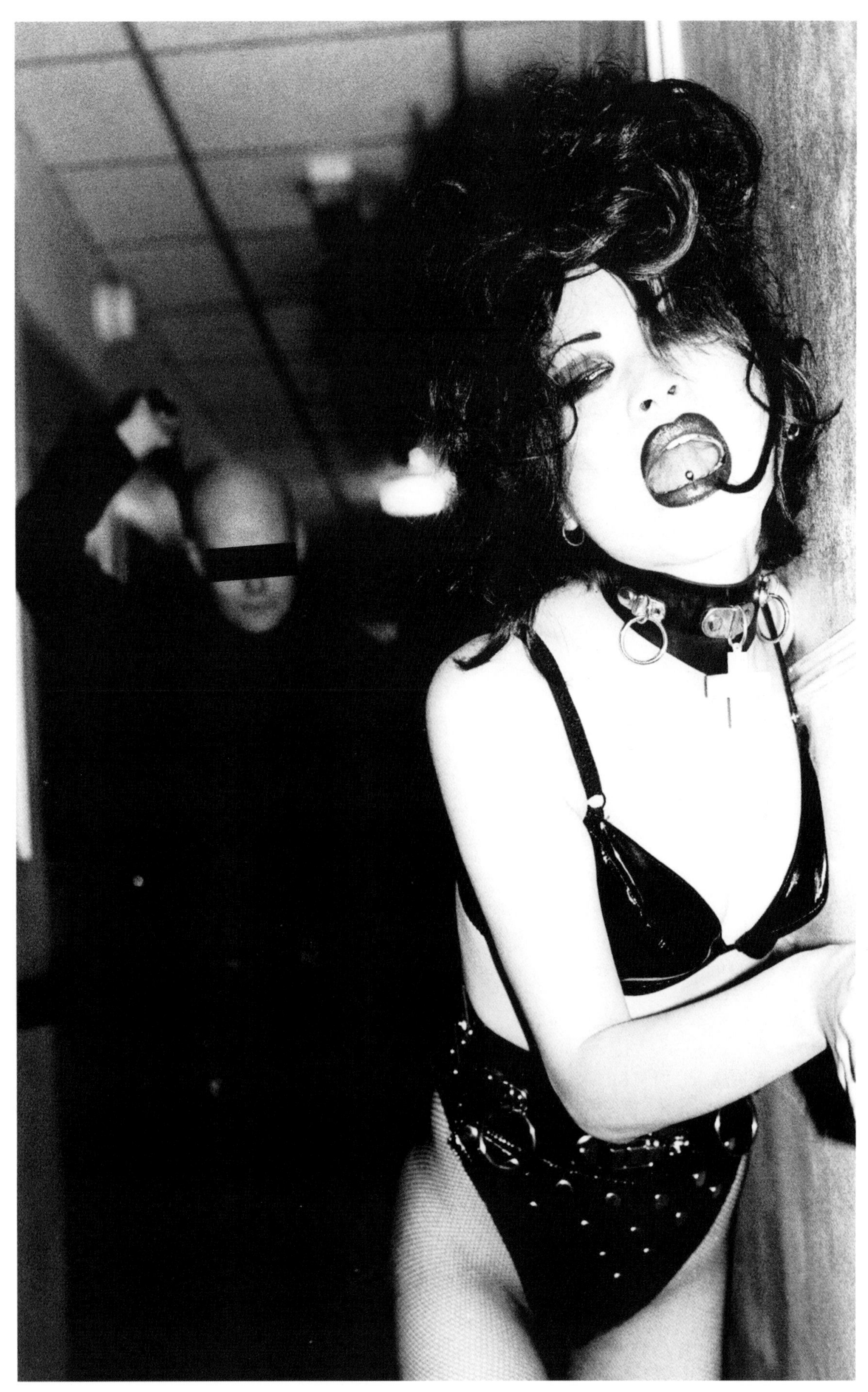

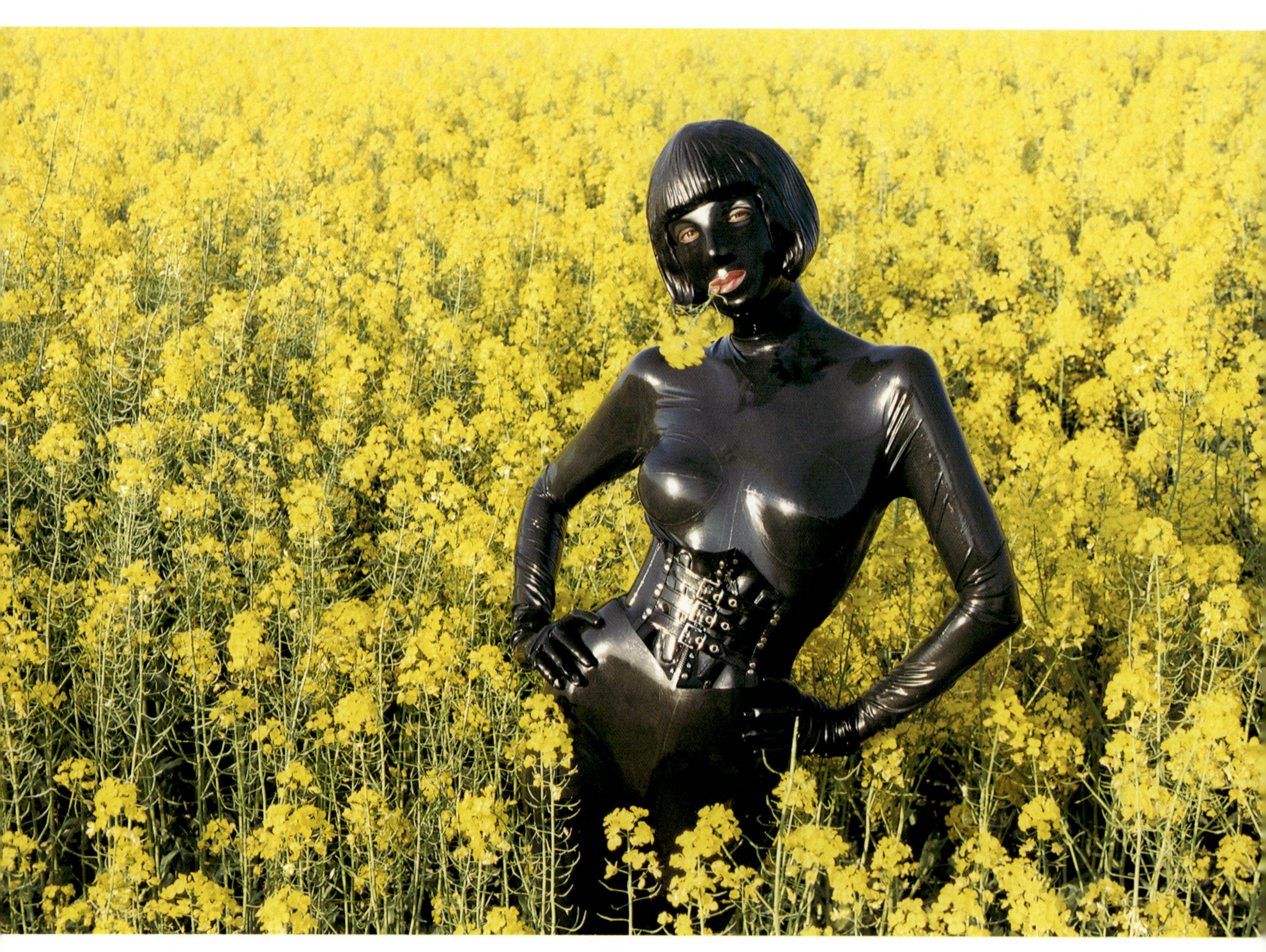

 Peter W. Czernich

Opposite Peter W. Czernich

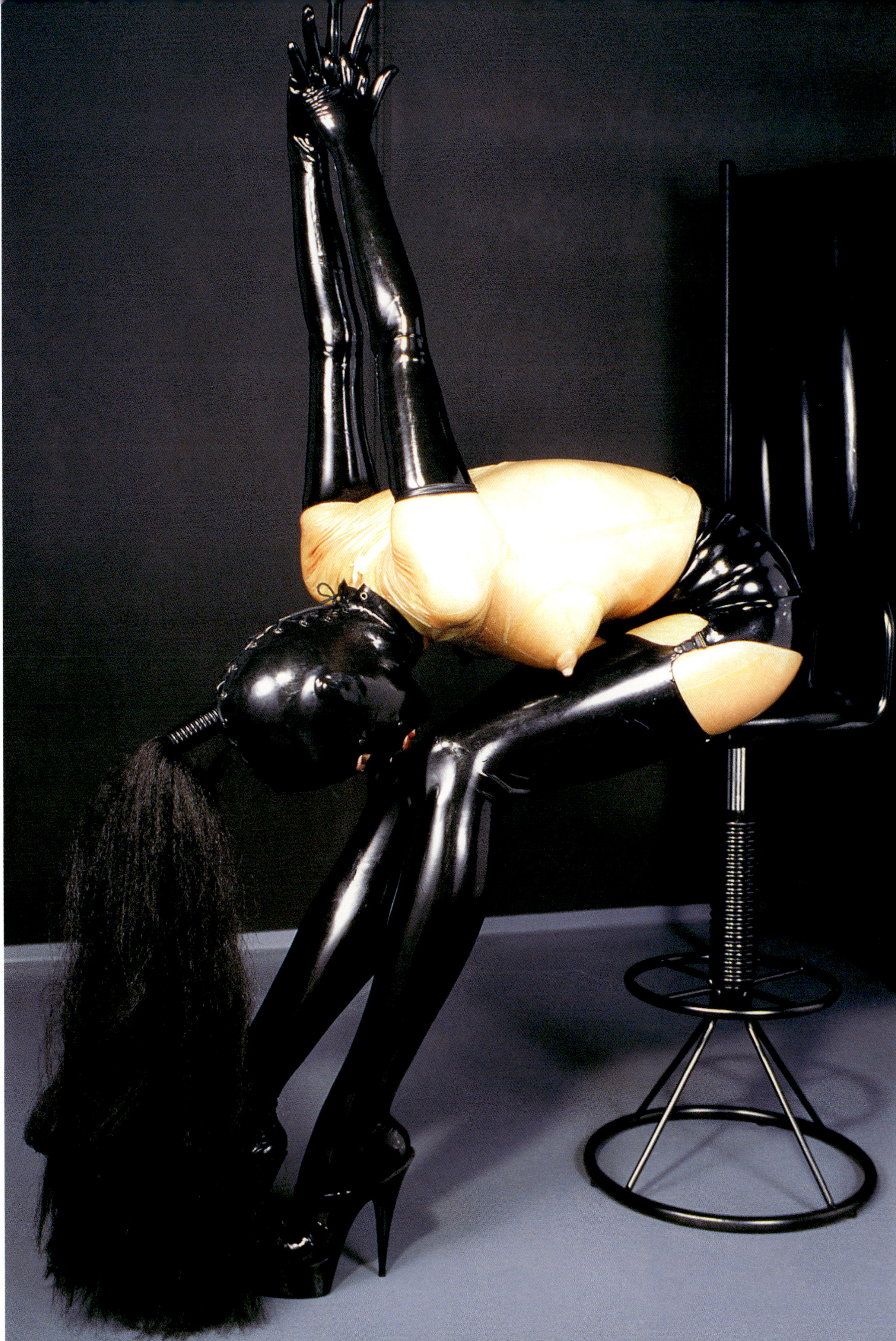

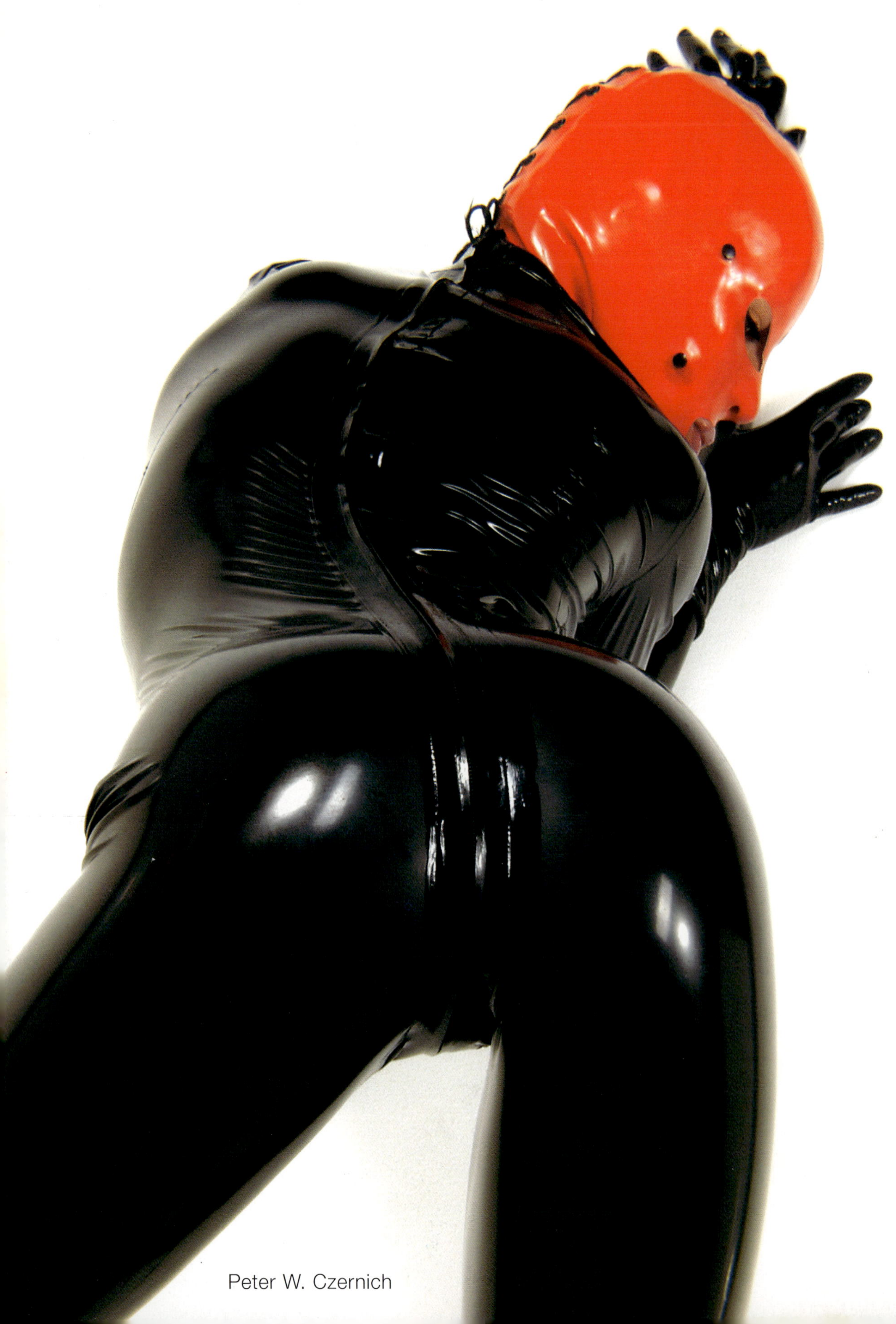

Peter W. Czernich

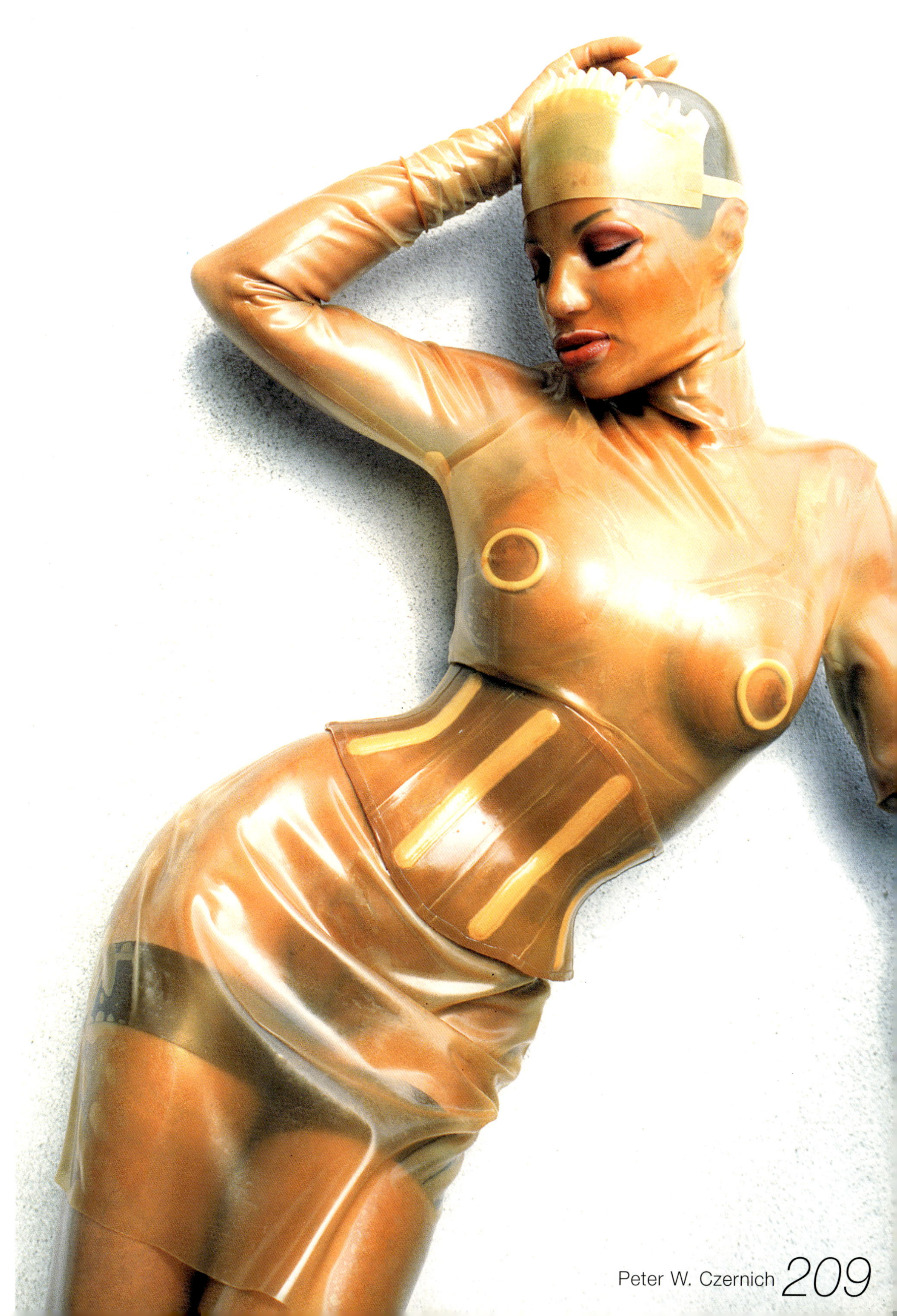

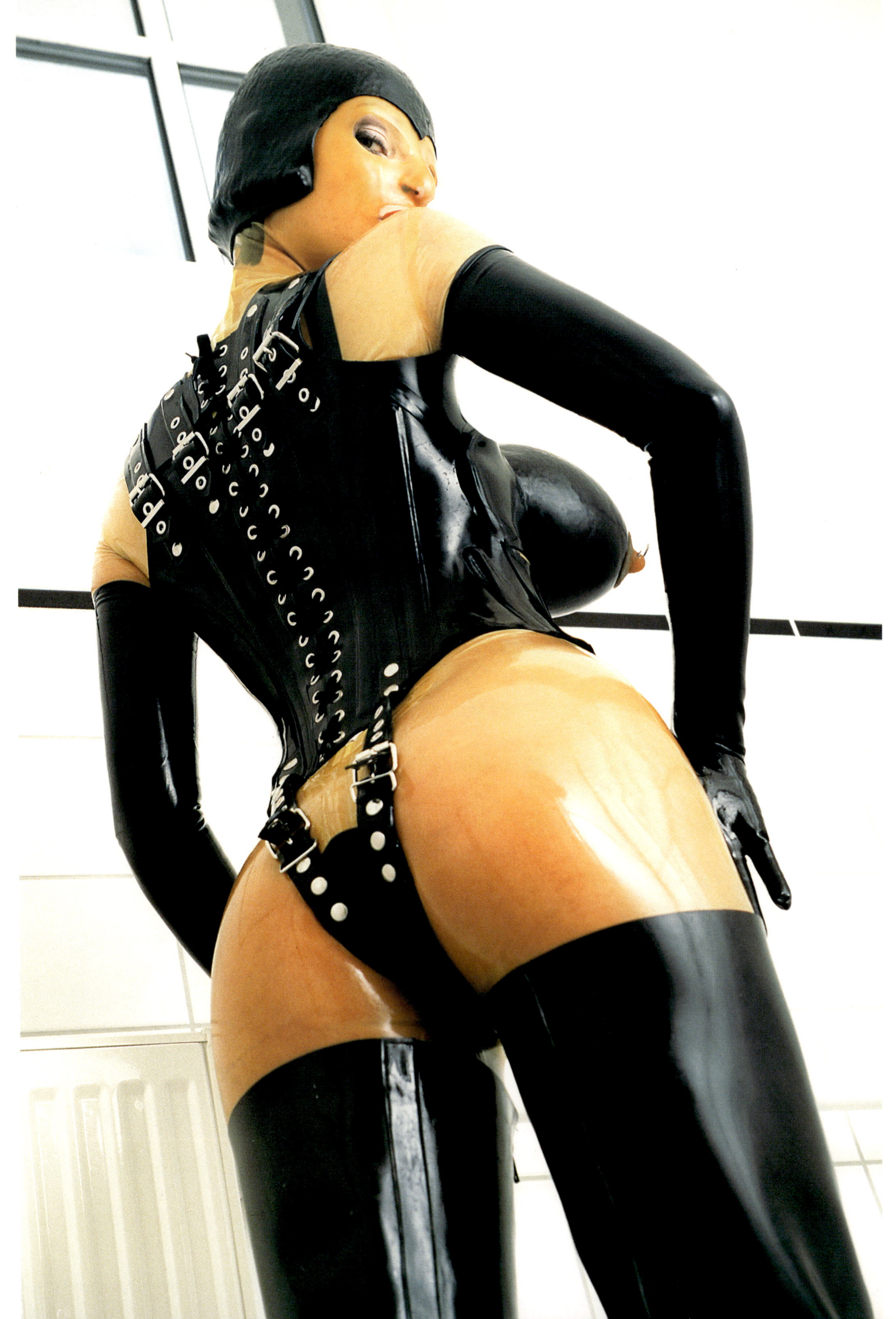

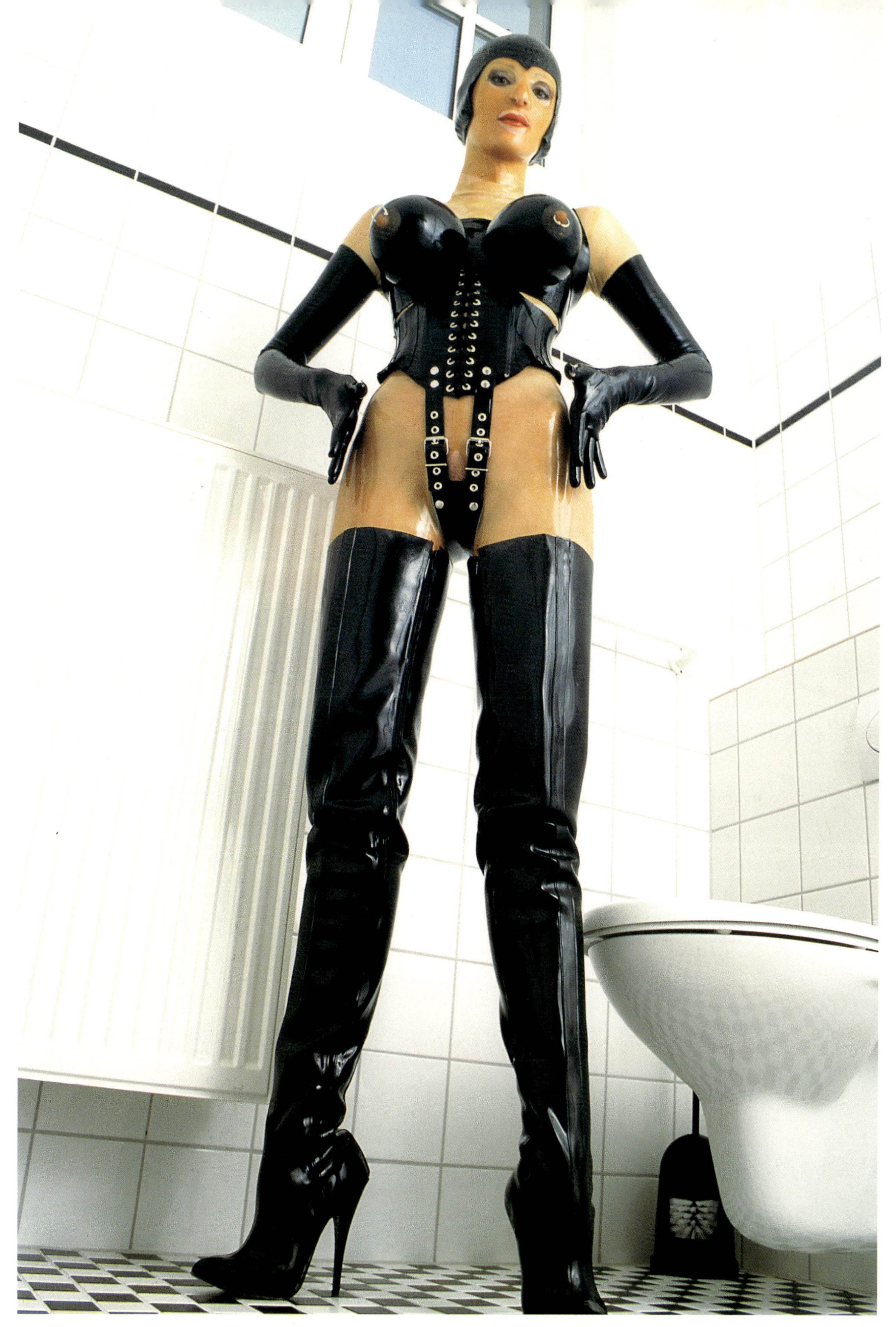

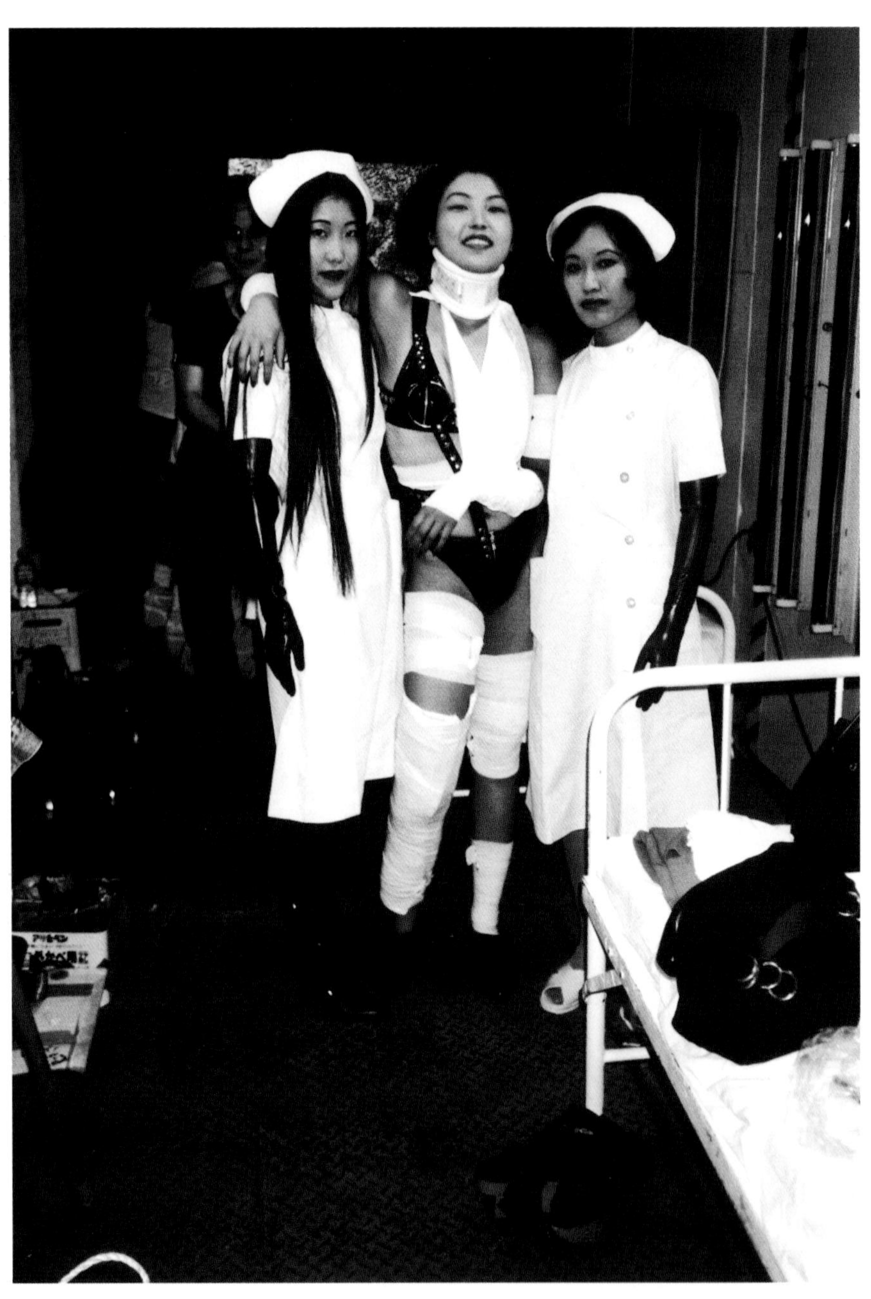

 Romain Slocombe

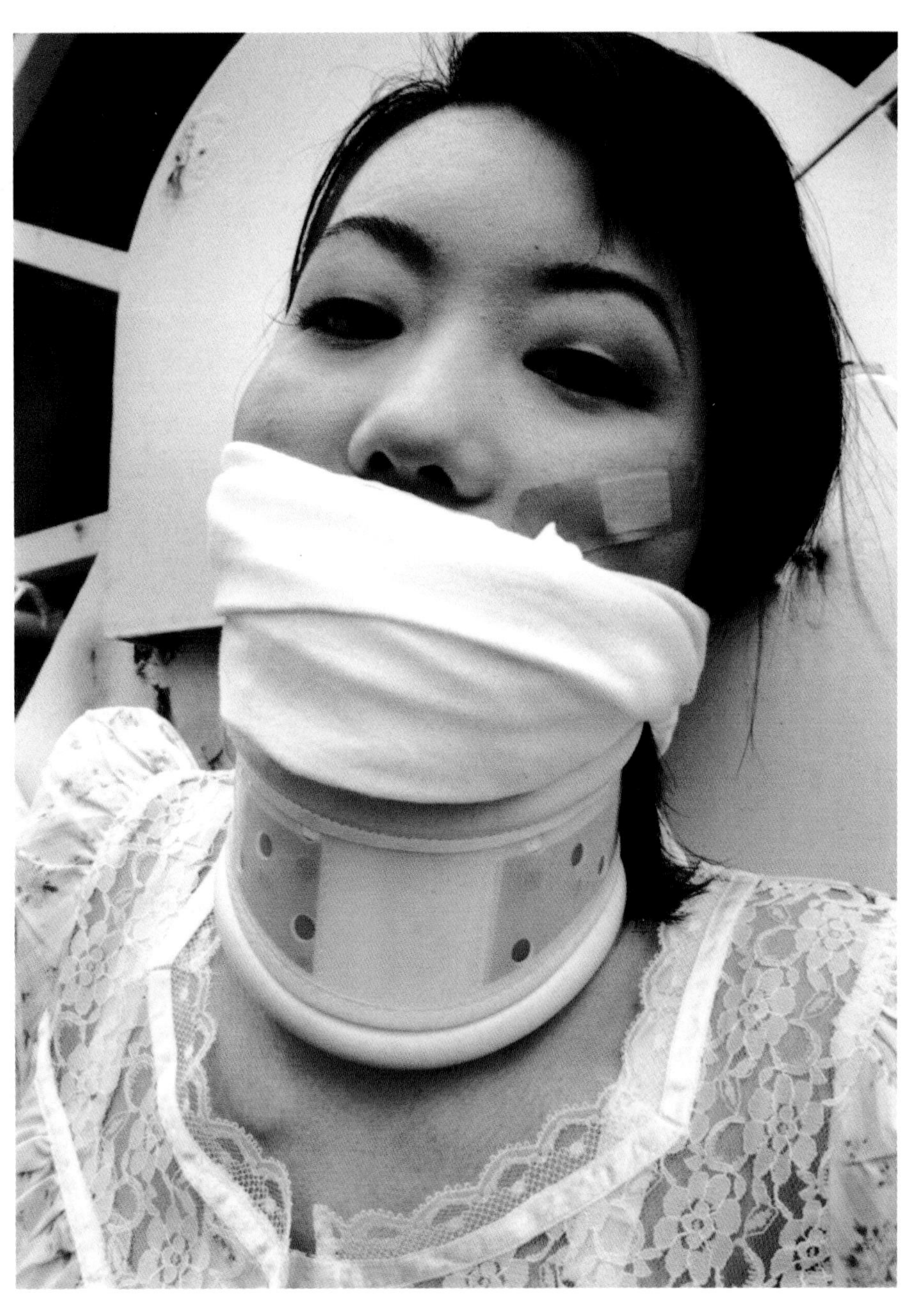

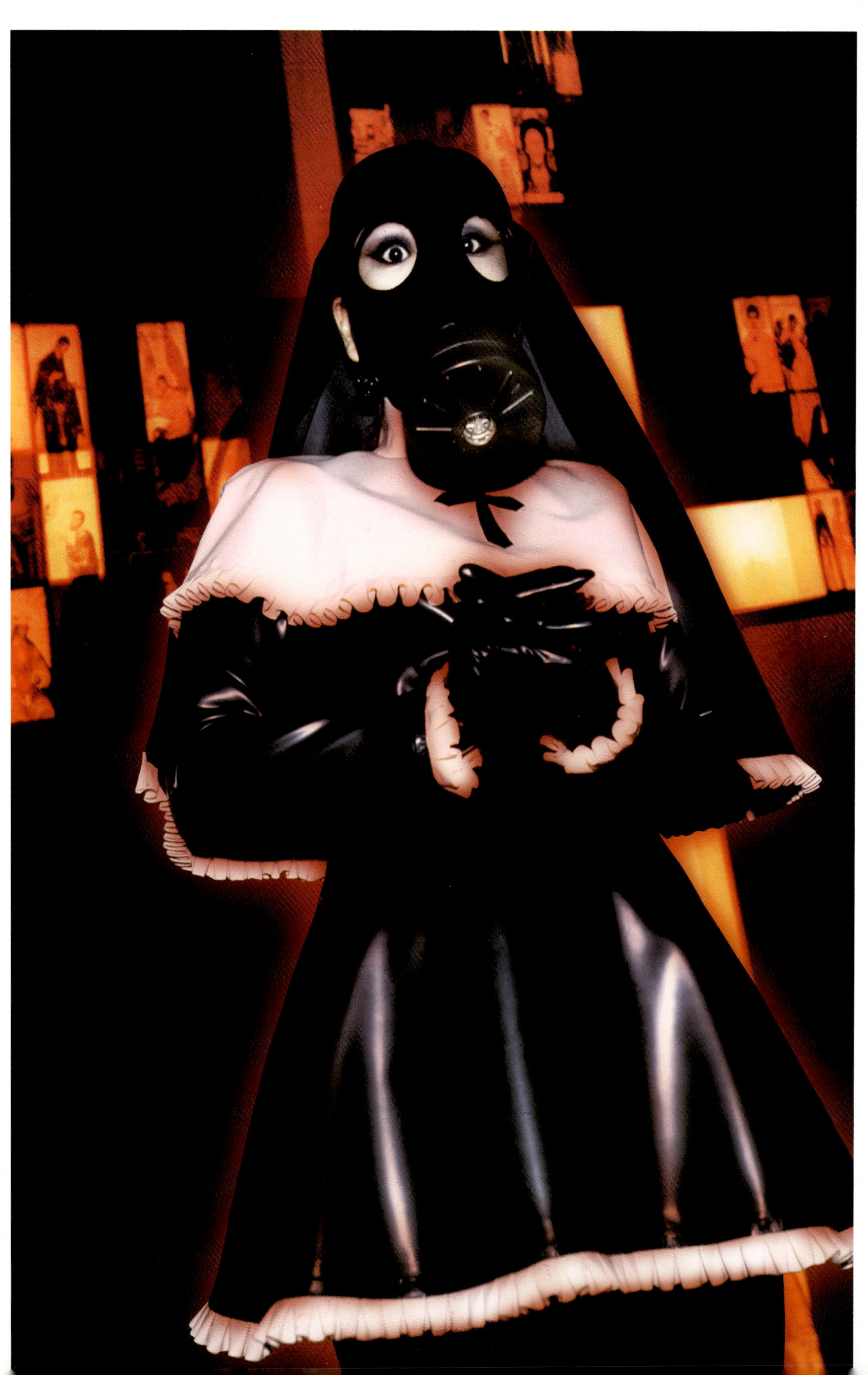

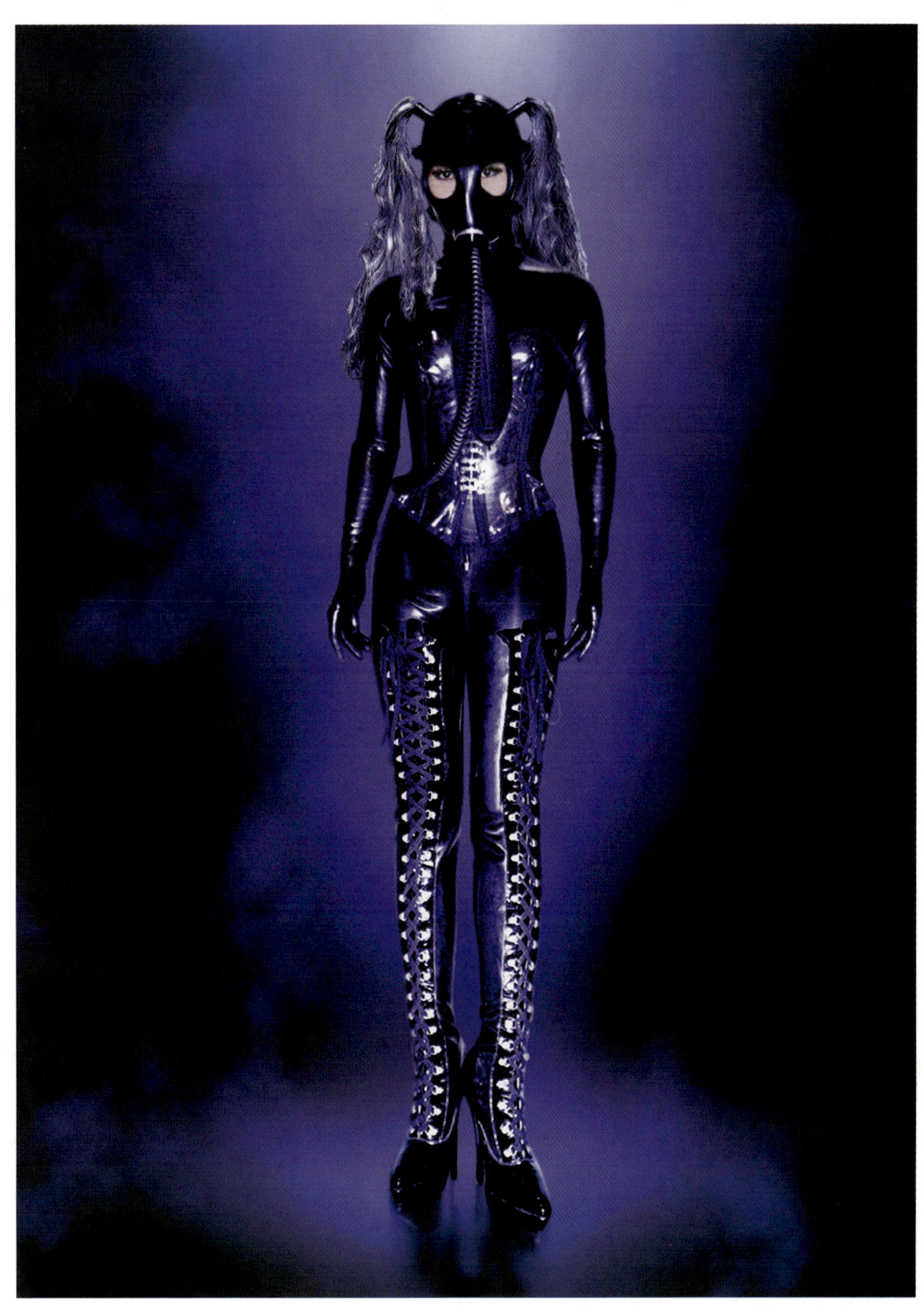

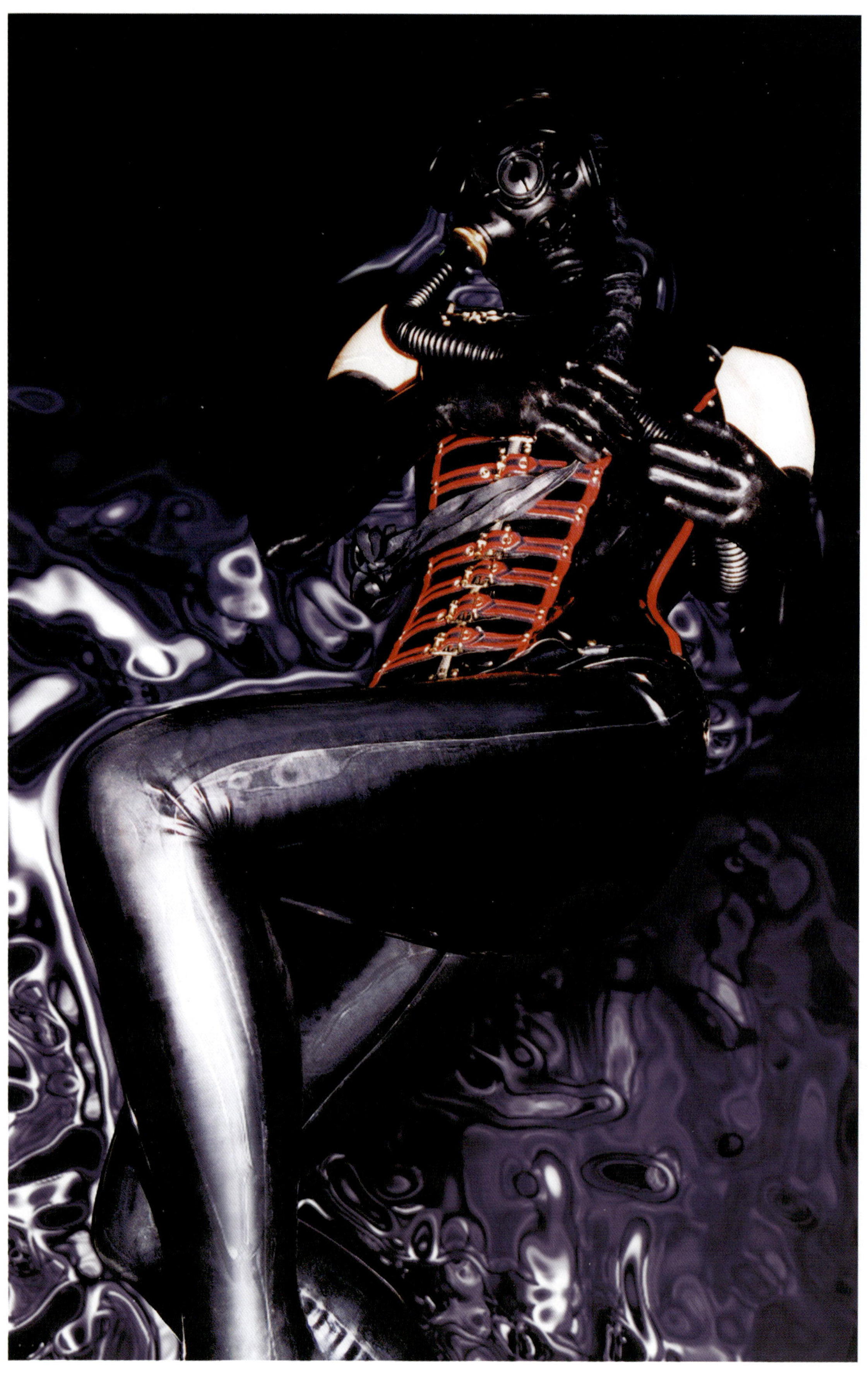

 Rubber Brain

Opposite Tony Ward

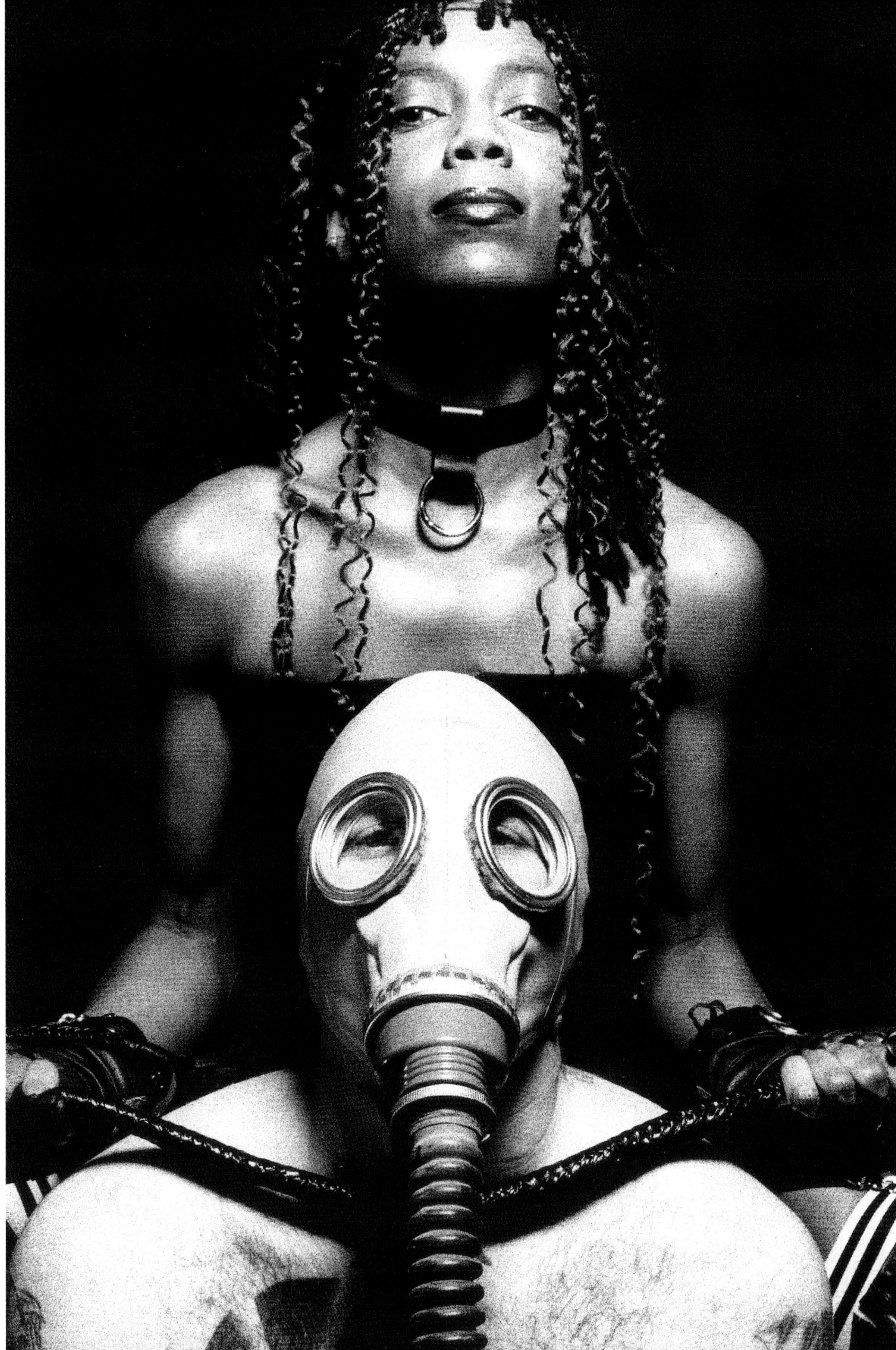

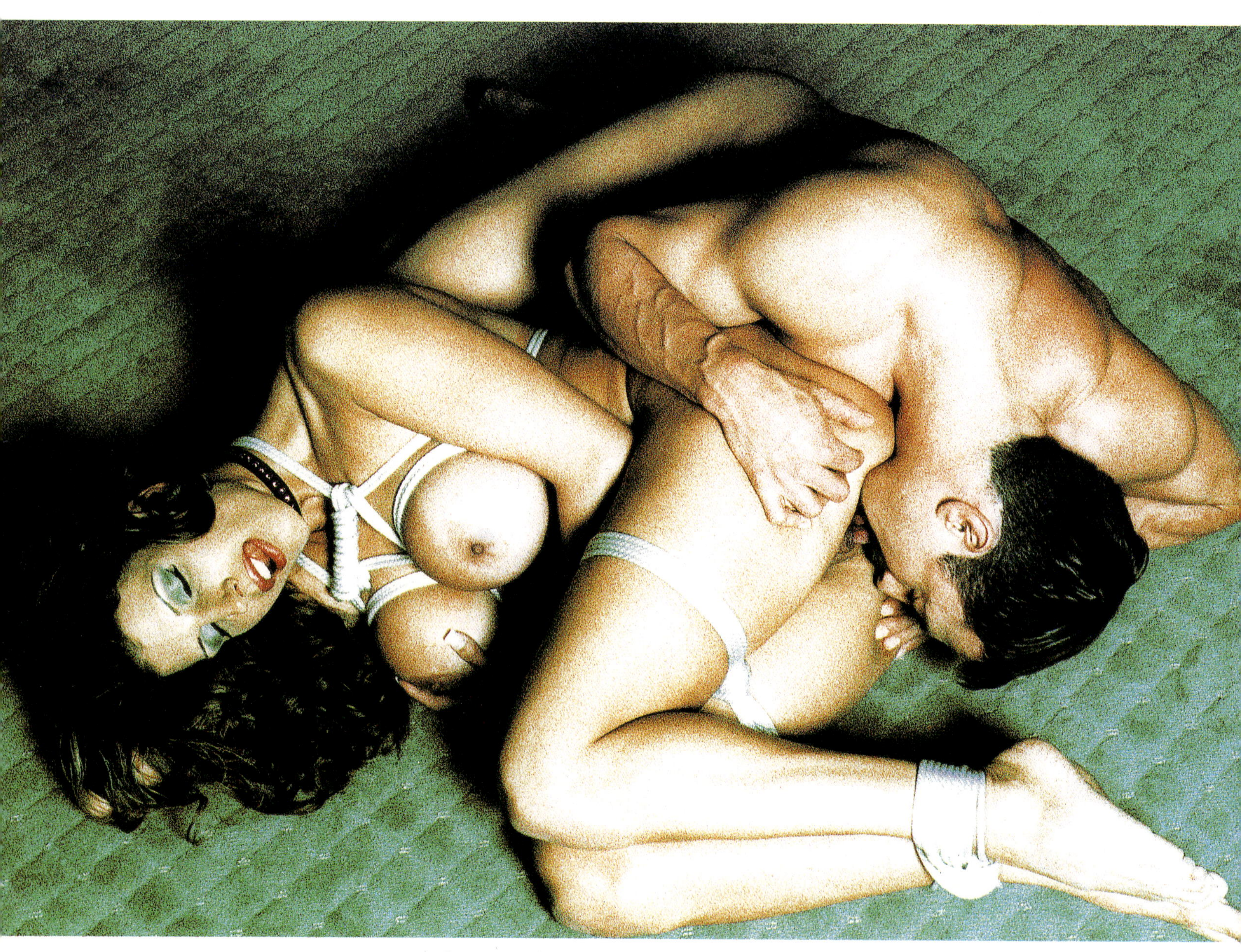



Opposite Tony Ward

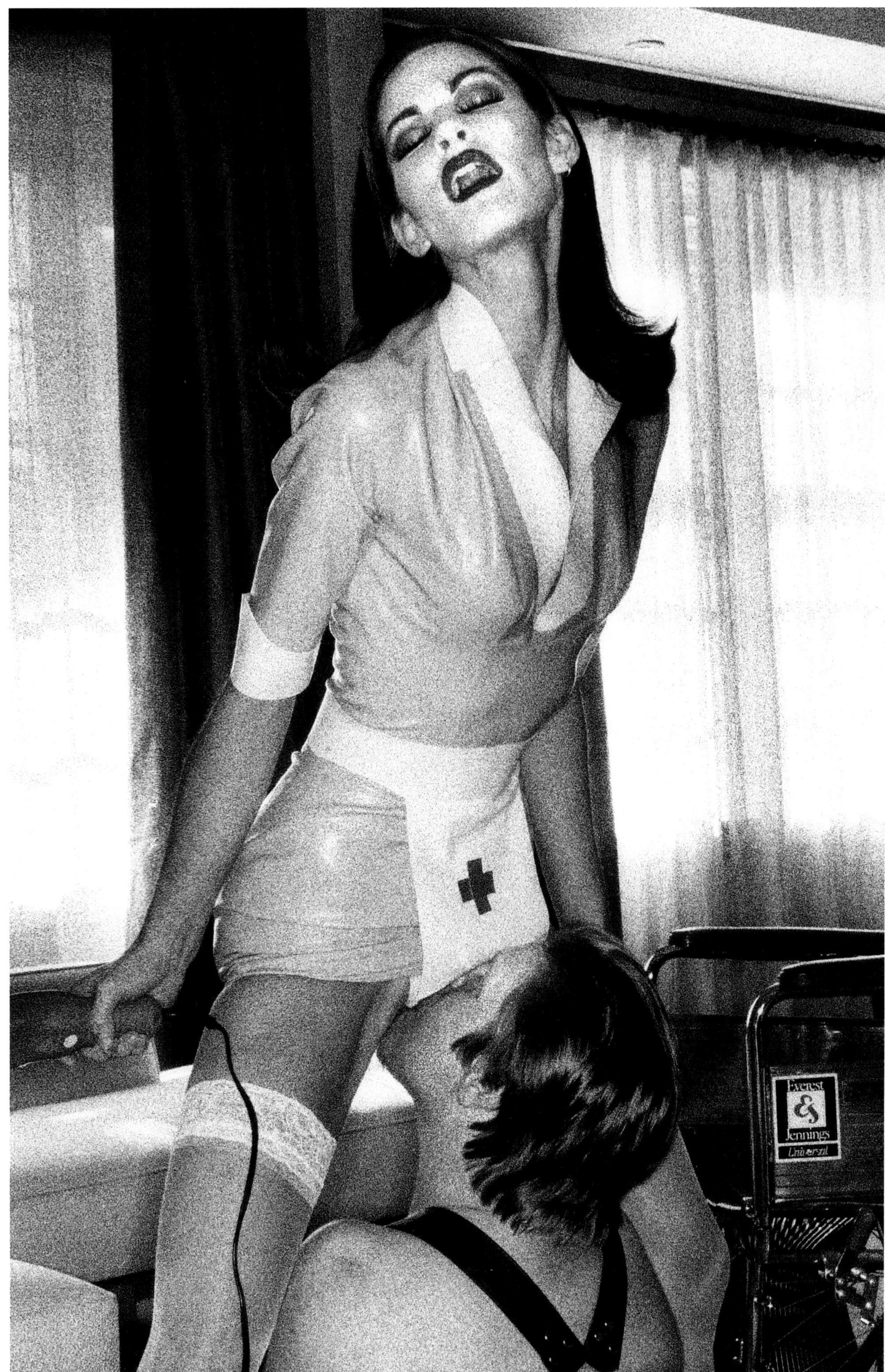

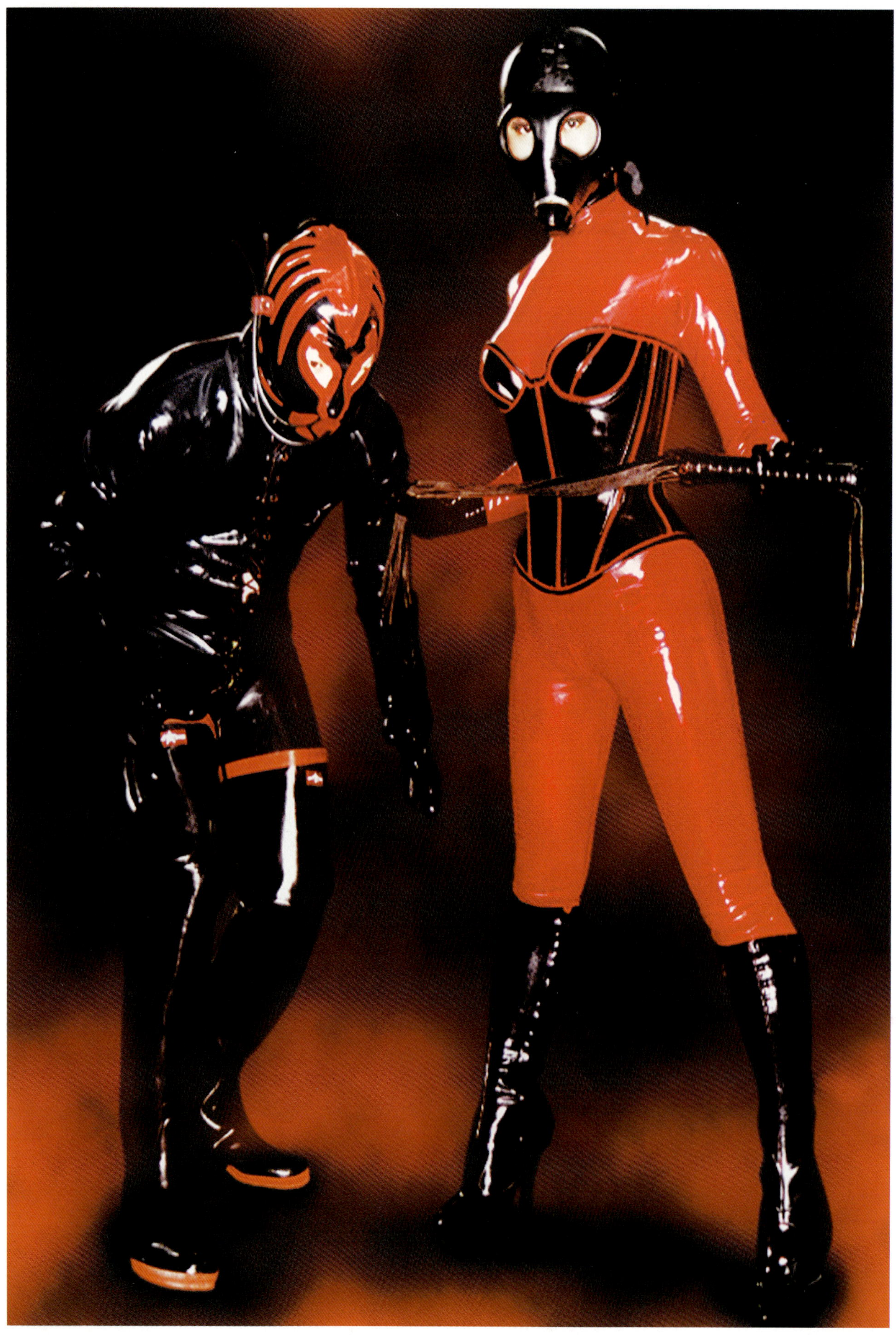



Opposite **Lee Higgs**

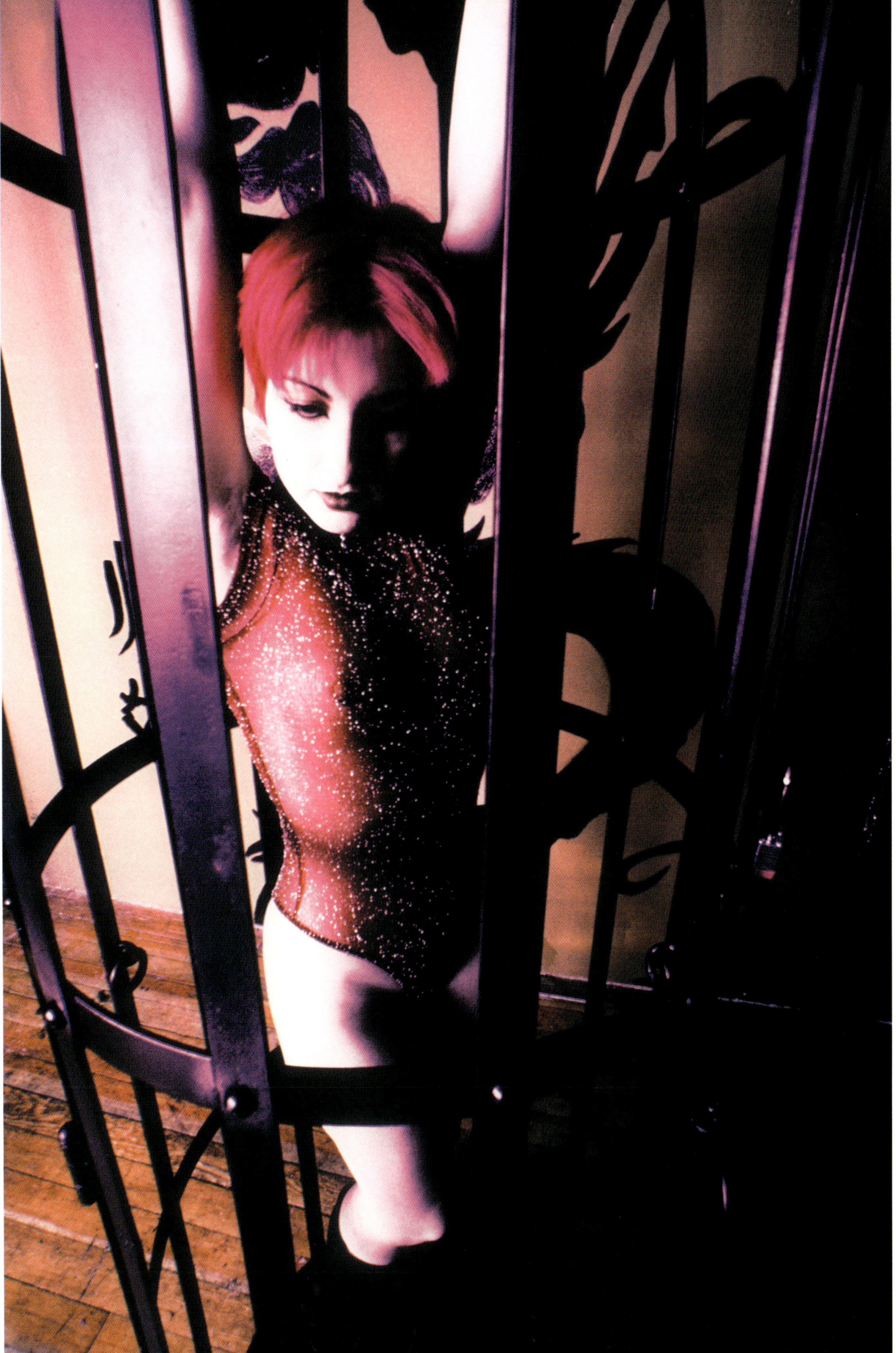

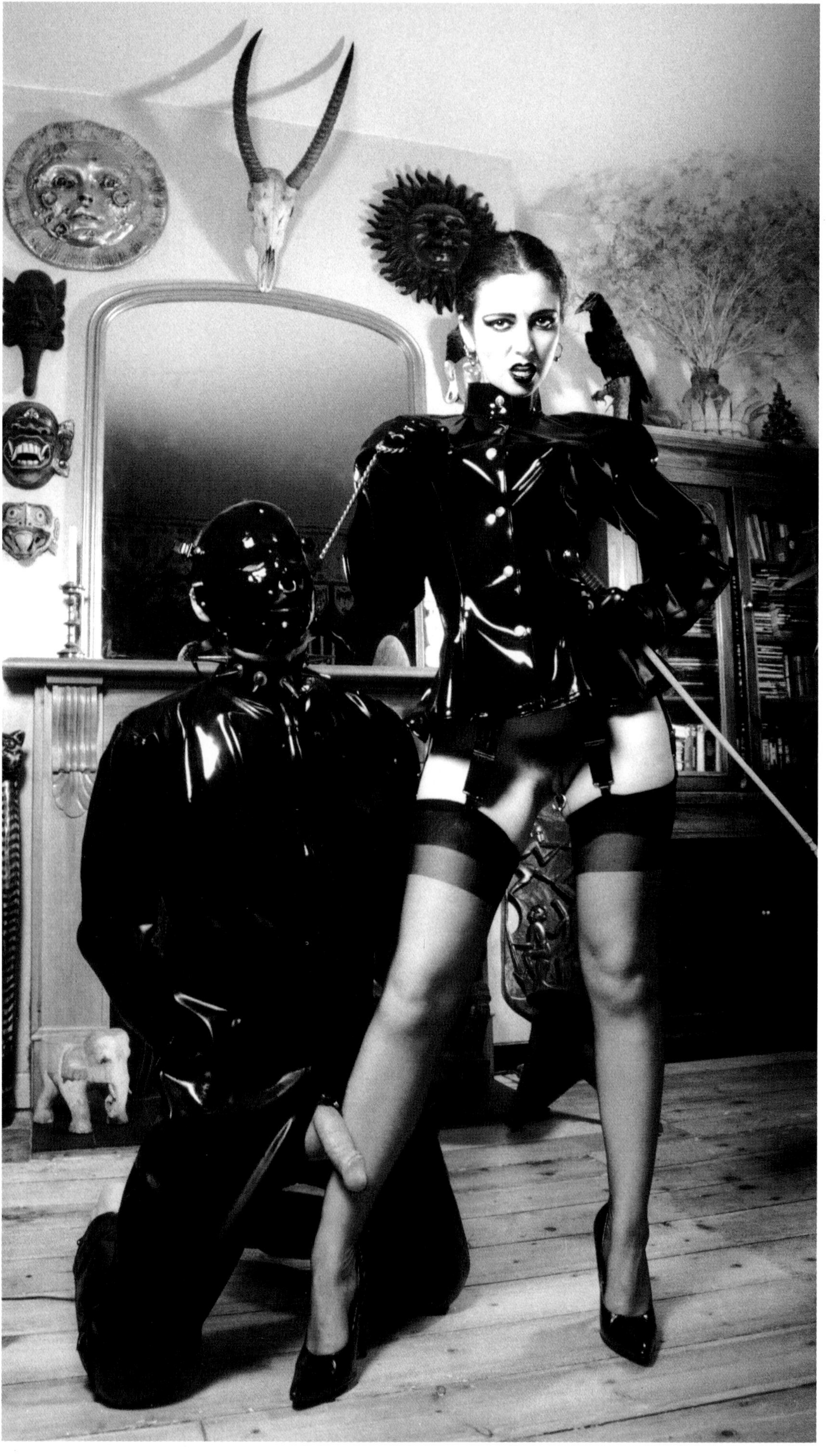



Opposite Trevor Watson

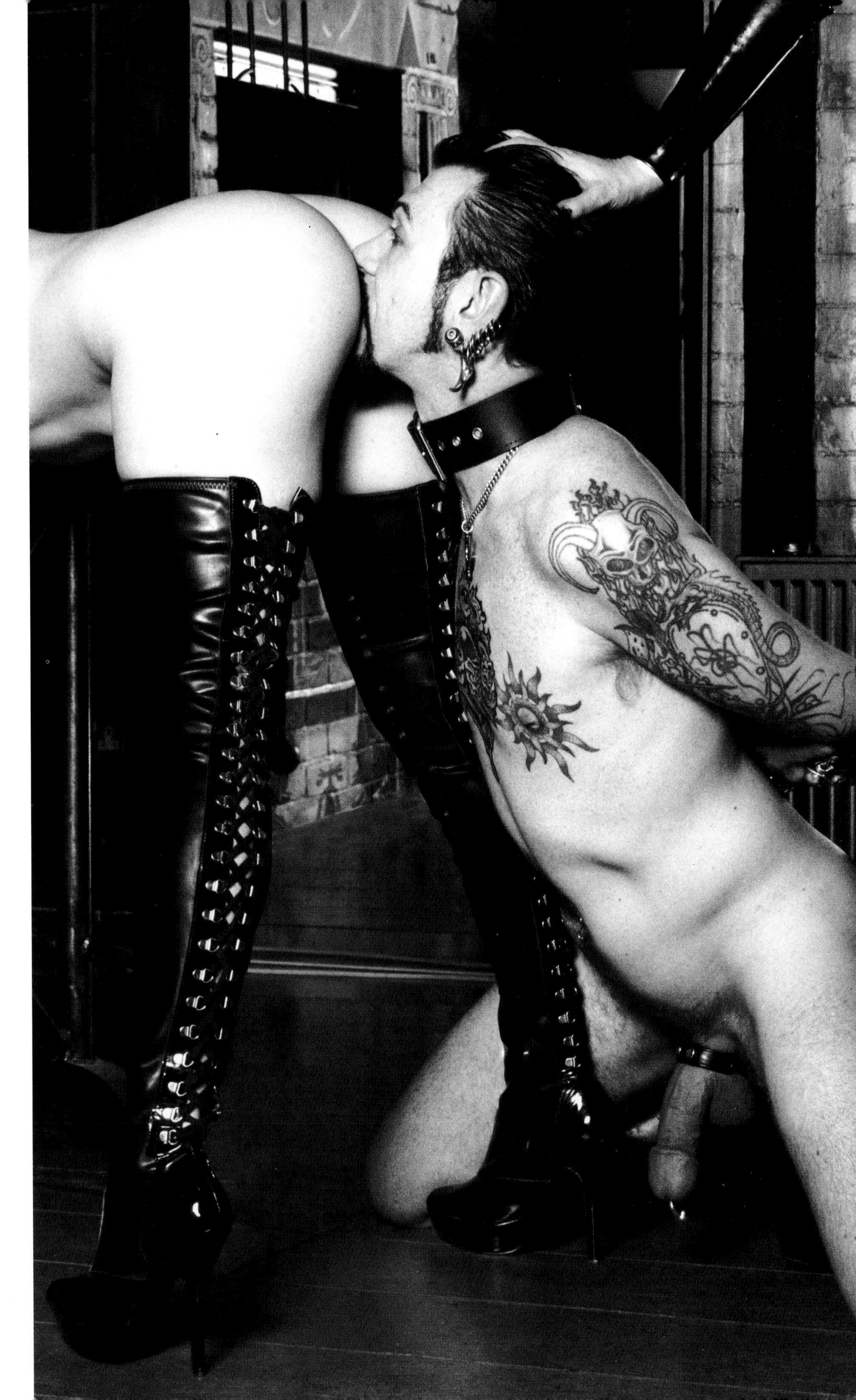

# CONTENTS BY PHOTOGRAPHER

The publishers would like to thank the following sources for their kind permission to reproduce the pictures in this book:


**CARLOS BATTS**
Before the Shower 69
Pretend Bondage 132
Time Out 133
Basement Games 134
Reptile Eden 135

**ALVA BERNADINE**
Cat Woman: Claws 1992 22
Cat Woman Jumping 1993 23

**BOB CARLOS CLARKE**
Rachel Weisz 26
Miss T 1980s 27
Charlie (*Loaded* Calendar) 2000 74
Nell (*Loaded* Calendar) 2000 75

**PETER W. CZERNICH**
Perfect Doll, July 2001 (Model: Natasha) 55
Bizarre Beauty 1998 (Model: Bianca) 65
Rapesfield 1997 (Model: Bianca) 206
Black Room 446-01 2000 (Model: Bianca) 207
Kiss Me!, July 2001 (Model: Natasha) 208
I C through U, June 2001 (Model: Natasha) 209
Benson Boobs, November 2000 (Model: Bianca) 210
Standing Tall, November 2000 (Model: Bianca) 211

**EMMA DELVES-BROUGHTON**
Katrina 1999 34
Devil 2001 35
Emily 1999 36
Roller Girl 2001 37
Cat Burglar 2000 146
Dungeon 2000 147
Valeria 2001 148–49
Gangster's Moll 2000 150

**JOHN DIETRICH**
Beguiled 106
Dita Blue 107
The Bargain 108
Lost Weekend 109
Dawn Witch 110
Sascha 111
Distant Cairo 112
Zastrozzi 113

**FETISH ART**
Notting Hill Gate 1998 86
Berliner Dom 1998 87

**FETISH EYES**
Photographer: Alikat 43
Photographer: Alikat 44
Photographer: Alikat 45
Photographer: Alikat 90
Photographer: Alikat 91
Photographer: Keital 186
Photographer: Keital 187

**JOHN FITZGERALD**
Untitled July 2001 50
Untitled July 2001 51

Untitled July 2001 52
Untitled September 2000 177
Untitled August 2001 190
Untitled 192
Untitled October 2000 193

**STEVE DIET GOEDDE**
Masuimi, Hollywood 2001 66
Emily Marilyn, Hollywood 2001 67
Natasha Sweet, Hollywood 2000 68
Zentai Girl, Hollywood 1999 197

**CHINA HAMILTON**
Whip Me Sweetly 1999 77
Presentation Sexually 1999 136
Historical Moment 1996 178
Metal Hell 2001 179
Within My Chains 1998 180
Soft Entity 1998 181

**ERIK HANSEN-HANSEN**
Untitled 1998 38
Untitled 1997 39
Upskirt # 2 2000 40
Upskirt # 1 2000 41
Trainspotting # 2 1999 42
Untitled 1998 88

**LEE HIGGS**
Zooey, December 2000 183
Restraint, December 2000 191
Tiffany and Myrna, March 2001 202
Tiffany, October 2000 203
Lilly & Zoe at Jade's Dungeon, December 1999 204
Natira, May 1999 221

**DAVID HINDLEY**
Rubberball 2000 28
New York 2001 182

**ALEXANDER HORN**
Nun in the Cellar, Bremen 1999 (Model: Bianca) 60
Blonde on the Bed, Bremen 1999 (Model: Greta) 158–59
Zipped Open – Taking a Peek, Bremen 2001 (Model: Bianca) 185
Blow-Up Girl at the Fountain, Bremen 2000 (Model: Bianca) 198
Hugging Christmas, Bremen 2000 (Model: Bianca) 199
Masked Greta, Bremen 1999 (Model: Greta) 200
Mirrored Rubberdoll, Hollywood 1997 (Model: Angel) 201

**JUSTICE HOWARD**
Untitled 1999 53
Untitled 1999 54
Untitled 1999 114
Untitled 1999 115

**KEVIN HUNDSNURCHER**
In the Park, July 2001 70
Milk, July 2001 116
Untitled, July 2000 117
Untitled, July 2000 118
Untitled, July 2000 119

**JAMES & JAMES**
Vanessa, House of Harlot 1999 100
Charlie, House of Harlot 1999 101
Libidex Hood 98 144

**SANDRA JENSEN**
Witch Lillith – The Bride of Death, Oslo 2000 (Model: Elisabeth Engebretsen) 63
The Amazon and Espen Thoresen Watching TV, Oslo 2001 for magazine *MANN* (Model: Lene Pedersen) 122
The Amazon and Bored Espen Thoresen, Oslo 2001 for magazine *MANN* (Model: Lene Pedersen) 123
Tomoko Haunted by Serial Killer, London 1999 205

**ROMAN KASPERSKI**
Untitled 2000 120
Untitled 1996 168
Untitled 1997 169
Untitled 1997 170
Untitled 1996 171

**RAIMUND LAVENDER**
Untitled, August 1999 167

**CRAIG MOREY**
Emeryville 1993 76
San Francisco 2001 138
San Francisco 1996 139
San Francisco 2001 140
San Francisco 2001 141

**CHRISTOPHE MOURTHÉ**
Teddy Bear in Paris 1999 71
Steps by Steps Paris 1998 78
Ingrid in Morocco 1999 79

**DAVE NAZ**
Catherine & Emily 2000 80
Taylor & Marnie 2001 81
Simone Kross Steps on Slave 2001 82
Torturella, Damien & Slave 2000 83
Antonia 2001 137
Simone Kross & Slave 2001 176

**NO MERCY**
Behind the Boots, 22 February 2000 160
Off Duty II, 29 April 2001 161
Finger Play, 22 May 2000 162
Taped, 18 July 2001 163
Cautious Approach, 17 January 2001 164
The Martyr, 17 January 2001 165
Off Duty I, 29 April 2001 166

**MARTIN PERREAULT**
Bath, March 2001 56–57
Vamp, November 1997 58
Sunbathing, January 2000 59
Friends, October 1997 105
Untitled, September 1997 145

**DORALBA PICERNO**
On Fire 30
Untitled 31
Angel 32
Police Woman No.3 84
Nurse No. 2 85
She Whips 89

**RUBBER BRAIN**
Red Moon 1998 (photo/YU, model/Miki 1998 © Rubber Brain) 64
Nun with Cross 2000 (photo/Mr.GumGum, model/Fumiyo 2000 © Rubber Brain) 214
Rubber Cyborg 1999 (photo & model/YU 1999 © Rubber Brain) 215
Melt Down 1999 (photo/Mr.GumGum, model/YU 1999 © Rubber Brain) 216
Red Mistress with Black Slave 1999 (Photo/Mr.GumGum, model/YU and F-ten 1999 © Rubber Brain) 220

**GARY & PIERRE SILVA**
Serena - Full Mask, November 1999 (Model: Serena) 46
Evil Family, February 2001 47
Full Blossom, February 2001 (Model: Mistress Isabella Sinclaire) 48
Sweet Aloma, April 2000 (Model: Sweet Aloma) 49
Dita on Polished Wood, February 2000 (Model: Dita von Teese) 92
Dita – Red Wall, April 2001 (Model: Dita von Teese) 93
Isabella Waiting, April 2000 (Model: Mistress Isabella Sinclaire) 94
Sitting Pretty, April 2000 (Models: Mistress Isabella Sinclaire and Sweet Aloma) 95
Isabella Mirror, December 1998 (Model: Mistress Isabella Sinclaire) 96
Mistress Aves, May 1995 (Model: Mistress Aves) 97
Red Room, September 1999 (Model: Mistress Isabella Sinclaire) 98
Sinful Daughter, July 2000 (Models: Mistress Sabrina Belladonna and Bella de Paul) 99
Faces, June 1999 (Models: Mistress Torturella and Master Damien) 188
Torture Table, April 2000 (Model: Sweet Aloma) 189

**ROMAIN SLOCOMBE**
Sawa Futaoka Tied Up by Nawashi Murakawa 2000 172
Aokigahara Forest near Mount Fuji 1996 173
Yuka, Yuki and Friend, after Performance at the Röntgen

Art Space 1994 212
Akiko, Sendai Harbour 1995 213

**DEL LAGRACE VOLCANO**
David, Transman, Berlin 1998 29
Ariane on the Wheel, London 2001 142
Persephone, London 1992 143
Ariane the Magical, London 2001 184

**TONY WARD**
The Nun 1998 61
Danny's 2001 62
Art & Shay 2000 121
Oxygen 1997 217
Art & Shay 2000 218
Todd & Paulette 1999 219

**TREVOR WATSON**
Untitled 1998 33
Untitled 2001 124
Untitled 2001 125
Untitled 1996 222
Untitled 2001 223

**JIM WEATHERS**
Payback is a... 2001 (Model: Rachel Paine tying Charisma) 102
Intimate Inquisition 2001 (Model: Jewel Evans straddles Sadie) 103
Mirror Mirror 2001 (Model: Molly Matthews being tied [photo by Jewel Evans]) 104
Double Cross 2000 (Model: Nicole Sheridan) 151
Homage to Sweet Gwendoline 2001 (Model: Dita von Teese) 152
Perfect Teese 2001 (Model: Dita von Teese and "Burt" [cat]) 153
Sweet Tangerine 2000 (Model: Nicole Sheridan) 154–155
Anticipation 2001 (Model: Jenna Lyte) 156
Pink Kittens 2001 (Model: Jenna Lyte with a very demure "Thumper" [cat]) 157

**BEN WESTWOOD**
Untitled 24
Untitled 25
Untitled 128
Untitled 129
Untitled 130
Untitled 131

**WHIPLASH!**
Untitled 194
Untitled 195
Untitled 196


Every effort has been made to acknowledge correctly and contact the source and/or copyright holder of each picture, and Carlton Books Limited apologises for any unintentional errors or omissions which will be corrected in future editions of this book.